LEVELS, TRENDS AND STRUCTURE OF WORKFORCE IN INDIA

LEVELS, TRENDS AND STRUCTURE OF WORKFORCE IN INDIA

A Census Based Study

R.B. Bhagat
K.C. Das

GYAN

Levels, Trends and Structure of Workforce in India

ISBN : 978-81-212-1154-3

Published in 2013 in India by
Gyan Publishing House
23, Main Ansari Road, Daryaganj,
New Delhi - 110002
Phones : 23282060, 23261060
Fax : (011) 23285914
E-mail: books@gyanbooks.com
website: gyanbooks.com

Laser Type Setting : Rajender Vashist, Delhi
Printed at : Chawla Offset Printers, Delhi

Contents

Preface

Indian economy has been predominantly agricultural. A major shift in the economic policy has taken place in 1991 with liberalisation, privatisation and globalisation of Indian economy. As a result, it has witnessed a series of reforms encompassing all major sectors of the economy, and has marked a steady break from the past policy regimes of control, regulation and licenses. This has boosted the economic growth as the economy grew on an average at the rate of nearly 6 per cent in 1990s. This was expected to bring about a major shift in the trend and pattern of work participation rates in rural and urban areas. The economists have generally relied on National Sample Survey (NSS) data for this purpose, and the wealth of information from various censuses are not taken seriously in analysing the trends in labour force.

The Census and NSS provide two different perspectives and approaches to undertand the labour market of the country. While Census attempts to classify the total population in terms of workers and non-workers which are further divided into several categories based on industrial and occupational classification of workforce, NSS tries to measure the employment and unemployment situation by time disposition. Both provide different perspectives, although complementary to understand the labour market. This book attempts to provide the utility of Census data in understanding the changing labour market in India.

We are immensely thankful to the International Institute Institute of Populational Sciences, Mumbai, for funding this project, and membes of Board of Studies and Academic Council for their suggestions and comments. We are thankful to our current Director Prof. F. Ram and former Director Late Prof P.N. Mari Bhat for their support in completing this project.

We would also like to put on record our deep apprecriation for the Libarry staff, Librarian – Mr D.D. Mestry, Assistant Librarian– Mr Pravin Kumar and Mr Vidhate for their help and co-operation.

This project work was possible due to hard work of our Research Staff Dr. Daliya Sebastian, Ms. Soumya Mohanty and Ms. Reecha Bohidar. We thank them for their help in the analysis of data, preparation of maps and their sincere effort in shaping the project report in the present form.

R.B. Bhagat
K.C. Das

1

Introduction

Changes in the size, composition and distribution of population are closely associated with the demographic structure of workforce. On the other hand, the workforce participation rates vary according to the stages of economic development, across cultures, age groups, and between sexes. Indian economy has been predominantly agricultural which contributes about one third to the total economy, and employs more than half of the workforce. The agriculture is understandably not able to absorb a significant number of additional workers. However, with modernisation, urbanisation and industrial development picking up, there is likely to be a shift in the occupational structure of the Indian workforce. Moreover, a major change in the economic policy has taken place in 1991 with the introduction of liberalisation of Indian economy. It was expected to bring a qualitative shift in the occupational structure of the workforce. Many have argued that the economic reforms have virtually stimulated economic growth during the last one decade. The economy has grown over 5 per cent per annum during the 1990s. But the implication of economic reforms and the outcome of high economic growth have however remained to be evaluated in terms of its impact on the level and composition of workforce. Economists have generally relied on aggregate data at the state level on the employment and unemployment released by the NSSO. Some recent studies show that there is no healthy impact of liberalisation on the growth of employment particularly in the rural sectors (Sundaram, 2001; Chadha and Sahu 2002). The overall growth rate in employment has slowed down in the 1990s compared to the 1980s (Papola 2004). The release of the 2001 Census data provides an opportunity to corroborate the findings emerging from NSS data.

This report presents an analysis of workforce data derived from censuses for the period 1981 to 2001. Earlier studies based on Census data show that work participation rates are significantly lower than the NSS rates of comparable rounds. This led to the conclusion that Census undercounts the workforce especially in case of women (Sinha 1982). Thus in this study, a comparison of the 2001 Census is also made with NSS 55th round (1999-2000). Some of the concepts used in the censuses are presented below:

1.1. Definition and Concepts

In recent Indian censuses, work is defined as participation in any economically productive activity with or without compensation, wages or profit. Such participation may be physical and/or mental in nature. Work involves not only the physical work but also includes supervision and direction given to other workers. However, the concept of 'economically productive activity' has considerable value loaded connotations, and influenced by the social desirability of what constitutes economically productive activity (for detail discussion, see Lauterbach 1977).

Work is taken as the basis to identify workers. The concept of work in Indian Census was introduced since 1961 Census, but the reference period was changed and the concept of main activity was introduced in 1971. The 1971 Census did record the marginal category of workforce. Thus, the figures of 1961 and 1971 Censuses were not comparable. On the other hand, we find that since 1981, the Census definition of work remains unchanged but more efforts have been made to enumerate female workforce in later censuses. In the 1981 Census, attempt was made to get a detailed profile of the working characteristics of the population. Also, usual status of the work was given emphasis instead of the current status of the work. A question was to divide the population who have worked any time and not worked at all during the last year. Those who have worked any time in the last one year were categorised as workers, and those who did not work at all were classified as non-workers. This type of classification of population into workers and non-workers category was followed in latter censuses as well. Workers were categoried into main and marginal workers since the 1981 Census.

Main Workers

All those workers who had worked for the major part of the year preceding the date of enumeration i.e. those who were engaged in any economically productive activity for 183 days (six months), and more during the last year, are termed as main workers.

Marginal Workers

All those workers who had worked any time in the year preceding enumeration but did not work for a major part the year i.e. those who worked less than 183 days or less than six months were termed as marginal workers.

Keeping in view the criticism of Census having failed to capture the women workforce fully, it is worthwhile to mention that the 2001 Census made a special effort to capture women workforce particularly engaged as unpaid family work by improving the instruction manual of enumerators. The manual included several sketches of unpaid work for sensitising the enumerators. Apart from various activities in agriculture, milching or milk production was included in work. The enumerators employed in backward and low literacy districts have been specially trained through Census Advisors to enumerate the women workforce (Sikri 2005).

1.1.2. Industrial Categories

In 1981 and 1991, workers were categorised into nine industrial categories, viz. (i) cultivators, (ii) agricultural labourers (iii) livestock, forestry, fishing, hunting, plantation, orchards and allied activities, (iv) mining and quarrying, (v) manufacturing and repairs- (a) household industries (b) other than household industries, (vi) construction, vii) trade and commerce, (vii) transport, storage and communication, (viii) services.

But, the 2001 Census provided information on four categories of workers only i.e. cultivators, agricultural labourers, household industries and other workers. The first two are related to agricultural activities while the rest are treated as non-agricultural workforce in this report.

I. Cultivators

According to Census definition, cultivators included persons engaged in cultivation of land owned or held from government or private persons or institutions for payment in money, kind or share. It includes effective supervisions or direction in cultivation. A person who has given out his/her land to another person or institution for cultivation, for money, kind or share of crop, and also does not even supervise or direct cultivation of land, will not be treated as cultivators.

II. Agricultural Labourers

The agricultural labourers are defined as a person who works on another person's land for wages in money or kind or share is regarded as agricultural labourers. He has no risk in the cultivation but merely works on another person's land on wages. The agricultural labourers are usually more economically and socially vulnerable group in our society.

III. Household Industry

A household industry is defined as an industry conducted by one or more numbers of the household at home or within the village in rural areas and only within the precincts of the house where the household lives in urban areas. The larger proportion of workers in the household industry should consist of household members. The industry should not be run on the scale of a registered factory, which would qualify to be registered under the Indian Factory Act.

III. Other Workers

All those who had worked in any field of economic activity other than cultivation, agricultural labourers or workers in the household industry are classified as other workers.

1.2. Some Earlier Findings

Demographic and non-demographic factors appear to be important in any analysis of labour force changes in developing countries. Under the demographic factors, high rate of population growth directly affects the work participation rates. On the other hand, the initial efforts to develop an economy, expansion of school enrolment, improved health and welfare services, increased urbanisation may be accompanied by declining trend in work participation rates and increase in the unemployment rates (Rayappa and Erpenshade: 1975). On the other hand, Census or labour force surveys in different countries across the globe highlight relatively low labour participation rates of women vis-à-vis men, and a significant variation in female work participation rates. Also, rural areas show higher participation than urban areas.

The work participation rates of the children and the aged are of special interest in the study of labour force studies. Subramaniam (1990) tried to find out the determinants of work force participation of rural children in India. According to him, agriculture is the major source of employment to the rural child labourers. Almost 83 per cent of child labourers were employed as agricultural workers, fishermen, hunters, loggers and related workers. Another 10 per cent of them were working in manufacturing and related field and only about 4 per cent are engaged in service sector. Subramaniam further showed that Andhra Pradesh has highest percentage of child labour and Kerala has the minimum in the country. He suggested that the work participation rate among rural children can be brought down by reducing the poverty gap between the rural-urban areas and taking steps to increase the attendance of school going children in the rural areas especially in the age group 10-14 years.

The worker population ratios have decreased in younger age groups because of increasing student population ratios in recent decades. The total workforce engaged in agricultural and allied activities has reduced. Also, there has been reduction in the size of workers in personal services by over 1.2 million in the aggregate. It represents low productivity, low income per worker sector. This reduction in the size and share of the personal services shows a positive development in the employment situation in the 1990s. The changes in the growth of workforce at the state level show a mixed trend in the 1990s but over all, there has been a decline in the growth of employment in the 1990s (Sundaram 2001).

Industrialisation measured in terms of the work force engaged in manufacturing sector or in non-agricultural activities shows that in spite of considerable progress in rural areas in electrification, transportation and communication networks and agro-processing industries, the share of non-agricultural workforce remains almost stagnant until recently (Visaria: 2003). However, this trend awaits confirmation from the Census 2001.

Dubey et.al (2004) observes the changes in the participation of women in the labour force in rural sector during the last two decades based on NSS 38th and 55th rounds. They found that more than 95 per cent of women are engaged as manual labour, and there is a reduction in women work participation rate during the study period. It further reveals that as economic status improves, the participation rate of female labour force declines. The paper emphasises the importance of education and level of economic development in raising the work participation rate of women, which is highly desirable for equity and balanced economic development.

Sundaram and Tendulkar (2004) reported that the worker population ratios are lower for males but higher for females in poor household despite higher child-women ratios and dependency burden. The low share of regular wage/ salary earning workers remained unchanged for the rural working poor, the only change was the rise in the share of manual workers at the cost of self-employment during the 1990s.

Several of the findings mentioned above are by and large acceptable, but the explanations for the trend and pattern of work participation rates are not easy to put forward due to the diversity of situations, as well as work participation rates being influenced by market and non-market factors like poverty and the prevailing norms of work by gender, age and social status in different parts of India. This work specifically attempts keeping in view the following objectives:

1.3. Objectives

1. To study the patterns and trends of work force growth at state and district levels during 1981-2001.
2. To study the changes in the workforce in terms of agricultural and non-agricultural sectors 1981-2001.

3. To study the changes in the composition of workforce by sex, age and educational levels 1981-2001

1.4. *Methodology*

The study analyses work force data at the state and district levels. The following indicators are calculated:

1. Crude work participation rates (CWPR)

It is defined as the ratio of total workers to the total population multiplied by 100. The crude work participation rates were calculated for the total, main, and marginal workers by sex and rural and urban residence.

Symbolically

$$CWPR = \frac{TW}{TP} \times 100$$

where,

CWPR = Crude Work Participation Rate

TW = Total workers

TP = Total population

2. Work participation rates in the working age group

The following indicator of working age group has been used in this study:

$$\frac{\text{Total Workers in 15-59 age groups}}{\text{Total Population in 15-59 age groups}} \times 100$$

3. Growth rate

Growth rate of workers has been calculated by using exponential growth rate method.

$$\text{Exponential growth rate} = \frac{1}{t} * \ln\left(\frac{P_t}{P_0}\right)$$

where, P_t = Population at time t, p_0

= Population at time 0

t = time period between 0 and t

4. Percentage of workers in non-agricultural sector

Percentage of workers in non-agricultural sector is calculated as follows:

$$\frac{\text{Total non-agricultural Workers}}{\text{Total workers}} \times 100$$

5. Age composition of workers (main and marginal workers) by residence and sex.

To calculate the age composition of workers, we clubbed the age group to three broad categories – those in age group 0-14 as child workers, age group 15-59 as adult workers and age group 60+ as old age workers.

$$\text{Share of Child Workers} = \frac{\text{Workers in age group 0-14}}{\text{Total Workers}} \times 100$$

$$\text{Share of Adult Workers} = \frac{\text{Workers in age group 15-59}}{\text{Total Workers}} \times 100$$

$$\text{Share of Old age Workers} = \frac{\text{Workers in age group 60+}}{\text{Total Workers}} \times 100$$

6. Educational level of Workers (main and marginal) by residence and sex.

To calculate educational level of workers, we have clubbed the educational levels into four categories – illiterate, primary, secondary and high school, and above. We calculated the share of workers by educational level by sex and rural-urban categories.

Share of Illiterate Workers =

$$\frac{\text{Number of illiterate Workers}}{\text{Total Workers}} \times 100$$

Likewise, we have calculated the share of educational level such as primary, secondary and high school, and above for both main and marginal workers.

1.5 Organisation of the Report

The report is organised in four chapters. The first chapter gives introductory in nature, the seconds presents the level, trends and composition of workforce by sex, age, education, and rural and urban areas. The third chapter provides a comparison of Census 2001 with NSS 55th round held in 1999-2000 in terms of indicators like work participation rates by main and marginal status of Census with that of the usual and subsidiary status of workforce derived from the NSS. Also, a comparison has been made in respect to the incidence of child labour, educational level of the workforce and share of workers in non-agricultural sector. The fourth chapter presents estimates of work participation rates and changes at the district from 1981 to 2001 along with the share of non-agricultural workforce both in main and marginal category based on 2001 Census. The final chapter summarises the findings emerging from the discussions of the earlier chapters.

1.6. Limitations

There are few limitations to this study:

Boundaries Changed

The study is based on 1981 to 2001 Census; so, we have clubbed the districts to take 1981 as a base. The new districts that are carved out of other districts have been clubbed to make them comparable to the districts in the 1991 and 2001 Census.

For example, Davangere is the new district formed in 2001 Census in Karnataka. Davangere is craved out from the three district namely Bellary, Shimoga and Chitradurga. Davangere is formed to acquire one taluk of Bellary district, two taluks of Shimoga district and three taluks of Chitradurga district. So, we clubbed the Davangere district with Chitradurga district. Similarly, it has been done in respect with other new districts carved out from 1991 to 2001. In 1981 Census was not held in Assam and in 1991 in Jammu and Kashmir. These states have been excluded in the study.

Broad Classification of Industrial Categories

There are nine-fold classification of workers in 1981 and 1991 but there are four broad categories available in 2001

Census. Due to non-availability of data in 2001, we have also clubbed the nine categories of workers into four categories in 1981 and 1991 Census.

Reorganisation of States

In 2000, three new states namely Jharkhand, Chhattisgarh and Uttarakhand were formed out of Bihar, Madhya Pradesh and Uttar Pradesh respectively for which separate data were available in 2001 Census. However, in order to make the figures comparable over Census years, these new states have been clubbed with their parent states.

2

Trend and Pattern of Work Participation

In this chapter, we have analysed the trends and patterns of work participation in India and states during the period 1981 to 2001 based on crude work participation rates by sex and residence. The age structure of the workers, their growth rates by main and marginal categories, their educational characteristics and the share of non-agricultural workers in the total workforce have also been analysed for the period 1981-2001.

2.1.1. Work Participation Rate (Main + Marginal), 1981-2001

Fig. 2.1.1 shows the crude work participation rate (Main+Marginal) by sex in India during the study period. It is observed that female work participation rate has gradually increased from 1981 to 2001 but at the same time, there is a little decline in the male work participation rate.

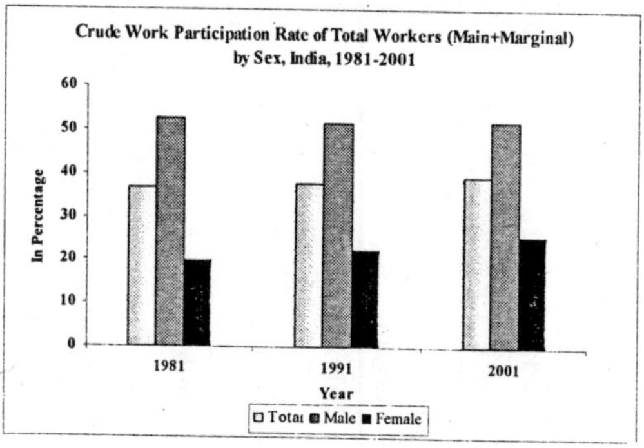

Fig. 2.1.1. Crude Work Participation Rate (Main + Marginal) by Sex in India, 1981-2001

Table 2.1.1. Crude Work Participation Rate (Main+Marginal), India and States, 1981-2001 (%)

Sl. No.	*State/Union Territories*	*1981*			*1991*			*2001*		
		Total	*Male*	*Female*	*Total*	*Male*	*Female*	*Total*	*Male*	*Female*
	India	36.77	52.65	19.77	37.46	51.55	22.25	39.26	51.93	25.68
01	Andaman & Nicobar	36.88	56.71	10.78	35.24	53.32	13.13	38.27	56.73	16.45
02	Andhra Pradesh	45.76	57.68	33.54	45.05	55.48	34.32	45.81	56.44	34.93
03	Arunachal Pradesh	52.63	58.63	45.67	46.24	53.76	37.49	43.97	50.69	36.45
04	Assam	NA	NA	NA	36.09	49.45	21.61	35.88	49.93	20.80
05	Bihar	32.35	50.18	13.50	32.16	47.92	14.86	33.88	47.73	18.84
06	Chandigarh	34.92	54.77	9.16	34.94	54.33	10.39	37.63	56.10	13.72
07	Dadra & Nagar Haveli	48.92	56.32	21.78	53.25	57.50	48.79	51.77	62.38	38.68
08	Delhi	32.19	52.67	6.84	31.64	51.72	7.36	32.80	52.21	9.15
09	Goa,Daman & Diu	35.19	48.20	21.93	35.47	49.72	20.73	39.63	56.13	21.89
10	Gujarat	37.27	52.91	20.66	40.23	53.57	25.96	42.10	55.02	28.03
11	Haryana	31.63	49.93	10.60	31.00	48.51	10.76	39.76	50.49	27.31
12	Himachal Pradesh	42.38	52.64	31.86	42.82	50.64	34.82	49.28	54.70	43.69
13	Jammu & Kashmir	44.26	55.81	31.31	NA	NA	NA	36.63	49.83	21.96

Sl .No.	State/ Union Territories	1981			1991			2001		
		Total	*Male*	*Female*	*Total*	*Male*	*Female*	*Total*	*Male*	*Female*
14	Karnataka	40.25	54.59	25.33	41.99	54.09	29.39	44.60	56.87	31.88
15	Kerala	30.53	44.89	16.61	31.43	47.58	15.85	32.32	50.36	15.28
16	Lakshadweep	24.39	39.24	9.16	26.43	44.17	7.60	25.33	42.51	7.19
17	Madhya Pradesh	42.92	54.48	30.64	42.82	52.26	32.68	42.75	51.62	33.10
18	Maharashtra	42.56	53.73	30.63	42.97	52.17	33.11	43.46	53.49	32.59
19	Manipur	43.20	46.80	39.48	42.18	45.27	38.96	44.79	48.91	40.51
20	Meghalaya	45.92	53.96	37.49	42.67	50.07	34.93	41.47	47.76	35.02
21	Mizoram	45.44	52.54	37.72	48.91	53.87	43.52	52.70	57.45	47.63
22	Nagaland	48.23	52.58	43.20	42.68	46.86	37.96	42.74	46.82	38.25
23	Odisha	38.01	55.86	19.81	37.53	53.79	20.79	38.88	52.75	24.62
24	Pondicherry	30.41	47.08	13.48	33.08	50.55	15.24	35.13	53.28	17.00
25	Punjab	31.50	53.76	6.16	30.87	54.22	4.40	37.58	54.10	18.68
26	Rajasthan	36.61	50.90	21.06	38.87	49.30	27.40	42.11	50.07	33.48

Sl.No.	State / Union Territories	1981			1991			2001		
		Total	Male	Female	Total	Male	Female	Total	Male	Female
27	Sikkim	48.30	57.22	37.61	41.51	51.26	30.41	48.72	57.58	38.59
28	Tamil Nadu	41.73	56.58	26.52	43.31	56.39	29.89	44.78	58.06	31.32
29	Tripura	32.27	50.71	12.78	31.14	47.55	13.76	36.29	50.81	21.02
30	Uttar Pradesh	29.46	52.67	8.57	32.20	49.68	12.32	32.70	46.77	17.08
31	West Bengal	29.34	48.71	8.07	32.19	51.40	11.25	36.78	54.23	18.08

Note: *Figures for 2001*

	Total	Male	Female
Chhattisgarh	46.54	52.97	40.04
Jharkhand	37.64	48.21	26.40
Uttarakhand	36.93	46.42	27.09

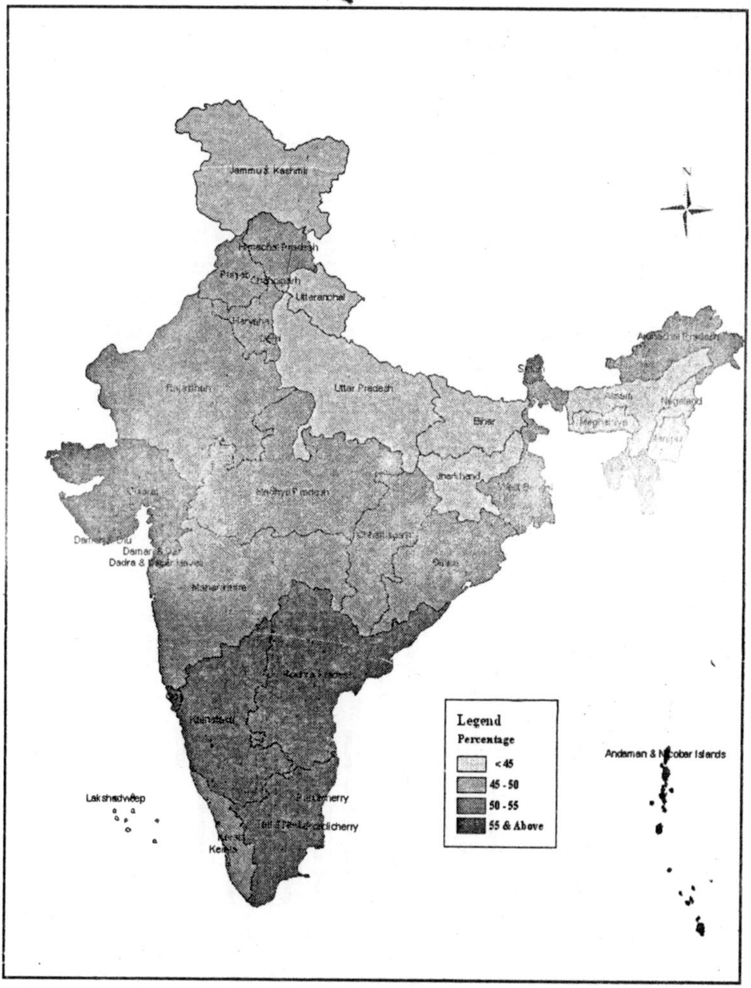

Map 2.1.1. Crude Work Participation Rate (Male), State, India, 2001

Map 2.1.1 shows the work participation rates of males in the states and union territories in 2001.It is seen that crude work participation rate is the highest in Dadra and Nagar Haveli (above 60 per cent). Almost all states of north and northeastern regions, the work participation rates of males is found to be below 50 per cent. Except Kerala, all the southern states show more than 55 per cent of male work participation rates in 2001. Map 2.1.2 shows the crude work participation rates of females in the states and union territories in 2001. Except Himachal Pradesh, in most of the states of northern India, the female work participation rate is low compared to western and south India (except Kerala). The north-eastern states, except Assam and Tripura, have much higher participation rates among females. The work participation rate of females is found the lowest in Lakshadweep followed by Delhi, whereas it is the highest in Mizoram followed by Himachal Pradesh, Manipur and Dadar Nagar Haveli.

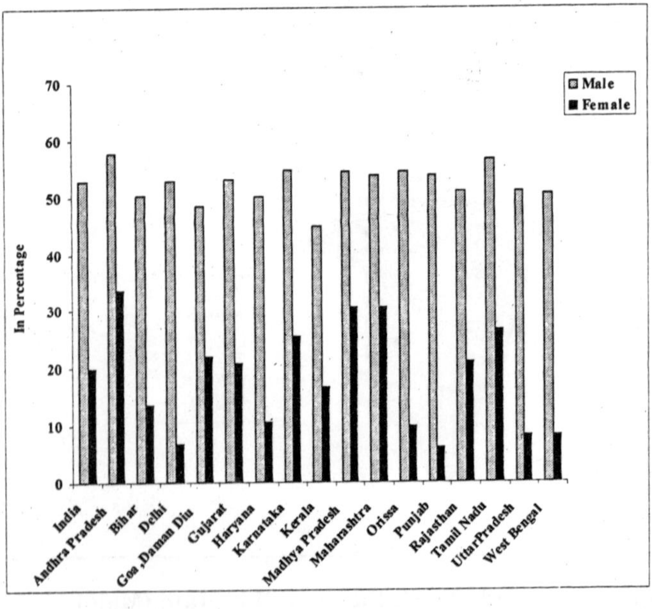

Fig. 2.1.2. Crude Work Participation Rate (Main + Marginal) in India and States, 1981

Figs. 2.1.2 through 2.1.5 show the crude work participation rate (Main+Marginal) for India and states from 1981 to 2001 by sex. It may also be seen that the work participation rate of females is lower than that of males during 1981-2001. However, the disparity by sex has been declining over the period 1981-2001. Among the EAG (Empowered Action Group) states, Bihar, Orissa and Uttar Pradesh have very low female work participation rates. Even in West Bengal, the work participation rate is quite low among the females. Andhra Pradesh shows very high participation rates along with Maharasthra, Madhya Pradesh, Karnataka and Tamil Nadu, and continues to show increase in the participation rates over the years 1981-2001.

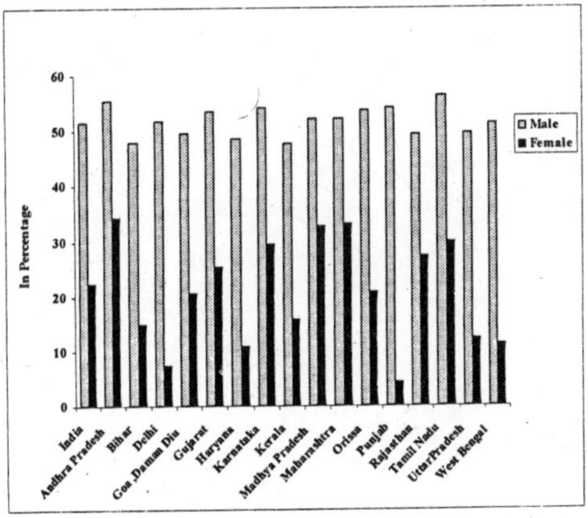

Fig. 2.1.3. Crude Work Participation Rate (Main + Marginal) in India and States, 1991

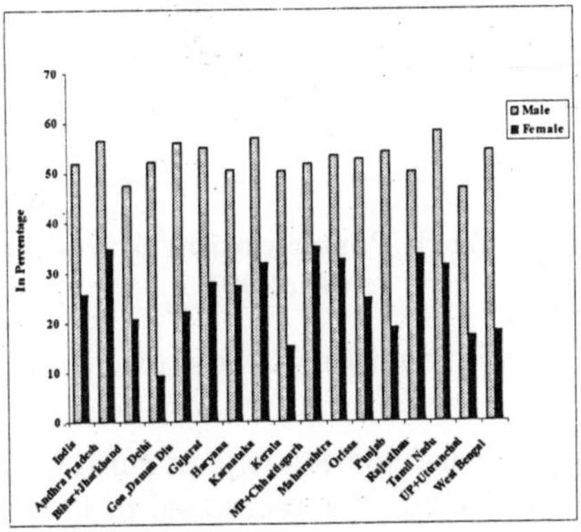

Fig. 2.1.4. Crude Work Participation Rate of Total Workers (Main + Marginal) in India and States, 2001.

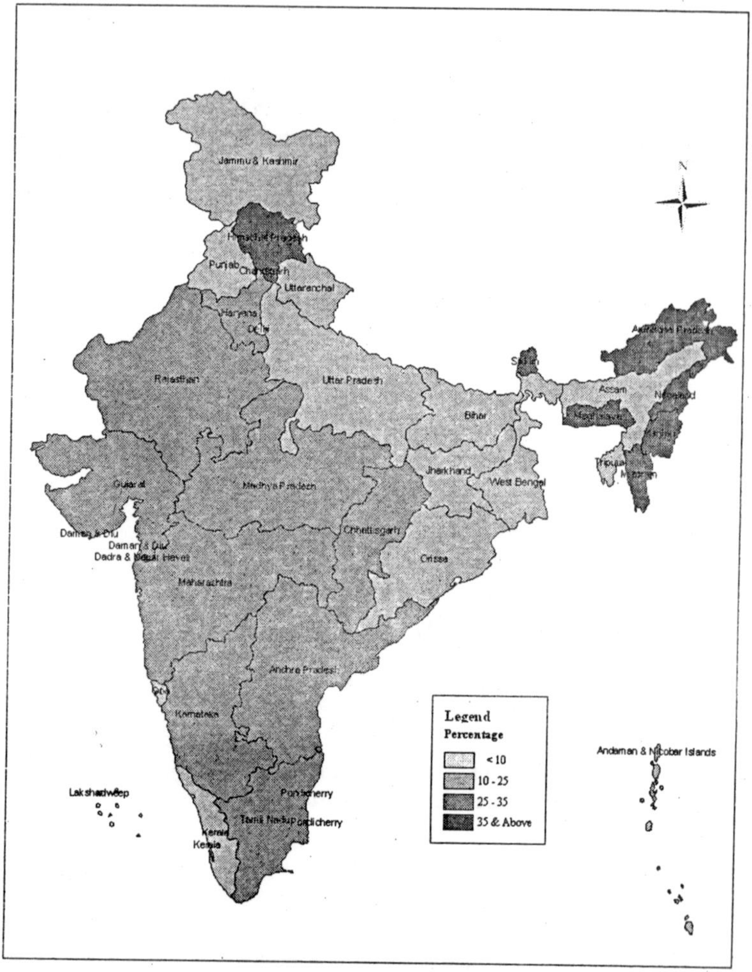

Map 2.1.2. Crude Work Participation Rate (Female), State, India, 2001

2.1.2. Work Participation Rates (Main+Marginal) by Residence

The crude work participation rate in rural India was around 39 per cent in 1981, which has increased to 40 per cent in 1991 and 42 per cent in 2001. This is true for both males and females (see Table 2.1.2). It is observed that in all EAG states,

Table 2.1.2. Crude Work Participation Rate (Main + Marginal) by Residence (Rural), India and States, 1981-2001

Sl. No.	*State / Union Territories*	*1981*			*1991*			*2001*		
		Total	*Male*	*Female*	*Total*	*Male*	*Female*	*Total*	*Male*	*Female*
	India	38.87	53.80	23.18	39.99	52.48	26.67	41.97	52.36	30.98
01	Andaman & Nicobar	37.03	56.40	12.01	35.41	53.02	14.36	39.20	57.05	18.50
02	Andhra Pradesh	50.19	60.19	40.03	50.29	57.92	42.48	50.92	58.48	43.24
03	Arunachal Pradesh	53.41	58.49	47.64	47.69	53.69	40.86	46.47	51.13	41.33
04	Assam	NA	NA	NA	36.73	49.30	23.27	36.45	49.77	22.28
05	Bihar	33.20	51.08	14.65	33.23	48.87	16.26	34.85	48.43	20.19
06	Chandigarh	36.17	58.58	3.59	41.54	64.43	5.34	43.41	63.96	10.32
07	Dadra & Nagar Haveli	49.42	56.39	42.31	54.29	57.42	51.05	53.85	61.29	45.10
08	Delhi	30.15	47.49	8.75	29.12	48.23	5.46	32.00	49.71	10.12
09	Goa,Daman & Diu	36.02	47.19	24.99	36.81	49.17	24.31	42.17	57.38	25.71
10	Gujarat	40.80	54.18	26.85	45.51	54.91	35.60	47.55	55.59	39.04
11	Haryana	32.75	49.84	12.29	31.87	48.51	12.62	43.13	50.88	34.18

Sl. No.	State/Union Territories	1981			1991			2001		
		Total	Male	Female	Total	Male	Female	Total	Male	Female
12	Himachal Pradesh	42.96	52.45	33.37	43.57	50.46	36.61	50.63	54.74	46.47
13	Jammu & Kashmir	47.73	57.27	37.08	NA	NA	NA	37.93	49.14	25.84
14	Karnataka	44.07	57.18	30.66	46.45	56.04	36.60	49.20	58.32	39.86
15	Kerala	31.25	45.23	17.72	32.09	47.88	16.80	32.56	50.22	15.88
16	Lakshadweep	25.25	39.01	11.29	25.28	42.86	6.96	23.77	40.70	6.07
17	Madhya Pradesh	46.31	56.38	35.78	46.83	53.96	39.26	47.11	53.08	40.68
18	Maharashtra	48.16	55.38	40.85	49.68	53.19	46.06	50.43	54.18	46.52
19	Manipur	45.96	48.45	43.38	45.22	47.12	43.22	46.72	50.07	43.20
20	Meghalaya	48.85	55.42	42.05	45.04	51.02	38.85	44.58	50.09	38.92
21	Mizoram	48.68	54.13	42.81	51.19	54.92	47.11	57.22	59.52	54.73
22	Nagaland	50.67	52.80	48.30	44.75	46.56	42.78	45.08	47.08	42.92
23	Odisha	38.90	56.68	21.09	38.75	54.68	22.62	40.33	53.38	27.10
24	Pondicherry	34.09	49.71	18.10	38.34	53.38	22.85	39.20	54.47	23.78
25	Punjab	32.14	54.45	6.90	31.22	55.05	4.37	39.73	54.45	23.15

Sl. No.	*State / Union Territories*	*1981*			*1991*			*2001*		
		Total	*Male*	*Female*	*Total*	*Male*	*Female*	*Total*	*Male*	*Female*
26	Rajasthan	39.07	52.18	24.99	42.04	50.12	33.25	45.94	50.82	40.70
27	Sikkim	49.55	56.61	41.37	41.74	50.90	31.47	49.75	57.75	40.67
28	Tamil Nadu	46.48	59.24	33.55	48.49	58.28	38.50	50.39	59.38	41.33
29	Tripura	32.84	51.33	13.28	31.54	47.52	14.58	37.11	50.61	22.86
30	Uttar Pradesh	31.46	51.49	9.04	33.46	50.51	14.16	34.10	47.84	18.89
31	West Bengal	29.35	48.72	8.89	33.18	52.09	13.07	37.93	54.30	20.70

Note:				
	Chhattisgarh	50.43	54.28	46.59
	Jharkhand	41.06	49.91	31.86
	Uttarakhand	39.63	45.99	33.32

except Rajasthan and Madhya Pradesh and some northern states/union territories like Haryana, Punjab, Chandigarh and Delhi, the female work participation was very low, and the gap between both the sexes was high. However, in the north-eastern states of India, the difference between male and female work participation rates is the lowest than rest of the country. Kerala and Lakshadweep stand discretely than rest of India as the work participation of females in the rural areas has shown a declining trend during the reference period.

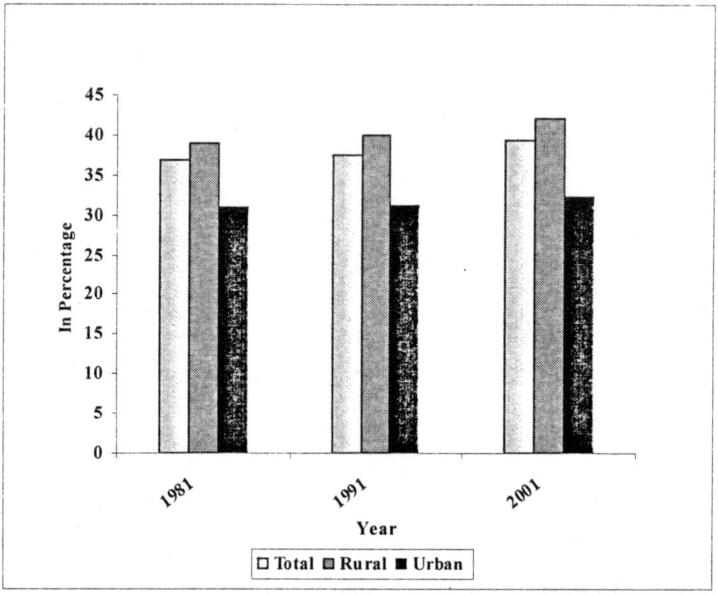

Fig. 2.1.5. Crude Work Participation Rate (Main + Marginal) by Residence in India, 1981-2001

Fig. 2.1.5 shows the crude work participation rates (Main+Marginal) by residence in India during 1981 to 2001. It depicts that the work participation rates remained almost static in the urban areas during 1981-1991, but increased slightly in 2001. While there has been a secular increase in participation rates among females in both rural and urban areas during 1981-2001, same is not true for males during the said period. In rural areas, male work participation has been declining throughout this period, whereas in urban areas, the increase has been noticed only during the last decade (1991-2001).

2.1.3. Work Participation Rates (Main Workers), 1981-2001

It has been mentioned earlier that workers are of two types based on the duration of work during the last year. As such, the main workers assume special importance as they are engaged in work during the major part of the year. Thus, the study of work participation rates based on main workers shows the extent of workforce fully employed. It is found that the crude work participation rate of female main workers is always lower than their male counterparts during the study period at the national level as well as in the states and union territories. However, an increase in crude work participation of female main workers is marked during 1981-91 but declined in 2001 At the national level, a declining trend observed in the work participation of male main workers is very obvious; it was around 52 per cent in 1981 which declined by 1 per cent in 1991 (51 per cent) and further declined by 5 per cent in 2001 (45 per cent) (see Fig. 2.1.6).

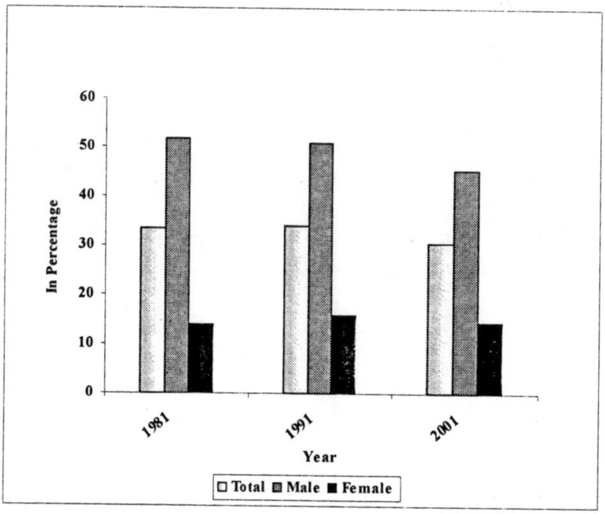

Fig. 2.1.6. Crude Work Participation Rate (Main) by Sex, India, 1981-2001

Table 2.1.3. Crude Work Participation Rate (Main+Marginal) by Residence (Urban) in India and States, 1981-2001

Sl. No.	*State / Union Territories*	*1981*			*1991*			*2001*		
		Total	*Male*	*Female*	*Total*	*Male*	*Female*	*Total*	*Male*	*Female*
	India	30.01	49.07	8.32	30.17	48.94	9.17	32.23	50.85	11.55
01	Andaman & Nicobar	36.48	57.56	7.20	34.78	54.13	9.60	36.33	56.09	12.09
02	Andhra Pradesh	31.20	49.58	11.81	30.82	48.92	11.94	32.22	51.10	12.62
03	Arunachal Pradesh	41.47	60.24	11.62	36.39	54.18	11.94	34.16	48.99	16.69
04	Assam	NA	NA	NA	30.92	50.52	7.52	31.98	51.03	10.29
05	Bihar	26.36	44.31	4.78	25.07	41.91	5.11	25.63	41.96	6.83
06	Chandigarh	34.83	54.50	9.46	34.18	53.05	10.89	36.97	55.12	14.06
07	Dadra & Nagar Haveli	41.94	55.30	26.84	41.98	58.21	22.10	44.74	65.74	14.35
08	Delhi	32.35	53.08	6.69	31.92	52.11	7.57	32.85	52.40	9.08
09	Goa,Daman & Diu	33.47	50.22	15.22	33.57	50.49	15.54	36.91	54.78	17.84
10	Gujarat	29.44	50.17	6.52	33.51	54.75	10.09	33.07	54.12	9.11

Sl. No.	State / Union Territories	1981			1991			2001		
		Total	Male	Female	Total	Male	Female	Total	Male	Female
10	Gujarat	29.44	50.17	6.52	33.51	54.75	10.09	33.07	54.12	9.11
11	Haryana	29.23	50.27	4.45	28.32	48.51	5.08	31.52	49.52	10.27
12	Himachal Pradesh	35.25	54.32	11.26	34.98	52.36	14.09	36.89	54.38	14.96
13	Jammu & Kashmir	31.27	50.41	9.39	NA	NA	NA	32.71	51.80	9.50
14	Karnataka	30.81	48.40	11.83	32.03	49.83	12.90	35.67	54.11	16.06
15	Kerala	27.42	43.42	11.76	29.61	46.76	13.02	31.65	50.78	13.55
16	Lakshadweep	23.39	39.50	6.65	27.31	45.17	8.10	27.28	44.75	8.61
17	Madhya Pradesh	29.62	47.29	9.63	29.55	46.80	10.24	30.64	47.64	11.70
18	Maharashtra	32.15	50.87	10.14	32.34	50.62	11.44	34.00	52.60	12.72
19	Manipur	35.52	42.21	28.61	34.18	40.33	27.88	38.71	45.17	32.28
20	Meghalaya	32.63	47.55	16.12	32.30	46.01	17.22	28.74	38.19	19.15
21	Mizoram	35.55	47.76	21.88	46.23	52.63	39.37	48.09	55.32	40.50
22	Nagaland	34.97	51.51	10.93	32.72	48.17	12.09	31.91	45.70	14.87

Sl. No.	State / Union Territories	1981			1991			2001		
		Total	*Male*	*Female*	*Total*	*Male*	*Female*	*Total*	*Male*	*Female*
23	Odisha	31.36	50.14	9.49	29.67	48.36	8.10	30.66	49.37	9.76
24	Pondicherry	27.05	44.67	9.30	30.12	48.96	10.99	33.08	52.68	13.61
25	Punjab	29.82	51.97	4.20	30.06	52.26	4.49	33.40	53.42	9.74
26	Rajasthan	27.37	45.52	5.88	28.17	46.60	7.22	29.56	47.64	9.24
27	Sikkim	41.81	60.09	15.58	39.20	54.53	18.75	40.49	56.27	21.42
28	Tamil Nadu	32.05	51.25	11.97	33.34	52.78	13.10	37.59	56.37	18.42
29	Tripura	27.60	45.64	8.73	28.89	47.68	9.27	32.32	51.78	12.09
30	Uttar Pradesh	27.29	47.46	3.46	27.14	46.37	4.78	27.08	44.77	6.85
31	West Bengal	29.30	48.70	5.59	29.59	49.64	6.21	33.82	54.07	11.13

Note:				
	Chhattisgarh	31.09	47.95	12.96
	Jharkhand	25.69	42.57	6.29
	Uttarakhand	29.09	47.58	7.28

Table 2.1.4. Crude Work Participation Rate (Main) in , India and States, 1981-2001

Sl. No.	*State / Union Territories*	*1981*			*1991*			*2001*		
		Total	*Male*	*Female*	*Total*	*Male*	*Female*	*Total*	*Male*	*Female*
	India	33.45	51.62	13.99	34.10	50.93	15.93	30.55	45.35	14.68
01	Andaman & Nicobar	33.21	54.59	5.07	32.35	52.25	8.03	31.98	50.70	9.85
02	Andhra Pradesh	42.26	57.12	27.02	42.77	55.14	30.05	38.10	50.71	25.21
03	Arunachal Pradesh	49.61	57.42	40.55	45.22	53.52	35.56	37.71	46.09	28.33
04	Assam	NA	NA	NA	31.19	48.38	12.57	26.59	42.35	9.68
05	Bihar	29.68	49.19	9.06	29.66	47.59	9.97	25.40	40.72	8.76
06	Chandigarh	34.69	54.50	8.98	34.83	54.24	10.28	36.51	54.77	12.87
07	Dadra & Nagar Haveli	40.81	55.11	26.14	43.91	55.94	31.26	43.70	58.62	25.30
08	Delhi	31.93	52.47	6.52	31.51	51.61	7.21	31.18	50.06	8.19
09	Goa,Daman & Diu	30.59	45.85	15.05	32.70	48.47	16.39	32.84	49.79	14.63
10	Gujarat	32.22	52.19	11.03	34.12	53.17	13.74	33.66	51.25	14.53

Sl No.	*State / Union Territories*	*1981*			*1991*			*2001*		
		Total	*Male*	*Female*	*Total*	*Male*	*Female*	*Total*	*Male*	*Female*
11	Haryana	28.35	48.94	4.69	28.66	48.26	6.01	29.62	43.62	13.37
12	Himachal Pradesh	34.36	49.61	18.71	34.41	49.08	19.36	32.36	43.30	21.08
13	Jammu & Kashmir	30.37	52.20	5.91	NA	NA	NA	25.19	41.30	7.28
14	Karnataka	36.76	53.90	18.95	38.45	53.53	22.73	36.71	51.92	20.92
15	Kerala	26.68	41.04	12.77	28.53	44.82	12.81	25.87	41.89	10.74
16	Lakshadweep	19.74	33.56	5.58	23.96	41.02	5.85	19.37	33.20	4.77
17	Madhya Pradesh	38.41	53.52	22.35	37.68	51.51	22.82	31.66	44.87	17.31
18	Maharashtra	38.71	52.51	23.98	39.29	51.25	26.47	36.87	48.65	24.10
19	Manipur	40.35	45.94	34.59	38.55	44.21	32.65	31.68	39.83	23.22
20	Meghalaya	43.44	53.12	33.29	40.32	49.54	30.67	32.21	40.40	23.80
21	Mizoram	41.73	50.38	32.33	42.09	49.59	33.95	40.83	49.29	31.82
22	Nagaland	47.53	51.91	42.45	42.29	46.69	37.32	35.63	40.73	30.01
23	Odisha	32.75	54.38	10.70	32.78	52.86	12.10	26.08	43.07	8.60
24	Pondicherry	28.66	46.02	11.03	32.41	50.11	14.34	32.54	50.52	14.57

Sl. No.	State / Union Territories	1981			1991			2001		
		Total	Male	Female	Total	Male	Female	Total	Male	Female
25	Punjab	29.35	53.14	2.27	30.07	54.12	2.79	32.23	49.97	11.92
26	Rajasthan	30.48	49.92	9.32	31.62	48.53	13.04	30.86	43.81	16.83
27	Sikkim	46.60	56.55	34.69	40.45	50.82	28.63	39.31	50.89	26.09
28	Tamil Nadu	39.30	55.85	22.36	40.82	56.10	25.13	38.13	52.28	23.79
29	Tripura	29.64	49.23	8.95	29.09	46.99	10.14	28.41	45.24	10.70
30	Uttar Pradesh	29.22	50.31	5.39	29.73	49.31	7.45	23.85	39.15	6.86
31	West Bengal	28.26	48.71	5.81	30.23	50.66	7.96	28.75	47.32	8.86

Note:				
	Chhattisgarh	33.92	45.44	22.28
	Jharkhand	24.02	37.22	10.00
	Uttarakhand	27.39	38.13	16.24

Figs. 2.1.7 through 2.1.9 further show that all the EAG states of India have very low work participation rates of females in the main work category except Madhya Pradesh where the rates are high. Among the southern states, Andhra Pradesh (about 27 per cent) shows the highest female work participation rate in both rural and urban areas in urban areas in 1981. It is interesting to see that all southern states experienced a marginal reduction in female work participation rate during 1991-2001. Among the states, the lowest percentage of male main workers has been observed in Uttar Pradesh (39.15) in 2001. The decline in male work participation rate from 1991 to 2001 is significantly high in Uttar Pradesh.

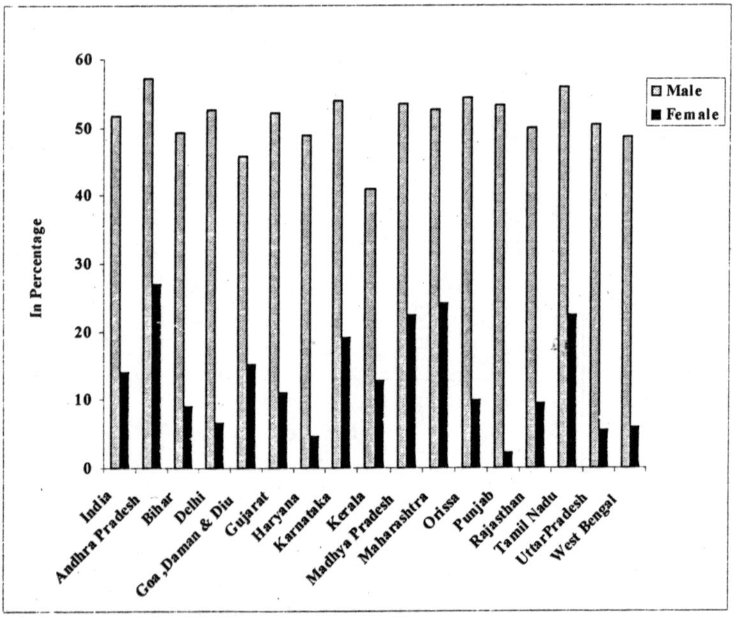

Fig. 2.1.7. Crude Work Participation Rate (Main) India and States, 1981

Further, it may be noted that except in Andhra Pradesh, Maharashtra and Tamil Nadu the gender disparity in workforce is high in the case of main workers. Punjab shows the highest disparity in work participation rate between the two sexes.

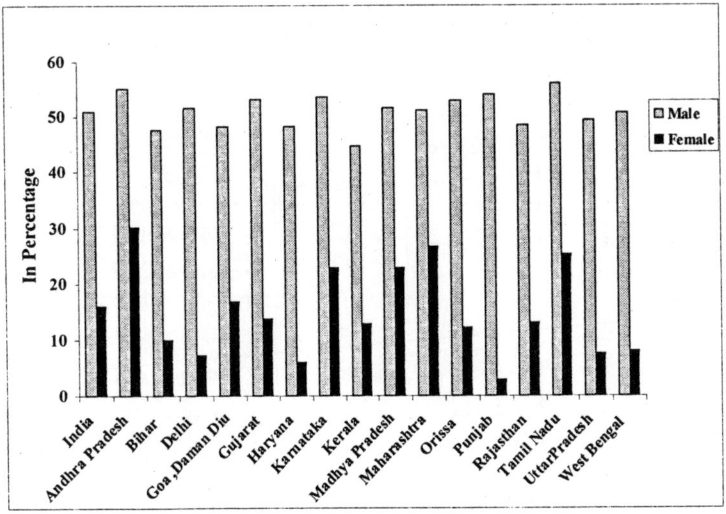

Fig. 2.1.8. Crude Work Participation (Main) India and States, 1991

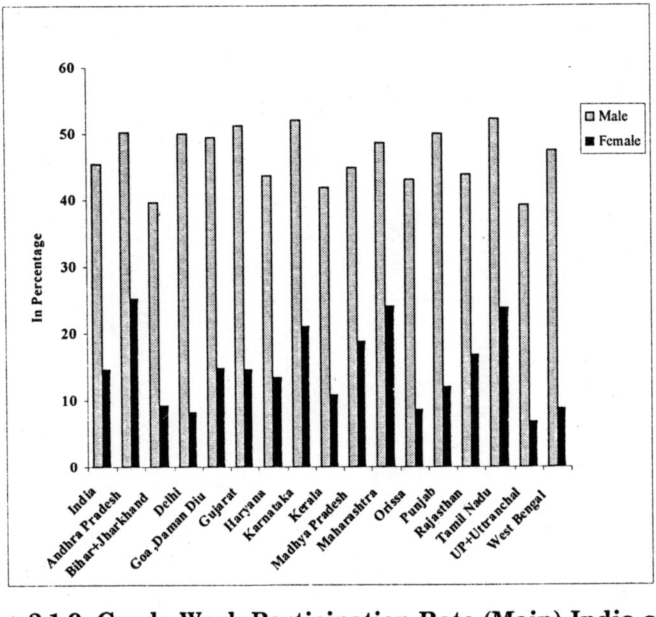

Fig. 2.1.9. Crude Work Participation Rate (Main) India and States, 2001

Table 2.1.5. Crude Work Participation Rate (Main) by Residence (Rural), India and States, 1981-2001

Sl.No.	State / Union Territories	1981			1991			2001		
		Total	Male	Female	Total	Male	Female	Total	Male	Female
	India	34.76	52.62	16.00	35.69	51.76	18.57	31.03	44.51	16.77
01	Andaman & Nicobar	32.26	53.80	4.45	31.66	51.78	7.61	30.70	49.29	9.13
02	Andhra Pradesh	45.86	59.56	31.95	47.36	57.52	36.96	41.49	51.93	30.87
03	Arunachal Pradesh	50.20	57.20	42.24	46.54	53.43	38.72	39.28	45.99	31.87
04	Assam	NA	NA	NA	31.30	48.14	13.26	26.15	41.46	9.86
05	Bihar	30.23	50.01	9.70	30.42	48.52	10.79	25.75	41.06	9.24
06	Chandigarh	35.85	58.37	3.12	41.36	64.34	5.01	41.47	61.77	8.77
07	Dadra & Nagar Haveli	41.18	55.39	26.68	44.37	55.76	32.57	44.20	56.77	29.41
08	Delhi	28.49	46.64	6.10	28.75	48.06	4.84	29.11	46.37	7.78
09	Goa,Daman & Diu	30.15	44.29	16.19	32.94	47.57	18.14	32.71	49.26	14.80
10	Gujarat	33.78	53.27	13.46	36.54	54.42	17.70	35.11	50.41	18.93
11	Haryana	28.21	48.64	4.89	28.85	48.20	6.46	30.20	42.71	15.78

Sl. No.	State / Union Territories	1981			1991			2001		
		Total	Male	Female	Total	Male	Female	Total	Male	Female
12	Himachal Pradesh	34.39	49.22	19.38	34.50	48.79	20.08	32.13	42.30	21.88
13	Jammu & Kashmir	30.76	52.86	6.12	NA	NA	NA	23.78	38.73	7.65
14	Karnataka	39.54	56.41	22.28	41.58	55.35	27.44	38.66	52.32	24.66
15	Kerala	27.10	41.19	13.47	30.75	48.07	14.06	25.44	40.96	10.78
16	Lakshadweep	18.89	31.23	6.36	21.94	37.78	5.42	17.56	30.47	4.07
17	Madhya Pradesh	40.87	55.30	25.78	40.38	53.07	26.93	33.30	45.23	20.44
18	Maharashtra	42.70	53.86	31.39	44.19	52.07	36.10	40.82	47.78	33.57
19	Manipur	43.35	47.72	38.85	41.74	46.05	37.20	32.69	40.26	24.74
20	Meghalaya	45.90	54.43	37.05	42.30	50.42	33.90	33.96	41.77	25.93
21	Mizoram	44.53	51.73	36.78	45.54	51.29	39.24	44.94	51.74	37.61
22	Nagaland	49.90	52.05	47.50	44.29	46.36	42.03	37.08	40.31	33.62
23	Odisha	33.10	55.10	11.07	33.37	53.67	12.83	25.82	42.55	8.86
24	Pondicherry	31.63	48.50	14.35	37.29	52.93	21.17	34.80	50.29	19.16
25	Punjab	29.29	53.66	1.72	30.11	54.92	2.16	32.70	49.35	13.95

Sl. .No.	*State / Union Territories*	*1981*			*1991*			*2001*		
		Total	*Male*	*Female*	*Total*	*Male*	*Female*	*Total*	*Male*	*Female*
26	Rajasthan	31.53	51.01	10.58	32.94	49.18	15.26	32.26	43.70	19.99
27	Sikkim	47.61	55.90	38.01	40.68	50.56	29.61	39.57	50.75	26.89
28	Tamil Nadu	43.20	58.35	27.85	45.07	57.92	31.97	40.98	51.79	30.08
29	Tripura	29.99	49.80	9.03	29.21	46.92	10.40	28.08	44.49	10.76
30	Uttar Pradesh	29.71	50.98	5.90	30.52	50.10	8.36	23.91	38.86	7.45
31	West Bengal	28.04	48.72	6.19	30.61	51.18	8.74	27.91	46.00	8.87

Note:				
	Chhattisgarh	35.42	45.61	25.27
	Jharkhand	24.47	36.95	11.50
	Uttarakhand	27.77	36.09	19.50.

2.1.4. Work Participation Rates, Main Workers, by Residence

The work participation rate by main worker status is higher in rural than urban areas (see Fig. 2.1.10). It may be noted from Table 2.1.5 that the work participation of rural male workers in the main work category has increased slightly in 1991 over 1981 but there is a noticeable decline in 2001 at the all India level. In case of rural females in the main work category, we find a slight increase in the work participation during 1981-91 but a decline in 2001 similar to males at all India level. The difference between rural males and females in the main work category is lower in most of the northeastern states and also in Andhra Pradesh, Madhya Pradesh, Maharashtra and Tamil Nadu. On the other hand in rural areas of the northern states and union territories like Punjab, Haryana, Jammu and Kashmir, Delhi and Chandigarh, the work participation of females in the main work category is not only lower than rest of the states and union territories but there is a wide gap between males and females in both rural and urban areas. A significant increase has been observed in the rural female work participation rates in 2001. For example, in case of Punjab, the work participation of rural females in the main work category was only around 2 per cent in 1981 and 1991 but it increased to 14 per cent in 2001. Same trend is also found in Haryana.

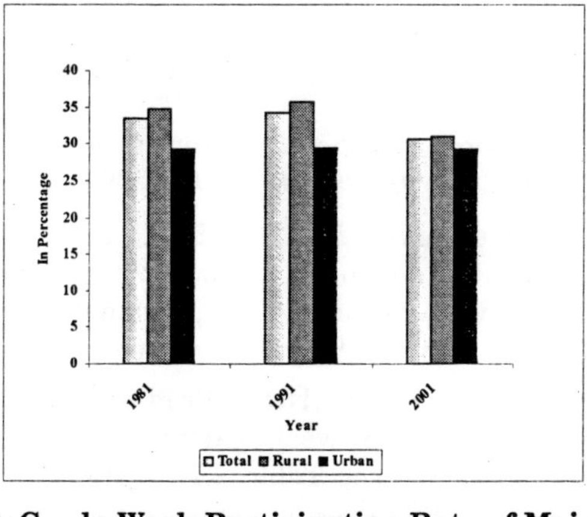

Fig. 2.1.10. Crude Work Participation Rate of Main Workers by Residence, India, 1981-2001

2.1.5. Work Participation Rates, Marginal Workers, 1981-2001

The work participation rate of marginal workers remains more or less constant during the period 1981 to1991, but there is a substantial increase in 2001 (see Fig. 2.1.11). It is found that the female workers show faster increase than the male workers during the reference period at the national level and also in most of the states and union territories.

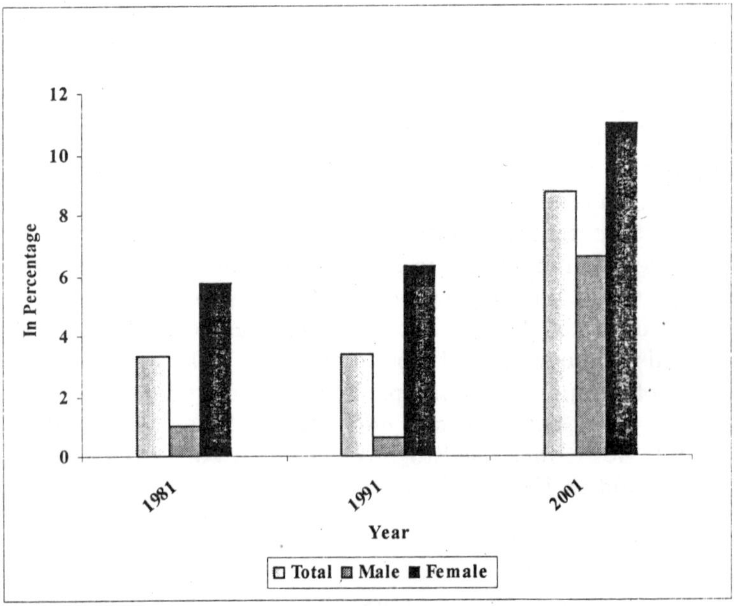

Fig. 2.1.11. Crude Work Participation Rate of Marginal Workers by Sex, India, 1981-2001

It may also be observed from Fig. 2.1.11 that during 1981-1991, there is a slight decline in the work participation rates of male marginal workers but in 2001, a remarkable increase is seen along with female marginal workers.

At the state level except Uttar Pradesh, all other EAG states have higher female work participation rates in the marginal work category (see Table 2.1.7). However, in 2001, the entire picture of male and female work participation rates in the marginal work category has changed. The work

Table 2.1.6. Crude Work Participation Rate (Main) by Residence (Urban) in India and States, 1981-2001

Sl. No.	State / Union Territories	1981			1991			2001		
		Total	Male	Female	Total	Male	Female	Total	Male	Female
	India	29.24	48.54	7.28	29.50	48.59	7.27	29.30	47.46	9.42
01	Andaman & Nicobar	35.86	56.71	6.89	34.27	53.50	9.25	34.61	53.53	11.48
02	Andhra Pradesh	30.40	49.27	10.49	30.30	48.71	11.09	29.11	47.48	10.52
03	Arunachal Pradesh	41.14	59.96	11.20	36.23	54.09	11.69	31.53	46.45	14.33
04	Assam	NA	NA	NA	30.39	50.22	6.71	29.62	48.26	8.79
05	Bihar	25.82	43.83	4.17	24.61	41.75	4.30	22.36	37.73	4.67
06	Chandigarh	34.61	54.23	9.30	34.08	52.95	10.80	35.94	53.89	13.59
07	Dadra & Nagar Haveli	35.77	51.38	18.12	38.89	57.73	15.82	42.01	64.31	9.93
08	Delhi	32.20	52.93	6.55	31.82	52.02	7.47	31.34	50.34	8.42
09	Goa, Daman & Diu	31.52	48.97	12.53	32.35	49.71	13.84	32.99	50.35	14.45
10	Gujarat	28.78	49.85	5.49	32.20	54.49	7.62	31.26	52.61	7.23
11	Haryana	28.88	50.01	3.99	28.08	48.43	4.65	28.20	45.84	7.66

Sl.		*1981*			*1991*			*2001*		
No.	*State / Union Territories*	*Total*	*Male*	*Female*	*Total*	*Male*	*Female*	*Total*	*Male*	*Female*
12	Himachal Pradesh	34.08	53.56	9.59	33.39	51.92	11.10	34.40	51.64	12.99
13	Jammu & Kashmir	28.92	49.75	5.11	NA	NA	NA	29.45	48.65	6.98
14	Karnataka	29.92	47.88	10.53	31.44	49.55	11.96	32.92	51.15	13.78
15	Kerala	24.86	40.37	9.67	27.66	44.57	11.30	27.10	44.54	10.71
16	Lakshadweep	20.74	36.24	4.65	25.53	43.50	6.19	21.63	36.58	5.67
17	Madhya Pradesh	28.74	46.80	8.31	28.71	46.46	8.82	27.12	43.88	8.47
18	Maharashtra	31.31	50.17	9.11	31.52	50.02	10.37	31.49	49.77	10.47
19	Manipur	32.00	40,99	22.71	30.17	39.29	20.82	28.50	38.45	18.95
20	Meghalaya	32.27	47.33	15.61	31.64	45.78	16.10	25.05	34.78	16.95
21	Mizoram	33.19	46.35	18.45	38.05	47.57	27.83	36.64	46.77	26.13
22	Nagaland	34.63	51.23	10.52	32.68	48.16	12.01	28.87	42.52	12.75
23	Odisha	30.11	49.38	7.65	28.93	47.90	7.03	27.56	45.93	7.29
24	Pondicherry	25.95	43.74	8.02	29.67	48.52	10.52	31.40	50.63	12.55

Sl. No.	*State / Union Territories*	*1981*			*1991*			*2001*		
		Total	*Male*	*Female*	*Total*	*Male*	*Female*	*Total*	*Male*	*Female*
25	Punjab	29.51	51.80	3.71	29.96	52.22	4.31	31.31	51.14	8.50
26	Rajasthan	26.54	45.22	4.45	27.18	46.36	5.36	26.29	44.15	6.51
27	Sikkim	41.36	59.59	15.21	38.08	53.24	17.87	37.21	51.92	19.83
28	Tamil Nadu	31.37	50.84	11.01	32.61	52.62	11.78	34.49	52.90	16.18
29	Tripura	26.83	44.61	8.25	28.45	47.38	8.68	30.02	48.92	10.67
30	Uttar Pradesh	26.99	47.30	2.99	26.56	46.19	3.75	23.62	40.22	4.63
31	West Bengal	28.87	48.70	4.66	29.23	49.34	5.79	30.90	50.61	9.21

Note:				
	Chhattisgarh	27.98	44.76	10.16
	Jharkhand	22.44	38.10	4.62
	Uttarakhand	26.29	43.61	6.16

Table 2.1.7. Crude Work Participation Rate (Marginal) in India and States, 1981-2001

Sl No.	State / Union Territories	1981			1991			2001		
		Total	Male	Female	Total	Male	Female	Total	Male	Female
	India	3.32	1.03	5.77	3.36	0.62	6.32	8.71	6.59	10.99
01	Andaman & Nicobar	3.67	2.12	5.71	2.88	1.07	5.10	6.29	6.03	6.60
02	Andhra Pradesh	3.50	0.56	6.53	2.28	0.35	4.27	7.70	5.74	9.72
03	Arunachal Pradesh	3.03	1.22	5.13	1.02	0.24	1.92	6.26	4.60	8.13
04	Assam	NA	NA	NA	4.89	1.07	9.04	9.29	7.58	11.12
05	Bihar	2.67	0.98	4.44	2.50	0.32	4.89	8.48	7.01	10.07
06	Chandigarh	0.23	0.27	0.18	0.10	0.10	0.11	1.12	1.33	0.85
07	Dadra & Nagar Haveli	8.11	1.20	15.19	9.34	1.56	17.53	8.07	3.77	13.38
08	Delhi	0.25	0.20	0.32	0.13	0.11	0.16	1.62	2.15	0.96
09	Goa,Daman & Diu	4.60	2.35	6.89	2.77	1.25	4.34	6.78	6.40	7.29
10	Gujarat	5.04	0.72	9.63	6.11	0.40	12.23	8.43	3.77	13.50

Sl No.	State/Union Territories	1981			1991			2001		
		Total	Male	Female	Total	Male	Female	Total	Male	Female
11	Haryana	3.28	0.99	5.91	2.34	0.25	4.75	10.14	6.86	13.94
12	Himachal Pradesh	8.01	3.02	13.14	8.42	1.56	15.45	16.92	11.40	22.61
13	Jammu & Kashmir	13.89	3.61	25.40	NA	NA	NA	11.44	8.53	14.68
14	Karnataka	3.49	0.70	6.38	3.55	0.56	6.66	7.90	4.95	10.96
15	Kerala	3.85	3.85	3.85	2.90	2.76	3.04	6.45	8.48	4.54
16	Lakshadweep	4.64	5.68	3.58	2.47	3.15	1.75	5.96	9.31	2.42
17	Madhya Pradesh	4.52	0.96	8.30	5.15	0.75	9.86	11.48	6.98	16.27
18	Maharashtra	3.85	1.22	6.65	3.68	0.92	6.64	6.60	4.85	8.49
19	Manipur	2.85	0.86	4.90	3.63	1.06	6.30	13.11	9.08	17.29
20	Meghalaya	2.49	0.85	4.21	2.35	0.53	4.25	9.27	7.36	11.22
21	Mizoram	3.71	2.15	5.40	6.82	4.28	9.57	11.87	8.16	15.82
22	Nagaland	0.70	0.66	0.74	0.39	0.17	0.64	7.12	6.10	8.24

Sl No.	State / Union Territories	1981			1991			2001		
		Total	Male	Female	Total	Male	Female	Total	Male	Female
23	Orissa	5.26	1.48	9.11	4.75	0.93	8.69	12.80	9.68	16.02
24	Pondicherry	1.75	1.06	2.45	0.67	0.44	0.90	2.59	2.76	2.43
25	Punjab	2.15	0.61	3.89	0.81	0.10	1.61	5.36	4.13	6.76
26	Rajasthan	6.13	0.98	11.74	7.25	0.77	14.36	11.25	6.26	16.66
27	Sikkim	1.70	0.68	2.93	1.07	0.43	1.78	9.41	6.69	12.51
28	Tamil Nadu	2.42	0.73	4.15	2.50	0.29	4.76	6.64	5.78	7.52
29	Tripura	2.62	1.48	3.83	2.05	0.56	3.63	7.89	5.57	10.32
30	Uttar Pradesh	0.24	2.36	3.18	2.47	0.36	4.87	8.85	7.62	10.22
31	West Bengal	1.91	1.58	2.26	1.96	0.74	3.29	8.03	6.91	9.22

Note:	Chhattisgarh	12.62	7.54	17.75
	Jharkhand	13.62	11.00	16.41
	Uttarakhand	9.55	8.29	10.85

participation rates of both sexes in marginal category have increased remarkably in most of the states and male and female disparity in the participation of marginal workforce has been reduced in 2001 Census (see Figs. 2.1.12 to 14). In all the three newly created states of 2001 (Uttarakhand, Chhattisgarh and Jharkhand), the work participation rates of both male and female workers in the marginal work category are found to be fairly high than their parent states

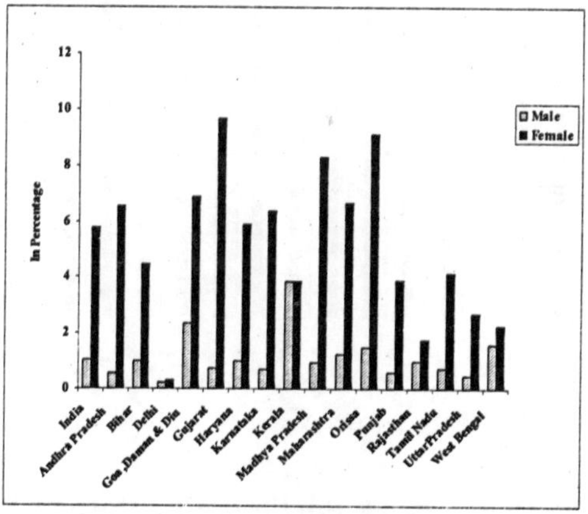

Fig. 2.1.12. Crude Work Participation Rate (Marginal) in India and States, 1981

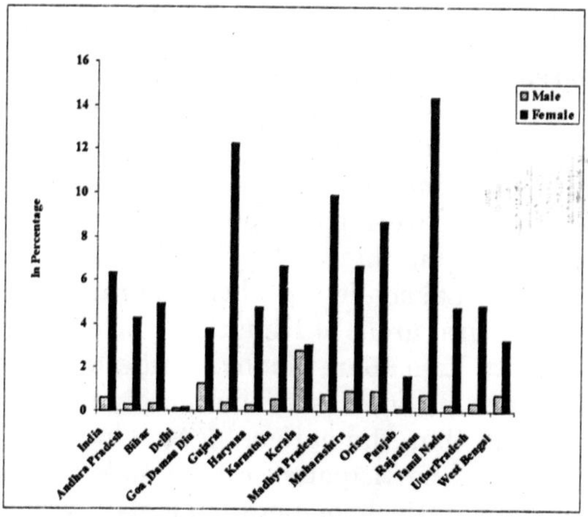

Fig. 2.1.13. Crude Work Participation Rate (Marginal) in India and States, 1991

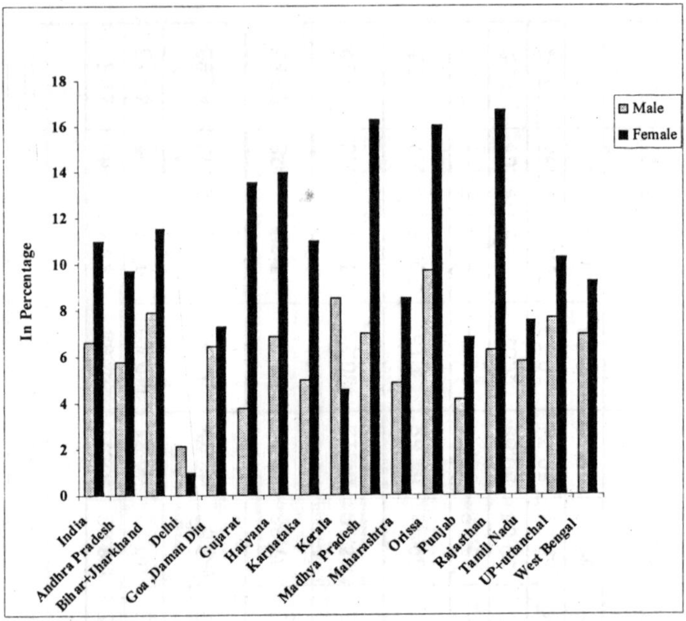

Fig. 2.1.14. Crude Work Participation Rate of Marginal Workers in India and States, 2001

2.1.6. Work Participation Rate, Marginal Workers by Residence

Rural areas have higher work participation rates in the marginal work category than the urban areas (see Fig. 2.1.15). This is also true for most of the states and union territories. Table 2.1.8 shows that in rural areas of all the states and union territories, the work participation rates in the marginal work category are quite higher for female than male workers except Kerala and Lakshadweep where the rate is high in case of males. In the rural areas of Himachal Pradesh, Jammu and Kashmir, Gujarat, Rajasthan, Madhya Pradesh and Orissa, the work participation of females in the marginal work category are always higher than the national level. On the other hand, in Kerala, the work participation rate of male workers (about 9 per cent) is comparatively higher than female workers (nearly 5 per cent) as per the 2001 Census.

Table 2.1.8. Crude Work Participation Rate (Marginal) by Residence (Rural) in India and States, 1981-2001

Sl. No.	*State / Union Territories*	*1981*			*1991*			*2001*		
		Total	*Male*	*Female*	*Total*	*Male*	*Female*	*Total*	*Male*	*Female*
	India	4.11	1.19	7.18	4.29	0.72	8.10	10.94	7.85	14.21
01	Andaman & Nicobar	4.76	2.60	7.56	3.75	1.24	6.75	8.51	7.76	9.37
02	Andhra Pradesh	4.33	0.63	8.08	2.93	0.40	5.52	9.43	6.54	12.37
03	Arunachal Pradesh	3.22	1.29	5.40	1.14	0.26	2.14	7.19	5.14	9.46
04	Assam	NA	NA	NA	5.44	1.17	10.01	10.30	8.31	12.42
05	Bihar	2.97	1.06	4.95	2.81	0.35	5.47	9.09	7.37	10.95
06	Chandigarh	0.31	0.21	0.47	0.18	0.09	0.33	1.94	2.19	1.55
07	Dadra & Nagar Haveli	8.24	1.00	15.63	9.92	1.66	18.48	9.65	4.53	15.68
08	Delhi	1.66	0.85	2.65	0.37	0.17	0.62	2.89	3.33	2.35
09	Goa, Daman & Diu	5.87	2.90	8.80	3.87	1.60	6.17	9.46	8.13	10.89
10	Gujarat	7.02	0.90	13.40	8.97	0.49	17.90	12.44	5.19	20.11

Sl. No.	*State / Union Territories*	*1981*			*1991*			*2001*		
		Total	*Male*	*Female*	*Total*	*Male*	*Female*	*Total*	*Male*	*Female*
11	Haryana	4.10	1.20	8.36	3.02	0.31	6.16	12.93	8.18	18.40
12	Himachal Pradesh	8.58	3.23	13.98	9.07	1.67	16.53	18.49	12.45	24.59
13	Jammu & Kashmir	16.96	4.41	30.97	NA	NA	NA	14.15	10.41	18.19
14	Karnataka	4.54	0.77	8.39	4.87	0.69	9.16	10.54	5.99	15.21
15	Kerala	4.15	4.04	4.25	3.36	3.11	3.61	7.12	9.26	5.10
16	Lakshadweep	6.36	7.78	4.93	3.35	5.08	1.54	6.21	10.23	2.00
17	Madhya Pradesh	5.44	1.08	10.00	6.44	0.88	12.34	13.81	7.85	20.24
18	Maharashtra	5.47	1.53	9.46	5.48	1.12	9.97	9.61	6.40	12.95
19	Manipur	2.61	0.73	4.54	3.48	1.07	6.01	14.03	9.81	18.46
20	Meghalaya	2.96	0.99	4.99	2.74	0.61	4.95	10.63	8.32	13.00
21	Mizoram	4.15	2.40	6.03	5.65	3.63	7.87	12.27	7.79	17.12
22	Nagaland	0.77	0.74	0.80	0.46	0.20	0.75	8.00	6.77	9.31

Sl. No.	*State / Union Territories*	*1981*			*1991*			*2001*		
		Total	*Male*	*Female*	*Total*	*Male*	*Female*	*Total*	*Male*	*Female*
23	Odisha	5.80	1.58	10.01	5.37	1.01	9.79	14.51	10.83	18.24
24	Pondicherry	2.46	1.22	3.74	1.06	0.45	1.68	4.40	4.17	4.62
25	Punjab	2.85	0.78	5.18	1.10	0.12	2.21	7.03	5.10	9.21
26	Rajasthan	7.54	1.16	14.40	9.10	0.94	17.99	13.68	7.12	20.72
27	Sikkim	1.94	0.71	3.36	1.06	0.34	1.87	10.17	6.99	13.78
28	Tamil Nadu	3.28	0.89	5.70	3.42	0.36	6.53	9.41	7.59	11.25
29	Tripura	2.85	1.54	4.25	2.34	0.60	4.18	9.03	6.12	12.10
30	Uttar Pradesh	1.75	0.51	3.14	2.94	0.41	5.81	10.28	8.45	12.30
31	West Bengal	2.26	1.84	2.70	2.57	0.91	4.33	10.02	8.30	11.83

Note:				
	Chhattisgarh	15.01	8.67	21.32
	Jharkhand	16.59	12.96	20.36
	Uttarakhand	11.86	9.90	13.82

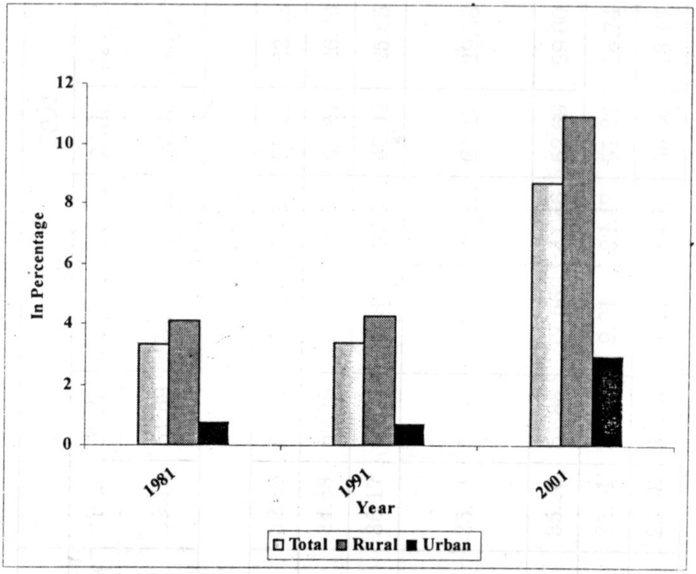

Fig. 2.1.15. Crude Work Participation Rate (Marginal) by Residence, India, 1981-2001

The work participation rates of females in marginal category are higher than the males in both rural and urban areas. Not only females are more engaged in marginal workforce and the rates are increasing rapidly even, It is also true for male workforce as well. (See Tables 2.1.8 and 2.1.9). The crude work participation rate (marginal) in the urban areas of India experienced around 2 per cent increase during 1991-2001- higher for males than females. Table 2.1.9 shows that the urban areas of northern states/union territories like Punjab, Haryana, Chandigarh and Delhi have very low work participation rates for both males and females in marginal categories. On the other hand, the north eastern states like Manipur and Mizoram show higher work participation rates in marginal category, and also females are much highly engaged as marginal workforce than males. Amongst the EAG states, the work participation rates of female workers in the marginal work category are much higher in the rural areas of Rajasthan, Madhya Pradesh and Orissa, and the differences between male and female are also found wide. The same is also true for Gujarat and Haryana.

Table 2.1.9. Crude Work Participation Rate (Marginal) by Residence (Urban) in India and States, 1981-2001

Sl. No.	*State / Union Territories*	*1981*			*1991*			*2001*		
		Total	*Male*	*Female*	*Total*	*Male*	*Female*	*Total*	*Male*	*Female*
	India	0.77	0.53	1.04	0.68	0.35	1.04	2.93	3.38	2.43
01	Andaman & Nicobar .	0.62	0.85	0.31	0.50	0.62	0.35	1.72	2.55	0.70
02	Andhra Pradesh	0.80	0.31	1.32	0.53	0.21	0.85	3.11	3.62	2.59
03	Arunachal Pradesh	0.33	0.28	0.43	0.16	0.09	0.26	2.63	2.54	2.74
04	Assam	NA	NA	NA	0.53	0.30	0.81	2.36	2.77	1.89
05	Bihar	0.54	0.47	0.61	0.46	0.17	0.81	3.27	4.24	2.16
06	Chandigarh	0.22	0.27	0.16	0.09	0.10	0.09	1.03	1.22	0.79
07	Dadra & Nagar Haveli	6.18	3.92	8.72	3.09	0.48	6.28	2.73	1.42	4.63
08	Delhi	0.14	0.15	0.14	0.10	0.10	0.11	1.52	2.06	0.86
09	Goa, Daman & Diu	1.95	1.26	2.70	1.22	0.77	1.70	4.02	4.54	3.46
10	Gujarat	0.66	0.32	1.03	1.31	0.26	2.46	1.80	1.51	2.14

Sl. No.	State / Union Territories	1981			1991			2001		
		Total	Male	Female	Total	Male	Female	Total	Male	Female
11	Haryana	0.35	0.26	0.46	0.24	0.07	0.43	3.32	3.68	2.89
12	Himachal Pradesh	1.17	0.76	1.67	1.60	0.44	2.98	2.49	2.74	2.18
13	Jammu & Kashmir	2.34	0.66	4.27	NA	NA	NA	3.26	3.15	3.40
14	Karnataka	0.89	0.51	1.29	0.60	0.28	0.94	2.75	2.95	2.54
15	Kerala	2.56	3.04	2.09	1.95	2.19	1.72	4.54	6.25	2.93
16	Lakshadweep	2.65	3.27	2.00	1.79	1.67	1.91	5.65	8.17	2.95
17	Madhya Pradesh	0.88	0.49	1.32	0.85	0.33	1.42	3.47	3.68	3.23
18	Maharashtra	0.85	0.69	1.03	0.82	0.61	1.07	2.51	2.83	2.14
19	Manipur	3.52	1.22	5.90	4.01	1.04	7.06	10.22	6.72	13.70
20	Meghalaya	0.36	0.22	0.51	0.66	0.23	1.13	3.70	3.41	3.99
21	Mizoram	2.36	1.41	3.43	8.18	5.06	11.54	11.45	8.55	14.50
22	Nagaland	0.34	0.29	0.41	0.04	0.02	0.08	3.04	3.17	2.89

Sl. No.	State / Union Territories	1981			1991			2001		
		Total	*Male*	*Female*	*Total*	*Male*	*Female*	*Total*	*Male*	*Female*
23	Odisha	1.26	0.75	1.84	0.74	0.46	1.07	3.10	3.44	2.73
24	Pondicherry	1.10	0.92	1.28	0.45	0.44	0.47	1.69	2.04	1.33
25	Punjab	0.31	0.17	0.49	0.10	0.04	0.17	2.09	2.28	1.87
26	Rajasthan	0.83	0.29	1.43	0.99	0.24	1.86	3.27	3.49	3.02
27	Sikkim	0.45	0.50	0.37	1.12	1.30	0.88	3.28	4.35	1.99
28	Tamil Nadu	0.68	0.41	0.96	0.73	0.16	1.32	3.10	3.47	2.73
29	Tripura	0.77	1.04	0.48	0.44	0.31	0.59	2.30	2.86	1.73
30	Uttar Pradesh	0.31	0.17	0.40	0.57	0.18	1.03	3.46	4.55	2.22
31	West Bengal	0.93	0.91	0.94	0.36	0.31	0.41	2.92	3.47	2.31

Note:			
Chhattisgarh	3.10	3.19	3.01
Jharkhand	3.25	4.47	1.84
Uttarakhand	2.80	3.97	1.42

Table 2.2.1. Work Participation Rate (Main+Marginal) Age 15-59, India and States, 1981-2001

Sl. No.	*State / Union Territories*	*Total*					
		1981		*1991*		*2001*	
		Male	*Female*	*Male*	*Female*	*Male*	*Female*
	India	85.27	31.85	82.81	35.86	80.71	40.02
01	Andaman & Nicobar	88.21	19.29	81.19	21.90	79.81	24.35
02	Andhra Pradesh	89.68	52.21	85.95	52.56	83.46	51.89
03	Arunachal Pradesh	91.37	74.62	86.33	63.55	81.27	60.64
04	Assam	NA	NA	80.48	37.00	77.82	33.25
05	Bihar	84.82	22.64	81.46	25.42	80.16	35.04
06	Chandigarh	81.52	14.67	81.02	16.63	80.13	21.19
07	Dadra & Nagar Haveli	94.10	67.62	91.26	77.67	91.80	61.23
08	Delhi	81.20	11.33	80.36	12.13	78.43	14.67
09	Goa, Daman & Diu	75.82	34.59	72.34	30.94	77.23	31.28
10	Gujarat	86.29	32.23	85.34	41.33	84.18	42.56
11	Haryana	85.27	17.78	81.78	18.56	80.89	43.60
12	Himachal Pradesh	86.50	51.16	79.96	55.14	79.93	63.44
13	Jammu & Kashmir	87.95	48.75	NA	NA	75.58	34.33
14	Karnataka	86.87	40.66	84.39	46.19	83.73	47.80
15	Kerala	72.05	26.63	71.80	24.04	73.35	22.45
16	Lakshadweep	71.08	16.28	73.98	12.94	67.76	11.93

Sl. No.	State / Union Territories	Total					
		1981		1991		2001	
		Male	Female	Male	Female	Male	Female
17	Madhya Pradesh	88.67	49.13	85.11	53.69	83.45	56.93
18	Maharashtra	85.49	48.87	82.46	52.61	80.41	46.93
19	Manipur	75.49	64.86	69.45	61.22	69.96	57.11
20	Meghalaya	87.15	62.22	83.75	60.43	79.77	58.30
21	Mizoram	85.73	75.47	84.85	71.90	84.77	71.36
22	Nagaland	77.31	66.08	71.11	60.10	68.87	56.72
23	Odisha	88.97	31.73	84.32	32.80	79.70	37.70
24	Pondicherry	77.15	21.81	76.70	23.40	76.77	24.93
25	Punjab	85.38	9.77	85.83	7.01	81.10	28.66
26	Rajasthan	86.66	35.57	84.38	46.05	83.73	54.99
27	Sikkim	88.50	61.86	81.70	51.53	83.12	57.63
28	Tamil Nadu	86.44	39.78	83.67	43.99	81.14	44.26
29	Tripura	82.31	21.39	77.14	23.23	76.33	32.69
30	Uttar Pradesh	85.15	1.34	82.92	20.76	77.93	28.28
31	West Bengal	80.16	13.38	80.92	18.18	81.54	28.13

Rural							
Sl. No.	State / Union Territories	1981		1991		2001	
		Male	Female	Male	Female	Male	Female
	India	88.37	37.73	85.54	43.64	83.35	49.47
01	Andaman & Nicobar	89.69	21.97	82.80	24.43	81.30	27.57
02	Andhra Pradesh	93.57	62.69	89.69	65.53	87.40	65.01
03	Arunachal Pradesh	91.99	77.67	87.08	69.54	82.91	69.60
04	Assam	NA	NA	81.59	40.50	78.61	36.32
05	Bihar	87.12	24.59	83.74	27.88	82.91	39.04
06	Chandigarh	3.50	4.15	91.93	8.95	89.01	17.43
07	Dadra & Nagar Haveli	94.54	27.46	91.93	81.62	92.59	72.88
08	Delhi	80.53	15.49	80.94	9.68	78.70	16.71
09	Goa, Daman & Diu	76.23	39.91	72.10	36.50	78.02	36.48
10	Gujarat	89.57	43.83	88.34	57.57	87.15	60.67
11	Haryana	86.94	20.89	83.03	22.19	83.11	55.78
12	Himachal Pradesh	87.36	52.00	80.40	58.34	80.64	67.87
13	Jammu & Kashmir	90.95	58.85	NA	NA	76.94	41.18
14	Karnataka	91.60	49.76	88.36	58.39	87.00	60.90
15	Kerala	28.21	28.61	72.63	25.79	73.30	23.44
16	Lakshadweep	72.60	20.46	71.73	11.78	65.68	10.48

		Rural					
Sl. No.	*State / Union Territories*	*1981*		*1991*		*2001*	
		Male	*Female*	*Male*	*Female*	*Male*	*Female*
17	Madhya Pradesh	92.51	58.74	88.50	65.25	87.31	70.74
18	Maharashtra	90.33	66.20	86.20	74.89	83.66	69.10
19	Manipur	77.68	70.91	72.18	67.77	72.08	61.40
20	Meghalaya	90.66	70.49	86.89	68.36	83.37	65.83
21	Mizoram	89.82	75.07	88.23	80.11	90.64	84.93
22	Nagaland	77.49	73.17	70.59	67.27	69.94	63.48
23	Orissa	90.68	33.77	86.38	35.84	81.64	41.97
24	Pondicherry	79.78	29.52	81.58	35.71	79.04	35.23
25	Punjab	87.08	10.92	87.51	6.89	82.99	35.87
26	Rajasthan	89.94	42.50	86.89	56.53	86.74	68.42
27	Sikkim	89.26	68.57	82.23	53.80	84.43	61.56
28	Tamil Nadu	90.31	50.42	87.11	57.19	84.06	58.99
29	Tripura	84.16	22.53	78.42	25.11	77.52	36.41
30	Uttar Pradesh	87.22	15.05	84.91	24.02	80.30	33.49
31	West Bengal	83.78	15.30	85.09	21.91	84.66	33.28

Sl. No.	State / Union Territories	Urban					
		1981		1991		2001	
		Male	Female	Male	Female	Male	Female
	India	76.79	11.15	75.94	14.49	74.89	17.61
01	Andaman & Nicobar	84.67	7.58	77.42	15.34	77.07	17.93
02	Andhra Pradesh	78.15	16.98	76.53	18.42	73.87	18.93
03	Arunachal Pradesh	85.12	9.96	82.20	20.29	76.23	27.49
04	Assam	NA	NA	73.48	11.09	73.54	14.77
05	Bihar	71.56	6.24	68.48	8.76	65.38	10.71
06	Chandigarh	81.00	10.95	79.57	17.33	78.97	21.53
07	Dadra & Nagar Haveli	88.38	36.88	85.47	34.71	89.70	22.31
08	Delhi	81.24	8.35	80.30	12.38	78.42	14.53
09	Goa, Daman & Diu	58.56	15.54	72.66	23.05	76.36	25.83
10	Gujarat	79.91	9.24	80.17	11.43	79.82	13.77
11	Haryana	80.24	6.15	78.36	8.49	76.06	16.32
12	Himachal Pradesh	79.49	13.08	76.36	21.57	74.96	21.94
13	Jammu & Kashmir	78.05	12.30	NA	NA	72.29	15.23
14	Karnataka	76.56	16.79	76.53	20.13	78.03	23.95
15	Kerala	73.44	20.24	69.60	19.32	73.49	19.69
16	Lakshadweep	69.42	11.60	75.69	13.86	70.28	13.64

		Rural					
Sl. No.	State / Union Territories	1981		1991		2001	
		Male	Female	Male	Female	Male	Female
17	Madhya Pradesh	75.78	13.16	75.21	16.68	73.39	18.84
18	Maharashtra	78.30	12.94	77.53	18.12	76.77	18.86
19	Manipur	80.53	52.89	62.23	44.18	64.22	46.01
20	Meghalaya	73.98	22.20	72.46	28.38	67.24	32.06
21	Mizoram	74.59	30.45	81.13	63.20	79.35	59.23
22	Nagaland	76.53	10.70	73.13	21.05	64.38	23.67
23	Odisha	78.28	12.08	73.07	12.65	70.43	14.45
24	Pondicherry	72.23	14.77	74.06	16.73	75.67	19.97
25	Punjab	81.38	5.83	82.09	7.28	77.82	15.27
26	Rajasthan	75.34	8.16	76.90	12.06	75.35	15.07
27	Sikkim	85.57	14.95	77.58	29.20	74.42	29.58
28	Tamil Nadu	78.75	17.07	77.54	19.19	77.68	26.18
29	Tripura	69.23	12.31	71.07	14.34	71.36	17.31
30	Uttar Pradesh	76.74	4.68	75.67	7.94	70.35	10.47
31	West Bengal	72.33	6.25	72.02	9.21	74.75	16.15

Table 2.3.1. Growth Rate of Total Workers (Main+Marginal) in India and States, 1981-2001

Sl. No.	State / Union Territories	1981-1991								
		Total			Rural			Urban		
		Total	Male	Female	Total	Male	Female	Total	Male	Female
	India	1.56	0.89	3.16	1.39	0.71	3.11	2.11	1.83	4.33
01	Andaman & Nicobar	3.51	3.03	6.36	3.46	2.95	6.13	3.64	3.23	7.38
02	Andhra Pradesh	2.01	1.79	2.38	1.71	1.34	2.25	3.47	3.40	3.76
03	Arunachal Pradesh	1.84	2.28	1.14	1.31	1.59	0.91	8.45	8.17	10.50
04	Assam	NA	NA	NA	NA	NA	NA	NA	NA	NA
05	Bihar	2.06	1.83	2.88	2.05	1.81	2.85	2.14	2.02	3.38
06	Chandigarh	3.52	3.32	4.99	9.72	9.62	11.86	2.90	2.62	4.75
07	Dadra & Nagar Haveli	3.74	3.22	4.43	3.64	2.96	4.49	5.29	6.16	2.91
08	Delhi	3.98	3.86	5.01	7.07	7.58	2.69	3.71	3.54	5.22
09	Goa, Daman & Diu	1.65	1.95	0.93	0.34	0.66	-0.28	4.08	4.00	4.36
10	Gujarat	2.69	2.09	4.17	2.59	1.72	4.21	4.25	3.82	7.32
11	Haryana	2.22	2.16	2.53	1.93	1.86	2.25	3.29	3.14	5.04
12	Himachal Pradesh	1.99	1.49	2.79	1.91	1.38	2.71	3.13	2.64	5.69
13	Jammu & Kashmir	NA	NA	NA	NA	NA	NA	NA	NA	NA
14	Karnataka	2.34	1.84	3.39	2.15	1.45	3.37	2.98	2.87	3.48
15	Kerala	1.63	1.90	0.89	1.23	1.57	0.33	5.53	5.44	5.84

Sl.		1981-1991								
		Total			Rural			Urban		
No.	State / Union Territories	Total	Male	Female	Total	Male	Female	Total	Male	Female
16	Lakshadweep	3.31	3.86	0.46	0.45	1.52	-4.54	6.02	5.98	6.25
17	Madhya Pradesh	2.35	2.01	2.97	2.12	1.63	2.87	3.69	3.55	4.38
18	Maharashtra	2.38	2.01	3.05	2.02	1.38	2.83	3.34	3.10	4.65
19	Manipur	-6.06	2.49	3.69	-5.52	2.39	3.38	-7.76	2.78	5.06
20	Meghalaya	2.11	2.08	2.14	1.96	1.94	1.99	3.03	2.77	3.83
21	Mizoram	4.05	3.58	4.78	0.50	0.22	0.86	12.22	10.36	15.70
22	Nagaland	3.23	3.18	3.30	3.01	2.90	3.14	4.83	4.47	6.99
23	Orissa	1.70	1.50	2.26	1.61	1.34	2.29	2.53	2.68	1.55
24	Pondicherry	3.74	3.64	4.10	1.26	0.83	2.38	5.99	5.88	6.55
25	Punjab	1.69	1.96	-1.44	1.34	1.72	-2.91	2.62	2.58	3.22
26	Rajasthan	3.10	2.23	5.08	3.00	1.93	5.06	3.63	3.41	5.41
27	Sikkim	0.99	1.17	0.65	1.60	2.10	0.75	-3.87	-4.50	-0.95
28	Tamil Nadu	1.80	1.41	2.61	1.67	1.12	2.60	2.18	2.06	2.71
29	Tripura	2.59	2.31	3.68	2.05	1.70	3.37	6.72	6.69	6.86
30	Uttar Pradesh	3.16	1.72	5.86	2.65	1.89	6.46	3.22	2.96	6.60
31	West Bengal	-4.47	-5.67	5.57	-4.24	-5.64	5.89	-5.12	-5.73	3.88

Sl. No.	State / Union Territories	1991-2001								
		Total			Rural			Urban		
		Total	Male	Female	Total	Male	Female	Total	Male	Female
	India	1.90	1.51	2.80	1.54	1.04	2.52	2.98	2.68	4.57
01	Andaman & Nicobar	3.21	2.85	4.82	2.55	2.13	4.23	4.84	4.50	7.03
02	Andhra Pradesh	1.52	1.49	1.55	1.41	1.35	1.49	1.96	1.93	2.09
03	Arunachal Pradesh	1.87	1.61	2.31	1.22	0.85	1.74	6.44	5.33	11.68
04	Assam	1.67	1.78	1.40	1.07	1.24	0.69	3.43	2.97	6.49
05	Bihar	0.11	-0.50	2.02	0.36	-0.23	2.08	-2.47	-2.82	0.42
06	Chandigarh	4.13	3.81	6.04	3.75	3.30	9.78	4.18	3.88	5.82
07	Dadra & Nagar Haveli	4.37	6.21	1.48	2.85	4.19	1.03	15.23	16.53	9.31
08	Delhi	4.18	3.95	5.95	1.11	0.46	6.35	4.45	4.25	5.92
09	Goa, Daman & Diu	2.78	3.07	2.01	1.78	2.29	0.64	4.15	4.02	4.58
10	Gujarat	2.03	1.93	2.26	1.44	1.11	1.96	2.33	2.50	1.28
11	Haryana	4.96	2.89	11.77	4.90	2.34	11.86	5.18	4.43	11.01
12	Himachal Pradesh	3.01	2.40	3.85	2.98	2.29	3.87	3.34	3.38	3.18
13	Jammu & Kashmir	NA	NA	NA	NA	NA	NA	NA	NA	NA
14	Karnataka	2.19	2.07	2.42	1.71	1.52	2.01	3.61	3.31	4.78
15	Kerala	1.18	1.36	0.63	0.49	0.67	-0.01	1.40	1.45	1.24

Sl. No.	State / Union Territories	1991-2001								
		Total			Rural			Urban		
		Total	Male	Female	Total	Male	Female	Total	Male	Female
16	Lakshadweep	1.16	1.18	1.06	3.37	3.48	2.60	-0.79	-0.90	-0.13
17	Madhya Pradesh	-0.96	-1.00	-0.88	-1.32	-1.46	-1.11	0.76	0.55	1.76
18	Maharashtra	2.15	2.35	1.82	1.57	1.67	1.45	3.45	3.34	4.00
19	Manipur	3.22	3.36	3.05	3.41	3.68	3.08	2.55	2.29	2.91
20	Meghalaya	2.33	2.05	2.75	2.39	2.27	2.54	1.99	0.91	4.62
21	Mizoram	3.31	3.12	3.56	3.02	2.65	3.48	3.67	3.67	3.66
22	Nagaland	4.99	4.84	5.18	4.98	4.94	5.03	5.02	4.41	7.78
23	Odisha	1.83	1.28	3.18	1.69	1.06	3.09	2.93	2.66	4.64
24	Pondicherry	2.47	2.29	3.07	1.35	1.23	1.63	3.20	2.89	4.51
25	Punjab	3.78	1.84	16.21	3.58	1.06	17.84	4.26	3.55	10.82
26	Rajasthan	3.30	2.58	4.57	3.32	2.50	4.52	3.19	2.88	5.25
27	Sikkim	4.45	4.03	5.22	4.38	3.95	5.13	5.16	4.71	6.72
28	Tamil Nadu	1.39	1.29	1.59	-0.15	-0.40	0.23	4.76	4.12	7.07
29	Tripura	2.99	2.10	5.73	2.88	1.86	5.79	3.65	3.33	5.20
30	Uttar Pradesh	1.90	1.18	4.68	1.84	1.01	4.65	2.18	1.89	4.94
31	West Bengal	2.97	2.09	6.48	2.90	1.93	6.22	3.18	2.51	7.89

2.1.7 Work Participation Rates (Main+Marginal) in Working Age-Group 15-59

Table 2.2.1 presents work participation rates in the working age group 15-59 for both rural and urban areas by sex. The picture is almost same as revealed by the crude work participation rates. The only difference that is important to be noted, is that the work participation when considered out of the working age gets doubled than that of the crude rates described in earlier sections. The declining trend in male work participation rates is very much confirmed from Table 2.2.1 and this is true for most of the states unlike female work participation rates which shows a significant increase at the national level as well as for most of the states and union territories. The declining trend in work participation rates of males is true for both rural and urban areas.

2.3. Growth Rates of Workers

2.3.1 Growth rate of all workers (Main +Marginal)

It may be seen from Fig. 2.3.1 and 2.3.2 that the growth rates of total workforce (Main+Marginal) by residence and sex have increased during 1981 to 2001. The growth rate of urban workers is significantly high for both sexes compared to the growth rates of rural workforce. It may further be noted that the growth rate of female workforce has shown a reduction during 1991-2001 compared to the decade 1981-91; on the other hand, the growth rates of male workers have doubled during the same period.

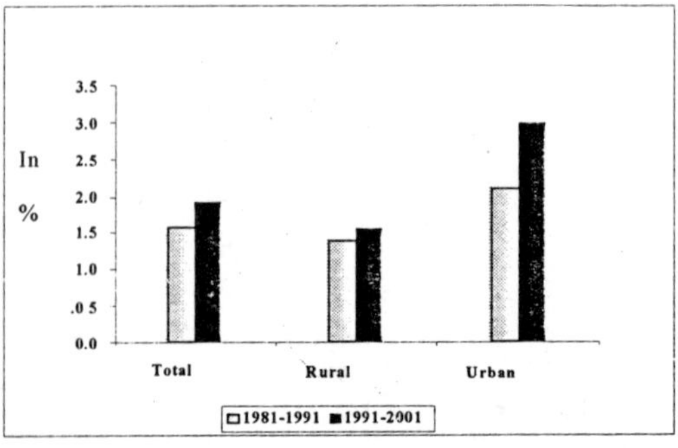

Fig. 2.3.1. Growth Rate (Main + Marginal) by Residence in India, 1981-2001

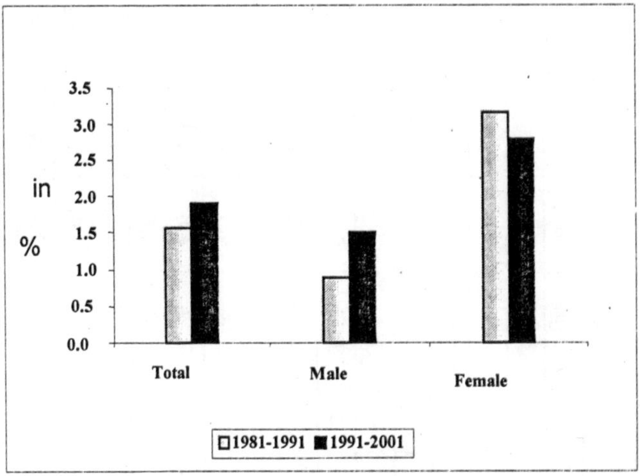

Fig. 2.3.2. Growth Rate of Total Workers (Main + Marginal) by Sex in India, 1981-2001

The growth rates of total female workforce were comparatively higher than the growth rates of total male workforce for the country as a whole and for states/union territories except Punjab, Sikkim, Kerala, Goa and Pondicherry during 1981-91. In most of the states also, the higher growth rates among female workforce continued during 1991-2001. Punjab shows the highest growth rate of female workforce followed by Haryana in the rural areas, whereas in the urban areas Haryana is ahead than Punjab during 1991-2001. Other developed states like Tamil Nadu, West Bengal and Karnataka also show very high growth rates in female workforce during 1991-2001. The higher growth rates of female workforce partly shows the success of Census in capturing women workforce in the rural areas, whereas higher growth rates in urban areas indicates increased participation of women folk in the production of goods and services in most of the states. Exception may be noted in Kerala which experienced a very low rate of growth for female workforce in both rural and urban areas, and same is also true for the male workforce during the last two decades. Among the male workers, the growth rates of male workers in the urban areas are higher than the rural male workers in most of the states and union territories during the period 1991-2001.

Table 2.3.2. Growth Rate of Main Workers in India and States, 1981-2001

Sl.		*1981-1991*								
		Total			*Rural*			*Urban*		
No.	*State / Union Territories*	*Total*	*Male*	*Female*	*Total*	*Male*	*Female*	*Total*	*Male*	*Female*
	India	2.16	1.96	3.36	2.05	1.67	3.25	3.17	3.00	4.37
01	Andaman & Nicobar	3.71	3.20	8.98	3.72	3.18	9.71	3.67	3.26	7.45
02	Andhra Pradesh	2.29	1.83	3.21	2.01	1.38	3.11	3.56	3.42	4.21
03	Arunachal Pradesh	2.21	2.45	1.81	1.69	1.76	1.57	8.55	8.20	11.12
04	Assam	NA	NA	NA	NA	NA	NA	NA	NA	NA
05	Bihar	2.11	1.96	2.88	2.10	1.95	2.87	2.16	2.09	3.03
06	Chandigarh	3.56	3.35	5.08	9.76	9.64	12.64	2.93	2.65	4.84
07	Dadra & Nagar Haveli	3.62	3.16	4.57	3.45	2.85	4.61	6.12	6.81	3.50
08	Delhi	4.02	3.88	5.28	7.50	7.73	5.09	3.72	3.55	5.29
09	Goa, Daman & Diu	2.23	2.20	2.35	1.01	0.96	1.14	4.31	4.10	5.15
10	Gujarat	2.49	2.15	4.07	2.30	1.80	4.15	4.08	3.83	6.25
11	Haryana	2.53	2.31	4.86	2.29	2.04	4.77	3.33	3.18	5.25
12	Himachal Pradesh	1.90	1.77	2.24	1.81	1.68	2.13	3.00	2.69	4.92
13	Jammu & Kashmir	NA	NA	NA	NA	NA	NA	NA	NA	NA
14	Karnataka	2.36	1.86	3.72	2.13	1.46	3.69	3.09	2.92	3.88
15	Kerala	2.01	2.20	1.39	1.61	1.88	0.79	5.83	5.69	6.38

Sl. No.	State / Union Territories	1981-1991								
		Total			Rural			Urban		
		Total	Male	Female	Total	Male	Female	Total	Male	Female
16	Lakshadweep	4.44	4.68	2.81	1.94	2.48	-1.30	6.54	6.46	7.14
17	Madhya Pradesh	2.18	2.04	2.54	1.89	1.66	2.38	3.70	3.59	4.37
18	Maharashtra	2.44	2.06	3.26	2.05	1.44	3.03	3.35	3.12	4.73
19	Manipur	-13.58	2.25	1.92	2.04	2.16	1.88	2.39	2.52	2.14
20	Meghalaya	2.10	2.14	2.03	1.96	2.01	1.89	2.93	2.77	3.47
21	Mizoram	3.40	3.17	3.84	0.22	-0.01	0.56	10.96	9.65	13.93
22	Nagaland	3.28	3.27	3.30	3.06	3.00	3.13	4.91	4.52	7.30
23	Odisha	1.84	1.60	3.01	1.73	1.44	3.06	2.69	2.74	2.29
24	Pondicherry	4.13	3.78	5.49	1.73	0.99	3.93	6.26	6.00	7.59
25	Punjab	2.13	2.05	3.99	1.90	1.84	3.94	2.70	2.60	4.06
26	Rajasthan	2.87	2.27	5.80	2.71	1.96	5.86	3.57	3.42	5.23
27	Sikkim	1.09	1.20	0.86	1.74	2.16	0.98	-4.05	-4.66	-1.19
28	Tamil Nadu	1.81	1.49	2.58	1.67	1.21	2.60	2.18	2.11	2.48
29	Tripura	2.76	2.49	4.19	2.19	1.87	3.85	6.84	6.85	6.78
30	Uttar Pradesh	2.44	2.10	5.47	2.30	1.91	5.45	3.12	2.96	5.64
31	West Bengal	2.88	2.57	5.39	2.95	2.60	5.48	2.71	2.50	5.03

Sl. No.	State / Union Territories	1991-2001								
		Total			*Rural*			*Urban*		
		Total	*Male*	*Female*	*Total*	*Male*	*Female*	*Total*	*Male*	*Female*
	India	0.40	0.32	0.65	-0.27	-0.39	0.09	2.27	2.07	3.50
01	Andaman & Nicobar	2.27	1.93	4.61	1.23	0.91	3.52	4.50	4.15	6.81
02	Andhra Pradesh	0.19	0.48	-0.38	-0.04	0.24	-0.49	1.11	1.24	0.54
03	Arunachal Pradesh	0.56	0.70	0.31	-0.22	-0.16	-0.32	5.62	4.81	9.65
04	Assam	0.13	0.35	-0.83	-0.63	-0.34	-1.84	2.84	2.48	5.59
05	Bihar	-1.96	-2.02	-1.65	-1.78	-1.81	-1.63	-3.63	-3.79	-1.97
06	Chandigarh	3.86	3.59	5.51	3.33	2.97	8.78	3.93	3.68	5.33
07	Dadra & Nagar Haveli	4.60	5.87	1.68	2.90	3.72	1.25	15.37	16.39	8.76
08	Delhi	3.71	3.55	5.05	0.29	-0.20	4.91	4.00	3.87	5.06
09	Goa, Daman & Diu	1.71	2.12	0.34	0.35	1.09	-1.96	3.39	3.33	3.62
10	Gujarat	1.45	1.29	2.06	0.59	0.22	1.69	2.17	2.26	1.40
11	Haryana	2.80	1.48	10.44	2.33	0.65	10.83	4.15	3.67	8.59
12	Himachal Pradesh	0.99	0.38	2.43	0.77	0.05	2.34	3.11	2.94	3.99
13	Jammu & Kashmir	NA	NA	NA	NA	NA	NA	NA	NA	NA
14	Karnataka	1.13	1.27	0.78	0.41	0.56	0.08	2.99	2.80	3.81
15	Kerala	-0.08	0.12	-0.76	-0.94	-0.75	-1.60	0.53	0.61	0.22

Sl. No.	State / Union Territories	1991-2001								
		Total			Rural			Urban		
		Total	Male	Female	Total	Male	Female	Total	Male	Female
16	Lakshadweep	-0.54	-0.55	-0.42	1.76	1.85	1.10	-2.43	-2.54	-1.64
17	Madhya Pradesh	-2.68	-2.26	-3.77	-3.31	-2.90	-4.22	-0.17	-0.20	0.02
18	Maharashtra	1.40	1.57	1.03	0.62	0.62	0.62	2.94	2.91	3.14
19	Manipur	0.66	1.55	-0.75	0.64	1.73	-0.99	0.73	0.95	0.31
20	Meghalaya	0.37	0.48	0.19	0.29	0.58	-0.16	0.82	0.03	2.96
21	Mizoram	2.26	2.42	2.00	1.78	1.93	1.56	2.90	3.00	2.69
22	Nagaland	3.26	3.48	2.93	3.13	3.43	2.76	4.03	3.69	5.69
23	Orissa	-0.81	-0.57	-1.93	-1.27	-1.02	-2.41	2.12	2.04	2.77
24	Pondicherry	1.91	1.84	2.14	0.44	0.52	0.24	2.83	2.58	3.92
25	Punjab	2.51	1.06	16.27	1.99	0.10	19.80	3.65	3.12	9.09
26	Rajasthan	2.25	1.41	5.12	2.22	1.18	5.20	2.38	2.17	4.26
27	Sikkim	2.57	2.88	1.90	2.35	2.72	1.60	4.60	4.15	6.23
28	Tamil Nadu	0.38	0.29	0.58	-1.48	-1.71	-1.09	4.12	3.52	6.53
29	Tripura	1.22	1.05	2.03	0.86	0.69	1.63	3.07	2.83	4.32
30	Uttar Pradesh	-0.47	-0.52	-0.11	-0.83	-0.87	-0.52	1.02	0.87	3.02
31	West Bengal	1.14	0.87	2.81	0.64	0.45	1.77	2.40	1.91	6.26

2.3.2. Growth Rates of Main Workers

Table 2.3.2 gives an idea about the growth rates of main workers during the study period. The growth rate of main workers declined during 1991-2001 period than 1981-1991 periods. At the national level, rural areas experienced a negative growth rate during the period 1991-2001. Among the EAG states, Bihar and Orissa have lower growth rate for male and female workers both in rural and urban areas than other EAG states during these two periods. Table 2.3.2 shows during 1991-2001, some of the state experienced negative growth in total main workers and it is mainly due to the negative growth of main workers in the rural areas.

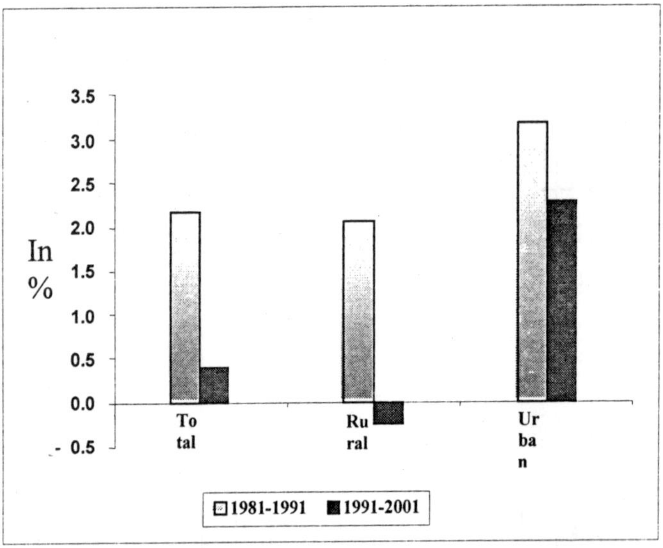

Fig. 2.2.3. Growth Rate of Main Workers by Residence in India, 1981-2001

Fig. 2.2.3 shows the growth rates of main workers by residence of India during 1981-2001.It may be noted that growth rates are remarkably higher in urban than rural areas, but show a tremendous decline from 1981-91 to 1991-2001 in both rural and urban areas. In the rural areas, there is even a negative growth in main work category during 1991-2001.

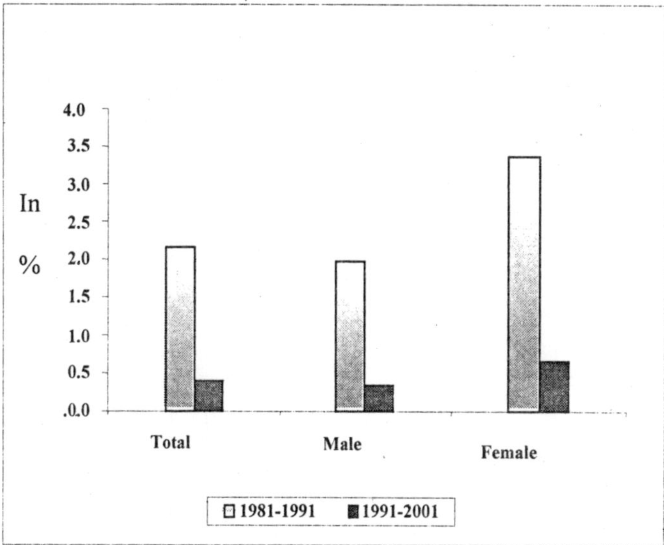

Fig. 2.2.4. Growth Rate of Main Workers by Sex in India, 1981-2001

Fig. 2.2.4 shows growth rates of main workers by sex of India during 1981-2001. It may be observed that growth rates have fallen both among male and female main workers from 1981-91 to 1991-2001.

2.3.3. Growth Rates of Marginal Workers

There was a decline in male marginal workforce during 1981-91, but female workforce showed a modest increase. However, the situation in the following decade has changed drastically with a spectacular rise in the marginal workforce during 1991-2001. The male marginal workforce grew as high as over 20 per cent per annum during the decade 1991-2001 in both rural and urban areas. On the other hand, female workforce grew also rapidly but half of the rates of male workforce in urban areas and nearly one-fourth of the rates of male marginal workforce in rural areas. This was precisely that the male marginal workforce experienced a negative growth during the previous decade. In all most all the states and union territories, male marginal workers have experienced a negative rate of growth in both rural and urban areas during

Table 2.3.3. Growth Rate of Marginal Workers in India and States, 1981-2001

Sl. No.	State / Union Territories	*1981-1991*								
		Total			*Rural*			*Urban*		
		Total	*Male*	*Female*	*Total*	*Male*	*Female*	*Total*	*Male*	*Female*
	India	1.43	-5.92	2.65	2.07	-3.40	2.78	1.50	-1.34	2.72
01	Andaman & Nicobar	1.55	-3.22	3.25	1.53	-3.82	3.21	2.02	0.75	5.71
02	Andhra Pradesh	-2.12	-2.55	-2.08	-2.21	-2.93	-2.15	-0.65	-0.37	-0.72
03	Arunachal Pradesh	-7.75	-13.06	-6.68	-7.89	-13.44	-6.79	2.60	-1.71	5.68
04	Assam	NA	NA	NA	NA	NA	NA	NA	NA	NA
05	Bihar	1.46	-8.82	2.87	1.47	-8.88	2.82	1.09	-7.93	5.49
06	Chandigarh	-4.43	-6.76	-1.02	2.96	0.56	4.23	-5.53	-7.36	-2.39
07	Dadra & Nagar Haveli	4.31	5.58	4.20	4.55	7.88	4.29	-1.65	-15.36	1.57
08	Delhi	-2.68	-2.37	-2.92	-7.54	-8.60	-7.15	0.31	-0.47	1.26
09	Goa, Daman & Diu	-3.50	-4.65	-3.12	-4.04	-5.70	-3.55	-0.62	-0.90	-0.48
10	Gujarat	3.85	-3.97	4.27	3.88	-4.66	4.27	9.82	1.02	11.64
11	Haryana	-0.97	-11.21	0.20	-0.98	-11.35	0.14	-0.34	-9.22	2.94
12	Himachal Pradesh	2.38	-4.76	3.52	2.33	-4.82	3.45	6.35	-2.47	9.25
13	Jammu & Kashmir	NA	NA	NA	NA	NA	NA	NA	NA	NA
14	Karnataka	2.09	-0.24	2.33	2.33	0.53	2.48	-1.42	-3.59	-0.61
15	Kerala	-1.48	-2.02	-0.98	-1.75	-2.30	-1.27	2.03	1.41	2.86

Sl. No.	State / Union Territories	1981-1991								
		Total			Rural			Urban		
		Total	Male	Female	Total	Male	Female	Total	Male	Female
16	Lakshadweep	-3.82	-3.23	-4.86	-5.99	-3.68	-11.35	0.53	-2.07	3.82
17	Madhya Pradesh	3.68	0.04	4.05	3.70	0.06	4.04	3.34	-0.15	4.50
18	Maharashtra	1.84	-0.56	2.25	1.74	-1.29	2.15	3.00	1.82	3.85
19	Manipur	4.98	4.74	5.03	5.31	6.33	5.13	-17.87	-14.12	-18.33
20	Meghalaya	9.44	10.22	9.08	3.09	4.21	2.57	22.03	22.18	21.96
21	Mizoram	2.28	-1.80	2.97	2.01	-2.15	2.69	9.10	3.38	10.99
22	Nagaland	-1.36	-9.41	3.16	-0.79	-8.82	3.73	-14.69	-23.69	-9.99
23	Odisha	0.82	-2.72	1.30	0.89	-2.79	1.37	-2.14	-1.79	-2.32
24	Pondicherry	-6.70	-5.86	-7.10	-8.38	-9.82	-7.95	-3.95	-2.52	-5.14
25	Punjab	-7.89	-16.51	-6.91	-7.85	-16.87	-6.88	-8.95	-12.92	-7.73
26	Rajasthan	4.18	0.21	4.47	4.15	0.14	4.43	5.19	1.16	5.94
27	Sikkim	-2.17	-2.17	-2.17	-2.74	-4.25	-2.40	5.88	5.96	5.72
28	Tamil Nadu	1.74	-7.67	2.78	1.66	-7.70	2.58	2.47	-7.57	4.97
29	Tripura	0.47	-6.82	2.39	0.46	-6.90	2.28	0.82	-5.93	8.22
30	Uttar Pradesh	1.21	-16.40	6.50	7.22	-0.11	8.13	9.53	3.90	11.17
31	West Bengal	2.49	-5.45	6.01	3.35	-4.95	6.76	-6.94	-8.52	-5.34

Sl. No.	State / Union Territories	1991-2001								
		Total			Rural			Urban		
		Total	Male	Female	Total	Male	Female	Total	Male	Female
	India	10.79	24.93	6.83	10.29	24.87	6.60	16.37	24.82	10.11
01	Andaman & Nicobar	10.18	19.52	5.14	9.72	19.74	4.97	16.67	18.29	11.52
02	Andhra Pradesh	13.51	29.39	9.59	12.98	29.26	9.39	19.31	29.99	12.62
03	Arunachal Pradesh	20.54	31.71	16.99	19.85	31.03	16.46	34.90	39.50	31.51
04	Assam	8.13	21.30	3.84	7.49	20.73	3.28	17.99	25.09	11.85
05	Bihar	11.81	30.29	6.88	11.64	30.37	6.85	16.82	29.09	7.99
06	Chandigarh	27.20	29.64	23.60	26.95	35.14	18.75	27.26	28.72	24.89
07	Dadra & Nagar Haveli	3.18	14.24	1.10	2.66	13.55	0.63	13.37	26.18	10.59
08	Delhi	29.15	34.04	21.96	20.69	29.82	13.51	31.26	34.71	25.11
09	Goa, Daman & Diu	10.62	18.07	6.61	9.35	16.97	5.78	14.88	20.66	10.11
10	Gujarat	4.80	24.16	2.49	4.35	24.70	2.22	5.67	20.03	0.89
11	Haryana	17.15	35.50	13.23	16.41	34.53	12.84	30.44	43.46	23.05
12	Himachal Pradesh	8.59	21.55	5.38	8.61	21.56	5.45	7.25	21.26	-0.58
13	Jammu & Kashmir	NA	NA	NA	NA	NA	NA	NA	NA	NA
14	Karnataka	9.60	23.35	6.60	8.87	22.74	6.22	17.85	26.12	12.57
15	Kerala	8.88	12.01	5.00	8.47	11.77	4.53	9.20	11.11	6.19

Sl. No.	State / Union Territories	1991-2001								
		Total			Rural			Urban		
		Total	Male	Female	Total	Male	Female	Total	Male	Female
16	Lakshadweep	10.40	12.40	4.87	10.16	10.99	6.60	10.74	15.08	3.60
17	Madhya Pradesh	6.73	21.05	3.70	6.24	20.53	3.48	14.64	24.63	8.66
18	Maharashtra	7.87	18.74	4.44	7.02	18.88	3.96	14.07	18.34	9.85
19	Manipur	15.47	24.06	12.74	17.02	25.24	14.30	10.65	19.84	8.08
20	Meghalaya	8.10	8.93	7.68	9.67	9.48	9.76	6.63	8.43	5.66
21	Mizoram	16.33	28.76	12.42	16.05	28.67	12.18	20.43	29.75	16.21
22	Nagaland	33.96	40.76	30.59	33.37	39.92	30.19	47.49	57.86	41.19
23	Odisha	11.39	24.87	7.60	11.23	25.03	7.51	16.88	22.47	12.17
24	Pondicherry	15.40	20.08	11.86	15.39	23.31	11.35	15.41	17.57	12.81
25	Punjab	20.75	39.34	16.11	19.70	38.38	15.46	33.63	44.95	26.80
26	Rajasthan	6.89	23.34	4.04	6.50	22.66	3.91	14.61	29.53	7.65
27	Sikkim	24.63	30.25	22.30	25.24	32.94	22.55	15.59	16.52	13.50
28	Tamil Nadu	10.84	30.81	5.70	9.60	29.85	4.96	18.06	34.11	10.95
29	Tripura	14.95	24.46	11.96	14.78	24.43	11.92	18.98	24.85	13.30
30	Uttar Pradesh	14.55	32.16	9.26	14.17	31.86	9.24	20.22	34.63	9.86
31	West Bengal	15.74	23.91	12.04	15.18	23.62	11.67	22.87	25.87	19.25

Table 2.3.3(a). Growth Rate of Marginal Workers by Main Activity 1991-2001

Sl. No.	State / Union Territories	*Cultivators*								
		Total			*Rural*			*Urban*		
		Total	*Male*	*Female*	*Total*	*Male*	*Female*	*Total*	*Male*	*Female*
	India	5.27	18.25	2.54	5.37	18.58	2.63	-0.33	7.41	-3.14
01	Andhra Pradesh	1.40	17.51	-2.13	1.44	17.59	-2.09	0.82	14.61	-4.81
02	Arunachal Pradesh	18.62	32.75	15.37	18.52	32.89	15.25	26.86	26.93	26.82
03	Assam	1.89	15.32	-1.80	1.92	15.42	-1.77	-5.13	3.23	-9.61
04	Bihar	9.52	25.82	5.95	9.67	26.19	6.11	-0.34	12.77	-6.13
05	Goa	5.37	12.35	2.94	5.55	12.94	3.02	3.78	7.84	2.11
06	Gujarat	1.92	19.50	0.45	2.01	19.97	0.52	-3.70	4.26	-4.86
07	Harayana	11.12	27.74	8.58	11.16	27.87	8.62	7.51	19.86	5.26
08	Himachal Pradesh	7.43	19.83	4.82	7.54	19.96	4.93	-5.86	4.29	-7.96
09	Jammu & Kashmir	NA	NA	NA	NA	NA	NA	NA	NA	NA
10	Karnataka	-1.08	9.79	-2.95	-1.08	9.87	-2.94	-1.13	7.19	-3.75
11	Kerala	-3.20	1.81	-8.32	-2.62	2.47	-7.78	-11.63	-7.20	-16.55
12	Madhya Pradesh	4.51	15.95	2.54	4.52	16.09	2.55	3.67	10.73	1.70
13	Maharashtra	1.75	12.92	-0.85	1.81	13.24	-0.80	-1.66	3.74	-3.99
14	Manipur	12.54	21.86	8.90	14.74	23.36	11.28	2.00	13.82	-2.46
15	Meghalaya	10.52	22.78	7.28	10.61	22.89	7.37	7.51	19.43	4.17

Sl. No.	State / Union Territories	Cultivators								
		Total			Rural			Urban		
		Total	Male	Female	Total	Male	Female	Total	Male	Female
16	Mizoram	5.14	5.29	5.06	8.69	8.47	8.80	-2.55	-1.40	-3.09
17	Nagaland	32.70	38.18	29.99	32.63	38.14	29.90	37.38	40.24	35.77
18	Odisha	6.08	18.34	1.92	6.14	18.56	1.97	1.00	8.21	-4.93
19	Punjab	9.35	29.72	6.31	9.33	30.03	6.32	10.56	22.40	6.09
20	Rajasthan	4.52	19.76	2.32	4.58	19.93	2.37	1.04	10.88	-0.57
21	Sikkim	23.89	34.37	20.99	24.01	34.90	21.07	-13.29	-17.35	-10.41
22	Tamil Nadu	-0.04	22.18	-4.87	0.09	22.40	-4.72	-1.96	19.16	-7.26
23	Tripura	7.44	17.38	5.24	7.60	17.71	5.39	-9.94	-0.26	-16.02
24	Uttar Pradesh	7.28	20.86	4.38	7.46	21.37	4.54	-2.89	5.37	-6.30
25	West Bengal	6.69	15.47	3.03	6.81	15.77	-19.89	-1.82	3.66	-7.09
26	Andaman & Nicobar	6.40	16.33	3.58	6.42	16.38	3.60	-6.06	2.88	-13.86
27	Chandigarh	40.43	37.26	44.77	46.15	49.97	43.50	25.65	17.92	0.00
28	Dadra & Nagar Haveli	-2.78	5.84	-4.18	-3.17	5.37	-4.57	5.15	17.81	3.53
29	Daman & Diu	-9.17	-1.49	-10.04	-8.77	-0.27	-9.69	-24.24	-19.81	-25.57
30	Delhi	16.39	25.57	13.17	15.79	27.12	12.27	20.32	20.19	20.42
31	Lakshadweep	0.00	0.00	0.00	0.00	0.00	0.00	0.00	0.00	0.00
32	Pondicherry	4.87	12.70	-0.83	4.14	14.35	-1.79	7.88	9.16	5.60

Sl. No.	State / Union Territories	Agricultural Labourers								
		Total			Rural			Urban		
		Total	Male	Female	Total	Male	Female	Total	Male	Female
	India	13.35	29.32	9.44	13.38	29.78	9.49	12.22	21.82	7.93
01	Andhra Pradesh	15.03	32.37	11.66	15.03	32.55	11.69	15.03	29.15	10.61
02	Arunachal Pradesh	17.25	24.19	14.40	17.17	23.77	14.44	18.46	32.54	13.76
03	Assam	12.95	26.27	8.00	13.00	26.47	8.03	6.98	12.67	3.29
04	Bihar	17.69	37.75	12.89	17.70	38.05	12.93	16.87	29.57	10.49
05	Goa	9.26	14.95	6.90	9.38	15.71	6.93	8.53	11.52	6.66
06	Gujarat	5.04	26.43	2.59	5.04	26.90	2.60	5.07	17.89	2.01
07	Harayana	18.03	36.99	13.84	17.85	37.02	13.68	24.13	36.36	19.80
08	Himachal Pradesh	12.54	21.55	7.83	12.68	21.68	8.01	5.28	15.90	-3.01
09	Jammu & Kashmir	NA	NA	NA	NA	NA	NA	NA	NA	NA
10	Karnataka	13.19	29.67	10.57	13.12	29.85	10.53	15.07	26.76	11.89
11	Kerala	5.98	9.07	2.55	6.54	9.76	2.98	0.61	2.65	-1.79
12	Madhya Pradesh	13.67	31.07	10.54	13.66	31.23	10.53	14.02	24.60	10.87
13	Maharashtra	9.56	21.36	6.86	9.57	21.67	6.86	9.38	16.94	6.81
14	Manipur	7.94	17.17	5.22	9.76	18.07	7.21	2.21	13.87	-0.93
15	Meghalaya	21.70	31.39	18.23	21.75	31.94	18.23	20.70	24.80	18.35

Sl. No.	State / Union Territories	Agricultural Labourers								
		Total			Rural			Urban		
		Total	Male	Female	Total	Male	Female	Total	Male	Female
16	Mizoram	6.01	6.39	5.79	7.39	7.37	7.40	5.34	5.91	4.99
17	Nagaland	28.06	36.95	24.01	27.87	36.83	23.80	42.30	43.17	41.59
18	Odisha	11.38	27.03	7.83	11.39	27.27	7.83	10.56	18.22	6.95
19	Punjab	15.69	34.80	9.73	15.51	34.82	9.69	20.06	34.53	11.13
20	Rajasthan	6.24	22.41	3.70	6.27	22.85	3.73	5.35	15.08	2.56
21	Sikkim	21.29	24.35	19.95	21.85	25.56	20.30	-23.42	-26.39	-20.79
22	Tamil Nadu	10.96	31.95	6.63	10.66	31.91	6.42	14.45	32.32	9.24
23	Tripura	16.55	25.11	14.06	16.66	25.33	14.19	8.27	17.74	-2.97
24	Uttar Pradesh	18.71	38.82	13.14	18.75	39.13	13.24	17.18	32.63	8.20
25	West Bengal	18.97	29.00	14.51	19.11	29.59	14.60	12.81	16.31	8.28
26	Andaman & Nicobar	4.22	14.45	-3.21	4.15	14.44	-3.24	10.46	14.55	1.54
27	Chandigarh	3.05	5.81	-1.63	16.23	23.51	3.68	-5.39	-6.69	-3.89
28	Dadra & Nagar Haveli	9.18	21.96	7.06	8.83	21.81	6.69	29.44	26.95	30.40
29	Daman & Diu	-2.11	5.19	-2.35	-1.60	5.85	-2.12	-8.27	-1.82	-4.46
30	Delhi	7.13	10.52	3.39	13.59	20.63	8.04	0.34	2.73	-2.89
31	Lakshadweep	0.00	0.00	0.00	0.00	0.00	0.00	0.00	0.00	0.00
32	Pondicherry	14.03	22.23	10.47	15.63	25.56	11.67	8.25	12.86	5.86

Sl. No.	State / Union Territories	Household Industry								
		Total			Rural			Urban		
		Total	Male	Female	Total	Male	Female	Total	Male	Female
	India	18.46	27.83	16.52	18.62	28.35	15.73	17.82	26.22	15.65
01	Andhra Pradesh	13.78	27.38	11.54	13.37	26.00	38.16	15.25	31.53	38.61
02	Arunachal Pradesh	43.26	63.08	40.24	42.35	0.00	38.85	48.18	46.05	49.09
03	Assam	23.12	29.30	22.24	24.04	30.26	23.19	12.89	22.27	10.68
04	Bihar	27.37	35.38	25.23	26.98	35.05	24.94	32.36	37.90	29.56
05	Goa	15.72	19.90	13.76	15.34	19.94	13.49	16.54	19.84	14.44
06	Gujarat	11.51	22.47	10.28	9.36	23.35	7.93	16.23	21.11	15.55
07	Harayana	29.92	39.18	27.87	29.12	37.89	27.18	32.85	44.00	30.40
08	Himachal Pradesh	24.94	31.20	22.61	25.16	31.43	22.83	20.74	27.04	18.18
09	Jammu & Kashmir	NA	NA	NA	NA	NA	NA	NA	NA	NA
10	Karnataka	16.65	25.99	15.06	16.70	26.88	15.05	16.53	24.32	15.07
11	Kerala	12.04	17.68	10.15	11.98	18.65	9.95	12.26	15.05	10.98
12	Madhya Pradesh	12.55	22.98	10.58	12.59	23.43	10.64	12.37	21.55	10.37
13	Maharashtra	15.46	17.58	14.81	16.11	20.13	14.97	14.39	13.97	14.53
14	Manipur	23.42	27.60	22.99	25.06	32.63	24.39	19.71	19.68	19.72
15	Meghalaya	33.09	46.50	30.82	33.66	48.47	31.40	28.41	38.16	25.32

Sl. No.	State / Union Territories	Household Industry								
		Total			*Rural*			*Urban*		
		Total	*Male*	*Female*	*Total*	*Male*	*Female*	*Total*	*Male*	*Female*
16	Mizoram	11.66	14.86	10.75	32.21	25.36	36.39	6.58	10.85	5.34
17	Nagaland	46.46	61.44	43.39	49.21	63.32	46.28	36.43	54.16	32.64
18	Odisha	15.91	24.62	14.49	15.86	24.92	14.45	17.02	21.69	15.31
19	Punjab	38.97	47.49	37.76	41.61	49.44	40.60	31.86	43.54	29.61
20	Rajasthán	18.82	30.56	16.62	18.72	30.33	16.55	19.12	31.19	16.81
21	Sikkim	32.20	32.58	31.96	39.28	39.02	39.45	4.64	9.16	0.69
22	Tamil Nadu	12.65	25.13	10.73	12.76	25.13	10.85	12.43	25.14	10.52
23	Tripura	19.23	28.05	18.09	19.26	28.88	18.09	18.88	21.88	18.12
24	Uttar Pradesh	25.77	39.70	22.28	26.64	39.87	23.32	22.93	39.15	18.83
25	West Bengal	17.70	23.26	16.75	17.16	22.14	16.38	21.87	28.42	19.94
26	Andaman & Nicobar	0.92	9.11	-1.23	0.56	8.34	-1.42	37.26	0.00	27.73
27	Chandigarh	44.90	42.39	46.15	35.09	28.03	37.99	52.04	51.65	52.23
28	Dadra & Nagar Haveli	14.31	27.08	11.81	13.86	30.45	9.71	15.34	10.99	15.69
29	Daman & Diu	7.53	-1.82	7.54	16.88	5.88	17.52	2.52	-7.73	2.91
30	Delhi	29.45	37.39	[illegible]	19.66	31.51	16.00	31.45	38.24	28.44
31	Lakshadweep	1.69	0.40	3.86	1.07	-2.17	11.72	2.39	4.94	0.06
32	Pondicherry	23.79	27.27	22.76	22.90	26.39	22.13	24.26	27.62	23.14

Sl. No.	State / Union Territories	Other Services								
		Total			Rural			Urban		
		Total	Male	Female	Total	Male	Female	Total	Male	Female
	India	21.34	28.22	15.99	20.55	28.45	15.77	23.16	27.88	16.84
01	Andhra Pradesh	18.46	18.99	17.94	14.17	16.44	17.38	22.93	23.28	19.25
02	Arunachal Pradesh	34.72	33.54	36.42	31.93	30.88	33.38	46.42	43.57	52.11
03	Assam	26.76	29.45	24.86	26.82	29.29	24.78	28.81	30.49	25.94
04	Bihar	33.51	41.81	25.45	32.05	41.28	24.50	40.12	43.28	32.87
05	Goa	19.85	22.43	16.69	17.60	20.25	14.58	23.67	25.74	20.74
06	Gujarat	10.74	26.11	7.50	9.03	28.29	6.55	17.93	26.79	13.62
07	Harayana	41.04	47.26	37.29	41.61	47.30	38.73	39.54	47.19	32.01
08	Himachal Pradesh	27.89	35.04	19.67	27.98	36.02	19.38	27.22	29.90	22.29
09	Jammu & Kashmir	NA	NA	NA	NA	NA	NA	NA	NA	NA
10	Karnataka	19.15	27.64	13.22	17.01	27.79	12.29	21.83	27.48	15.71
11	Kerala	14.08	15.78	11.23	14.59	16.63	11.41	12.70	13.70	10.69
12	Madhya Pradesh	19.30	27.78	13.34	2.35	25.90	12.16	23.38	29.71	16.14
13	Maharashtra	16.61	20.94	11.47	16.56	23.90	10.91	16.65	19.37	12.12
14	Manipur	34.01	36.04	32.84	34.95	38.04	33.30	32.39	33.02	31.98
15	Meghalaya	28.67	39.69	24.03	28.55	40.99	23.94	28.87	36.86	24.33

Sl. No.	State / Union Territories	Other Services								
		Total			Rural			Urban		
		Total	Male	Female	Total	Male	Female	Total	Male	Female
16	Mizoram	17.87	20.54	16.36	24.05	25.18	23.32	17.03	19.85	15.48
17	Nagaland	57.89	68.36	51.67	55.98	64.77	50.98	64.85	84.90	54.56
18	Odisha	22.34	28.53	17.76	21.95	29.20	17.31	24.38	26.23	21.54
19	Punjab	48.56	52.88	46.23	49.32	53.53	47.48	46.40	51.71	41.22
20	Rajasthan	25.19	35.93	19.90	25.76	35.73	21.68	23.85	36.24	14.16
21	Sikkim	29.37	28.01	31.05	35.00	35.63	34.45	17.40	17.48	17.21
22	Tamil Nadu	23.50	33.40	15.75	20.38	30.32	13.08	27.10	36.72	19.05
23	Tripura	26.05	29.17	23.33	26.06	29.34	23.45	26.01	28.53	22.56
24	Uttar Pradesh	27.34	41.62	17.85	26.94	41.40	18.84	28.29	41.99	14.53
25	West Bengal	20.93	25.37	17.54	19.05	23.59	16.29	28.03	29.22	25.79
26	Andaman & Nicobar	22.70	25.17	19.51	24.30	28.23	20.39	16.98	18.22	12.88
27	Chandigarh	28.99	31.54	25.18	27.01	36.49	16.62	29.37	30.81	27.05
28	Dadra & Nagar Haveli	22.20	29.94	18.69	21.58	29.04	18.39	25.04	31.01	20.18
29	Daman & Diu	5.14	18.94	-1.56	13.52	29.96	4.88	-1.65	9.26	-5.87
30	Delhi	32.78	36.54	25.79	25.32	32.79	16.15	33.88	36.97	27.64
31	Lakshadweep	15.07	17.82	6.22	14.45	16.83	4.76	16.05	19.65	8.76
32	Pondicherry	17.42	18.93	14.97	16.08	20.31	11.12	17.97	18.48	16.99

1981-91 (see Table 2.3.3). During 1991-2001, the entire picture in the growth of marginal workers has changed in most of the states and union territories. Rise in the growth rates of marginal workforce is consistent with decline in main workforce during the decade 1991-2001. The developed states like Punjab, Haryana, Delhi and Tamil Nadu shows a very high growth rate of male marginal workforce during the decade 1991-2001 in both rural and urban area. It seems that most of the jobs generated after the implementation of new economic policy are of part time nature. What is the impact of such jobs on the level of real income of the people? One may not expect very positive results because most of such jobs originate in the unorganised sector.

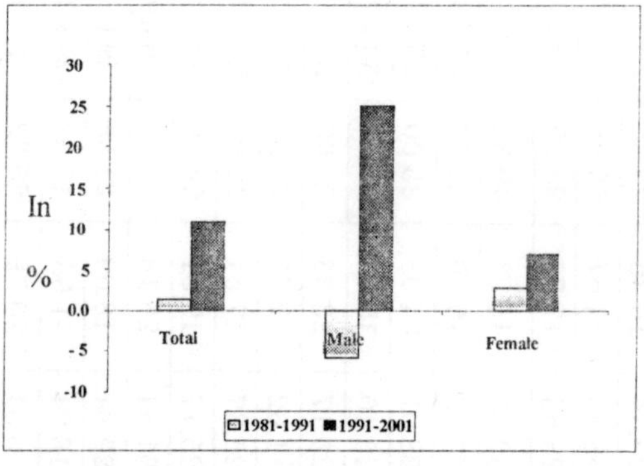

Fig. 2.3.5. Growth Rate of Marginal Workers by Sex in India, 1981-2001

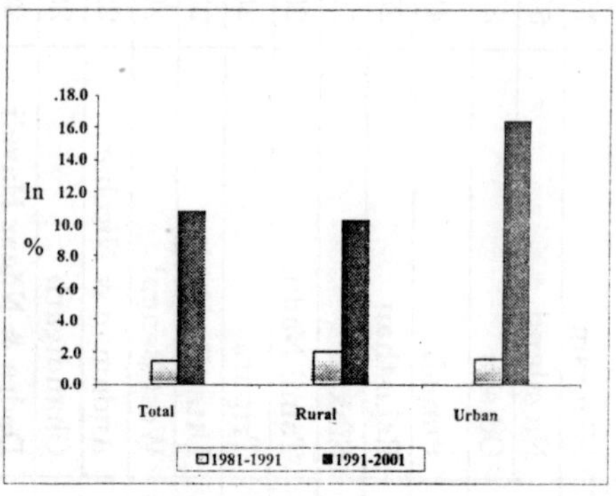

Fig. 2.3.6. Growth rate of Marginal Workers by Residence in India, 1981-2001

Further, the marginalisation in a segment of the workforce has been rapid in the urban compared to the rural areas, and this is true for most of the states and union territories (see Fig. 2.3.6 and Table 2.3.3).

It would be interesting to know in which sector of the economy the marginal workforce is engaged more. The data available from 2001 Census allows disaggregation by four industrial categories – cultivators, agricultural labourer, household industry and other services. It may be seen that marginal workforce among male has grown faster in all categories except cultivators. The male marginal workforce engaged as agricultural labourer, household industry and in other services has grown nearly 30 per cent per annum compared to its half or less among female workforce (see Table 2.3.3 a). The male-female differentials in growth rates are very conspicuous in all categories but the marginalisation of male force has been far greater in agricultural categories when compared to female workforce. Females show high level of marginal work force in household and other service categories compared to agricultural occupations, but even then the growth rates remains lower than that of the male workforce in all categories. Both among males and females, the growth of marginal workforce has been slow among those who returned as cultivators. For females, this even shows a negative growth in urban areas at the all India level and also in the states of Kerala and Karnataka and union territories of Dadra & Nagar Haveli and Daman & Diu. This indicates about the processes of switching over of the erstwhile cultivators to agricultural labourers. In nutshell, we find that other services show very high growth rate followed by household industry and agricultural labourer. More importantly, marginal workforce engaged in household industry has grown very faster in some of the developed states like Punjab, Haryana, Delhi and Chandigarh in both rural and urban areas. Same pattern is also observed in some of the lagging states like Bihar, Assam and Rajashtan and Uttar Pradesh. A high level of marginalisation of workforce is very distinctly observed in several states of northeast India particularly notable among them are the states of Arunanchal Pradesh, Nagaland and Manipur and Meghalaya.

2.4. Workforce in Non-Agricultural Sector

2.4.1. All Non-agricultural Workers (Main+Marginal)

The share of workforce in non-agricultural sector has increased considerably over the decades at the national level and for most of the states and union territories (see Table 2.4.1). When the share is computed for male and female workers separately it is found that the share in non-agricultural activities has increased and the difference between sexes remained more or less similar (see also Fig. 2.4.1). In 1981, around one-third of the total male workers were engaged in non-agricultural activities which went up to half of the total male workers in 2001. North eastern states like Assam, Meghalaya and Mizoram have lower share of non-agricultural workforce than the national level. Table 2.4.1 also depicts that among the northern states/union territories, Delhi and Chandigarh have higher percentages of non-agricultural workers being more urbanised, and the states like Punjab and Haryana have gained around 20 per cent increase in non-agricultural workforce during 1981-2001. The EAG states have not done good as the share of both male and female non-agricultural workers to total workers is found to be low compared to the national level Figs. Among the southern states, Kerala has the highest percentage share of non-agricultural workers. In 1981, Kerala had about half of the total workers engaged in non-agricultural activities, which went up to as high as three-fourth in 2001.

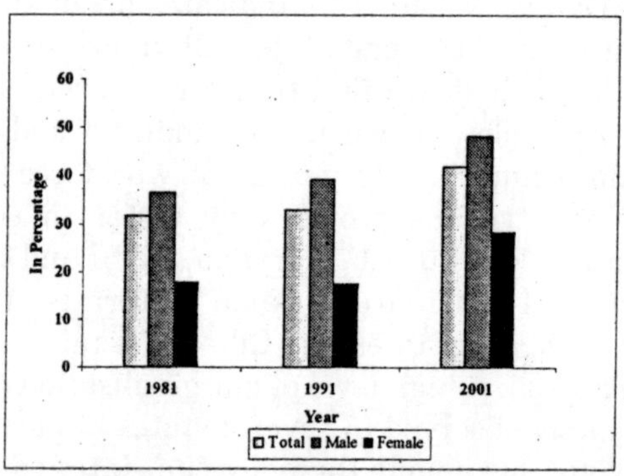

Fig. 2.4.1. Percentage of Total Non-Agricultural Workers to Total Workers, India, 1981-2001

2.4.2. Rural Non-agricultural Worker (Main +Marginal)

India is predominantly an agricultural country. Hence, a very low percentage of rural workforce is engaged in the non-agricultural sector. At the national level, around one fifth of the rural workforce were engaged in non-agricultural activities in 1981 that increased by 10 percentage points in 2001 (27 per cent). The change from 1981 to 2001 has been gradual as the increase in the non-agricultural workforce increased by nearly 5 percentage points in each decade since 1981. On the other hand, gender differential has not been gradual, but most of the increase in the female workforce in non-agricultural activities has occurred during the last decade only. In the rural areas of the EAG states, a low share of both male and female in non-agricultural activities was observed compared to the national level. On the other hand, except Madhya Pradesh, all EAG states have achieved a perceptible increase in the share of non-agricultural workers in rural areas. Among the southern states, Karnataka has the lowest percentage of non-agricultural workers in rural areas during the last two decades and in case of Kerala almost half of the rural workers were in non-agricultural category even in 1981, which is reported, nearly two-third in 200. It is evident from Table 2.4.2 that the non-agricultural sector is expanding in most of the states, but very slow in the states of Bihar, Madhya Pradesh and Maharashtra.

2.4.3. Urban Non-agricultural Workers (Main +Marginal)

In urban areas, nearly one-tenth of the workforce are employed in non-agricultural sector. Nearly 15 per cent women are engaged in agricultural activities i.e. twice the men in urban areas. However, in most of the states, the share of the non-agricultural workforce has been increasing except Tamil Nadu. Some of northeastern states like Manipur and Mizoram show much higher level of agricultural workforce even in the urban areas (see Table 2.4.3).

2.4.4. Main Non-agricultural Workers

The share of main workers in non-agricultural sector has also increased considerably over the decades at the national level and for all the states and union territories. As per 1981 Census, around one third of the main workers are engaged in

Table 2.4.1. Percentage of Total Non-agricultural Workers to Total Workers, India and States, 1981-2001

Sl. No	State / Union Territories	1981			1991			2001		
		Total	*Male*	*Female*	*Total*	*Male*	*Female*	*Total*	*Male*	*Female*
	India	29.66	33.72	17.46	32.87	39.01	17.54	42.50	48.53	29.22
01	Andaman & Nicobar Islands	79.24	79.41	78.04	75.45	77.92	63.18	80.46	82.61	71.76
02	Andhra Pradesh	29.29	36.53	16.52	30.55	38.82	16.81	37.84	46.20	24.15
03	Arunachal Pradesh	25.08	38.61	4.94	33.86	47.77	10.65	38.26	50.05	19.98
04	Assam	NA	NA	NA	32.68	36.51	23.17	47.64	49.55	42.73
05	Bihar	19.90	22.47	9.77	18.06	21.17	7.07	22.75	25.85	14.25
06	Chandigarh	98.07	97.89	99.48	98.20	98.02	99.41	99.21	99.24	99.01
07	Dadra & Nagar Haveli	23.51	34.25	8.49	25.27	39.49	7.66	52.52	69.01	19.86
08	Delhi	97.13	97.37	94.89	97.91	97.97	97.44	98.83	99.04	97.41
09	Goa,Daman & Diu	64.98	74.92	42.72	72.91	80.71	53.56	84.63	89.90	70.27
10	Gujarat	36.33	43.18	17.69	39.16	48.24	19.13	48.42	55.68	32.90
11	Haryana	35.75	39.55	15.15	39.30	43.56	17.06	48.71	54.99	35.23
12	Himachal Pradesh	24.29	35.13	5.88	27.04	40.83	6.47	31.53	47.23	11.24
13	Jammu & Kashmir	28.21	37.89	8.87	NA	NA	NA	51.04	55.41	40.12
14	Karnataka	33.12	38.09	21.99	34.63	41.71	21.06	44.29	51.08	31.84
15	Kerala	55.83	59.77	45.54	60.03	62.26	53.56	77.20	78.36	73.61

Sl. No	State / Union Territories	1981			1991			2001		
		Total	Male	Female	Total	Male	Female	Total	Male	Female
16	Lakshadweep	93.62	97.96	74.56	100.03	100.00	100.21	100.00	100. 0	100.0
17	Madhya Pradesh	22.33	28.26	11.12	22.60	30.00	9.90	28.51	35.77	16.27
18	Maharashtra	35.64	47.34	13.76	37.85	51.21	15.31	45.04	56.78	23.02
19	Manipur	25.51	33.15	30.69	29.79	36.14	22.08	47.81	49.89	45.19
20	Meghalaya	26.45	32.45	17.40	30.76	37.33	20.91	34.16	39.15	27.10
21	Mizoram	25.37	34.97	10.82	32.31	40.76	20.96	39.40	45.53	31.50
22	Nagaland	26.56	41.34	5.72	25.73	38.39	8.10	31.62	41.32	18.39
23	Odisha	23.44	25.86	16.49	24.70	28.57	14.39	35.23	39.45	25.98
24	Pondicherry	57.53	63.44	36.60	63.13	68.47	45.07	75.73	79.99	62.62
25	Punjab	39.53	40.65	28.42	43.67	43.67	43.65	61.05	58.81	68.26
26	Rajasthan	26.95	33.09	10.81	26.05	35.38	7.59	34.09	44.76	16.81
27	Sikkim	33.11	23.70	50.26	33.84	40.98	20.13	43.64	52.41	28.71
28	Tamil Nadu	37.70	44.82	22.13	38.83	47.08	22.84	50.67	58.46	36.24
29	Tripura	30.64	32.66	22.13	36.80	39.70	26.19	49.17	53.86	37.29
30	Uttar Pradesh	22.77	25.22	12.79	25.80	28.75	12.26	34.11	37.25	24.30
31	West Bengal	44.02	44.36	41.68	45.75	47.01	39.49	55.85	56.51	53.74

Table 2.4.2. Percentage of Non-agricultural Workers (Rural) to Total Rural Workers, India and States, 1981-2001

Sl. No.	State / Union Territories	1981			1991			2001		
		Total	Male	Female	Total	Male	Female	Total	Male	Female
	India	17.13	19.40	11.22	18.95	22.75	10.96	27.23	30.80	20.73
01	Andaman & Nicobar Islands	72.09	71.84	73.61	66.9	69.6	54.8	71.88	74.34	63.17
02	Andhra Pradesh	18.96	23.42	12.15	22.1	28.8	12.7	24.96	30.43	17.46
03	Arunachal Pradesh	21.37	33.84	3.99	27.2	40.1	8.0	27.11	37.42	13.27
04	Assam	NA	NA	NA	26.3	28.7	20.7	40.86	41.59	39.13
05	Bihar	12.79	14.32	7.25	11.3	13.2	4.8	17.60	19.72	12.15
06	Chandigarh	81.33	81.17	85.17	91.2	91.1	93.6	95.52	95.95	91.56
07	Dadra & Nagar Haveli	21.18	31.35	7.37	21.5	34.7	6.2	42.94	59.97	15.79
08	Delhi	67.07	69.21	52.77	84.1	84.8	75.6	88.36	90.43	75.94
09	Goa,Daman & Diu	53.12	64.13	32.60	60.6	70.4	40.5	74.86	82.91	55.59
10	Gujarat	18.56	21.97	11.39	20.9	25.6	13.2	28.76	31.18	25.08
11	Haryana	22.00	25.00	8.12	24.7	28.5	8.0	35.17	38.94	28.67
12	Himachal Pradesh	19.78	29.64	4.11	22.4	35.3	4.5	26.43	41.25	8.80
13	Jammu & Kashmir	18.39	25.81	5.61	NA	NA	NA	38.90	41.29	33.98
14	Karnataka	18.76	21.04	14.42	19.0	22.9	12.8	26.51	30.49	20.58
15	Kerala	49.35	53.13	40.02	49.1	50.8	44.6	71.31	72.42	68.02

Sl. No.	*State / Union Territories*	*1981*			*1991*			*2001*		
		Total	*Male*	*Female*	*Total*	*Male*	*Female*	*Total*	*Male*	*Female*
16	Lakshadweep	93.62	97.96	74.56	100.03	100.00	100.21	100.00	100. 0	100.0
17	Madhya Pradesh	22.33	28.26	11.12	22.60	30.00	9.90	28.51	35.77	16.27
18	Maharashtra	35.64	47.34	13.76	37.85	51.21	15.31	45.04	56.78	23.02
19	Manipur	25.51	33.15	30.69	29.79	36.14	22.08	47.81	49.89	45.19
20	Meghalaya	26.45	32.45	17.40	30.76	37.33	20.91	34.16	39.15	27.10
21	Mizoram	25.37	34.97	10.82	32.31	40.76	20.96	39.40	45.53	31.50
22	Nagaland	26.56	41.34	5.72	25.73	38.39	8.10	31.62	41.32	18.39
23	Odisha	23.44	25.86	16.49	24.70	28.57	14.39	35.23	39.45	25.98
24	Pondicherry	57.53	63.44	36.60	63.13	68.47	45.07	75.73	79.99	62.62
25	Punjab	39.53	40.65	28.42	43.67	43.67	43.65	61.05	58.81	68.26
26	Rajasthan	26.95	33.09	10.81	26.05	35.38	7.59	34.09	44.76	16.81
27	Sikkim	33.11	23.70	50.26	33.84	40.98	20.13	43.64	52.41	28.71
28	Tamil Nadu	37.70	44.82	22.13	38.83	47.08	22.84	50.67	58.46	36.24
29	Tripura	30.64	32.66	22.13	36.80	39.70	26.19	49.17	53.86	37.29
30	Uttar Pradesh	22.77	25.22	12.79	25.80	28.75	12.26	34.11	37.23	24.30
31	West Bengal	44.02	44.36	41.68	45.75	47.01	39.49	55.85	56.51	53.74

Table 2.4.3. Percentage of Non-agricultural Workers (Urban) to Total Urban Workers, India and States, 1981-2001

Sl. No.	*State / Union Territories*	*1981*			*1991*			*2001*		
		Total	*Male*	*Female*	*Total*	*Male*	*Female*	*Total*	*Male*	*Female*
	India	81.28	82.19	76.24	86.66	88.86	73.71	92.44	93.95	85.32
01	Andaman & Nicobar Islands	99.56	99.55	99.67	99.3	99.3	99.4	99.56	99.56	99.59
02	Andhra Pradesh	83.91	87.93	66.14	83.5	87.4	66.7	91.82	93.97	83.24
03	Arunachal Pradesh	93.29	95.78	72.83	93.6	95.3	82.2	93 69	96.00	85.39
04	Assam	NA	NA	NA	93.7	94.5	87.1	97.54	97.87	95.65
05	Bihar	82.75	84.04	68.32	77.7	79.8	56.7	82.42	84.57	67.74
06	Chandigarh	99.25	99.18	99.82	99.2	99.1	99.7	99.70	99.73	99.57
07	Dadar & Nagar Haveli	61.86	73.68	34.33	77.9	87.2	47.7	91.36	94.97	67.73
08	Delhi	99.30	99.34	98.92	99.3	99.3	99.2	99.57	99.64	99.12
09	Goa,Daman & Diu	91.66	95.13	79.21	92.0	94.5	83.3	96.51	97.76	92.50
10	Gujarat	90.87	92.53	76.80	82.0	86.6	54.3	95.47	96.52	88.61
11	Haryana	90.00	90.33	85.60	89.4	89.8	86.0	94.07	95.23	87.70
12	Himachal Pradesh	90.91	93.17	77.18	89.5	93.4	72.1	95.66	97.35	88.08
13	Jammu & Kashmir	84.43	88.76	57.82	NA	NA	NA	93.85	94.50	89.92
14	Karnataka	83.65	86.38	71.61	85.4	88.0	74.6	91.82	93.45	86.09
15	Kerala	87.86	89.54	81.81	83.5	85.1	78.1	94.49	95.11	92.31

Sl. No.	State/Union Territories	1981			1991			2001		
		Total	Male	Female	Total	Male	Female	Total	Male	Female
16	Lakshadweep	99.91	99.95	99.51	100.0	100.0	100.0	100.0	100.0	100.0
17	Madhya Pradesh	85.66	88.30	70.97	83.4	86.7	66.7	88.38	90.89	77.29
18	Maharashtra	91.44	93.80	77.55	91.4	93.9	78.6	94.65	96.19	87.27
19.	Manipur	36.13	75.82	66.45	54.1	60.2	45.2	77.40	78.37	76.06
20	Meghalaya	94.07	95.33	89.96	92.1	94.2	85.7	90.81	92.91	86.37
21	Mizoram	74.84	76.53	72.48	54.4	62.8	42.4	68.58	73.33	61.81
22	Nagaland	92.31	95.40	71.19	88.8	92.5	69.4	94.43	96.71	86.70
23	Odisha	83.17	85.42	69.36	84.3	86.3	70.6	92.49	93.64	86.18
24	Pondicherry	86.45	89.09	73.65	85.7	87.1	79.0	93.51	94.26	90.70
25	Punjab	88.70	88.78	87.56	88.4	88.1	92.7	94.14	94.18	93.88
26	Rajasthan	85.88	87.98	67.02	85.6	88.6	63.0	92.18	94.65	78.40
27	Sikkim	98.03	98.20	97.09	98.5	98.7	97.6	99.56	99.64	99.32
28	Tamil Nadu	88.00	90.42	77.17	87.5	90.2	76.3	85.98	89.05	76.76
29	Tripura	91.28	92.12	86.70	89.9	89.4	92.5	96.70	96.45	97.75
30	Uttar Pradesh	84.77	84.91	82.41	81.7	82.4	73.7	90.52	91.06	86.48
31	West Bengal	95.20	95.42	92.81	94.3	94.5	92.4	97.49	97.63	96.78

Table 2.4.4. Percentage of Total Non-agricultural Workers (Main) to Total Main Workers, India and States, 1981-2001

Sl. No.	State / Union Territories	1981			1991			2001		
		Total	*Male*	*Female*	*Total*	*Male*	*Female*	*Total*	*Male*	*Female*
	India	32.69	36.66	20.68	35.19	39.26	21.19	46.61	50.29	34.47
01	Andaman & Nicobar Islands	79.88	79.49	85.35	78.51	78.42	79.26	83.99	84.21	82.70
02	Andhra Pradesh	30.47	36.63	17.14	31.39	38.86	17.30	40.70	47.67	26.56
03	Arunachal Pradesh	26.25	39.00	5.32	34.51	47.88	11.10	40.85	51.97	20.70
04	Assam	NA	NA	NA	37.01	37.00	37.06	53.38	52.48	57.53
05	Bihar	20.93	22.64	11.13	19.29	21.23	9.11	29.10	31.21	19.23
06	Chandigarh	98.07	97.89	99.51	98.24	98.04	99.55	99.32	99.31	99.33
07	Dadra & Nagar Haveli	27.37	34.72	11.46	30.08	40.43	10.63	59.21	71.75	23.58
08	Delhi	97.43	97.45	97.31	98.03	98.01	98.17	99.03	99.14	98.20
09	Goa,Daman & Diu	71.44	76.91	54.43	76.06	81.07	61.16	90.93	92.92	83.73
10	Gujarat	39.89	43.47	21.90	43.71	48.39	24.34	54.42	57.46	42.88
11	Haryana	39.21	40.09	28.74	42.22	43.72	28.32	54.62	57.23	44.75
12	Himachal Pradesh	29.19	36.71	8.72	33.45	42.05	11.11	42.70	54.60	17.53
13	Jammu & Kashmir	39.65	40.19	34.31	NA	NA	NA	59.69	60.23	56.53
14	Karnataka	34.97	38.16	25.53	36.88	41.88	24.60	48.51	52.30	38.89
15	Kerala	58.70	61.01	51.50	62.22	63.36	58.35	80.48	80.96	78.73

Sl. No.	*State / Union Territories*	*1981*			*1991*			*2001*		
		Total	*Male*	*Female*	*Total*	*Male*	*Female*	*Total*	*Male*	*Female*
16	Lakshadweep	99.99	99.97	99.73	100	100	100	100	100	100
17	Madhya Pradesh	23.80	28.69	12.11	24.73	30.19	11.52	31.82	36.93	18.77
18	Maharashtra	38.25	47.81	15.92	40.38	51.54	17.23	48.71	58.54	25.47
19	Manipur	6.57	33.00	29.61	31.55	36.74	24.21	50.31	53.45	44.41
20	Meghalaya	9.43	3.95	18.60	32.18	37.64	22.95	37.22	41.37	29.78
21	Mizoram	32.85	38.57	24.19	35.37	43.23	22.92	41.04	46.89	31.40
22	Nagaland	26.91	41.83	5.76	25.94	38.52	8.16	33.13	43.51	17.34
23	Odisha	25.30	26.08	21.26	27.00	28.76	19.10	42.30	42.85	39.53
24	Pondicherry	59.39	63.79	40.76	63.65	68.51	46.30	77.91	81.22	66.65
25	Punjab	41.97	40.96	68.81	44.74	43.73	66.93	62.33	59.44	75.49
26	Rajasthan	31.09	33.41	17.59	31.20	35.79	12.43	39.26	46.54	18.93
27	Sikkim	33.75	23.63	53.53	34.35	41.00	20.89	48.20	55.08	33.01
28	Tamil Nadu	39.05	45.01	23.81	40.52	47.17	25.29	54.53	60.86	40.70
29	Tripura	32.71	33.23	29.66	38.53	39.87	31.93	53.87	55.39	47.22
30	Uttar Pradesh	22.58	26.31	16.94	27.80	29.36	16.01	38.44	39.41	32.25
31	West Bengal	45.01	44.91	45.90	47.04	47.20	45.90	60.57	59.33	67.38

non-agricultural activities, however, the percentage increased remarkably to more than 40 per cent in 2001 at the all India level (Table 2.4.4).

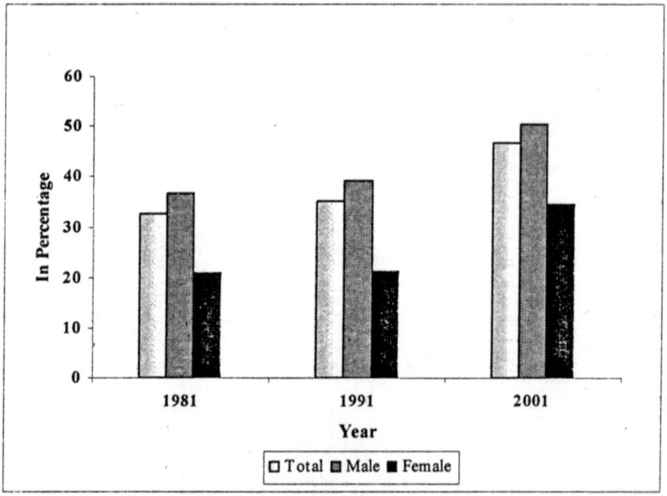

Fig. 2.4.1. Percentage of Total Non-Agricultural Workers (Main) to Total Main Workers, India, 1981-2001

In the case of both male and female main workers the percentage of non-agricultural workers was almost static during 1981 to 1991, but there has been a significant increase during the period 1991-2001. As increase has been more or less same, gender gap in non-agricultural workforce remained almost unchanged (see Fig. 2.4.1).

Most of the EAG states have lower percentage of non-agricultural male and female workers in the main work category than at the national level. States like Punjab, Gujarat, Maharashtra, West Bengal and Kerala have higher percentage of non-agricultural main workers than the other states. These states have gained more than 10 percentage points increase in the non-agricultural workforce during the period 1991-2001.

The share of non-agricultural workers in main work category is very low in rural areas. At the national level, around one fifth of the rural workers in the main work category are non-agricultural workers in 1981, and it remained

Table 2.4.5. Percentage of Rural Non-agricultural Workers (Main) to Rural Main Workers, India and States, 1981-2001

Sl. No.	*State / Union Territories*	*1981*			*1991*			*2001*		
		Total	*Male*	*Female*	*Total*	*Male*	*Female*	*Total*	*Male*	*Female*
	India	19.02	20.84	12.73	19.97	22.45	12.59	29.37	31.66	22.95
01	Andaman & Nicobar Islands	72.07	71.71	77.70	70.27	70.23	70.58	75.43	75.86	72.77
02	Andhra Pradesh	19.60	23.46	12.27	19.03	23.59	11.78	26.79	31.42	18.93
03	Arunachal Pradesh	22.39	34.17	4.27	27.80	40.20	8.35	28.92	38.97	13.27
04	Assam	NA	NA	NA	30.03	29.09	33.71	45.53	43.93	52.55
05	Bihar	13.33	14.39	7.66	12.00	13.26	5.85	20.85	22.26	14.75
06	Chandigarh	81.29	81.19	84.02	91.28	91.14	94.01	96.27	96.39	94.99
07	Dadra & Nagar Haveli	24.73	31.71	9.97	25.81	35.53	8.56	49.26	62.93	18.29
08	Delhi	69.75	69.93	68.05	84.56	84.92	80.05	90.33	91.41	82.53
09	Goa, Daman & Diu	60.10	66.41	43.06	64.44	70.76	48.23	84.07	87.49	71.90
10	Gujarat	20.04	22.13	11.42	23.22	25.99	14.27	32.16	32.21	32.03
11	Haryana	24.52	25.37	14.89	27.06	28.63	13.52	39.11	40.30	35.35
12	Himachal Pradesh	24.00	31.04	5.91	27.94	36.34	7.34	36.33	48.23	13.15
13	Jammu & Kashmir	27.15	27.65	22.33	NA	NA	NA	45.25	45.05	46.29
14	Karnataka	19.82	21.06	16.60	20.28	22.94	14.76	29.06	31.05	24.78
15	Kerala	52.23	54.30	46.09	54.35	55.31	51.23	74.79	75.21	73.32

Sl. No	State / Union Territories	1981			1991			2001		
		Total	Male	Female	Total	Male	Female	Total	Male	Female
16	Lakshadweep	99.98	99.97	100.0	100.0	100.0	100.00	100.0	100.00	100.00
17	Madhya Pradesh	12.60	14.96	7.32	11.92	14.83	5.86	16.12	18.86	10.15
18	Maharashtra	17.00	22.92	6.70	17.13	24.46	6.27	21.09	27.97	9.90
19	Manipur	23.07	23.48	22.56	23.87	28.90	17.32	39.55	43.58	32.16
20	Meghalaya	17.08	20.35	12.11	21.73	25.50	15.92	25.34	28.79	19.53
21	Mizoram	97.62	98.18	96.86	16.83	24.32	6.11	16.33	21.74	8.25
22	Nagaland	18.48	30.86	3.39	16.28	25.74	4.90	23.22	31.73	11.78
23	Odisha	18.08	18.39	16.53	19.19	20.28	14.56	32.49	32.54	32.25
24	Pondicherry	33.74	38.56	17.06	31.97	38.22	15.86	48.65	54.70	32.79
25	Punjab	23.75	23.08	47.69	26.44	25.84	43.55	46.38	40.31	69.60
26	Rajasthan	18.51	19.91	11.27	17.44	20.65	6.21	25.71	31.31	12.64
27	Sikkim	26.27	34.67	11.96	28.28	34.38	16.60	42.20	49.29	27.14
28	Tamil Nadu	21.45	25.23	13.43	22.50	26.65	14.84	32.71	37.48	24.50
29	Tripura	26.00	26.70	21.92	29.38	30.88	22.19	44.35	46.09	36.91
30	Uttar Pradesh	13.68	14.11	9.55	15.52	16.54	8.62	24.33	24.63	22.63
31	West Bengal	26.17	25.34	33.02	29.79	29.08	34.24	44.48	42.36	55.75

Table 2.4.6. Percentage of Urban Non-agricultural Workers (Main) to Urban Main Workers, India and States, 1981-2001

Sl. No.	*State / Union Territories*	*1981*			*1991*			*2001*		
		Total	*Male*	*Female*	*Total*	*Male*	*Female*	*Total*	*Male*	*Female*
	India	88.85	90.18	78.77	88.38	89.73	79.39	93.72	94.63	88.66
01	Andaman & Nicobar Islands	99.58	99.55	99.86	99.41	99.36	99.80	99.65	99.63	99.72
02	Andhra Pradesh	84.43	87.99	66.79	83.90	87.42	67.76	93.41	94.79	87.00
03	Arunachal Pradesh	93.46	95.82	73.31	93.30	95.39	80.00	94.91	96.63	87.89
04	Assam	NA	NA	NA	94.58	94.75	93.06	98.05	98.16	97.33
05	Bihar	83.36	84.24	72.29	78.87	80.01	65.76	89.93	90.67	83.07
06	Chandigarh	99.25	99.18	99.84	99.21	99.11	99.80	99.72	99.74	99.62
07	Dadra & Nagar Haveli	69.75	77.93	43.54	82.79	87.68	60.91	94.49	95.74	82.87
08	Delhi	99.33	99.34	99.15	99.39	99.38	99.47	99.62	99.67	99.26
09	Goa, Daman & Diu	94.09	95.83	86.70	92.91	94.64	86.35	98.19	98.64	96.51
10	Gujarat	91.49	92.57	80.59	91.87	92.94	81.91	96.27	96.78	92.04
11	Haryana	90.44	90.45	90.28	89.89	89.80	91.02	95.32	95.71	92.56
12	Himachal Pradesh	92.77	93.74	85.94	93.27	93.88	89.87	97.33	98.03	93.85
13	Jammu & Kashmir	89.54	89.61	88.76	NA	NA	NA	95.73	95.73	95.72
14	Karnataka	84.22	86.45	73.32	85.92	88.09	76.24	92.87	93.84	89.06
15	Kerala	89.91	90.51	84.38	85.09	85.94	81.87	95.72	96.04	94.43

Sl. No.	State / Union Territories	1981			1991			2001		
		Total	Male	Female	Total	Male	Female	Total	Male	Female
16	Lakshadweep	100.00	99.97	99.76	100.00	100.00	100.00	100.00	100.00	100.00
17	Madhya Pradesh	86.34	88.44	72.96	84.46	86.85	70.40	90.83	92.16	83.69
18	Maharashtra	92.01	93.93	79.55	92.02	94.00	81.12	95.52	96.53	90.05
19	Manipur	71.21	75.50	63.22	59.52	61.24	56.21	82.64	82.28	83.38
20	Meghalaya	94.37	95.40	90.90	93.38	94.51	89.83	94.25	94.99	92.45
21	Mizoram	99.67	99.78	99.41	61.32	67.32	50.32	72.01	75.85	64.82
22	Nagaland	93.02	95.80	73.30	88.88	92.50	69.47	96.15	97.69	90.24
23	Odisha	84.71	85.80	76.53	85.41	86.55	76.50	94.48	94.70	92.92
24	Pondicherry	87.92	89.51	79.76	86.05	87.24	80.50	94.19	94.58	92.61
25	Punjab	89.22	88.88	94.70	88.59	88.12	95.25	94.68	94.59	95.33
26	Rajasthan	87.15	88.11	75.77	87.42	88.84	73.51	93.74	95.02	84.01
27	Sikkim	98.27	98.41	97.49	99.05	99.08	98.94	99.59	99.64	99.42
28	Tamil Nadu	88.37	90.50	78.10	88.54	90.26	80.53	87.48	89.96	79.32
29	Tripura	91.83	92.68	87.00	90.54	89.59	95.98	97.12	96.85	98.41
30	Uttar Pradesh	85.00	84.96	85.68	84.75	84.84	83.49	92.10	92.16	91.55
31	West Bengal	95.67	95.71	95.21	94.70	94.71	94.59	98.03	98.05	97.87

approximately same in 1991 but a noticeable increase is marked as more than one-fourth of total rural workers in the main work category are engaged in non-agricultural workers in 2001. However, the inequality in the percentage of male and female rural non-agricultural workers remained more or less same during the reference period (Table 2.4.5). This is also true for urban areas (see Table 2.4.6).

2.4.5. Marginal Non-agricultural Workers

The percentage of non-agricultural workers to total marginal workers was 13 per cent in 1981, which declined to 10 per cent in 1991 at the national level. However, the share of marginal workers in non-agricultural sector has increased remarkably to one-fourth in 2001 (see Fig. 2.4.2 and Table 2.4.7). Among the major states of India, Kerala has the highest percentage of marginal workers in non-agricultural sector i.e. around 36 per cent in 1981, increased to around 39 per cent in 1991, and further increased remarkably to 64 per cent in 2001. The states like Jammu and Kashmir, Punjab, Haryana and Himachal Pradesh have very low share of marginal workers in non-agricultural sector in 1981; however, in 2001, Punjab has more than half of its marginal workers in non-agricultural sector whereas around one-third in case of Haryana and Jammu and Kashmir. The percentage of marginal workers in non-agricultural sector is comparatively lower than the national level in all the EAG states during the study period. Males have generally higher share in marginal workers employed in the non-agricultural sector compared to females. But in the states of Punjab and West Bengal, there are higher percentages of female marginal workers in non-agricultural sector compared to males in 2001 (Table 2.4.7). Further, rural and urban scenario in the composition of marginal workers is presented in Tables 2.4.8 and 2.4.9.

Table 2.4.7. Percentage of Total Non-agricultural Workers (Marginal) to Total Marginal Workers, India and States, 1981-2001

Sl. No.	*State / Union Territories*	*1981*			*1991*			*2001*		
		Total	*Male*	*Female*	*Total*	*Male*	*Female*	*Total*	*Male*	*Female*
	India	12.98	18.58	9.69	10.00	25.35	8.37	25.79	33.70	20.69
01	Andaman & Nicobar Islands	73.41	77.23	71.55	41.06	53.51	37.86	62.72	69.48	55.35
02	Andhra Pradesh	14.97	26.76	13.94	14.86	31.98	13.43	23.62	33.22	17.80
03	Arunachal Pradesh	5.93	20.22	1.99	5.00	23.37	2.33	22.46	30.48	17.42
04	Assam	NA	NA	NA	5.05	14.19	3.88	30.80	32.74	29.38
05	Bihar	8.36	14.14	7.01	3.50	11.83	2.89	15.90	20.69	12.30
06	Chandigarh	97.88	97.96	97.72	86.04	85.39	86.75	95.98	96.61	94.83
07	Dadra & Nagar Haveli	4.09	12.82	3.38	2.67	5.89	2.37	16.64	27.42	12.84
08	Delhi	59.08	76.40	45.75	69.29	76.30	63.59	95.05	96.67	90.73
09	Goa, Daman & Diu	22.07	36.17	17.16	26.55	45.12	21.01	54.43	66.49	43.05
10	Gujarat	13.59	22.78	12.86	13.76	28.10	13.26	24.25	31.65	21.97
11	Haryana	5.79	13.21	4.36	3.42	13.51	2.80	31.45	40.82	26.03
12	Himachal Pradesh	3.25	9.23	1.84	0.81	2.44	0.65	10.19	19.43	5.36
13	Jammu & Kashmir	3.18	4.60	2.96	NA	NA	NA	31.34	31.75	31.07
14	Karnataka	13.62	32.71	11.46	10.32	25.52	8.99	24.70	38.41	18.22
15	Kerala	35.95	46.47	25.75	38.54	44.43	33.38	63.99	65.50	61.34

Sl. No.	*State / Union Territories*	*1981*			*1991*			*2001*		
		Total	*Male*	*Female*	*Total*	*Male*	*Female*	*Total*	*Male*	*Female*
16	Lakshadweep	66.51	85.91	34.97	100.00	100.00	100.00	100.00	100.00	100.00
17	Madhya Pradesh	9.86	21.23	8.46	6.99	17.00	6.16	15.62	24.33	11.53
18	Maharashtra	9.46	27.24	5.98	10.81	32.36	7.63	25.21	39.15	16.69
19	Manipur	2.08	3.19	1.95	11.08	11.28	11.04	42.03	34.06	46.12
20	Meghalaya	8.91	13.52	7.93	6.44	8.07	6.22	23.31	26.12	21.53
21	Mizoram	5.77	5.21	6.01	13.41	12.19	14.01	33.72	37.34	31.70
22	Nagaland	2.89	2.43	3.37	3.67	2.04	4.15	24.20	26.85	22.06
23	Odisha	11.85	17.53	10.91	8.85	17.98	7.84	20.78	24.34	18.56
24	Pondicherry	27.13	48.26	17.81	38.12	63.51	25.45	48.41	57.56	37.99
25	Punjab	6.15	13.32	4.87	3.95	13.72	3.28	53.30	51.16	54.80
26	Rajasthan	6.36	16.64	5.43	3.57	9.81	3.20	19.85	32.43	14.63
27	Sikkim	15.38	29.30	11.53	14.58	38.74	7.90	24.26	31.96	19.48
28	Tamil Nadu	15.74	30.48	13.08	11.19	31.16	9.92	28.36	36.69	21.91
29	Tripura	7.19	13.71	4.53	12.27	25.35	10.14	31.83	41.09	26.59
30	Uttar Pradesh	7.46	10.68	6.85	7.31	13.12	6.82	23.99	31.02	18.16
31	West Bengal	29.41	27.58	30.82	25.89	33.70	23.98	39.02	37.52	40.25

Table 2.4.8. Percentage of Rural Non-agricultural Workers (Marginal) to Rural Marginal Workers, India and States, 1981-2001

Sl. No.	*State / Union Territories*	*1981*			*1991*			*2001*		
		Total	*Male*	*Female*	*Total*	*Male*	*Female*	*Total*	*Male*	*Female*
	India	8.59	16.98	7.83	7.80	17.86	6.84	19.85	24.50	17.14
01	Andaman & Nicobar Islands	72.23	74.55	71.21	38.48	45.43	36.95	59.22	64.87	53.73
02	Andhra Pradesh	12.19	19.08	11.64	11.98	22.99	11.17	16.83	22.56	13.75
03	Arunachal Pradesh	5.44	19.09	1.73	4.59	21.64	2.21	17.15	23.58	13.29
04	Assam	NA	NA	NA	4.58	12.76	3.56	28.80	29.72	28.14
05	Bihar	7.21	10.61	6.45	3.24	10.06	2.77	13.81	17.29	11.30
06	Chandigarh	86.67	77.14	92.73	85.12	81.08	86.90	81.38	84.47	75.15
07	Dadar & Nagar Haveli	3.45	11.27	2.94	2.28	5.13	2.02	14.27	23.49	11.11
08	Delhi	21.00	29.48	17.64	44.74	56.49	40.70	68.61	76.94	53.96
09	Goa, Daman & Diu	17.27	29.29	13.35	19.94	38.78	14.99	43.15	55.33	33.32
10	Gujarat	11.45	12.51	11.37	13.76	28.10	13.26	19.02	21.11	18.45
11	Haryana	4.62	9.86	3.66	3.42	13.51	2.80	25.96	31.83	22.92
12	Himachal Pradesh	2.88	8.28	1.62	1.41	4.43	1.11	9.25	17.68	4.92
13	Jammu & Kashmir	2.51	3.79	2.31	NA	NA	NA	27.76	26.93	28.28
14	Karnataka	9.57	19.44	8.64	7.63	15.65	7.01	17.15	25.61	13.71
15	Kerala	30.55	41.19	20.76	32.47	36.55	29.08	58.81	60.07	56.66

Sl. No.	State / Union Territories	1981 Total	1981 Male	1981 Female	1991 Total	1991 Male	1991 Female	2001 Total	2001 Male	2001 Female
16	Lakshadweep	54.80	80.87	13.04	99.60	100.00	98.24	100.00	100.00	100.00
17	Madhya Pradesh	7.66	14.82	6.85	5.34	11.26	4.89	10.19	13.82	8.66
18	Maharashtra	4.35	12.35	3.05	5.60	13.98	4.63	14.23	21.89	10.34
19	Manipur	5.40	5.67	5.35	9.96	7.86	10.36	36.91	28.74	41.14
20	Meghalaya	7.31	10.04	6.75	5.22	5.67	5.17	19.69	21.49	18.59
21	Mizoram	2.16	3.11	1.76	2.44	2.81	2.26	11.65	13.53	10.71
22	Nagaland	1.53	0.82	2.27	2.80	1.79	3.09	19.78	20.57	19.18
23	Odisha	10.85	14.60	10.25	8.18	15.00	7.46	18.71	21.04	17.30
24	Pondicherry	15.10	31.08	9.79	20.87	39.76	15.66	23.48	29.84	17.65
25	Punjab	4.71	9.67	3.86	2.83	9.55	2.40	47.97	42.67	51.29
26	Rajasthan	5.23	13.12	4.55	2.57	6.85	2.32	15.43	23.61	12.36
27	Sikkim	12.66	22.68	10.20	7.74	20.21	5.20	21.48	27.07	18.19
28	Tamil Nadu	10.10	18.80	8.73	7.87	23.41	6.99	17.70	22.83	14.22
29	Tripura	5.05	9.25	3.44	10.99	21.85	9.33	28.63	36.38	24.52
30	Uttar Pradesh	5.28	6.32	5.09	5.53	9.73	5.20	18.76	23.24	15.37
31	West Bengal	21.87	17.51	25.01	23.86	29.08	22.69	32.84	28.19	36.30

Table 2.4.9. Percentage of Urban Non-agricultural Workers (Marginal) to Urban Marginal Workers, India and States, 1981-2001

Sl. No.	*State / Union Territories*	*1981*			*1991*			*2001*		
		Total	*Male*	*Female*	*Total*	*Male*	*Female*	*Total*	*Male*	*Female*
	India	27.45	75.47	50.87	47.46	67.74	40.33	80.23	85.31	72.51
01	Andaman & Nicobar Islands	98.71	99.59	95.38	93.65	96.20	87.83	97.90	97.94	97.75
02	Andhra Pradesh	64.27	77.57	61.00	58.50	78.04	53.51	77.19	83.41	68.32
03	Arunachal Pradesh	73.19	85.71	60.29	24.58	54.24	10.00	78.20	83.47	72.70
04	Assam	NA	NA	NA	43.00	56.38	37.05	90.65	92.49	87.56
05	Bihar	53.17	65.92	41.30	13.96	35.48	8.72	65.10	71.21	52.95
06	Chandigarh	98.94	99.08	98.65	86.24	85.90	86.70	99.14	99.35	98.76
07	Dadar & Nagar Haveli	16.16	18.06	15.19	16.02	32.26	14.50	44.33	63.34	35.12
08	Delhi	93.46	97.51	88.08	79.40	80.25	78.45	98.67	98.99	97.74
09	Goa, Daman & Diu	52.32	67.85	44.46	56.13	63.21	52.69	82.81	87.98	75.56
10	Gujarat	63.99	85.16	56.73	26.48	65.16	21.89	82.01	87.83	77.28
11	Haryana	54.27	67.76	45.38	36.69	62.90	31.57	83.49	89.23	74.81
12	Himachal Pradesh	36.41	52.96	26.93	10.70	36.73	6.08	73.02	84.82	54.59
13	Jammu & Kashmir	21.38	24.62	20.81	NA	NA	NA	77.01	76.09	78.07
14	Karnataka	64.53	80.41	57.71	59.54	79.00	53.34	79.54	87.01	70.31
15	Kerala	73.88	76.66	69.92	61.33	67.57	53.64	87.16	88.44	84.58

Sl. No.	State/Union Territories	1981			1991			2001		
		Total	Male	Female	Total	Male	Female	Total	Male	Female
16	Lakshadweep	99.19	99.68	98.36	100.00	100.00	100.00	100.00	100.00	100.00
17	Madhya Pradesh	63.36	75.13	58.44	48.61	66.23	43.98	74.25	84.14	61.48
18	Maharashtra	70.51	83.92	59.91	65.79	83.62	54.27	83.54	90.19	73.36
19	Manipur	1.33	2.31	1.23	13.63	20.67	12.56	62.37	55.82	65.62
20	Meghalaya	68.04	81.27	61.69	28.60	35.01	27.16	64.69	69.07	60.81
21	Mizoram	25.15	16.00	29.36	22.27	20.13	23.28	57.63	59.68	56.34
22	Nagaland	19.80	22.66	16.92	47.31	15.79	55.41	79.05	84.82	70.91
23	Odisha	46.25	60.33	39.54	40.24	57.43	31.61	74.97	79.74	68.22
24	Pondicherry	51.70	69.03	39.07	60.76	77.35	45.05	80.92	86.29	72.78
25	Punjab	40.13	57.83	33.14	33.63	47.94	30.27	86.27	85.40	87.52
26	Rajasthan	45.05	67.28	39.84	34.55	48.27	32.56	79.73	89.97	66.36
27	Sikkim	76.09	73.51	81.01	79.23	83.58	70.71	99.22	99.61	98.20
28	Tamil Nadu	71.00	80.98	66.53	41.20	64.27	38.25	69.27	75.23	61.74
29	Tripura	71.93	67.59	81.65	49.55	63.79	41.81	91.17	89.60	93.79
30	Uttar Pradesh	64.41	70.86	61.74	44.23	44.37	44.21	81.91	84.26	76.46
31	West Bengal	80.54	80.24	80.89	64.40	68.19	61.12	92.01	91.71	92.52

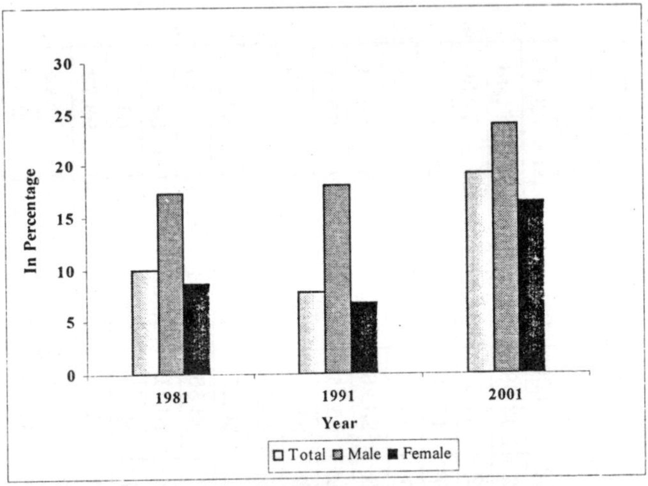

Fig. 2.4.2. Percentage of Total Non-Agricultural Workers to Total Marginal Workers, India, 1981-2001

The percentage of marginal non-agricultural workers to urban marginal workers was around 27 per cent in 1981, which increased to around 47 per cent in 1991 and hopped to 80 per cent in 2001 at the national level. Table 2.4.9 depicts that all the states and union territories have experienced noticeable increase in the percentage of marginal workers in the non-agricultural sector in the post reform period. Developed states like Maharashtra, West Bengal and Tamil Nadu have higher percentages of urban marginal workers in non-agricultural sector than the national average in 1981 but the percentage share declined by 10 to 15 percentage points in 199, but a remarkable increase is noticed in these states in 2001.

2.5. Age Composition

2.5.1. Age Composition of All Workers (Main+Marginl),

It may be observed from Table 2.5.1 that the percentage of workers in the age below 14 has declined during the period 1981-2001. All states and union territories demonstrate this trend, but females show higher incidence of child labour than males. The Census 2001 shows that southern states have lowest incidence of child labour with Kerala showing the least one. On the other hand, north-eastern states like Meghalaya,

Table 2.5.1. Age Composition of Total Workers (Main+ Marginal), India and States, 1981-2001

Sl. No.	State / Union Territories	1981					
		Male			Female		
		0-14	15-59	60+	0-14	15-59	60+
	India	4.48	87.60	7.92	8.79	86.53	4.68
01	Andaman & Nicobar	1.61	94.91	3.48	3.80	94.15	2.05
02	Andhra Pradesh	6.79	85.52	7.69	10.05	84.93	5.02
03	Arunachal Pradesh	3.92	89.95	6.13	7.60	87.40	5.01
04	Assam	NA	NA	NA	NA	NA	NA
05	Bihar	4.15	86.29	9.57	7.72	87.18	5.10
06	Chandigarh	1.15	96.15	2.70	2.12	96.73	1.15
07	Dadra and Nagar Haveli	5.56	89.63	4.82	9.33	87.40	3.27
08	Delhi	1.20	94.97	3.83	2.05	95.63	2.32
09	Goa, Daman & Diu	1.54	93.02	5.45	4.53	90.47	4.99
10	Gujarat	3.81	90.30	5.89	7.70	88.75	3.55
11	Haryana	3.74	88.25	8.02	10.24	87.34	2.42
12	Himachal Pradesh	3.52	85.40	11.08	8.84	86.54	4.62
13	Jammu & Kashmir	7.47	84.79	7.74	14.31	81.92	3.77
14	Karnataka	6.25	86.65	7.10	10.55	85.27	4.18
15	Kerala	0.85	91.32	7.83	4.32	91.06	4.62
16	Lakshadweep	0.39	95.42	4.19	1.37	97.64	0.99
17	Madhya Pradesh	6.20	85.93	7.86	10.33	84.09	5.57
18	Maharashtra	4.40	88.85	6.75	8.53	86.98	4.49
19	Manipur	2.41	88.53	9.05	4.37	89.61	6.02
20	Meghalaya	6.86	86.27	6.87	8.03	87.53	4.44
21	Mizoram	2.14	93.50	4.36	3.84	93.82	2.35
22	Nagaland	3.34	86.24	10.42	5.78	84.27	9.95
23	Odisha	5.88	86.78	7.33	10.25	85.53	4.22
24	Pondicherry	1.64	91.29	7.07	3.10	91.93	4.97
25	Punjab	3.75	87.35	8.90	7.61	88.06	4.33
26	Rajasthan	4.97	88.41	6.62	10.66	86.18	3.16
27	Sikkim	3.72	90.58	5.70	9.05	86.94	4.01
28	Tamil Nadu	3.76	89.11	7.13	7.16	88.24	4.60
29	Tripura	2.97	87.67	9.36	6.52	88.96	4.52
30	Uttar Pradesh	3.77	85.73	10.50	7.37	86.17	6.46
31	West Bengal	3.24	90.68	6.08	6.69	89.77	3.54

Sl. No.	*State / Union Territories*	*1991*					
		Male			*Female*		
		0-14	*15-59*	*60+*	*0-14*	*15-59*	*60+*
	India	3.09	88.99	7.92	5.84	89.24	4.91
01	Andaman & Nicobar	1.03	94.78	4.19	2.51	95.01	2.48
02	Andhra Pradesh	4.31	88.16	7.53	7.60	87.50	4.89
03	Arunachal Pradesh	2.12	91.70	6.18	4.77	89.94	5.29
04	Assam	3.61	89.06	7.33	5.16	91.57	3.27
05	Bihar	2.87	87.89	9.24	5.30	89.83	4.87
06	Chandigarh	0.78	96.56	2.65	1.17	97.65	1.18
07	Dadra and Nagar Haveli	4.39	91.18	4.43	7.97	88.56	3.47
08	Delhi	0.89	95.64	3.47	1.14	96.51	2.35
09	Goa, Daman & Diu	0.92	94.03	5.00	2.11	93.48	4.61
10	Gujarat	2.30	92.16	5.53	5.04	91.19	3.77
11	Haryana	1.72	90.04	8.24	4.40	90.69	4.91
12	Himachal Pradesh	1.71	87.36	10.92	3.80	90.01	6.19
13	Jammu & Kashmir	NA	NA	NA	NA	NA	NA
14	Karnataka	4.02	88.84	7.14	7.39	88.17	4.44
15	Kerala	0.29	91.71	8.00	0.66	93.70	5.64
16	Lakshadweep	0.24	94.75	5.01	0.32	97.68	2.01
17	Madhya Pradesh	3.73	88.06	8.21	6.64	87.92	5.44
18	Maharashtra	2.21	90.80	6.98	4.74	90.02	5.24
19	Manipur	1.65	88.51	9.85	2.72	90.66	6.62
20	Meghalaya	4.28	88.34	7.38	5.04	90.12	4.84
21	Mizoram	4.11	89.97	5.91	5.92	89.70	4.38
22	Nagaland	2.59	87.05	10.36	4.06	87.41	8.53
23	Odisha	2.84	88.99	8.17	6.40	89.20	4.40
24	Pondicherry	0.86	93.23	5.91	1.47	93.80	4.73
25	Punjab	9.78	82.67	7.55	12.26	83.51	4.23
26	Rajasthan	2.90	90.19	6.91	7.75	88.38	3.87
27	Sikkim	2.48	90.50	7.02	4.99	90.65	4.36
28	Tamil Nadu	1.75	90.51	7.74	3.64	91.19	5.17
29	Tripura	1.42	89.26	9.32	3.75	91.14	5.11
30	Uttar Pradesh	2.69	86.99	10.31	5.28	88.32	6.40
31	West Bengal	2.68	91.07	6.26	6.18	90.27	3.56

Sl. No.	State/Union Territories	2001					
		Male			Female		
		0-14	15-59	60+	0-14	15-59	60+
	India	2.46	89.23	8.31	4.59	88.98	6.42
01	Andaman & Nicobar	1.09	94.34	4.57	2.88	93.39	3.74
02	Andhra Pradesh	2.95	89.54	7.52	5.49	89.01	5.50
03	Arunachal Pradesh	2.78	90.61	6.61	5.47	88.80	5.73
04	Assam	3.12	89.15	7.73	5.15	90.21	4.64
05	Bihar	3.48	86.40	10.12	5.44	88.16	6.41
06	Chandigarh	0.94	96.04	3.02	1.97	95.64	2.39
07	Dadra and Nagar Haveli	2.26	94.49	3.25	6.68	89.23	4.09
08	Delhi	0.83	95.70	3.47	1.53	95.14	3.32
09	Goa, Daman & Diu	0.60	94.45	4.94	1.41	93.10	5.49
10	Gujarat	1.65	92.59	5.76	3.64	91.61	4.75
11	Haryana	2.36	90.84	6.80	4.46	90.13	5.41
12	Himachal Pradesh	3.12	86.73	10.15	4.23	87.67	8.10
13	Jammu & Kashmir	3.37	87.87	8.77	8.01	86.58	5.41
14	Karnataka	2.89	89.78	7.33	4.62	89.71	5.67
15	Kerala	0.21	92.05	7.74	0.39	93.13	6.48
16	Lakshadweep	0.17	95.14	4.68	0.19	97.81	2.00
17	Madhya Pradesh	3.30	88.42	8.28	5.55	87.97	6.48
18	Maharashtra	1.49	90.43	8.08	2.55	88.69	8.75
19	Manipur	2.71	87.65	9.64	3.50	89.11	7.39
20	Meghalaya	5.06	87.61	7.33	6.29	87.96	5.75
21	Mizoram	4.89	88.49	6.62	6.57	87.69	5.74
22	Nagaland	4.76	87.16	8.08	6.32	86.89	6.78
23	Odisha	1.87	88.64	9.49	4.35	89.49	6.16
24	Pondicherry	0.46	93.92	5.62	0.85	93.17	5.99
25	Punjab	1.68	89.36	8.96	2.82	90.16	7.02
26	Rajasthan	3.83	89.15	7.02	7.79	87.15	5.07
27	Sikkim	4.99	88.02	7.00	8.45	86.57	4.98
28	Tamil Nadu	1.25	89.58	9.17	1.99	90.58	7.43
29	Tripura	1.37	89.94	8.69	3.16	90.57	6.26
30	Uttar Pradesh	2.93	86.32	10.76	5.66	86.39	7.95
31	West Bengal	2.22	91.08	6.69	5.08	90.30	4.63

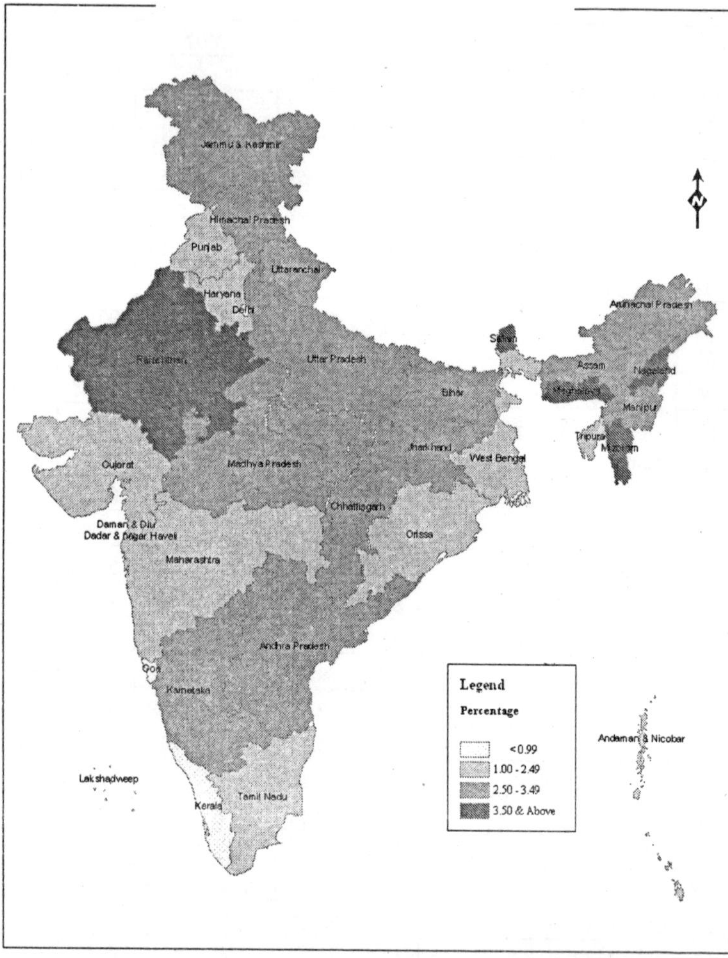

Map 2.2.1. Percentage of Child Labour (Male), State, India, 2001

Mizoram and Nagaland show high level of participation of children in the labour force. Meghalaya has the highest proportion of male workers, which has more than 5 per cent of male child workers in 2001. In the case of female workers, the incidence of child labour is up to 8 per cent of the workforce in the states of Jammu and Kashmir and Sikkim.

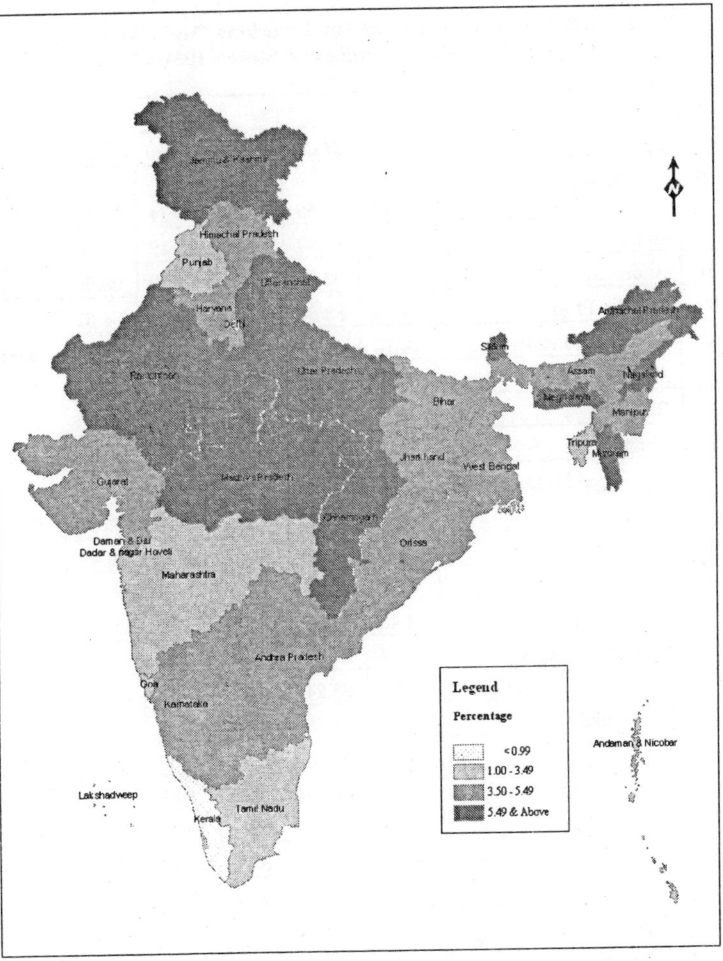

Map 2.2.2. Percentage of Child Labour (Female), State, India, 2001

The percentage of the total male and female workers in the working age group i.e. 15 to 59 age group varies between 85 per cent to 95 per cent in most of the states and union territories. Amongst major states, the percentage of male total workers in the age group 15-59 is highest in Gujarat (92.05 per cent), but the percentage of female total workers is highest in Kerala (93.13 per cent) in 2001. The proportion of both male and female workers in the age group 60 and above has increased

Table 2.5.2. Age Composition of Total Workers (Main+Marginal) by Residence (Rural), India and States, 1981-2001

Sl. No.	State / Union Territories	1981					
		Male			Female		
		0-14	15-59	60+	0-14	15-59	60+
	India	5.25	85.97	8.78	9.12	86.05	4.83
01	Andaman & Nicobar	1.81	93.91	4.28	4.20	93.56	2.24
02	Andhra Pradesh	7.76	83.84	8.40	10.36	84.61	5.03
03	Arunachal Pradesh	4.15	89.31	6.54	7.64	87.30	5.06
04	Assam	NA	NA	NA	NA	NA	NA
05	Bihar	4.45	85.49	10.06	7.85	87.08	5.08
06	Chandigarh	12.65	35.88	51.47	6.24	92.57	1.20
07	Dadra and Nagar Haveli	5.55	89.60	4.85	9.30	87.39	3.30
08	Delhi	1.39	92.21	6.40	5.45	91.86	2.69
09	Goa, Daman & Diu	1.80	92.07	6.14	4.43	90.49	5.09
10	Gujarat	4.84	88.46	6.71	8.21	88.31	3.48
11	Haryana	4.43	86.91	8.66	9.70	76.10	14.19
12	Himachal Pradesh	3.78	84.61	11.61	9.27	85.92	4.81
13	Jammu & Kashmir	8.35	83.24	8.41	15.66	80.52	3.82
14	Karnataka	7.36	84.75	7.89	11.15	84.68	4.17
15	Kerala	0.89	90.76	8.35	2.08	93.14	4.78
16	Lakshadweep	2.33	93.40	4.27	1.48	97.45	1.07
17	Madhya Pradesh	7.20	84.36	8.43	10.57	83.94	5.50
18	Maharashtra	6.07	85.76	8.17	9.17	86.30	4.52
19	Manipur	2.84	87.82	9.34	4.79	89.33	5.88
20	Meghalaya	7.98	84.67	7.35	8.39	87.12	4.48
21	Mizoram	2.55	92.78	4.68	4.20	93.48	2.32
22	Nagaland	3.79	84.13	12.09	5.87	83.77	10.36
23	Odisha	6.31	85.98	7.71	10.44	85.37	4.19
24	Pondicherry	1.59	90.04	8.37	3.44	92.09	4.47
25	Punjab	4.50	85.65	9.85	8.82	86.62	4.56
26	Rajasthan	5.72	87.29	7.00	10.99	85.93	3.08
27	Sikkim	4.12	89.53	6.35	9.22	86.61	4.16
28	Tamil Nadu	4.40	87.52	8.08	7.35	87.93	4.72
29	Tripura	3.20	87.05	9.76	6.53	88.82	4.65
30	Uttar Pradesh	4.09	84.64	11.27	7.65	85.85	6.50
31	West Bengal	4.01	89.33	6.66	6.53	90.10	3.37

Sl. No.	State / Union Territories	1991					
		Male			Female		
		0-14	15-59	60+	0-14	15-59	60+
	India	3.74	87.34	8.92	6.66	88.33	5.01
01	Andaman & Nicobar	1.17	93.77	5.06	2.89	94.28	2.84
02	Andhra Pradesh	8.35	83.45	8.20	10.59	84.62	4.78
03	Arunachal Pradesh	2.30	90.79	6.91	4.77	89.77	5.46
04	Assam	3.93	88.40	7.67	5.01	91.67	3.32
05	Bihar	3.06	87.28	9.66	5.37	89.74	4.89
06	Chandigarh	0.95	96.15	2.89	3.07	94.38	2.56
07	Dadra and Nagar Haveli	4.70	90.65	4.65	8.10	88.35	3.56
08	Delhi	0.72	95.69	3.59	1.88	95.17	2.95
09	Goa, Daman & Diu	0.82	93.43	5.76	2.09	93.30	4.61
10	Gujarat	3.03	90.17	6.81	5.51	90.53	3.96
11	Haryana	1.98	88.89	9.13	4.73	90.18	5.09
12	Himachal Pradesh	1.83	86.60	11.57	3.87	89.83	6.30
13	Jammu & Kashmir	NA	NA	NA	NA	NA	NA
14	Karnataka	4.80	86.98	8.22	7.84	87.60	4.56
15	Kerala	0.30	91.01	8.69	0.66	93.61	5.73
16	Lakshadweep	0.22	94.45	5.33	0.26	97.37	2.37
17	Madhya Pradesh	6.67	84.50	8.83	9.04	85.55	5.41
18	Maharashtra	3.04	88.05	8.91	5.15	89.40	5.45
19	Manipur	1.96	88.16	9.88	3.02	90.51	6.47
20	Meghalaya	5.04	86.93	8.03	5.32	89.74	4.95
21	Mizoram	4.80	88.79	6.41	6.79	88.73	4.48
22	Nagaland	3.02	84.86	12.11	4.16	86.99	8.85
23	Odisha	3.08	88.25	8.67	6.53	89.06	4.41
24	Pondicherry	0.73	91.37	7.89	1.43	93.65	4.92
25	Punjab	2.50	88.65	8.85	5.68	89.39	4.93
26	Rajasthan	3.38	89.10	7.52	7.99	88.14	3.87
27	Sikkim	2.53	90.05	7.43	4.95	90.54	4.52
28	Tamil Nadu	2.07	88.99	8.94	3.72	90.87	5.41
29	Tripura	1.59	88.42	9.99	3.83	90.76	5.41
30	Uttar Pradesh	2.83	85.98	11.19	5.92	87.58	6.50
31	West Bengal	5.39	87.74	6.88	5.79	90.11	4.10

Sl. No.	State / Union Territories	2001					
		Male			Female		
		0-14	15-59	60+	0-14	15-59	60+
	India	2.96	87.63	9.41	4.87	88.56	6.57
01	Andaman & Nicobar	1.38	92.82	5.80	3.46	92.11	4.43
02	Andhra Pradesh	3.40	88.33	8.28	5.69	88.78	5.53
03	Arunachal Pradesh	3.25	88.90	7.85	5.36	88.45	6.19
04	Assam	3.45	88.51	8.04	5.07	90.26	4.67
05	Bihar	3.64	86.00	10.35	5.46	88.15	6.39
06	Chandigarh	1.12	96.50	2.38	3.66	93.27	3.07
07	Dadra and Nagar Haveli	2.87	93.40	3.73	7.11	88.68	4.21
08	Delhi	0.79	95.85	3.36	1.65	94.36	3.99
09	Goa, Daman & Diu	0.58	94.00	5.42	1.31	92.43	6.26
10	Gujarat	2.12	91.08	6.80	3.83	91.41	4.76
11	Haryana	2.91	89.56	7.53	4.76	89.68	5.56
12	Himachal Pradesh	3.43	85.74	10.84	4.32	87.44	8.24
13	Jammu & Kashmir	4.17	86.17	9.65	8.54	85.86	5.61
14	Karnataka	3.48	88.00	8.52	4.98	89.08	5.94
15	Kerala	0.22	91.43	8.35	0.39	92.93	6.68
16	Lakshadweep	0.17	95.43	4.40	0.29	98.14	1.57
17	Madhya Pradesh	4.03	86.85	9.12	5.87	87.67	6.45
18	Maharashtra	2.06	86.84	11.10	2.79	87.72	9.49
19	Manipur	3.17	87.32	9.51	3.98	88.96	7.06
20	Meghalaya	5.82	86.38	7.81	6.68	87.45	5.87
21	Mizoram	6.64	86.09	7.27	8.36	85.83	5.82
22	Nagaland	5.30	85.85	8.84	6.34	86.58	7.07
23	Odisha	2.03	87.83	10.14	4.43	89.39	6.18
24	Pondicherry	0.41	91.96	7.63	0.70	92.74	6.57
25	Punjab	1.88	87.93	10.19	2.85	89.73	7.42
26	Rajasthan	4.60	87.76	7.64	8.09	86.81	5.09
27	Sikkim	5.33	87.31	7.36	8.51	86.33	5.16
28	Tamil Nadu	1.45	87.87	10.69	2.00	90.25	7.75
29	Tripura	1.54	89.18	9.28	3.12	90.39	6.49
30	Uttar Pradesh	3.18	85.12	11.70	5.65	86.30	8.05
31	West Bengal	2.64	90.50	6.86	5.25	90.30	4.45

Table 2.5.3. Age Composition of Total Workers (Main+Marginal) by Residence (Urban), India and States, 1981-2001

Sl. No.	*State / Union Territories*	*1981*					
		Male			*Female*		
		0-14	*15-59*	*60+*	*0-14*	*15-59*	*60+*
	India	1.98	92.74	5.28	4.83	89.68	5.49
01	Andaman & Nicobar	1.05	97.59	1.36	1.81	97.06	1.14
02	Andhra Pradesh	2.98	92.12	4.90	6.44	88.63	4.93
03	Arunachal Pradesh	1.19	97.61	1.19	4.63	94.29	1.08
04	Assam	NA	NA	NA	NA	NA	NA
05	Bihar	1.86	92.30	5.84	4.74	89.69	5.57
06	Chandigarh	1.14	96.36	2.50	2.02	96.83	1.15
07	Dadra and Nagar Haveli	5.53	90.07	4.40	9.98	87.39	2.64
08	Delhi	1.19	95.16	3.65	1.70	96.01	2.29
09	Goa, Daman & Diu	1.02	94.95	4.04	2.87	52.89	44.24
10	Gujarat	1.43	94.57	3.99	2.90	92.93	4.18
11	Haryana	1.32	92.92	5.76	2.22	94.66	3.12
12	Himachal Pradesh	0.82	93.79	5.39	2.86	94.22	2.92
13	Jammu & Kashmir	3.76	91.32	4.93	9.34	88.38	2.29
14	Karnataka	17.43	55.56	27.01	6.59	89.14	4.27
15	Kerala	0.68	93.84	5.48	2.19	93.44	4.37
16	Lakshadweep	0.37	95.62	4.00	1.15	98.04	0.82
17	Madhya Pradesh	1.71	93.01	5.29	4.62	89.77	5.60
18	Maharashtra	1.26	94.65	4.08	3.13	88.24	8.63
19	Manipur	1.05	90.81	8.14	2.61	90.78	6.61
20	Meghalaya	1.35	93.33	5.32	3.55	92.48	3.97
21	Mizoram	2.55	92.78	4.68	1.62	95.85	2.53
22	Nagaland	1.11	96.76	2.13	5.27	92.58	2.15
23	Odisha	2.48	93.14	4.38	6.81	88.39	4.80
24	Pondicherry	1.69	92.57	5.73	2.51	91.63	5.86
25	Punjab	1.73	91.95	6.33	2.36	94.32	3.32
26	Rajasthan	1.90	93.05	5.05	5.24	90.31	4.45
27	Sikkim	1.92	95.27	2.81	6.30	92.05	1.65
28	Tamil Nadu	2.28	92.81	4.91	6.04	90.04	3.92
29	Tripura	0.90	93.35	5.75	6.45	90.66	2.90
30	Uttar Pradesh	2.23	91.02	6.76	4.03	90.01	5.96
31	West Bengal	1.19	94.27	4.54	7.42	88.23	4.35

Sl. No.	State / Union Territories	1991					
		Male			Female		
		0-14	15-59	60+	0-14	15-59	60+
	India	1.44	93.68	4.88	3.58	92.31	4.12
01	Andaman & Nicobar	0.69	97.39	1.92	0.90	98.18	0.93
02	Andhra Pradesh	2.01	93.56	4.43	4.53	90.89	4.58
03	Arunachal Pradesh	1.00	97.35	1.65	4.86	94.23	0.90
04	Assam	1.23	93.96	4.81	9.07	88.90	2.03
05	Bihar	1.46	92.42	6.12	3.60	91.92	4.48
06	Chandigarh	0.76	96.63	2.62	1.08	97.81	1.11
07	Dadra and Nagar Haveli	1.38	96.35	2.26	4.46	94.33	1.20
08	Delhi	0.91	95.63	3.46	1.08	96.62	2.30
09	Goa, Daman & Diu	0.99	95.02	3.99	2.16	94.05	3.79
10	Gujarat	1.13	95.28	3.59	2.53	94.06	3.41
11	Haryana	0.91	93.56	5.53	1.90	94.53	3.57
12	Himachal Pradesh	0.62	94.19	4.91	1.68	95.03	3.11
13	Jammu & Kashmir	NA	NA	NA	NA	NA	NA
14	Karnataka	2.12	93.40	4.48	4.43	91.91	3.66
15	Kerala	0.23	93.73	6.04	0.67	94.01	5.32
16	Lakshadweep	0.25	94.98	4.77	0.35	97.88	1.76
17	Madhya Pradesh	1.17	93.58	5.25	3.11	91.60	5.29
18	Maharashtra	0.90	95.16	3.94	1.93	94.20	3.87
19	Manipur	0.66	89.60	9.73	1.50	91.28	7.21
20	Meghalaya	2.39	93.14	4.47	5.04	90.12	4.84
21	Mizoram	3.27	91.43	5.30	4.72	91.05	4.23
22	Nagaland	0.77	96.35	2.88	2.19	95.43	2.38
23	Odisha	1.19	94.06	4.74	3.82	92.00	4.18
24	Pondicherry	0.95	94.37	4.68	1.52	93.97	4.51
25	Punjab	1.18	92.93	5.90	1.82	95.45	2.72
26	Rajasthan	1.20	94.07	4.73	3.97	92.13	3.90
27	Sikkim	2.04	94.42	3.55	5.73	92.75	1.52
28	Tamil Nadu	1.23	93.74	5.03	3.20	93.04	3.76
29	Tripura	0.48	93.91	5.61	3.02	94.46	2.51
30	Uttar Pradesh	2.02	91.45	6.53	4.53	90.17	5.30
31	West Bengal	1.00	94.26	4.74	4.68	91.81	3.52

Sl. No.	State / Union Territories	2001					
		Male			Female		
		0-14	15-59	60+	0-14	15-59	60+
	India	1.17	93.34	5.49	2.76	91.78	5.46
01	Andaman & Nicobar	0.48	97.46	2.06	0.99	97.52	1.49
02	Andhra Pradesh	1.59	93.20	5.21	3.70	91.03	5.27
03	Arunachal Pradesh	1.05	96.84	2.11	6.54	92.23	1.23
04	Assam	1.13	93.01	5.86	6.25	89.50	4.25
05	Bihar	1.88	90.19	7.93	4.87	88.37	6.76
06	Chandigarh	0.92	95.97	3.11	1.84	95.82	2.33
07	Dadra and Nagar Haveli	0.51	97.62	1.87	1.70	95.63	2.67
08	Delhi	0.84	95.69	3.48	1.52	95.21	3.27
09	Goa, Daman & Diu	0.63	94.96	4.41	1.57	94.11	4.32
10	Gujarat	0.86	95.11	4.03	2.32	93.07	4.61
11	Haryana	0.98	94.04	4.98	2.07	93.72	4.21
12	Himachal Pradesh	0.56	95.02	4.41	1.42	95.09	3.50
13	Jammu & Kashmir	1.13	92.56	6.32	3.72	92.50	3.78
14	Karnataka	1.67	93.46	4.87	2.88	92.75	4.37
15	Kerala	0.19	93.78	6.03	0.37	93.79	5.84
16	Lakshadweep	0.18	94.82	5.00	0.09	97.52	2.40
17	Madhya Pradesh	1.08	93.21	5.71	2.43	90.83	6.75
18	Maharashtra	0.72	95.23	4.05	1.38	93.53	5.09
19	Manipur	1.27	88.69	10.04	1.81	89.63	8.56
20	Meghalaya	1.52	93.37	5.11	3.38	91.77	4.85
21	Mizoram	2.94	91.17	5.89	4.16	90.20	5.64
22	Nagaland	2.05	93.64	4.32	6.06	91.20	2.74
23	Odisha	0.93	93.39	5.67	3.03	91.16	5.80
24	Pondicherry	0.49	94.95	4.56	0.98	93.54	5.49
25	Punjab	1.28	92.13	6.59	2.68	92.10	5.22
26	Rajasthan	1.19	93.94	4.87	3.45	91.89	4.66
27	Sikkim	2.19	93.77	4.04	7.54	90.21	2.25
28	Tamil Nadu	0.99	91.88	7.13	1.98	91.49	6.53
29	Tripura	0.54	93.60	5.86	3.55	92.16	4.29
30	Uttar Pradesh	1.92	91.09	6.99	5.68	87.43	6.89
31	West Bengal	1.17	92.56	6.27	4.25	90.26	5.49

T able 2.5.4. Age Composition of Main Workers, India and States, 1981-2001

Sl. No.	State / Union Territories	1981					
		Male			Female		
		0-14	15-59	60+	0-14	15-59	60+
	India	4.19	87.88	7.93	8.36	86.86	4.78
01	Andaman & Nicobar	1.14	95.66	3.20	2.96	94.73	2.31
02	Andhra Pradesh	6.58	85.76	7.66	10.30	84.71	4.98
03	Arunachal Pradesh	3.39	90.55	6.06	7.07	88.02	4.92
04	Assam	NA	NA	NA	NA	NA	NA
05	Bihar	3.82	86.53	9.65	7.11	87.41	5.48
06	Chandigarh	1.13	96.18	2.69	2.11	96.76	1.13
07	Dadra and Nagar Haveli	4.81	90.37	4.82	9.12	87.74	3.14
08	Delhi	1.18	94.99	3.82	1.92	95.79	2.29
09	Goa, Daman & Diu	1.30	93.47	5.22	4.49	91.01	4.50
10	Gujarat	3.51	90.59	5.90	8.17	87.91	3.92
11	Haryana	3.41	88.53	8.06	9.68	87.69	2.63
12	Himachal Pradesh	2.33	86.40	11.28	8.96	86.86	4.18
13	Jammu & Kashmir	5.20	86.97	7.83	13.88	82.94	3.18
14	Karnataka	6.00	86.93	7.07	10.30	85.57	4.13
15	Kerala	0.68	91.76	7.56	2.01	93.72	4.28
16	Lakshadweep	0.23	96.30	3.46	1.35	97.65	0.99
17	Madhya Pradesh	5.70	86.44	7.86	9.77	84.56	5.67
18	Maharashtra	4.05	89.22	6.73	7.91	87.75	4.34
19	Manipur	2.25	88.63	9.12	4.28	89.61	6.11
20	Meghalaya	6.32	86.76	6.92	7.49	88.04	4.47
21	Mizoram	1.56	94.09	4.35	1.16	98.12	0.72
22	Nagaland	3.01	86.47	10.52	6.21	82.17	11.62
23	Odisha	5.36	87.32	7.32	9.13	86.38	4.49
24	Pondicherry	1.56	91.45	6.99	3.44	90.88	5.68
25	Punjab	3.61	87.49	8.90	4.50	91.48	4.03
26	Rajasthan	4.48	88.93	6.59	12.48	84.28	3.24
27	Sikkim	3.46	90.84	5.71	9.11	87.10	3.79
28	Tamil Nadu	3.61	89.27	7.12	7.06	88.30	4.64
29	Tripura	2.72	87.84	9.44	6.37	88.99	4.64
30	Uttar Pradesh	3.61	85.85	10.54	6.99	86.12	6.89
31	West Bengal	3.08	90.82	6.10	6.30	90.23	3.47

Sl. No.	State / Union Territories	1991					
		Male			Female		
		0-14	15-59	60+	0-14	15-59	60+
	India	2.56	89.54	7.90	5.33	89.89	4.78
01	Andaman & Nicobar	0.73	95.15	4.12	1.67	96.24	2.09
02	Andhra Pradesh	4.18	88.34	7.48	7.72	87.44	4.84
03	Arunachal Pradesh	2.05	91.78	6.18	4.63	90.10	5.28
04	Assam	3.39	89.30	7.31	5.09	91.95	2.95
05	Bihar	2.74	88.03	9.24	5.10	89.93	4.97
06	Chandigarh	0.78	96.58	2.64	1.14	97.71	1.15
07	Dadra and Nagar Haveli	3.16	92.59	4.24	6.74	90.32	2.94
08	Delhi	0.88	95.66	3.46	1.07	96.62	2.31
09	Goa, Daman & Diu	0.82	94.29	4.90	2.07	93.98	3.95
10	Gujarat	2.16	92.34	5.50	4.67	91.90	3.42
11	Haryana	1.63	90.15	8.22	4.28	91.12	4.61
12	Himachal Pradesh	1.07	88.05	10.88	3.44	91.10	5.46
13	Jammu & Kashmir	NA	NA	NA	NA	NA	NA
14	Karnataka	3.76	89.15	7.09	7.13	88.65	4.21
15	Kerala	0.25	91.96	7.79	0.65	94.24	5.11
16	Lakshadweep	0.15	95.63	4.23	0.07	98.22	1.71
17	Madhya Pradesh	3.28	88.54	8.18	5.82	88.70	5.47
18	Maharashtra	1.91	91.19	6.91	4.04	91.22	4.74
19	Manipur	1.43	88.75	9.82	2.57	90.92	6.51
20	Meghalaya	4.01	88.62	7.37	4.82	90.38	4.80
21	Mizoram	1.74	92.50	5.76	2.95	93.19	3.86
22	Nagaland	2.54	87.08	10.38	4.04	87.36	8.60
23	Odisha	2.58	89.33	8.09	5.67	90.04	4.29
24	Pondicherry	0.85	93.27	5.88	1.44	93.86	4.70
25	Punjab	2.10	89.91	7.99	3.87	92.49	3.63
26	Rajasthan	2.47	90.67	6.86	7.84	88.60	3.56
27	Sikkim	2.36	90.64	7.00	4.93	90.78	4.29
28	Tamil Nadu	1.71	90.58	7.71	3.65	91.24	5.11
29	Tripura	1.31	89.40	9.29	3.52	91.58	4.91
30	Uttar Pradesh	2.52	87.18	10.31	4.74	88.77	6.49
31	West Bengal	2.47	91.33	6.21	5.83	90.87	3.31

Sl. No.	State / Union Territories	2001					
		Male			Female		
		0-14	15-59	60+	0-14	15-59	60+
	India	1.50	90.16	8.34	3.02	90.57	6.42
01	Andaman & Nicobar	0.45	95.09	4.46	1.00	96.02	2.98
02	Andhra Pradesh	2.44	90.15	7.41	4.89	89.77	5.33
03	Arunachal Pradesh	1.35	92.14	6.51	3.22	91.22	5.57
04	Assam	1.63	90.26	8.11	3.18	91.72	5.10
05	Bihar	2.16	88.11	9.73	3.79	89.70	6.51
06	Chandigarh	0.80	96.25	2.95	1.61	96.12	2.27
07	Dadra and Nagar Haveli	1.27	95.65	3.08	4.30	91.83	3.87
08	Delhi	0.72	95.82	3.46	1.18	95.60	3.21
09	Goa, Daman & Diu	0.44	95.00	4.55	1.20	94.29	4.51
10	Gujarat	1.03	93.21	5.76	2.18	93.13	4.68
11	Haryana	1.00	92.32	6.68	1.80	93.24	4.96
12	Himachal Pradesh	0.55	89.64	9.81	1.02	91.06	7.92
13	Jammu & Kashmir	1.53	89.56	8.92	5.36	89.20	5.43
14	Karnataka	2.13	90.52	7.35	3.51	91.04	5.45
15	Kerala	0.17	92.41	7.42	0.33	93.95	5.72
16	Lakshadweep	0.10	96.69	3.21	0.14	98.80	1.06
17	Madhya Pradesh	1.63	90.01	8.35	2.90	90.63	6.47
18	Maharashtra	0.93	91.24	7.83	1.61	90.31	8.09
19	Manipur	1.31	88.95	9.74	2.09	89.92	7.98
20	Meghalaya	3.03	89.32	7.65	3.98	89.99	6.04
21	Mizoram	1.20	92.35	6.45	1.81	93.01	5.19
22	Nagaland	2.61	88.84	8.55	3.76	88.80	7.44
23	Odisha	0.87	89.62	9.51	2.55	90.95	6.50
24	Pondicherry	0.41	94.17	5.42	0.75	93.60	5.65
25	Punjab	1.26	89.80	8.95	2.13	90.84	7.03
26	Rajasthan	1.53	91.53	6.94	4.25	90.88	4.87
27	Sikkim	2.27	90.80	6.93	4.71	90.53	4.76
28	Tamil Nadu	1.06	89.94	9.00	1.79	90.96	7.25
29	Tripura	0.72	90.60	8.68	2.25	91.45	6.31
30	Uttar Pradesh	1.73	87.03	11.24	3.63	87.34	9.03
31	West Bengal	1.29	91.95	6.75	3.78	91.35	4.87

Table 2.5.5. Age Composition of Main Workers by Residence(Rural), India and States, 1981-2001

Sl. No.	State / Union Territories	1981					
		Male			Female		
		0-14	15-59	60+	0-14	15-59	60+
	India	4.90	86.30	8.80	8.85	86.32	4.83
01	Andaman & Nicobar	1.33	94.38	4.29	3.68	93.42	2.90
02	Andhra Pradesh	7.51	84.11	8.37	10.68	84.34	4.98
03	Arunachal Pradesh	3.58	89.95	6.47	7.10	87.92	4.98
04	Assam	NA	NA	NA	NA	NA	NA
05	Bihar	4.09	85.75	10.15	7.25	87.28	5.47
06	Chandigarh	1.30	93.46	5.25	6.65	92.24	1.11
07	Dadra and Nagar Haveli	4.92	90.24	4.85	9.04	87.79	3.17
08	Delhi	1.25	92.33	6.42	5.31	92.00	2.69
09	Goa, Daman & Diu	1.44	92.63	5.93	4.19	91.20	4.61
10	Gujarat	4.43	88.85	6.72	8.61	87.78	3.61
11	Haryana	4.03	87.23	8.73	11.42	86.08	2.50
12	Himachal Pradesh	2.49	85.65	11.86	9.20	86.57	4.24
13	Jammu & Kashmir	5.64	85.79	8.57	20.71	76.04	3.25
14	Karnataka	7.05	85.08	7.87	11.01	84.87	4.11
15	Kerala	0.70	91.22	8.08	1.96	93.71	4.33
16	Lakshadweep	0.24	96.50	3.26	1.61	97.37	1.02
17	Madhya Pradesh	6.62	84.95	8.43	10.19	84.15	5.66
18	Maharashtra	5.59	86.23	8.18	8.61	87.04	4.36
19	Manipur	2.69	87.91	9.40	4.75	89.29	5.96
20	Meghalaya	7.35	85.24	7.41	7.85	87.63	4.52
21	Mizoram	1.92	93.42	4.66	3.68	94.32	2.00
22	Nagaland	3.41	84.36	12.23	5.41	84.25	10.34
23	Odisha	5.75	86.55	7.71	9.36	86.18	4.46
24	Pondicherry	1.46	90.24	8.30	3.36	92.12	4.52
25	Punjab	4.33	85.81	9.86	6.73	88.47	4.80
26	Rajasthan	5.13	87.89	6.98	13.31	83.60	3.09
27	Sikkim	3.81	89.83	6.36	9.30	86.76	3.95
28	Tamil Nadu	4.20	87.71	8.08	7.24	87.97	4.79
29	Tripura	2.92	87.23	9.85	6.34	88.81	4.85
30	Uttar Pradesh	3.91	84.76	11.33	7.35	85.69	6.97
31	West Bengal	3.83	89.46	6.71	6.30	90.32	3.38

Sl. No.	State / Union Territories	1991					
		Male			Female		
		0-14	15-59	60+	0-14	15-59	60+
	India	2.99	88.09	8.92	5.66	89.44	4.90
01	Andaman & Nicobar	0.76	94.26	4.99	1.98	95.42	2.60
02	Andhra Pradesh	4.87	86.68	8.45	8.07	87.07	4.86
03	Arunachal Pradesh	2.22	90.87	6.91	4.61	89.93	5.45
04	Assam	3.69	88.65	7.65	4.82	92.17	3.02
05	Bihar	2.91	87.43	9.66	5.20	89.80	5.01
06	Chandigarh	0.93	96.18	2.89	2.65	95.02	2.33
07	Dadra and Nagar Haveli	3.35	92.20	4.45	6.80	90.16	4.14
08	Delhi	0.70	95.73	3.57	1.85	95.34	2.80
09	Goa, Daman & Diu	0.71	93.65	5.64	2.03	93.79	4.18
10	Gujarat	2.70	90.83	6.46	5.12	91.45	4.18
11	Haryana	1.87	89.02	9.11	4.85	90.26	3.43
12	Himachal Pradesh	1.13	87.33	11.54	3.54	90.86	5.60
13	Jammu & Kashmir	NA	NA	NA	NA	NA	NA
14	Karnataka	4.45	87.38	8.17	7.65	88.02	4.33
15	Kerala	0.27	91.26	8.47	0.65	94.14	5.21
16	Lakshadweep	0.07	95.84	4.09	0.17	98.82	1.02
17	Madhya Pradesh	3.88	87.15	8.97	6.13	88.39	5.49
18	Maharashtra	2.58	88.60	8.81	4.43	90.67	4.91
19	Manipur	1.73	88.39	9.87	2.89	90.73	6.38
20	Meghalaya	4.71	87.25	8.03	5.09	89.99	4.91
21	Mizoram	2.43	91.37	6.20	3.92	92.19	3.88
22	Nagaland	2.96	84.90	12.14	4.14	86.93	8.93
23	Odisha	2.79	88.62	8.59	5.84	89.86	4.30
24	Pondicherry	0.71	91.42	7.86	1.41	93.68	4.92
25	Punjab	2.47	88.69	8.84	5.63	89.90	4.47
26	Rajasthan	2.85	89.68	7.47	8.27	88.20	3.54
27	Sikkim	2.42	90.19	7.39	4.89	90.67	4.44
28	Tamil Nadu	1.94	89.06	9.00	3.71	90.91	5.38
29	Tripura	1.46	88.58	9.96	3.59	91.12	5.30
30	Uttar Pradesh	2.65	86.17	11.18	4.83	88.55	6.63
31	West Bengal	3.05	90.18	6.77	6.13	90.60	3.27

Sl. No.	*State / Union Territories*	*2001*					
		Male			*Female*		
		0-14	*15-59*	*60+*	*0-14*	*15-59*	*60+*
	India	1.73	88.72	9.55	3.16	90.18	6.66
01	Andaman & Nicobar	0.45	93.81	5.74	1.19	94.91	3.90
02	Andhra Pradesh	2.81	88.99	8.19	5.09	89.55	5.36
03	Arunachal Pradesh	1.53	90.67	7.81	2.98	90.96	6.06
04	Assam	1.76	89.71	8.53	2.84	91.94	5.22
05	Bihar	2.31	87.50	10.19	3.82	89.63	6.56
06	Chandigarh	0.91	96.82	2.27	2.82	94.37	2.82
07	Dadra and Nagar Haveli	1.57	94.86	3.57	4.54	91.47	3.99
08	Delhi	0.60	96.12	3.28	1.00	95.05	3.95
09	Goa, Daman & Diu	0.42	94.76	4.82	1.09	93.62	5.28
10	Gujarat	1.22	91.88	6.90	2.26	93.04	4.71
11	Haryana	1.11	91.43	7.46	1.86	92.95	5.19
12	Himachal Pradesh	0.56	88.81	10.63	1.01	90.77	8.21
13	Jammu & Kashmir	1.79	88.13	10.08	5.92	88.11	5.97
14	Karnataka	2.48	88.89	8.63	3.79	90.39	5.82
15	Kerala	0.17	91.78	8.05	0.33	93.73	5.94
16	Lakshadweep	0.08	96.97	2.96	0.29	98.97	0.73
17	Madhya Pradesh	1.91	88.79	9.30	3.06	90.46	6.49
18	Maharashtra	1.18	87.90	10.93	1.71	89.39	8.90
19	Manipur	1.52	88.76	9.72	2.44	89.94	7.62
20	Meghalaya	3.54	88.21	8.25	4.28	89.51	6.21
21	Mizoram	1.73	91.24	7.03	2.47	92.31	5.23
22	Nagaland	2.87	87.66	9.47	3.71	88.49	7.80
23	Odisha	0.90	88.80	10.30	2.59	90.78	6.63
24	Pondicherry	0.38	92.25	7.37	0.58	93.30	6.11
25	Punjab	1.36	88.40	10.25	2.10	90.27	7.63
26	Rajasthan	1.74	90.67	7.60	4.43	90.66	4.91
27	Sikkim	2.31	90.38	7.31	4.49	90.51	5.00
28	Tamil Nadu	1.20	88.20	10.60	1.77	90.57	7.66
29	Tripura	0.78	89.89	9.34	2.05	91.18	6.77
30	Uttar Pradesh	1.81	85.75	12.45	3.53	87.09	9.38
31	West Bengal	1.44	91.61	6.95	3.79	91.61	4.61

Table 2.5.6. Age Composition of Main Workers by Residence(Urban), India and States, 1981-2001

Sl. No.	State/Union Territories	1981					
		Male			Female		
		0-14	15-59	60+	0-14	15-59	60+
	India	1.82	93.20	4.98	4.70	90.89	4.41
01	Andaman & Nicobar	1.00	97.63	1.37	1.61	97.20	1.19
02	Andhra Pradesh	2.92	92.20	4.88	6.48	88.51	5.02
03	Arunachal Pradesh	1.17	97.64	1.19	4.75	94.19	1.06
04	Assam	NA	NA	NA	NA	NA	NA
05	Bihar	1.79	92.36	5.85	4.49	89.79	5.72
06	Chandigarh	1.12	96.39	2.49	2.01	96.86	1.13
07	Dadra and Nagar Haveli	3.29	92.25	4.46	10.71	86.73	2.55
08	Delhi	1.18	95.18	3.64	1.67	96.07	2.26
09	Goa, Daman & Diu	0.95	95.13	3.92	5.36	90.47	4.17
10	Gujarat	1.39	94.62	3.99	2.75	93.03	4.22
11	Haryana	1.27	92.97	5.76	1.94	94.86	3.19
12	Himachal Pradesh	0.72	93.94	5.34	2.31	95.03	2.66
13	Jammu & Kashmir	3.50	91.60	4.89	9.19	89.05	1.76
14	Karnataka	3.03	92.16	4.81	6.52	89.27	4.21
15	Kerala	0.62	94.09	5.29	2.29	93.75	3.97
16	Lakshadweep	0.23	96.10	3.66	0.94	98.13	0.94
17	Madhya Pradesh	1.62	93.11	5.27	4.42	89.82	5.76
18	Maharashtra	1.19	94.75	4.06	2.93	88.02	9.05
19	Manipur	0.83	90.95	8.23	2.04	91.15	6.81
20	Meghalaya	1.09	94.50	4.41	3.49	92.57	3.94
21	Mizoram	0.37	96.33	3.31	0.87	96.78	2.35
22	Nagaland	1.01	96.88	2.11	4.60	93.32	2.08
23	Odisha	2.35	93.31	4.34	6.43	88.66	4.91
24	Pondicherry	1.65	92.70	5.65	2.43	91.93	5.64
25	Punjab	1.69	91.97	6.33	1.76	95.17	3.07
26	Rajasthan	1.85	93.12	5.03	4.79	90.60	4.61
27	Sikkim	1.90	95.29	2.80	6.30	92.16	1.54
28	Tamil Nadu	2.25	92.86	4.89	6.08	90.05	3.86
29	Tripura	0.83	93.43	5.73	6.62	90.63	2.75
30	Uttar Pradesh	2.19	91.05	6.76	3.73	91.14	5.13
31	West Bengal	1.13	94.35	4.52	6.33	89.77	3.89

Sl. No.	State / Union Territories	1991					
		Male			Female		
		0-14	15-59	60+	0-14	15-59	60+
	India	1.27	93.87	4.86	3.05	92.96	3.99
01	Andaman & Nicobar	0.67	97.44	1.90	0.93	98.17	0.90
02	Andhra Pradesh	1.98	93.61	4.41	4.53	90.85	4.62
03	Arunachal Pradesh	1.00	97.35	1.65	4.96	94.14	0.90
04	Assam	1.21	93.99	4.80	9.75	88.41	1.84
05	Bihar	1.43	92.46	6.11	3.36	92.25	4.39
06	Chandigarh	0.75	96.64	2.61	1.07	97.83	1.10
07	Dadra and Nagar Haveli	1.34	96.43	2.23	5.16	94.24	0.60
08	Delhi	0.90	95.65	3.45	1.02	96.71	2.28
09	Goa, Daman & Diu	0.50	49.75	49.75	2.14	94.33	3.52
10	Gujarat	1.09	95.33	3.58	2.11	94.50	3.39
11	Haryana	0.89	93.60	5.51	1.86	94.75	3.39
12	Himachal Pradesh	0.51	94.60	4.89	1.45	96.16	2.39
13	Jammu & Kashmir	NA	NA	NA	NA	NA	NA
14	Karnataka	2.08	93.47	4.45	4.40	91.98	3.62
15	Kerala	0.22	93.91	5.87	0.66	94.54	4.80
16	Lakshadweep	0.20	95.48	4.32	0.00	97.81	2.19
17	Madhya Pradesh	1.09	93.67	5.23	2.67	91.98	5.35
18	Maharashtra	0.85	95.24	3.92	1.78	94.48	3.75
19	Manipur	0.50	89.85	9.65	1.09	91.77	7.14
20	Meghalaya	0.68	95.05	4.27	2.22	94.02	3.76
21	Mizoram	0.86	93.94	5.20	1.38	94.81	3.81
22	Nagaland	0.76	96.36	2.88	2.17	95.44	2.39
23	Odisha	1.14	94.16	4.70	3.58	92.33	4.10
24	Pondicherry	0.94	94.41	4.65	1.48	94.07	4.45
25	Punjab	1.16	92.95	5.89	1.75	95.64	2.62
26	Rajasthan	1.15	94.14	4.71	3.64	92.62	3.74
27	Sikkim	1.89	94.52	3.59	5.66	92.92	1.42
28	Tamil Nadu	1.21	93.77	5.02	3.31	93.03	3.66
29	Tripura	0.48	93.94	5.58	3.07	94.60	2.34
30	Uttar Pradesh	1.95	91.54	6.52	3.91	90.82	5.27
31	West Bengal	0.95	94.32	4.73	4.57	91.97	3.47

Sl. No.	State / Union Territories	2001					
		Male			Female		
		0-14	15-59	60+	0-14	15-59	60+
	India	0.95	93.65	5.40	2.25	92.53	5.23
01	Andaman & Nicobar	0.45	97.47	2.08	0.69	97.93	1.39
02	Andhra Pradesh	1.37	93.49	5.13	3.31	91.55	5.14
03	Arunachal Pradesh	0.73	97.23	2.04	5.34	93.53	1.13
04	Assam	0.95	93.19	5.85	5.88	89.99	4.14
05	Bihar	1.15	92.20	6.65	3.38	90.73	5.89
06	Chandigarh	0.79	96.17	3.05	1.53	96.23	2.23
07	Dadra and Nagar Haveli	0.44	97.82	1.74	1.66	95.80	2.54
08	Delhi	0.73	95.80	3.47	1.20	95.64	3.16
09	Goa, Daman & Diu	0.46	95.27	4.27	1.32	95.00	3.68
10	Gujarat	0.74	95.28	3.98	1.85	93.58	4.58
11	Haryana	0.76	94.33	4.91	1.47	94.76	3.77
12	Himachal Pradesh	0.46	95.31	4.23	1.12	96.03	2.85
13	Jammu & Kashmir	0.91	92.90	6.19	3.23	93.39	3.38
14	Karnataka	1.44	93.71	4.85	2.50	93.34	4.16
15	Kerala	0.16	94.06	5.78	0.33	94.59	5.07
16	Lakshadweep	0.12	96.41	3.47	0.00	98.65	1.35
17	Madhya Pradesh	0.77	93.77	5.47	1.71	91.91	6.37
18	Maharashtra	0.62	95.40	3.98	1.18	94.11	4.72
19	Manipur	0.68	89.50	9.82	0.99	89.88	9.13
20	Meghalaya	0.88	94.05	5.07	2.12	92.89	4.99
21	Mizoram	0.59	93.62	5.79	0.85	94.02	5.13
22	Nagaland	1.41	94.25	4.34	4.34	92.94	2.72
23	Odisha	0.71	93.77	5.53	2.28	92.20	5.52
24	Pondicherry	0.42	95.13	4.44	0.88	93.82	5.30
25	Punjab	1.08	92.37	6.56	2.23	92.78	4.99
26	Rajasthan	0.89	94.28	4.83	2.40	93.08	4.52
27	Sikkim	1.98	94.00	4.03	7.22	90.76	2.03
28	Tamil Nadu	0.89	92.12	6.99	1.83	91.91	6.27
29	Tripura	0.47	93.79	5.74	3.22	92.78	4.00
30	Uttar Pradesh	1.45	91.60	6.95	4.28	88.85	6.87
31	West Bengal	0.95	92.74	6.31	3.76	90.67	5.58

Table 2.5.7. Age Composition of Marginal Workers, India and States, 1981-2001

Sl. No.	State / Union Territories	1981					
		Male			Female		
		0-14	15-59	60+	0-14	15-59	60+
00	India	19.11	73.41	7.48	9.54	86.03	4.42
01	Andaman & Nicobar	11.06	85.30	3.64	4.54	93.64	1.83
02	Andhra Pradesh	28.06	60.97	10.97	10.33	83.70	5.97
03	Arunachal Pradesh	29.25	61.46	9.29	11.78	82.50	5.72
04	Assam	NA	NA	NA	NA	NA	NA
05	Bihar	20.58	73.87	5.55	8.97	86.72	4.32
06	Chandigarh	4.96	90.95	4.09	2.83	94.90	2.27
07	Dadra and Nagar Haveli	39.59	55.99	4.42	9.69	86.81	3.50
08	Delhi	6.54	88.12	5.33	4.63	92.33	3.05
09	Goa, Daman & Diu	6.67	83.92	9.41	4.62	89.31	6.07
10	Gujarat	25.75	68.67	5.58	7.67	88.96	3.37
11	Haryana	19.93	74.22	5.85	10.69	87.06	2.25
12	Himachal Pradesh	23.17	69.03	7.81	8.67	86.08	5.25
13	Jammu & Kashmir	40.24	53.32	6.44	14.41	81.68	3.90
14	Karnataka	26.12	64.78	9.10	11.27	84.38	4.35
15	Kerala	2.66	86.73	10.62	2.39	91.40	6.21
16	Lakshadweep	1.30	90.22	8.48	1.41	97.61	0.98
17	Madhya Pradesh	34.15	57.65	8.21	11.37	83.58	5.04
18	Maharashtra	19.38	73.23	7.39	10.74	84.20	5.06
19	Manipur	11.14	83.62	5.25	5.03	89.54	5.43
20	Meghalaya	40.93	54.69	4.38	12.30	83.49	4.21
21	Mizoram	15.70	79.48	4.83	7.16	88.69	4.15
22	Nagaland	29.25	68.21	2.55	28.57	67.93	3.50
23	Odisha	25.08	67.13	7.80	11.57	84.53	3.91
24	Pondicherry	5.28	84.32	10.40	3.55	91.37	5.08
25	Punjab	16.02	75.26	8.71	9.42	86.07	4.51
26	Rajasthan	30.06	62.24	7.71	9.22	87.69	3.09
27	Sikkim	25.87	68.88	5.24	8.33	85.07	6.60
28	Tamil Nadu	15.25	76.97	7.78	7.70	87.91	4.39
29	Tripura	11.33	81.82	6.80	6.88	88.88	4.24
30	Uttar Pradesh	21.49	73.08	5.43	8.15	86.26	5.59
31	West Bengal	8.08	86.51	5.41	7.69	88.60	3.71

Sl. No.	State / Union Territories	1991					
		Male			Female		
		0-14	15-59	60+	0-14	15-59	60+
	India	19.54	69.48	10.98	6.59	88.15	5.26
01	Andaman & Nicobar	15.77	76.71	7.52	3.84	93.08	3.08
02	Andhra Pradesh	25.37	60.12	14.51	6.78	87.90	5.31
03	Arunachal Pradesh	17.54	75.36	7.10	7.41	87.03	5.56
04	Assam	13.38	78.33	8.29	5.25	91.03	3.72
05	Bihar	22.21	67.92	9.87	5.71	89.63	4.66
06	Chandigarh	5.17	87.36	7.47	4.11	92.72	3.16
07	Dadra and Nagar Haveli	48.73	40.11	11.16	10.16	85.42	4.42
08	Delhi	7.47	85.82	6.71	4.19	91.72	4.09
09	Goa, Daman & Diu	3.73	87.26	9.01	2.27	91.84	5.89
10	Gujarat	21.16	68.75	10.09	5.45	90.38	4.17
11	Haryana	18.60	69.25	12.15	4.56	90.15	5.30
12	Himachal Pradesh	21.98	65.73	12.29	4.25	88.64	7.12
13	Jammu & Kashmir	NA	NA	NA	NA	NA	NA
14	Karnataka	29.00	59.27	11.73	8.25	86.54	5.21
15	Kerala	0.79	87.72	11.49	0.69	91.43	7.88
16	Lakshadweep	1.43	83.41	15.16	1.14	95.88	2.97
17	Madhya Pradesh	34.38	55.33	10.28	8.51	86.12	5.37
18	Maharashtra	19.42	69.36	11.22	7.51	85.22	7.26
19	Manipur	10.46	78.54	11.00	3.49	89.33	7.18
20	Meghalaya	30.30	61.83	7.86	6.63	88.25	5.12
21	Mizoram	31.63	60.67	7.70	16.43	77.34	6.23
22	Nagaland	17.52	77.35	5.13	4.99	90.40	4.61
23	Odisha	17.96	69.55	12.49	7.41	88.04	4.55
24	Pondicherry	2.44	88.12	9.43	1.97	92.74	5.29
25	Punjab	16.94	69.93	13.12	5.68	88.95	5.37
26	Rajasthan	29.64	60.23	10.12	7.67	88.17	4.16
27	Sikkim	15.67	74.68	9.66	5.86	88.55	5.59
28	Tamil Nadu	10.06	76.66	13.28	3.62	90.87	5.51
29	Tripura	10.69	77.26	12.05	4.39	89.93	5.68
30	Uttar Pradesh	26.88	62.03	11.09	6.11	87.64	6.25
31	West Bengal	17.04	73.28	9.68	6.90	88.97	4.13

Sl. No.	State / Union Territories	2001					
		Male			Female		
		0-14	15-59	60+	0-14	15-59	60+
	India	9.22	82.70	8.08	6.78	86.82	6.40
01	Andaman & Nicobar	6.32	88.15	5.53	5.69	89.43	4.88
02	Andhra Pradesh	7.39	84.14	8.47	7.06	87.01	5.94
03	Arunachal Pradesh	17.33	75.01	7.65	13.43	80.25	6.31
04	Assam	11.63	82.81	5.56	6.92	88.86	4.23
05	Bihar	9.59	82.62	7.80	6.94	87.49	5.57
06	Chandigarh	6.21	88.24	5.56	6.52	89.59	3.89
07	Dadra and Nagar Haveli	17.36	76.80	5.84	11.18	84.32	4.50
08	Delhi	3.41	92.97	3.62	4.48	91.26	4.25
09	Goa, Daman & Diu	1.86	90.19	7.95	1.84	90.70	7.47
10	Gujarat	10.01	84.23	5.77	5.24	89.95	4.81
11	Haryana	10.95	81.51	7.53	7.04	87.11	5.85
12	Himachal Pradesh	12.85	75.73	11.43	7.22	84.51	8.26
13	Jammu & Kashmir	12.42	79.54	8.04	9.47	85.14	5.40
14	Karnataka	10.75	82.11	7.13	6.76	87.14	6.09
15	Kerala	0.43	90.24	9.33	0.52	91.17	8.31
16	Lakshadweep	0.45	89.67	9.88	0.28	95.87	3.86
17	Madhya Pradesh	13.48	78.98	7.53	8.10	85.37	6.53
18	Maharashtra	7.08	82.30	10.62	5.01	84.52	10.47
19	Manipur	8.93	81.91	9.17	5.20	88.12	6.68
20	Meghalaya	16.93	77.59	5.48	11.10	83.74	5.16
21	Mizoram	27.06	65.32	7.62	16.29	76.84	6.87
22	Nagaland	18.99	76.04	4.97	15.32	80.21	4.47
23	Odisha	6.34	84.25	9.40	5.33	88.69	5.97
24	Pondicherry	1.43	89.45	9.12	1.43	90.56	8.01
25	Punjab	6.70	84.13	9.17	4.09	88.90	7.01
26	Rajasthan	19.75	72.68	7.58	11.42	83.32	5.26
27	Sikkim	25.80	66.69	7.51	16.48	78.06	5.45
28	Tamil Nadu	2.98	86.28	10.74	2.65	89.35	7.99
29	Tripura	6.79	84.47	8.74	4.16	89.62	6.22
30	Uttar Pradesh	8.77	83.30	7.93	6.67	86.09	7.24
31	West Bengal	8.50	85.22	6.28	6.36	89.26	4.39

Table 2.5.8. Age Composition of Marginal Workers by Residence(Rural), India and States, 1981-2001

Sl. No.	*State / Union Territories*	*1981*					
		Male			*Female*		
		0-14	*15-59*	*60+*	*0-14*	*15-59*	*60+*
	India	20.86	71.54	7.60	9.68	85.90	4.41
01	Andaman & Nicobar	11.84	84.25	3.91	4.51	93.64	1.85
02	Andhra Pradesh	30.55	58.11	11.34	9.11	85.66	5.23
03	Arunachal Pradesh	29.65	60.94	9.41	11.82	82.44	5.74
04	Assam	NA	NA	NA	NA	NA	NA
05	Bihar	21.47	72.97	5.57	9.01	86.68	4.31
06	Chandigarh	21.74	71.74	6.52	3.57	94.64	1.79
07	Dadra and Nagar Haveli	40.98	54.30	4.71	9.75	86.71	3.54
08	Delhi	8.74	85.77	5.50	5.78	91.52	2.70
09	Goa, Daman & Diu	7.31	83.09	9.60	4.87	89.18	5.95
10	Gujarat	28.64	65.70	5.66	7.81	88.84	3.35
11	Haryana	20.53	73.71	5.76	10.80	86.96	2.24
12	Himachal Pradesh	23.51	68.67	7.83	8.69	86.05	5.26
13	Jammu & Kashmir	40.96	52.64	6.40	14.59	81.47	3.94
14	Karnataka	30.06	60.58	9.36	11.52	84.16	4.32
15	Kerala	2.84	86.07	11.09	2.46	91.33	6.20
16	Lakshadweep	1.06	90.20	8.74	1.32	97.55	1.13
17	Madhya Pradesh	32.99	59.49	7.52	11.55	83.39	5.06
18	Maharashtra	22.98	69.18	7.84	11.05	83.87	5.08
19	Manipur	12.62	82.14	5.24	5.12	89.68	5.20
20	Meghalaya	42.70	53.24	4.06	12.46	83.35	4.19
21	Mizoram	16.07	78.70	5.23	7.43	88.30	4.27
22	Nagaland	30.08	67.65	2.27	29.02	67.52	3.46
23	Odisha	26.03	66.14	7.83	11.64	84.46	3.90
24	Pondicherry	6.60	82.23	11.17	3.73	91.99	4.27
25	Punjab	16.34	74.57	9.08	9.51	86.01	4.48
26	Rajasthan	31.41	60.89	7.70	9.28	87.65	3.07
27	Sikkim	28.47	66.11	5.42	8.37	85.02	6.61
28	Tamil Nadu	17.30	74.74	7.96	7.87	87.74	4.38
29	Tripura	12.01	81.14	6.85	6.93	88.85	4.22
30	Uttar Pradesh	22.08	72.54	5.39	8.21	86.17	5.62
31	West Bengal	8.76	85.88	5.36	7.10	89.53	3.37

Sl. No.	State / Union Territories	1991					
		Male			Female		
		0-14	15-59	60+	0-14	15-59	60+
	India	21.63	66.88	11.49	6.68	88.04	5.28
01	Andaman & Nicobar	18.25	73.52	8.23	3.91	92.99	3.10
02	Andhra Pradesh	28.42	55.87	15.71	6.91	87.70	5.39
03	Arunachal Pradesh	18.23	74.36	7.41	7.52	86.86	5.63
04	Assam	13.67	77.98	8.35	5.27	91.01	3.72
05	Bihar	23.18	66.90	9.92	5.72	89.62	4.66
06	Chandigarh	16.22	78.38	5.41	9.52	84.52	5.95
07	Dadra and Nagar Haveli	49.95	38.75	11.30	10.37	85.16	4.47
08	Delhi	6.79	84.74	8.46	2.10	93.83	4.08
09	Goa, Daman & Diu	3.97	86.84	9.19	2.27	91.85	5.88
10	Gujarat	24.03	65.05	10.92	5.48	90.33	4.19
11	Haryana	19.10	69.15	11.75	4.61	90.10	5.29
12	Himachal Pradesh	22.19	65.40	12.41	4.27	88.59	7.14
13	Jammu & Kashmir	NA	NA	NA	NA	NA	NA
14	Karnataka	32.60	55.13	12.28	8.41	86.34	5.25
15	Kerala	0.86	87.12	12.02	0.69	91.59	7.72
16	Lakshadweep	1.37	84.13	14.51	0.59	92.35	7.06
17	Madhya Pradesh	37.06	52.38	10.56	8.60	86.01	5.38
18	Maharashtra	24.44	62.41	13.15	7.78	84.82	7.41
19	Manipur	11.81	77.90	10.30	3.83	89.10	7.07
20	Meghalaya	32.41	60.00	7.59	6.85	87.97	5.18
21	Mizoram	38.31	52.36	9.33	21.06	71.47	7.47
22	Nagaland	17.55	77.23	5.22	4.98	90.32	4.70
23	Odisha	18.84	68.42	12.74	7.45	88.01	4.54
24	Pondicherry	2.86	85.39	11.75	1.75	93.26	4.99
25	Punjab	16.72	70.60	12.69	5.74	88.89	5.37
26	Rajasthan	31.09	58.68	10.23	7.75	88.09	4.15
27	Sikkim	18.82	68.29	12.90	5.80	88.52	5.68
28	Tamil Nadu	10.91	75.09	14.00	3.76	90.64	5.60
29	Tripura	11.53	76.18	12.29	4.44	89.87	5.70
30	Uttar Pradesh	27.52	61.31	11.17	6.08	87.64	6.28
31	West Bengal	18.16	71.79	10.05	6.92	88.95	4.12

Sl. No.	State / Union Territories	2001					
		Male			Female		
		0-14	15-59	60+	0-14	15-59	60+
	India	10.10	81.51	8.38	6.92	86.68	6.40
01	Andaman & Nicobar	7.17	86.67	6.16	5.69	89.35	4.95
02	Andhra Pradesh	8.03	83.03	8.95	7.20	86.85	5.95
03	Arunachal Pradesh	18.62	73.19	8.18	13.49	79.85	6.65
04	Assam	11.99	82.47	5.54	6.89	88.89	4.21
05	Bihar	9.98	82.10	7.92	6.95	87.49	5.56
06	Chandigarh	6.48	88.30	5.22	7.69	88.02	4.29
07	Dadra and Nagar Haveli	18.88	75.43	5.69	11.90	83.47	4.62
08	Delhi	3.46	92.18	4.36	3.81	92.07	4.12
09	Goa, Daman & Diu	1.52	89.48	9.00	1.60	90.80	7.60
10	Gujarat	10.93	83.24	5.83	5.33	89.85	4.82
11	Haryana	12.29	79.86	7.85	7.26	86.87	5.88
12	Himachal Pradesh	13.12	75.35	11.53	7.26	84.47	8.27
13	Jammu & Kashmir	13.29	78.69	8.02	9.75	84.81	5.44
14	Karnataka	12.12	80.24	7.64	6.93	86.93	6.14
15	Kerala	0.44	89.88	9.68	0.52	91.23	8.25
16	Lakshadweep	0.45	90.91	8.64	0.30	96.45	3.25
17	Madhya Pradesh	14.93	77.30	7.77	8.30	85.19	6.51
18	Maharashtra	8.63	78.97	12.40	5.31	83.83	10.86
19	Manipur	9.96	81.39	8.65	5.76	87.83	6.40
20	Meghalaya	17.80	76.74	5.46	11.28	83.50	5.22
21	Mizoram	39.22	51.92	8.86	21.51	71.36	7.13
22	Nagaland	19.98	74.94	5.07	15.41	80.02	4.57
23	Odisha	6.49	84.00	9.51	5.34	88.70	5.96
24	Pondicherry	0.74	88.49	10.76	1.17	90.35	8.49
25	Punjab	6.97	83.41	9.61	4.04	88.87	7.09
26	Rajasthan	22.01	70.07	7.92	11.67	83.05	5.27
27	Sikkim	27.31	64.94	7.75	16.57	77.96	5.47
28	Tamil Nadu	3.12	85.61	11.27	2.61	89.41	7.98
29	Tripura	7.27	83.90	8.83	4.11	89.66	6.23
30	Uttar Pradesh	9.25	82.57	8.17	6.61	86.12	7.27
31	West Bengal	9.21	84.40	6.38	6.37	89.30	4.33

Table 2.5.9: Age Composition of Marginal Workers by Residence (Urban), India and States, 1981-2001

Sl. No.	State / Union Territories	1981					
		Male			Female		
		0-14	15-59	60+	0-14	15-59	60+
	India	7.06	86.32	6.62	6.24	89.04	4.72
01	Andaman & Nicobar	4.12	95.06	0.82	6.06	93.94	0.00
02	Andhra Pradesh	11.57	79.89	8.54	6.19	89.61	4.21
03	Arunachal Pradesh	5.71	91.43	2.86	1.49	97.01	1.49
04	Assam	NA	NA	NA	NA	NA	NA
05	Bihar	7.65	87.04	5.31	6.41	89.01	4.58
06	Chandigarh	5.21	90.80	3.99	2.68	94.97	2.35
07	Dadra and Nagar Haveli	34.72	61.81	3.47	8.45	88.73	2.82
08	Delhi	5.56	89.18	5.26	2.89	93.55	3.56
09	Goa, Daman & Diu	3.69	87.79	8.51	2.82	90.32	6.86
10	Gujarat	8.33	86.54	5.14	3.65	92.39	3.97
11	Haryana	10.24	82.50	7.26	4.58	92.94	2.48
12	Himachal Pradesh	7.30	85.91	6.79	6.00	89.57	4.43
13	Jammu & Kashmir	23.07	69.53	7.40	9.51	87.57	2.92
14	Karnataka	11.98	79.87	8.15	7.18	88.04	4.78
15	Kerala	1.60	90.50	7.89	1.75	92.00	6.25
16	Lakshadweep	1.94	90.29	7.77	1.63	97.83	0.54
17	Madhya Pradesh	10.57	83.05	6.38	5.91	89.49	4.60
18	Maharashtra	6.36	87.69	5.95	5.58	89.21	5.21
19	Manipur	8.71	86.03	5.26	4.79	89.34	5.87
20	Meghalaya	7.02	82.46	10.53	5.26	89.98	4.75
21	Mizoram	13.81	83.43	2.76	5.70	90.79	3.51
22	Nagaland	18.59	75.38	6.03	22.73	73.23	4.04
23	Odisha	11.17	81.53	7.30	8.39	87.26	4.35
24	Pondicherry	3.68	86.84	9.48	3.03	89.71	7.26
25	Punjab	12.11	83.69	4.20	6.93	87.82	5.25
26	Rajasthan	10.55	81.70	7.75	6.64	89.42	3.94
27	Sikkim	4.64	92.05	3.31	6.33	87.34	6.33
28	Tamil Nadu	6.39	86.65	6.96	5.56	89.90	4.54
29	Tripura	3.68	89.96	6.36	3.56	91.01	5.43
30	Uttar Pradesh	13.45	80.51	6.03	6.17	89.21	4.62
31	West Bengal	4.48	89.80	5.72	12.81	80.56	6.63

Sl. No.	State / Union Territories	1991					
		Male			Female		
		0-14	15-59	60+	0-14	15-59	60+
	India	7.51	84.45	8.04	4.47	90.55	4.98
01	Andaman & Nicobar	2.66	93.54	3.80	0.00	98.26	1.74
02	Andhra Pradesh	9.74	81.95	8.31	4.57	91.40	4.03
03	Arunachal Pradesh	5.08	93.22	1.69	0.00	99.07	0.93
04	Assam	4.70	88.61	6.68	3.40	92.97	3.62
05	Bihar	9.16	81.65	9.19	4.90	90.17	4.93
06	Chandigarh	3.86	88.42	7.72	2.16	95.69	2.16
07	Dadra and Nagar Haveli	6.45	87.10	6.45	2.72	94.56	2.72
08	Delhi	7.60	86.04	6.36	5.56	90.35	4.09
09	Goa, Daman & Diu	3.04	88.45	8.51	2.26	91.76	5.98
10	Gujarat	9.86	83.32	6.81	4.64	91.84	3.52
11	Haryana	12.05	70.58	17.37	2.35	92.10	5.55
12	Himachal Pradesh	14.06	77.84	8.10	2.52	91.66	5.82
13	Jammu & Kashmir	NA	NA	NA	NA	NA	NA
14	Karnataka	9.43	81.80	8.77	4.79	91.02	4.18
15	Kerala	0.53	89.98	9.49	0.70	90.51	8.79
16	Lakshadweep	1.59	81.75	16.67	1.50	98.13	0.37
17	Madhya Pradesh	11.46	80.60	7.94	5.87	89.17	4.96
18	Maharashtra	5.42	88.75	5.84	3.45	91.50	5.05
19	Manipur	6.78	80.30	12.92	2.72	89.85	7.43
20	Meghalaya	6.82	82.32	10.86	2.32	93.77	3.90
21	Mizoram	25.98	67.70	6.32	12.78	81.96	5.25
22	Nagaland	15.79	84.21	0.00	5.48	94.52	0.00
23	Odisha	6.30	84.55	9.15	5.44	89.83	4.74
24	Pondicherry	2.20	89.72	8.08	2.41	91.69	5.90
25	Punjab	18.87	64.34	16.79	3.72	90.85	5.42
26	Rajasthan	10.68	80.55	8.77	4.93	90.71	4.36
27	Sikkim	8.06	90.11	1.83	7.14	89.29	3.57
28	Tamil Nadu	6.43	83.35	10.22	2.24	93.11	4.65
29	Tripura	1.52	89.09	9.39	2.39	92.50	5.11
30	Uttar Pradesh	21.00	68.68	10.32	6.79	87.79	5.43
31	West Bengal	8.66	84.47	6.87	6.19	89.58	4.22

Sl. No.	State / Union Territories	2001					
		Male			Female		
		0-14	15-59	60+	0-14	15-59	60+
	India	4.10	89.59	6.31	4.68	89.00	6.32
01	Andaman & Nicobar	1.04	97.32	1.65	5.56	91.41	3.03
02	Andhra Pradesh	4.37	89.38	6.24	5.24	88.95	5.81
03	Arunachal Pradesh	7.34	89.12	3.54	12.63	85.61	1.76
04	Assam	4.41	89.58	6.01	8.02	87.16	4.82
05	Bihar	4.65	89.11	6.24	6.42	87.65	5.92
06	Chandigarh	6.15	88.22	5.63	6.29	89.90	3.81
07	Dadra and Nagar Haveli	3.47	89.37	7.16	1.79	95.26	2.95
08	Delhi	3.40	93.07	3.53	4.61	91.11	4.28
09	Goa, Daman & Diu	2.52	91.54	5.94	2.62	90.36	7.02
10	Gujarat	5.09	89.49	5.43	3.88	91.38	4.75
11	Haryana	3.77	90.44	5.79	3.64	90.96	5.40
12	Himachal Pradesh	2.51	89.74	7.75	3.12	89.61	7.26
13	Jammu & Kashmir	4.38	87.37	8.25	4.70	90.69	4.61
14	Karnataka	5.56	89.22	5.21	4.89	89.60	5.51
15	Kerala	0.40	91.77	7.83	0.52	90.84	8.63
16	Lakshadweep	0.44	87.75	11.81	0.26	95.36	4.38
17	Madhya Pradesh	4.08	89.94	5.98	4.12	88.97	6.91
18	Maharashtra	2.48	92.15	5.37	2.39	90.63	6.99
19	Manipur	4.70	84.03	11.27	2.98	89.27	7.75
20	Meghalaya	8.85	85.53	5.62	8.69	87.05	4.27
21	Mizoram	15.65	77.90	6.46	10.16	83.28	6.56
22	Nagaland	9.81	86.18	4.01	13.74	83.42	2.84
23	Odisha	3.94	88.45	7.61	5.03	88.41	6.56
24	Pondicherry	2.13	90.44	7.43	1.88	90.91	7.21
25	Punjab	5.59	87.04	7.36	4.62	89.14	6.24
26	Rajasthan	4.97	89.67	5.36	5.71	89.34	4.96
27	Sikkim	5.02	90.80	4.17	11.02	84.37	4.61
28	Tamil Nadu	2.58	88.16	9.26	2.87	89.06	8.07
29	Tripura	1.82	90.32	7.86	5.57	88.42	6.01
30	Uttar Pradesh	5.44	88.26	6.30	7.89	85.49	6.62
31	West Bengal	4.35	89.96	5.69	6.16	88.70	5.14

fastly, particularly in the last decade 1991-2001. It is worrying to note that poor states like Bihar and Uttar Pradesh show very high participation of the elderly in 2001. Uttar Pradesh further shows a very high proportion of rural male workers (12 per cent) among the elderly in 2001, up from 1981.

The pattern of child labour described above may also be seen from Maps 2.2.1 and 2.2.2. Tables 2.5.2 and 2.5.3 present that child labour is higher in rural than urban areas and same pattern is true for the elderly participation as well. Tables 2.5.4 through 2.5.9 depicts that children are more engaged as marginal workers both in rural and urban areas and same is by and large true for the elderly population as well.

2.6. Educational Levels

2.6.1. Distribution of All Workers by Educational Levels

There has been a fast increase in the educational level of all workers during 1981-2001. The increase in educational level of workforce has been much faster during 1991-2001 compared to earlier decade. It may be seen from Table 2.6.1 that the literacy level among male workers was about 50 per cent in 1981, which increased to 57 per cent in 1991 and has gone up dramatically to 71 per cent in 2001. Similarly, among female workforce, only one-tenth of the workforce was literate in 1981, which increased to one-third of the female workforce in 2001. Similar effect is also seen when we analyse the education level of workers as well. For example, the percentage of total male workers with educational level matric and above was 5 per cent in 1981 at the national level; it reached 9 per cent in 1991 and much steeper rise of 27 per cent in 2001. In the case of female workers, the increase is observed from 2 to 3 per cent from 1981 to 1991 and further to 9 per cent in 2001. While trend in the educational level of workers is increasing, the educational level reveals that human resources need to be developed more in the coming decades. At least half the male workforce should be matriculate by 2020, and we strive to achieve one-third of the female workforce to be matriculate by that time.

As expected, Kerala shows the highest per cent of literate male workers throughout the reference period (Table 2.6.1).

Table 2.6.1. Percentage Distribution of Total workers according to education, India and States, 1981-2001

Sl. No.	State / Union Territories	*1981*					
		Male			*Female*		
		L	*BM*	*AM*	*L*	*BM*	*AM*
	India	49.60	43.92	5.68	14.55	12.75	1.80
01	Andaman & Nicobar	65.41	57.83	7.58	44.43	32.19	12.24
02	Andhra Pradesh	39.40	34.90	4.50	7.51	6.78	0.74
03	Arunachal Pradesh	30.39	26.31	4.08	4.33	3.82	0.52
04	Assam	NA	NA	NA	NA	NA	NA
05	Bihar	38.31	34.28	4.03	4.82	4.12	0.70
06	Chandigarh	71.73	44.92	26.81	65.90	16.77	49.14
07	Dadra and Nagar Haveli	40.13	36.62	3.51	8.24	7.76	0.47
08	Delhi	74.71	49.57	25.13	58.19	18.51	39.68
09	Goa, Daman & Diu	69.18	58.85	10.34	32.94	27.72	5.23
10	Gujarat	58.79	54.00	4.79	18.93	17.53	1.40
11	Haryana	50.73	44.38	6.35	14.78	10.57	4.21
12	Himachal Pradesh	55.08	49.18	5.90	24.47	22.93	1.54
13	Jammu & Kashmir	37.25	32.20	5.05	9.75	8.49	1.26
14	Karnataka	51.77	46.18	5.59	16.48	14.94	1.55
15	Kerala	85.26	75.48	9.78	60.26	53.52	6.74
16	Lakshadweep	82.83	75.64	7.19	59.01	52.59	6.42
17	Madhya Pradesh	42.42	36.67	5.76	6.59	5.76	0.83
18	Maharashtra	63.62	56.58	7.04	31.10	29.42	1.68
19	Manipur	56.35	48.32	8.03	20.60	18.20	2.40
20	Meghalaya	42.12	37.96	4.16	26.70	24.54	2.16
21	Mizoram	81.81	76.14	5.67	69.92	68.03	1.89
22	Nagaland	49.98	45.73	4.25	21.70	20.89	0.81
23	Odisha	50.86	48.57	2.29	7.33	6.62	0.71
24	Pondicherry	70.06	62.69	7.37	25.31	20.43	4.87
25	Punjab	47.32	40.91	6.40	27.77	17.17	10.60
26	Rajasthan	44.09	28.81	15.28	3.89	2.96	0.93
27	Sikkim	46.99	42.60	4.40	14.75	13.35	1.41
28	Tamil Nadu	63.45	58.27	5.19	20.74	19.28	1.46
29	Tripura	56.12	50.78	5.34	18.37	14.34	4.03
30	Uttar Pradesh	39.77	33.61	6.16	8.76	6.38	2.38
31	West Bengal	54.10	47.47	6.64	15.76	11.83	3.92

Sl. No.	State / Union Territories	1991					
		Male			Female		
		L	BM	AM	L	BM	AM
	India	56.90	47.65	9.25	21.80	18.67	3.13
01	Andaman & Nicobar	71.35	60.96	10.40	56.57	44.84	11.73
02	Andhra Pradesh	44.81	36.65	8.16	11.90	10.30	1.60
03	Arunachal Pradesh	44.14	36.35	7.79	12.25	10.51	1.75
04	Assam	53.63	47.39	6.24	29.33	26.83	2.50
05	Bihar	42.80	35.86	6.95	8.77	7.37	1.39
06	Chandigarh	76.68	45.66	31.03	76.63	19.10	57.53
07	Dadra and Nagar Haveli	45.99	39.51	6.47	32.19	30.91	1.29
08	Delhi	77.56	47.22	30.33	67.59	18.19	49.40
09	Goa, Daman & Diu	79.38	59.17	20.21	63.14	41.90	21.24
10	Gujarat	66.33	57.28	9.04	26.99	23.74	3.26
11	Haryana	61.07	51.61	9.46	22.99	16.17	6.81
12	Himachal Pradesh	67.66	59.46	8.20	37.01	34.34	2.67
13	Jammu & Kashmir	NA	NA	NA	NA	NA	NA
14	Karnataka	58.49	49.09	9.41	33.61	30.84	2.78
15	Kerala	88.07	79.15	8.92	68.42	58.03	10.39
16	Lakshadweep	90.13	79.61	10.52	81.06	68.68	12.38
17	Madhya Pradesh	50.81	40.42	10.39	29.51	28.21	1.30
18	Maharashtra	71.33	57.96	13.37	37.12	33.51	3.60
19	Manipur	62.99	50.68	12.31	35.49	30.48	5.02
20	Meghalaya	48.23	40.88	7.35	37.05	32.99	4.06
21	Mizoram	84.59	77.34	7.25	81.48	77.73	3.75
22	Nagaland	57.84	51.05	6.78	35.42	33.15	2.27
23	Odisha	58.14	50.71	7.43	34.95	33.39	1.56
24	Pondicherry	79.05	64.39	14.65	41.91	31.37	10.54
25	Punjab	58.50	50.03	8.47	52.88	37.26	15.63
26	Rajasthan	47.27	38.67	8.60	36.89	35.95	0.94
27	Sikkim	55.57	49.09	6.47	31.02	27.46	3.57
28	Tamil Nadu	66.84	58.66	8.18	35.29	32.22	3.07
29	Tripura	73.37	67.57	5.80	47.41	43.54	3.87
30	Uttar Pradesh	48.41	38.35	10.06	34.23	32.11	2.12
31	West Bengal	60.09	50.09	10.00	35.70	31.69	4.01

Sl. No.	*State / Union Territories*	*2001*					
		Male			*Female*		
		L	*BM*	*AM*	*L*	*BM*	*AM*
	India	70.50	40.71	26.61	35.70	24.07	8.65
01	Andaman & Nicobar	83.80	53.94	29.01	68.71	39.09	28.87
02	Andhra Pradesh	62.00	33.60	25.24	27.81	19.50	5.72
03	Arunachal Pradesh	59.14	35.28	22.37	25.55	17.90	6.45
04	Assam	67.33	41.96	23.32	43.28	27.63	14.00
05	Bihar	54.19	28.06	22.34	15.44	9.68	3.89
06	Chandigarh	82.61	28.44	53.21	72.72	12.97	58.56
07	Dadra and Nagar Haveli	67.37	34.40	31.95	18.52	12.13	5.93
08	Delhi	84.92	31.54	52.41	69.77	15.71	52.82
09	Goa, Daman & Diu	86.13	40.25	44.29	63.69	29.95	32.19
10	Gujarat	76.12	45.52	29.71	37.43	26.77	9.88
11	Haryana	74.44	38.07	35.22	38.13	24.64	12.25
12	Himachal Pradesh	82.35	43.59	37.33	58.82	38.68	18.65
13	Jammu & Kashmir	59.90	28.70	28.07	27.56	14.02	10.07
14	Karnataka	70.11	38.29	30.17	37.88	25.50	11.08
15	Kerala	94.48	60.79	32.58	82.14	50.51	30.15
16	Lakshadweep	94.18	60.46	28.73	89.40	47.07	34.47
17	Madhya Pradesh	71.19	46.30	20.82	31.47	22.04	4.08
18	Maharashtra	82.70	44.38	36.14	49.33	35.24	12.16
19	Manipur	78.42	38.04	37.21	50.76	26.89	21.37
20	Meghalaya	62.59	42.89	16.12	51.25	38.17	9.83
21	Mizoram	91.12	69.79	19.13	85.95	70.75	12.68
22	Nagaland	64.82	37.44	24.78	47.29	31.77	13.18
23	Odisha	70.64	47.21	21.19	25.89	19.35	5.20
24	Pondicherry	87.00	42.91	42.48	56.98	30.51	24.96
25	Punjab	70.25	33.21	35.86	50.88	27.56	21.55
26	Rajasthan	70.59	45.20	20.45	27.47	18.71	2.83
27	Sikkim	73.70	50.27	20.73	50.65	36.74	12.40
28	Tamil Nadu	78.67	42.11	26.05	46.50	29.05	10.62
29	Tripura	77.12	58.86	16.86	42.90	34.01	7.35
30	Uttar Pradesh	62.64	34.84	24.54	23.50	15.03	5.82
31	West Bengal	73.14	50.45	20.94	40.32	30.73	8.01

In the case of female workers highest percentage of literates was shown in Mizoram.

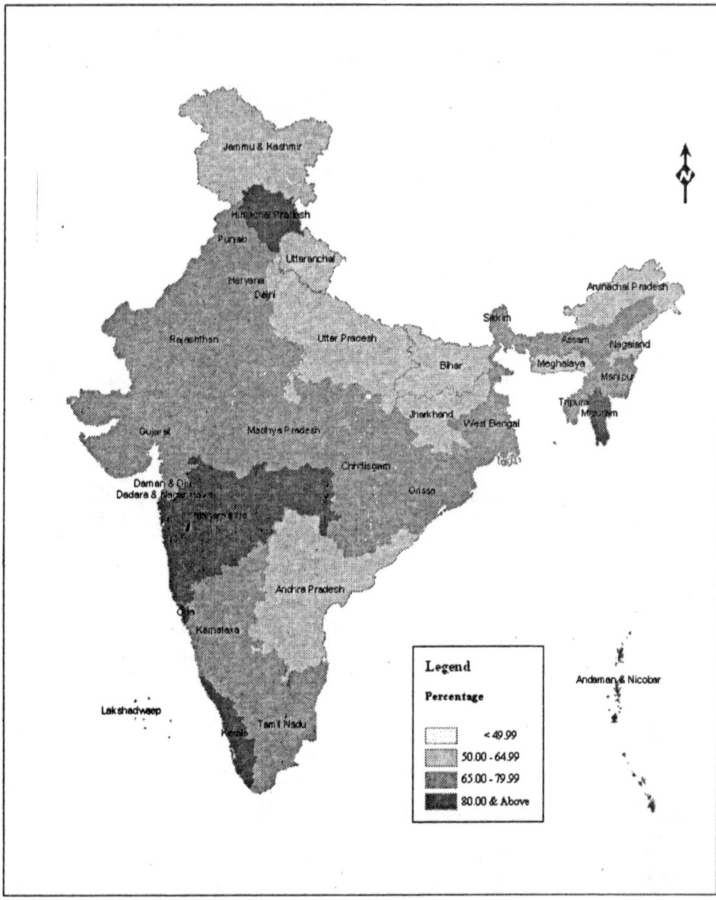

Map 2.3.1. Percentage of literate workers to total male workers of State and Union Territories of India in 2001

Map 2.3.1 shows the percentage of literate workers to total male workers for the states and union territories in 2001. It is observed from the map that the percentage of literate total male workers is highest in Kerala. On the other hand, Jammu Kashmir, Uttarakhand, Utter Pradesh, Bihar, Jharkhand, Andhra Pradesh and some north eastern states show very low percentage of literates among male workers.

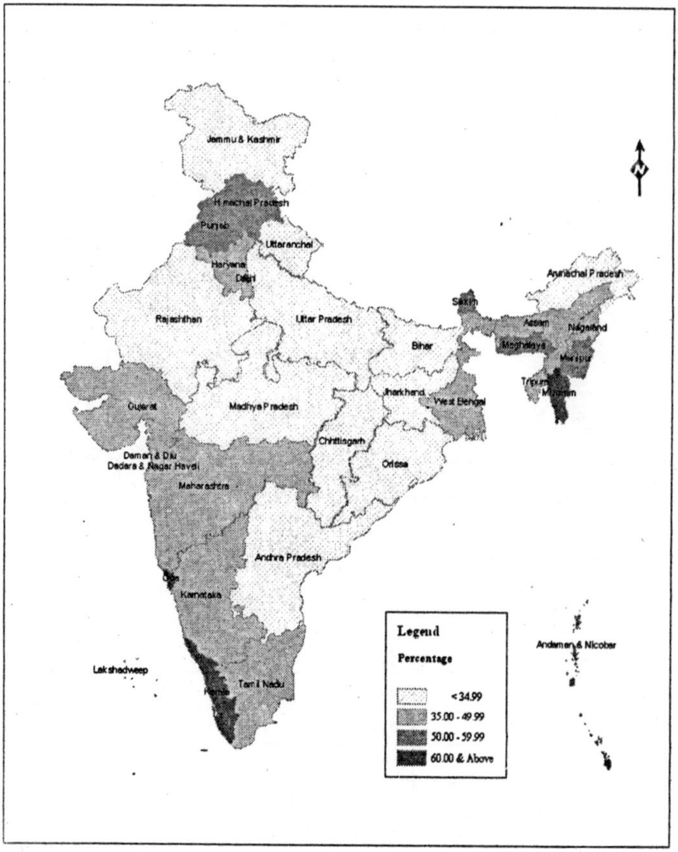

Map 2.3.2. Percentage of literate workers to total female workers of State and Union Territories of India in 2001

Similarly, Map 2.3.2 shows that the percentage of literates among female workers is very high in Mizoram and Kerala, whereas the lower percentages of literates to total female workers have been found in Jammu and Kashmir, most of the EAG states and in the states of northeastern India. As expected, urban areas shows higher educational level than the rural areas in both main and marginal categories. However, the increase in educational level has been faster in rural than urban areas.

Table 2.6.2. Percentage Distribution of Total workers according to education, (Rural) India and States, 1981-2001

Sl. No.	State / Union Territories	1981					
		Male			Female		
		L	BM	AM	L	BM	AM
	India	42.71	40.07	2.64	11.71	11.23	0.48
01	Andaman & Nicobar	60.89	55.83	5.06	36.24	31.01	5.22
02	Andhra Pradesh	32.78	30.86	1.92	6.11	5.96	0.15
03	Arunachal Pradesh	27.35	24.18	3.16	3.86	3.52	0.33
04	Assam	NA	NA	NA	NA	NA	NA
05	Bihar	34.65	32.17	2.48	3.81	3.58	0.23
06	Chandigarh	48.78	44.32	4.45	6.81	5.61	1.21
07	Dadra and Nagar Haveli	37.61	34.72	2.90	7.21	6.91	0.30
08	Delhi	64.43	51.24	13.19	20.62	15.27	5.34
09	Goa, Daman & Diu	64.59	57.43	7.17	28.85	25.91	2.93
10	Gujarat	50.64	48.93	1.71	16.30	16.03	0.27
11	Haryana	44.22	40.80	3.42	9.98	9.00	0.98
12	Himachal Pradesh	52.74	48.54	4.20	23.48	22.67	0.80
13	Jammu & Kashmir	32.72	30.15	2.57	7.88	7.59	0.29
14	Karnataka	44.83	42.45	2.39	13.43	13.15	0.28
15	Kerala	83.34	78.79	4.55	58.16	53.11	5.06
16	Lakshadweep	81.47	76.20	5.28	61.60	57.67	3.93
17	Madhya Pradesh	35.78	33.15	2.63	5.29	5.14	0.14
18	Maharashtra	55.54	52.70	2.84	29.31	29.07	0.24
19	Manipur	51.61	46.58	5.02	18.42	17.20	1.23
20	Meghalaya	35.48	34.49	0.99	23.65	23.28	0.37
21	Mizoram	78.42	75.21	3.21	66.97	66.42	0.55
22	Nagaland	44.60	42.03	2.57	20.13	19.74	0.40
23	Odisha	48.10	47.32	0.78	6.51	6.24	0.26
24	Pondicherry	60.63	57.50	3.13	14.25	13.31	0.94
25	Punjab	40.29	37.07	3.23	19.48	15.57	3.91
26	Rajasthan	30.08	27.75	2.33	2.47	2.30	0.17
27	Sikkim	42.22	39.79	2.43	11.95	11.50	0.45
28	Tamil Nadu	54.33	52.51	1.82	16.39	16.03	0.35
29	Tripura	52.56	49.53	3.02	13.89	12.57	1.32
30	Uttar Pradesh	35.58	31.70	3.87	5.98	5.50	0.48
31	West Bengal	48.26	44.86	3.40	9.47	8.50	0.97

Sl. No.	State / Union Territories	1991					
		Male			Female		
		L	BM	AM	L	BM	AM
	India	50.17	45.01	5.16	18.28	17.21	1.06
01	Andaman & Nicobar	67.39	59.59	7.80	52.59	46.12	6.47
02	Andhra Pradesh	37.11	33.12	4.00	9.82	9.37	0.45
03	Arunachal Pradesh	39.21	33.26	5.96	10.47	9.55	0.92
04	Assam	49.88	45.75	4.13	27.89	26.40	1.49
05	Bihar	38.98	34.22	4.76	7.37	6.77	0.60
06	Chandigarh	60.88	54.48	6.40	34.69	27.72	6.97
07	Dadra and Nagar Haveli	42.16	37.46	4.70	31.48	30.67	0.81
08	Delhi	73.22	54.18	19.03	40.03	26.23	13.80
09	Goa, Daman & Diu	77.45	57.07	20.37	49.82	34.11	15.71
10	Gujarat	58.79	54.33	4.47	24.16	22.89	1.28
11	Haryana	55.65	50.43	5.23	16.98	15.22	1.76
12	Himachal Pradesh	65.69	59.82	5.87	35.77	34.26	1.51
13	Jammu & Kashmir	NA	NA	NA	NA	NA	NA
14	Karnataka	51.11	46.51	4.59	31.55	30.53	1.02
15	Kerala	86.97	79.72	7.26	66.12	58.07	8.05
16	Lakshadweep	87.80	78.35	9.45	75.45	63.77	11.69
17	Madhya Pradesh	44.00	38.11	5.88	28.83	28.45	0.38
18	Maharashtra	64.11	54.91	9.20	34.52	33.16	1.36
19	Manipur	58.55	49.63	8.91	32.28	28.98	3.31
20	Meghalaya	41.15	36.83	4.32	33.86	32.02	1.83
21	Mizoram	76.33	72.25	4.08	74.14	72.20	1.94
22	Nagaland	51.90	47.42	4.48	33.19	31.83	1.36
23	Odisha	55.47	49.85	5.62	34.64	33.70	0.94
24	Pondicherry	69.06	61.87	7.19	26.02	23.91	2.10
25	Punjab	52.77	48.25	4.53	46.54	40.24	6.30
26	Rajasthan	39.66	35.24	4.42	36.51	36.27	0.23
27	Sikkim	52.86	47.81	5.04	28.74	26.37	2.37
28	Tamil Nadu	58.90	54.60	4.29	31.99	30.60	1.39
29	Tripura	71.75	68.53	3.22	45.07	43.75	1.32
30	Uttar Pradesh	44.79	37.68	7.11	33.27	32.37	0.90
31	West Bengal	52.92	47.79	5.13	32.67	31.43	1.25

Sl. No.	State / Union Territories	2001					
		Male			Female		
		L	BM	AM	L	BM	AM
	India	65.29	42.47	19.49	32.14	23.80	5.39
01	Andaman & Nicobar	81.54	57.98	22.64	64.58	44.60	19.25
02	Andhra Pradesh	56.51	35.27	17.84	25.45	19.35	3.51
03	Arunachal Pradesh	52.53	34.76	16.25	22.04	17.34	3.55
04	Assam	63.91	42.65	19.08	41.32	27.88	11.79
05	Bihar	51.91	28.14	19.95	14.45	9.48	3.14
06	Chandigarh	78.70	38.98	38.96	52.02	28.01	23.09
07	Dadra and Nagar Haveli	59.21	34.96	23.43	14.61	10.73	3.45
08	Delhi	84.00	36.35	46.84	59.18	24.66	33.54
09	Goa, Daman & Diu	84.82	46.17	36.97	59.34	34.68	22.98
10	Gujarat	69.56	47.87	20.72	34.21	26.55	6.93
11	Haryana	70.93	40.73	28.97	35.40	25.50	8.66
12	Himachal Pradesh	81.43	45.47	34.49	58.14	39.33	17.32
13	Jammu & Kashmir	54.12	30.59	20.18	23.73	14.21	6.06
14	Karnataka	63.56	40.85	20.77	33.41	25.41	6.68
15	Kerala	93.81	62.90	29.73	80.17	52.85	25.80
16	Lakshadweep	92.57	62.76	25.27	87.00	49.36	32.84
17	Madhya Pradesh	66.68	48.67	13.00	29.62	21.92	1.97
18	Maharashtra	77.73	49.25	25.98	45.79	36.76	7.03
19	Manipur	75.40	40.13	31.74	47.72	28.17	16.83
20	Meghalaya	57.40	43.29	10.08	47.53	38.51	5.55
21	Mizoram	86.29	72.03	11.36	78.14	69.55	5.24
22	Nagaland	60.75	37.19	20.87	44.97	31.99	10.62
23	Odisha	68.09	48.97	16.69	24.41	19.32	3.76
24	Pondicherry	80.40	47.74	31.06	42.54	30.80	10.54
25	Punjab	65.17	35.20	28.70	47.04	29.47	15.83
26	Rajasthan	66.50	47.00	14.25	26.14	18.60	1.45
27	Sikkim	72.25	51.19	18.20	48.91	37.45	9.93
28	Tamil Nadu	72.07	44.38	18.09	40.67	28.19	6.61
29	Tripura	74.02	59.80	12.69	38.76	33.14	4.03
30	Uttar Pradesh	59.93	36.14	20.41	21.09	14.70	3.83
31	West Bengal	68.78	53.42	13.59	35.79	30.52	3.77

Table 2.6.3. Percentage Distribution of Total workers according to education, (Urban) India and States, 1981-2001

Sl. No.	State / Union Territories	1981					
		Male			Female		
		L	BM	AM	L	BM	AM
	India	72.87	56.91	15.95	41.15	27.01	14.14
01	Andaman & Nicobar	77.42	63.14	14.28	83.67	37.82	45.85
02	Andhra Pradesh	66.67	51.54	15.13	23.49	16.06	7.43
03	Arunachal Pradesh	66.88	51.76	15.12	38.10	24.60	13.50
04	Assam	NA	NA	NA	NA	NA	NA
05	Bihar	66.60	50.62	15.98	27.92	16.47	11.45
06	Chandigarh	73.94	44.98	28.97	73.75	18.25	55.50
07	Dadra and Nagar Haveli	72.10	60.78	11.32	29.89	25.75	4.14
08	Delhi	75.43	49.46	25.97	62.23	18.85	43.38
09	Goa, Daman & Diu	77.99	61.58	16.42	47.71	34.21	13.50
10	Gujarat	77.80	65.83	11.97	43.71	31.68	12.03
11	Haryana	74.01	57.19	16.83	61.59	25.88	35.71
12	Himachal Pradesh	79.82	55.94	23.88	64.36	33.10	31.26
13	Jammu & Kashmir	56.24	40.81	15.43	37.90	22.10	15.80
14	Karnataka	71.41	56.76	14.64	36.46	26.60	9.86
15	Kerala	92.21	63.54	28.66	74.04	56.23	17.82
16	Lakshadweep	84.33	75.03	9.29	55.76	46.22	9.54
17	Madhya Pradesh	72.65	52.66	19.99	26.39	15.13	11.26
18	Maharashtra	79.37	64.14	15.22	48.03	32.77	15.26
19	Manipur	71.47	53.86	17.61	29.81	22.45	7.36
20	Meghalaya	76.14	55.72	20.42	64.06	39.90	24.16
21	Mizoram	93.09	79.22	13.86	88.07	77.91	10.16
22	Nagaland	76.70	64.10	12.60	65.34	53.05	12.29
23	Odisha	72.33	58.29	14.03	22.20	13.39	8.81
24	Pondicherry	79.71	68.00	11.71	44.79	32.98	11.81
25	Punjab	66.19	51.25	14.94	63.76	24.13	39.63
26	Rajasthan	80.21	31.53	48.67	27.21	13.72	13.49
27	Sikkim	68.25	55.10	13.16	58.37	41.99	16.38
28	Tamil Nadu	85.05	71.90	13.16	48.09	39.68	8.40
29	Tripura	88.68	62.13	26.55	71.07	35.21	35.86
30	Uttar Pradesh	60.05	42.83	17.22	41.24	16.66	24.58
31	West Bengal	69.21	54.20	15.01	46.60	28.21	18.40

Sl. No.	State / Union Territories	1991					
		Male			Female		
		L	BM	AM	L	BM	AM
	India	77.24	55.61	21.63	52.14	31.25	20.89
01	Andaman & Nicobar	81.72	64.52	17.20	80.88	37.03	43.85
02	Andhra Pradesh	69.35	47.91	21.43	32.23	19.37	12.86
03	Arunachal Pradesh	74.67	55.52	19.15	58.38	35.35	23.03
04	Assam	81.44	59.59	21.84	67.32	38.25	29.08
05	Bihar	71.10	47.97	23.13	39.64	20.79	18.84
06	Chandigarh	79.13	44.29	34.84	78.78	18.66	60.12
07	Dadra and Nagar Haveli	84.48	60.12	24.36	52.82	37.67	15.15
08	Delhi	78.01	46.49	31.52	69.99	17.49	52.50
09	Goa, Daman & Diu	82.31	62.34	19.97	78.14	50.67	27.47
.10	Gujarat	81.38	63.19	18.19	54.16	31.91	22.25
11	Haryana	77.70	55.25	22.45	68.54	23.39	45.15
12	Himachal Pradesh	85.96	56.08	29.88	74.29	36.79	37.50
13	Jammu & Kashmir	NA	NA	NA	NA	NA	NA
14	Karnataka	76.76	55.45	21.31	49.29	33.17	16.12
15	Kerala	91.25	77.53	13.73	77.33	57.87	19.46
16	Lakshadweep	91.83	80.53	11.30	84.86	72.01	12.85
17	Madhya Pradesh	76.70	49.17	27.53	39.88	24.67	15.21
18	Maharashtra	83.36	63.04	20.32	56.73	36.16	20.57
19	Manipur	76.81	53.92	22.90	47.33	36.00	11.33
20	Meghalaya	82.57	60.50	22.07	71.85	43.53	28.32
21	Mizoram	94.78	83.61	11.17	92.77	86.23	6.54
22	Nagaland	83.09	66.52	16.57	78.36	58.56	19.80
23	Odisha	77.04	56.83	20.20	42.60	25.78	16.82
24	Pondicherry	85.37	65.99	19.38	60.50	40.09	20.41
25	Punjab	72.77	54.48	18.29	74.46	27.09	47.38
26	Rajasthan	74.67	51.03	23.64	44.28	29.61	14.67
27	Sikkim	78.54	59.93	18.60	73.65	47.81	25.84
28	Tamil Nadu	83.63	67.25	16.39	55.42	42.06	13.36
29	Tripura	86.14	59.96	26.18	76.65	40.91	35.74
30	Uttar Pradesh	64.19	41.25	22.94	47.85	28.34	19.50
31	West Bengal	77.60	55.72	21.88	57.26	33.57	23.69

Sl. No.	State / Union Territories	2001					
		Male			Female		
		L	BM	AM	L	BM	AM
	India	84.09	36.11	45.20	60.21	25.92	31.14
01	Andaman & Nicobar	88.45	45.67	42.05	82.10	21.22	60.03
02	Andhra Pradesh	78.65	28.53	47.66	48.58	20.80	25.27
03	Arunachal Pradesh	83.18	37.16	44.61	59.82	23.40	34.72
04	Assam	88.06	37.73	49.03	72.07	24.04	46.44
05	Bihar	76.02	27.25	45.14	40.60	14.91	22.86
06	Chandigarh	83.18	26.90	55.29	74.27	11.84	61.22
07	Dadra and Nagar Haveli	90.80	32.78	56.42	64.53	28.53	35.07
08	Delhi	84.99	31.21	52.79	70.62	15.00	54.35
09	Goa, Daman & Diu	87.59	33.58	52.51	70.29	22.80	46.13
10	Gujarat	87.05	41.62	44.70	60.39	28.35	30.89
11	Haryana	83.24	31.41	50.91	60.00	17.75	40.97
12	Himachal Pradesh	90.06	27.86	61.10	80.35	18.35	60.74
13	Jammu & Kashmir	75.87	23.47	49.89	58.63	12.52	42.58
14	Karnataka	83.59	33.03	49.50	59.42	25.93	32.30
15	Kerala	96.39	54.84	40.62	88.74	42.68	44.72
16	Lakshadweep	95.98	57.88	32.62	91.57	44.99	35.94
17	Madhya Pradesh	84.98	39.04	44.73	49.29	23.20	24.29
18	Maharashtra	89.33	37.89	49.71	66.83	27.75	37.54
19	Manipur	87.77	31.57	54.11	61.33	22.42	37.19
20	Meghalaya	86.76	41.04	44.26	79.17	35.67	41.99
21	Mizoram	96.52	67.28	27.82	96.48	72.35	22.71
22	Nagaland	84.98	38.66	44.15	79.34	28.79	48.54
23	Odisha	85.62	36.93	47.54	49.76	19.88	28.50
24	Pondicherry	90.46	40.39	48.47	69.36	30.26	37.34
25	Punjab	80.09	29.36	49.71	68.08	19.01	47.14
26	Rajasthan	84.60	39.03	41.75	46.44	20.36	22.53
27	Sikkim	85.43	42.80	41.33	77.62	25.62	50.84
28	Tamil Nadu	87.50	39.07	36.71	62.77	31.44	21.80
29	Tripura	91.95	54.38	36.82	79.60	41.76	36.78
30	Uttar Pradesh	73.44	29.68	41.02	49.65	18.65	27.41
31	West Bengal	84.11	42.98	39.43	62.04	31.71	28.32

Table 2.6.4. Percentage Distribution of Main workers according to education, India and States, 1981-2001

Sl. No.	State / Union Territories	1981					
		Male			Female		
		L	BM	AM	L	BM	AM
	India	49.32	43.63	5.68	15.44	12.99	2.45
01	Andaman & Nicobar	65.52	57.77	7.75	59.70	35.03	24.66
02	Andhra Pradesh	39.37	34.89	4.48	7.20	6.31	0.89
03	Arunachal Pradesh	30.14	26.01	4.13	3.94	3.38	0.56
04	Assam	NA	NA	NA	NA	NA	NA
05	Bihar	38.08	34.09	3.98	4.71	3.72	0.99
06	Chandigarh	71.80	44.93	26.87	66.46	16.73	49.72
07	Dadra and Nagar Haveli	40.11	36.58	3.53	9.04	8.28	0.76
08	Delhi	74.72	49.57	25.16	59.62	18.24	41.38
09	Goa, Daman & Diu	69.29	58.62	10.67	33.69	26.41	7.28
10	Gujarat	58.71	53.93	4.78	20.24	17.74	2.50
11	Haryana	50.42	44.08	6.33	21.93	12.86	9.08
12	Himachal Pradesh	53.58	47.68	5.90	22.87	20.58	2.29
13	Jammu & Kashmir	35.89	30.72	5.17	16.96	10.97	5.99
14	Karnataka	51.64	46.11	5.52	16.68	14.70	1.98
15	Kerala	85.44	75.03	10.41	59.31	50.86	8.45
16	Lakshadweep	85.00	76.97	8.03	62.46	54.93	7.53
17	Madhya Pradesh	42.31	36.57	5.74	6.83	5.75	1.09
18	Maharashtra	63.55	56.50	7.06	33.55	31.55	2.00
19	Manipur	56.06	48.19	7.87	20.74	18.27	2.47
20	Meghalaya	41.87	37.66	4.21	26.83	24.41	2.42
21	Mizoram	81.26	75.69	5.57	68.83	66.81	2.02
22	Nagaland	49.52	45.26	4.26	20.88	20.08	0.80
23	Odisha	50.79	48.52	2.27	7.24	5.97	1.27
24	Pondicherry	70.09	62.68	7.41	27.02	21.17	5.85
25	Punjab	47.32	40.90	6.41	49.00	21.01	28.00
26	Rajasthan	44.09	28.62	15.47	5.64	3.62	2.02
27	Sikkim	46.83	42.41	4.43	14.82	13.30	1.52
28	Tamil Nadu	63.42	58.24	5.18	20.95	19.27	1.69
29	Tripura	56.02	50.69	5.33	20.07	14.59	5.48
30	Uttar Pradesh	39.53	33.44	6.09	10.18	6.75	3.43
31	West Bengal	53.99	47.39	6.61	16.65	11.43	5.23

Sl. No.	State / Union Territories	1991					
		Male			Female		
		L	BM	AM	L	BM	AM
	India	56.80	47.52	9.28	22.34	18.29	4.05
01	Andaman & Nicobar	72.27	61.63	10.64	65.39	40.60	24.79
02	Andhra Pradesh	44.78	36.62	8.16	11.34	9.58	1.76
03	Arunachal Pradesh	44.12	36.31	7.81	12.08	10.27	1.81
04	Assam	53.57	47.29	6.28	28.43	24.80	3.64
05	Bihar	42.79	35.84	6.95	8.54	6.66	1.88
06	Chandigarh	76.79	45.70	31.09	77.24	18.69	58.56
07	Dadra and Nagar Haveli	45.80	39.06	6.74	12.37	10.11	2.26
08	Delhi	77.68	47.26	30.42	68.44	17.16	51.28
09	Goa, Daman & Diu	79.33	59.34	19.99	65.25	42.87	22.38
10	Gujarat	66.36	57.30	9.06	28.76	23.26	5.49
11	Haryana	61.05	51.59	9.46	28.25	16.68	11.57
12	Himachal Pradesh	67.38	59.09	8.29	36.65	32.69	3.96
13	Jammu & Kashmir	NA	NA	NA	NA	NA	NA
14	Karnataka	58.72	49.26	9.46	24.17	20.58	3.59
15	Kerala	92.80	83.40	9.39	77.40	63.99	13.41
16	Lakshadweep	90.83	79.73	11.10	84.13	68.60	15.53
17	Madhya Pradesh	50.88	40.26	10.62	11.97	9.70	2.27
18	Maharashtra	72.13	58.55	13.58	30.87	26.36	4.51
19	Manipur	63.74	51.17	12.57	30.37	24.18	6.18
20	Meghalaya	48.20	40.72	7.48	33.54	28.47	5.07
21	Mizoram	83.67	76.16	7.51	80.14	75.87	4.27
22	Nagaland	57.90	51.11	6.80	34.95	32.65	2.30
23	Odisha	58.45	50.86	7.59	13.56	10.09	3.47
24	Pondicherry	79.11	64.37	14.73	42.68	31.56	11.12
25	Punjab	58.54	50.06	8.48	56.46	25.94	30.52
26	Rajasthan	47.23	38.43	8.80	8.16	5.48	2.68
27	Sikkim	55.67	49.14	6.53	28.70	24.81	3.88
28	Tamil Nadu	67.03	58.82	8.21	29.86	26.26	3.59
29	Tripura	73.80	67.93	5.87	46.10	40.30	5.80
30	Uttar Pradesh	48.42	38.29	10.13	14.11	10.04	4.07
31	West Bengal	60.45	50.25	10.20	23.84	17.06	6.78

Sl. No.	State / Union Territories	2001					
		Male			Female		
		L	BM	AM	L	BM	AM
00	India	71.27	40.22	27.87	38.34	23.78	11.29
01	Andaman & Nicobar	83.93	52.61	30.43	73.70	31.01	41.76
02	Andhra Pradesh	62.94	33.54	26.30	28.23	18.99	6.64
03	Arunachal Pradesh	59.65	34.68	23.51	24.14	15.89	7.08
04	Assam	67.67	41.49	24.10	41.05	22.35	16.70
05	Bihar	54.76	27.94	23.04	15.37	8.43	4.80
06	Chandigarh	82.77	28.13	53.67	73.47	11.94	60.31
07	Dadra and Nagar Haveli	68.66	34.15	33.47	18.58	11.05	6.95
08	Delhi	85.44	31.00	53.48	71.70	14.31	56.15
09	Goa, Daman & Diu	87.14	39.01	46.57	67.51	25.59	40.42
10	Gujarat	76.55	45.20	30.48	39.54	25.97	12.64
11	Haryana	75.07	36.94	37.00	39.03	21.53	16.08
12	Himachal Pradesh	81.56	41.74	38.33	55.74	34.82	19.03
13	Jammu & Kashmir	61.24	27.39	30.92	34.23	11.04	18.99
14	Karnataka	70.63	38.07	30.95	39.32	24.93	13.04
15	Kerala	94.99	59.61	34.31	83.43	47.23	34.72
16	Lakshadweep	95.16	56.29	33.46	93.39	38.89	47.19
17	Madhya Pradesh	71.88	45.72	22.07	32.01	20.46	5.99
18	Maharashtra	83.12	43.77	37.18	48.85	33.63	13.25
19	Manipur	78.72	37.10	38.33	51.48	25.33	23.24
20	Meghalaya	63.58	42.34	17.58	52.41	36.42	12.42
21	Mizoram	90.86	69.14	19.38	86.23	69.94	13.93
22	Nagaland	63.97	35.99	25.31	43.89	28.62	12.84
23	Orissa	72.14	47.48	22.47	29.55	18.27	9.73
24	Pondicherry	87.48	42.51	43.36	58.91	29.93	27.43
25	Punjab	70.94	32.78	37.00	53.54	26.47	25.10
26	Rajasthan	70.52	44.02	21.50	26.41	16.18	4.03
27	Sikkim	73.47	48.72	22.12	49.14	32.15	15.32
28	Tamil Nadu	79.47	41.89	26.96	48.08	29.06	11.85
29	Tripura	77.43	58.70	17.34	45.71	32.89	11.13
30	Uttar Pradesh	63.42	34.26	25.93	26.43	13.82	9.30
31	West Bengal	73.50	49.93	21.82	41.72	27.43	12.47

Table 2.6.5. Percentage Distribution of Main workers according to education (Rural), India and States, 1981-2001

Sl. No.	State / Union Territories	1981					
		Male			Female		
		L	BM	AM	L	BM	AM
00	India	42.29	39.69	2.60	11.71	11.08	0.63
01	Andaman & Nicobar	60.94	55.74	5.20	46.49	33.33	13.16
02	Andhra Pradesh	32.71	30.83	1.89	5.54	5.37	0.17
03	Arunachal Pradesh	27.01	23.82	3.20	3.41	3.06	0.35
04	Assam	NA	NA	NA	NA	NA	NA
05	Bihar	34.34	31.93	2.41	3.34	3.02	0.31
06	Chandigarh	48.75	44.31	4.45	6.88	5.64	1.23
07	Dadra and Nagar Haveli	37.78	34.88	2.91	7.61	7.12	0.49
08	Delhi	64.20	51.11	13.09	18.40	12.06	6.34
09	Goa, Daman & Diu	64.50	57.06	7.44	28.14	23.89	4.25
10	Gujarat	50.41	48.76	1.66	15.68	15.24	0.44
11	Haryana	43.67	40.34	3.33	11.83	9.77	2.07
12	Himachal Pradesh	50.97	46.87	4.10	21.24	20.17	1.08
13	Jammu & Kashmir	30.73	28.20	2.53	8.31	7.13	1.18
14	Karnataka	44.63	42.34	2.29	12.77	12.46	0.31
15	Kerala	83.39	78.67	4.73	56.68	50.31	6.37
16	Lakshadweep	84.61	78.54	6.07	60.64	56.44	4.20
17	Madhya Pradesh	35.57	33.00	2.57	5.20	5.03	0.17
18	Maharashtra	55.29	52.52	2.77	31.68	31.41	0.27
19	Manipur	51.36	46.46	4.90	18.59	17.35	1.24
20	Meghalaya	35.09	34.09	1.00	23.47	23.06	0.41
21	Mizoram	77.68	74.65	3.03	65.65	65.13	0.52
22	Nagaland	43.99	41.42	2.56	19.31	18.92	0.38
23	Orissa	47.97	47.24	0.73	5.85	5.37	0.48
24	Pondicherry	60.46	57.40	3.06	14.13	13.01	1.12
25	Punjab	40.19	36.99	3.20	32.78	18.16	14.61
26	Rajasthan	29.79	27.50	2.29	2.72	2.37	0.35
27	Sikkim	41.98	39.53	2.44	11.80	11.32	0.48
28	Tamil Nadu	54.18	52.42	1.76	16.03	15.63	0.39
29	Tripura	52.40	49.44	2.96	14.13	12.30	1.84
30	Uttar Pradesh	35.26	31.49	3.77	6.20	5.56	0.64
31	West Bengal	47.93	44.69	3.25	8.66	7.39	1.27

Sl. No.	State / Union Territories	1991					
		Male			Female		
		L	BM	AM	L	BM	AM
	India	50.00	44.86	5.14	17.75	16.49	1.26
01	Andaman & Nicobar	68.27	60.29	7.99	57.79	42.19	15.60
02	Andhra Pradesh	37.05	33.07	3.98	9.04	8.58	0.46
03	Arunachal Pradesh	39.18	33.20	5.97	10.21	9.26	0.95
04	Assam	49.74	45.61	4.13	26.07	24.11	1.96
05	Bihar	38.95	34.19	4.75	6.61	5.88	0.74
06	Chandigarh	60.91	54.51	6.40	32.84	25.53	7.32
07	Dadra and Nagar Haveli	41.73	36.85	4.88	10.61	9.30	1.31
08	Delhi	73.40	54.28	19.12	37.86	21.34	16.52
09	Goa, Daman & Diu	77.28	57.35	19.93	48.70	33.62	15.07
10	Gujarat	58.79	54.34	4.45	23.92	22.00	1.91
11	Haryana	55.59	50.38	5.21	17.98	15.19	2.79
12	Himachal Pradesh	65.33	59.43	5.91	34.75	32.70	2.05
13	Jammu & Kashmir	NA	NA	NA	NA	NA	NA
14	Karnataka	51.19	46.64	4.55	19.37	18.54	0.83
15	Kerala	91.89	84.33	7.56	74.85	64.66	10.19
16	Lakshadweep	89.03	78.54	10.49	78.50	64.00	14.50
17	Madhya Pradesh	43.86	37.84	6.01	9.56	8.96	0.60
18	Maharashtra	64.75	55.44	9.31	26.15	24.92	1.24
19	Manipur	59.07	50.03	9.03	26.92	23.15	3.76
20	Meghalaya	40.94	36.54	4.40	29.22	26.95	2.27
21	Mizoram	75.13	70.94	4.19	73.47	71.34	2.14
22	Nagaland	51.93	47.45	4.48	32.62	31.27	1.35
23	Odisha	55.70	49.96	5.74	11.45	9.39	2.06
24	Pondicherry	69.12	61.91	7.21	25.93	23.72	2.21
25	Punjab	52.79	48.27	4.52	39.93	25.97	13.96
26	Rajasthan	39.32	34.81	4.51	4.83	4.33	0.51
27	Sikkim	52.90	47.83	5.07	26.10	23.55	2.55
28	Tamil Nadu	59.02	54.73	4.29	24.76	23.39	1.37
29	Tripura	72.16	68.92	3.24	42.21	40.29	1.92
30	Uttar Pradesh	44.75	37.61	7.14	10.44	9.06	1.37
31	West Bengal	53.09	47.88	5.21	15.21	13.40	1.81

Sl. No.	State / Union Territories	2001					
		Male			Female		
		L	BM	AM	L	BM	AM
	India	65.54	42.18	20.02	32.98	23.59	6.12
01	Andaman & Nicobar	81.39	56.70	23.73	68.43	37.38	30.06
02	Andhra Pradesh	57.19	35.42	18.42	25.32	18.87	3.83
03	Arunachal Pradesh	52.59	34.03	17.07	19.85	15.09	3.62
04	Assam	63.75	42.27	19.24	36.87	22.43	12.39
05	Bihar	52.25	28.05	20.40	13.59	8.10	3.39
06	Chandigarh	78.75	38.62	39.37	50.65	26.25	23.44
07	Dadra and Nagar Haveli	60.39	34.83	24.72	14.17	9.87	3.76
08	Delhi	84.48	35.70	47.96	60.25	22.07	37.11
09	Goa, Daman & Diu	85.65	45.07	38.94	61.80	30.14	29.99
10	Gujarat	69.63	47.66	21.01	34.49	26.01	7.62
11	Haryana	70.94	39.77	29.93	33.70	22.85	9.42
12	Himachal Pradesh	80.24	43.91	34.78	54.23	35.94	16.36
13	Jammu & Kashmir	54.41	29.17	22.07	24.84	11.04	9.39
14	Karnataka	63.69	40.84	20.93	32.91	24.80	6.72
15	Kerala	94.34	61.98	31.23	81.14	50.17	29.44
16	Lakshadweep	93.48	58.88	29.51	91.80	42.02	43.92
17	Madhya Pradesh	66.89	48.41	13.38	28.67	20.23	2.32
18	Maharashtra	77.80	48.99	26.28	44.02	35.48	6.47
19	Manipur	75.40	39.29	32.40	47.01	26.97	16.79
20	Meghalaya	57.92	42.94	10.80	47.68	37.32	6.47
21	Mizoram	86.09	71.45	11.61	78.99	70.69	5.28
22	Nagaland	59.17	35.49	20.91	41.02	28.85	9.72
23	Odisha	69.28	49.69	17.18	25.91	18.22	6.14
24	Pondicherry	81.14	47.65	31.88	43.61	30.58	11.82
25	Punjab	65.58	34.85	29.49	48.34	29.21	17.16
26	Rajasthan	65.80	45.80	14.60	23.88	15.92	1.51
27	Sikkim	71.70	49.54	19.36	46.44	32.81	11.93
28	Tamil Nadu	72.62	44.44	18.49	41.28	28.22	6.99
29	Tripura	74.11	59.77	12.80	38.44	31.38	5.21
30	Uttar Pradesh	60.25	35.68	21.21	21.22	13.21	4.78
31	West Bengal	68.61	53.22	13.62	33.42	26.52	5.15

Table 2.6.6. Percentage Distribution of Main workers according to education (Urban), India and States, 1981-2001

Sl. No.	State / Union Territories	1981					
		Male			Female		
		L	BM	AM	L	BM	AM
	India	72.90	56.87	16.02	42.94	27.08	15.87
01	Andaman & Nicobar	77.33	63.00	14.33	84.69	38.25	46.43
02	Andhra Pradesh	66.71	51.56	15.15	24.15	15.87	8.27
03	Arunachal Pradesh	66.90	51.78	15.12	38.42	24.55	13.86
04	Assam	NA	NA	NA	NA	NA	NA
05	Bihar	66.72	50.68	16.05	29.01	16.00	13.01
06	Chandigarh	74.02	44.99	29.03	74.33	18.20	56.13
07	Dadra and Nagar Haveli	71.35	59.43	11.92	35.43	29.64	5.79
08	Delhi	75.45	49.46	25.99	62.78	18.71	44.07
09	Goa, Daman & Diu	78.14	61.50	16.64	49.49	33.60	15.89
10	Gujarat	77.88	65.88	12.00	45.77	31.75	14.02
11	Haryana	74.06	57.19	16.87	65.46	26.17	39.29
12	Himachal Pradesh	79.79	55.85	23.94	67.43	31.85	35.58
13	Jammu & Kashmir	56.17	40.64	15.53	56.37	28.44	27.93
14	Karnataka	71.43	56.77	14.66	37.49	26.62	10.87
15	Kerala	92.54	62.35	30.19	75.27	54.18	21.09
16	Lakshadweep	85.39	75.41	9.98	65.41	52.47	12.94
17	Madhya Pradesh	72.72	52.68	20.04	27.52	14.81	12.71
18	Maharashtra	79.44	64.14	15.30	49.38	32.79	16.59
19	Manipur	71.26	53.79	17.47	30.95	22.63	8.32
20	Meghalaya	76.15	55.71	20.43	64.21	39.43	24.78
21	Mizoram	92.94	79.09	13.85	88.75	77.36	11.38
22	Nagaland	76.74	64.13	12.62	65.68	52.98	12.69
23	Odisha	72.41	58.30	14.11	23.52	12.94	10.59
24	Pondicherry	79.91	68.07	11.84	47.90	34.40	13.50
25	Punjab	66.24	51.29	14.95	68.89	24.49	44.40
26	Rajasthan	80.28	31.46	48.82	32.56	15.15	17.42
27	Sikkim	68.37	55.15	13.22	59.07	42.34	16.72
28	Tamil Nadu	85.13	71.92	13.21	49.11	40.03	9.08
29	Tripura	88.91	62.05	26.86	71.77	34.55	37.22
30	Uttar Pradesh	60.05	42.83	17.23	45.22	17.20	28.01
31	West Bengal	69.36	54.24	15.12	49.69	28.12	21.57

Sl. No.	State / Union Territories	1991					
		Male			Female		
		L	BM	AM	L	BM	AM
	India	77.23	55.54	21.69	53.39	30.45	22.95
01	Andaman & Nicobar	82.48	65.07	17.41	83.37	36.84	46.53
02	Andhra Pradesh	69.35	47.91	21.44	32.37	18.79	13.58
03	Arunachal Pradesh	74.71	55.54	19.17	59.10	35.58	23.52
04	Assam	81.50	59.59	21.91	67.99	36.26	31.73
05	Bihar	71.16	47.98	23.17	41.98	20.32	21.67
06	Chandigarh	79.25	44.33	34.91	79.29	18.37	60.92
07	Dadra and Nagar Haveli	85.08	60.41	24.66	55.28	29.86	25.42
08	Delhi	78.13	46.52	31.61	70.63	16.86	53.77
09	Goa, Daman & Diu	82.35	62.27	20.08	79.48	50.81	28.67
10	Gujarat	81.43	63.21	18.22	56.39	30.46	25.93
11	Haryana	77.72	55.26	22.46	71.79	23.02	48.77
12	Himachal Pradesh	85.97	56.01	29.96	76.35	32.58	43.77
13	Jammu & Kashmir	NA	NA	NA	NA	NA	NA
14	Karnataka	77.09	55.65	21.44	49.33	31.28	18.05
15	Kerala	95.33	80.80	14.52	85.81	61.77	24.04
16	Lakshadweep	92.03	80.53	11.50	88.02	71.77	16.24
17	Madhya Pradesh	77.12	49.29	27.82	37.06	17.41	19.65
18	Maharashtra	84.20	63.63	20.58	58.44	34.77	23.68
19	Manipur	78.35	54.72	23.63	46.40	28.97	17.43
20	Meghalaya	82.91	60.67	22.24	75.01	43.12	31.89
21	Mizoram	94.56	82.82	11.74	92.45	84.24	8.21
22	Nagaland	83.11	66.53	16.58	78.76	58.72	20.04
23	Odisha	77.59	57.10	20.48	40.53	19.12	21.41
24	Pondicherry	85.43	65.94	19.49	61.65	40.44	21.22
25	Punjab	72.80	54.50	18.30	76.48	25.89	50.59
26	Rajasthan	74.94	51.12	23.82	40.83	16.84	23.99
27	Sikkim	79.95	60.63	19.32	76.03	47.86	28.17
28	Tamil Nadu	83.84	67.40	16.44	56.82	41.45	15.37
29	Tripura	86.62	60.18	26.44	80.43	40.46	39.97
30	Uttar Pradesh	64.32	41.27	23.05	47.63	18.94	28.69
31	West Bengal	77.96	55.88	22.08	58.46	31.74	26.71

Sl. No.	State / Union Territories	2001					
		Male			Female		
		L	BM	AM	L	BM	AM
	India	84.89	35.55	46.57	63.58	24.71	35.59
01	Andaman & Nicobar	88.63	45.05	42.84	82.74	20.08	61.82
02	Andhra Pradesh	79.62	28.08	49.15	51.32	19.96	28.89
03	Arunachal Pradesh	83.91	36.92	45.65	62.95	23.05	38.36
04	Assam	88.62	37.29	50.04	74.41	21.76	51.09
05	Bihar	77.38	26.92	46.84	46.92	14.21	29.66
06	Chandigarh	83.35	26.62	55.73	74.98	10.99	62.76
07	Dadra and Nagar Haveli	91.19	32.30	57.27	68.13	24.30	42.80
08	Delhi	85.51	30.68	53.85	72.47	13.78	57.43
09	Goa, Daman & Diu	88.71	32.64	54.60	73.68	20.66	51.68
10	Gujarat	87.32	41.36	45.24	62.41	25.80	35.40
11	Haryana	84.47	30.48	53.07	66.11	14.81	50.01
12	Himachal Pradesh	90.60	26.97	62.53	81.97	15.33	65.38
13	Jammu & Kashmir	77.23	23.21	51.61	70.19	11.04	55.75
14	Karnataka	84.21	32.64	50.55	62.08	25.39	35.51
15	Kerala	96.67	53.37	42.40	90.10	38.70	50.05
16	Lakshadweep	96.89	53.62	37.51	94.86	35.99	50.20
17	Madhya Pradesh	85.99	38.12	46.70	54.30	21.99	30.53
18	Maharashtra	89.74	37.28	50.73	68.88	25.95	41.36
19	Manipur	88.39	30.70	55.64	65.69	20.11	43.74
20	Meghalaya	87.70	39.77	46.49	81.33	30.92	48.83
21	Mizoram	96.35	66.49	28.34	96.68	68.85	26.41
22	Nagaland	86.05	38.30	45.58	81.39	25.62	53.77
23	Odisha	86.54	36.34	49.08	56.26	18.71	36.14
24	Pondicherry	90.67	39.92	49.15	70.64	29.44	39.39
25	Punjab	80.78	28.99	50.80	71.06	17.23	51.87
26	Rajasthan	85.56	38.33	43.47	52.57	18.82	30.09
27	Sikkim	87.08	42.43	43.32	79.61	24.75	53.73
28	Tamil Nadu	88.01	38.72	37.50	64.29	31.05	23.41
29	Tripura	92.23	53.93	37.54	81.85	40.39	40.51
30	Uttar Pradesh	75.02	29.08	43.24	56.77	17.38	35.68
31	West Bengal	84.64	42.44	40.51	63.52	29.81	31.64

Table 2.6.7. Percentage Distribution of Marginal workers according to education, India and States, 1981-2001

Sl. No.	*State / Union Territories*	*1981*					
		Male			*Female*		
		L	*BM*	*AM*	*L*	*BM*	*AM*
	India	66.79	61.36	5.42	12.40	12.18	0.22
01	Andaman & Nicobar	65.52	57.77	7.75	59.70	35.03	24.66
02	Andhra Pradesh	39.37	34.89	4.48	7.20	6.31	0.89
03	Arunachal Pradesh	30.14	26.01	4.13	3.94	3.38	0.56
04	Assam	NA	NA	NA	NA	NA	NA
05	Bihar	38.08	34.09	3.98	4.71	3.72	0.99
06	Chandigarh	71.80	44.93	26.87	66.46	16.73	49.72
07	Dadra and Nagar Haveli	40.11	36.58	3.53	9.04	8.28	0.76
08	Delhi	74.72	49.57	25.16	59.62	18.24	41.38
09	Goa, Daman & Diu	69.29	58.62	10.67	33.69	26.41	7.28
10	Gujarat	58.71	53.93	4.78	20.24	17.74	2.50
11	Haryana	50.42	44.08	6.33	21.93	12.86	9.08
12	Himachal Pradesh	53.58	47.68	5.90	22.87	20.58	2.29
13	Jammu & Kashmir	35.89	30.72	5.17	16.96	10.97	5.99
14	Karnataka	51.64	46.11	5.52	16.68	14.70	1.98
15	Kerala	85.44	75.03	10.41	59.31	50.86	8.45
16	Lakshadweep	85.00	76.97	8.03	62.46	54.93	7.53
17	Madhya Pradesh	42.31	36.57	5.74	6.83	5.75	1.09
18	Maharashtra	63.55	56.50	7.06	33.55	31.55	2.00
19	Manipur	56.06	48.19	7.87	20.74	18.27	2.47
20	Meghalaya	41.87	37.66	4.21	26.83	24.41	2.42
21	Mizoram	81.26	75.69	5.57	68.83	66.81	2.02
22	Nagaland	49.52	45.26	4.26	20.88	20.08	0.80
23	Odisha	50.79	48.52	2.27	7.24	5.97	1.27
24	Pondicherry	70.09	62.68	7.41	27.02	21.17	5.85
25	Punjab	47.32	40.90	6.41	49.00	21.01	28.00
26	Rajasthan	44.09	28.62	15.47	5.64	3.62	2.02
27	Sikkim	46.83	42.41	4.43	14.82	13.30	1.52
28	Tamil Nadu	63.42	58.24	5.18	20.95	19.27	1.69
29	Tripura	56.02	50.69	5.33	20.07	14.59	5.48
30	Uttar Pradesh	39.53	33.44	6.09	10.18	6.75	3.43
31	West Bengal	53.99	47.39	6.61	16.65	11.43	5.23

Sl. No.	State / Union Territories	1991					
		Male			Female		
		L	BM	AM	L	BM	AM
	India	64.90	57.72	7.17	20.45	19.66	0.79
01	Andaman & Nicobar	72.27	61.63	10.64	41.88	40.14	1.74
02	Andhra Pradesh	44.78	36.62	8.16	15.86	15.33	0.53
03	Arunachal Pradesh	44.12	36.31	7.81	15.37	14.84	0.53
04	Assam	53.57	47.29	6.28	30.58	29.66	0.92
05	Bihar	42.79	35.84	6.95	9.24	8.83	0.41
06	Chandigarh	76.79	45.70	31.09	46.69	32.18	14.51
07	Dadra and Nagar Haveli	45.80	39.06	6.74	10.34	9.97	0.37
08	Delhi	77.68	47.26	30.42	39.90	27.56	12.35
09	Goa, Daman & Diu	79.33	59.34	19.99	52.71	37.11	15.60
10	Gujarat	66.36	57.30	9.06	25.01	24.27	0.74
11	Haryana	61.05	51.59	9.46	16.32	15.53	0.79
12	Himachal Pradesh	67.38	59.09	8.29	37.46	36.41	1.05
13	Jammu & Kashmir	NA	NA	NA	NA	NA	NA
14	Karnataka	58.72	49.26	9.46	26.79	26.03	0.76
15	Kerala	92.80	83.40	9.39	79.64	76.68	2.96
16	Lakshadweep	90.83	79.73	11.10	70.78	68.95	1.83
17	Madhya Pradesh	50.88	40.26	10.62	10.72	10.25	0.47
18	Maharashtra	72.13	58.55	13.58	36.96	35.81	1.16
19	Manipur	63.74	51.17	12.57	27.34	23.53	3.81
20	Meghalaya	48.20	40.72	7.48	28.98	28.44	0.54
21	Mizoram	83.67	76.16	7.51	86.66	84.89	1.77
22	Nagaland	57.90	51.11	6.80	47.11	44.48	2.62
23	Odisha	58.45	50.86	7.59	12.79	12.60	0.19
24	Pondicherry	79.11	64.37	14.73	29.71	28.36	1.36
25	Punjab	58.54	50.06	8.48	26.12	25.19	0.93
26	Rajasthan	47.23	38.43	8.80	6.20	5.95	0.25
27	Sikkim	55.67	49.14	6.53	24.73	23.82	0.91
28	Tamil Nadu	67.03	58.82	8.21	32.20	31.00	1.20
29	Tripura	73.80	67.93	5.87	25.01	24.19	0.81
30	Uttar Pradesh	48.42	38.29	10.13	12.74	11.61	1.14
31	West Bengal	60.45	50.25	10.20	32.61	31.28	1.33

Sl. No.	State / Union Territories	2001					
		Male			Female		
		L	BM	AM	L	BM	AM
	India	65.22	44.06	17.95	32.15	24.45	5.11
01	Andaman & Nicobar	82.76	64.89	17.25	61.23	51.21	9.52
02	Andhra Pradesh	53.75	34.14	15.88	26.68	20.83	3.32
03	Arunachal Pradesh	53.89	41.36	10.70	30.53	25.05	4.20
04	Assam	65.38	44.65	18.84	45.30	32.39	11.57
05	Bihar	50.85	28.76	18.18	15.50	10.80	3.07
06	Chandigarh	76.70	40.09	35.85	63.09	26.11	36.12
07	Dadra and Nagar Haveli	47.62	38.13	8.81	18.41	14.16	3.99
08	Delhi	72.98	43.99	27.84	53.54	27.54	24.75
09	Goa, Daman & Diu	78.27	49.79	26.61	55.99	38.78	15.54
10	Gujarat	70.34	49.90	19.27	35.12	27.64	6.86
11	Haryana	70.46	45.23	24.03	37.27	27.65	8.55
12	Himachal Pradesh	85.33	50.57	33.53	61.69	42.29	18.30
13	Jammu & Kashmir	53.29	35.15	14.07	23.87	15.67	5.15
14	Karnataka	64.67	40.62	22.04	35.10	26.60	7.30
15	Kerala	92.01	66.67	24.04	79.05	58.36	19.21
16	Lakshadweep	90.71	75.17	12.07	81.59	63.05	9.62
17	Madhya Pradesh	66.65	50.07	12.56	30.87	23.80	1.96
18	Maharashtra	78.46	50.58	25.75	50.57	39.42	9.34
19	Manipur	77.11	42.20	32.22	49.87	28.78	19.11
20	Meghalaya	56.77	46.12	7.52	48.83	41.82	4.44
21	Mizoram	92.70	73.66	17.59	85.38	72.39	10.13
22	Nagaland	70.45	47.05	21.28	59.21	42.80	14.37
23	Odisha	63.97	46.04	15.48	23.88	19.95	2.72
24	Pondicherry	78.28	50.23	26.38	45.17	34.06	9.93
25	Punjab	61.98	38.34	22.13	45.95	29.59	14.93
26	Rajasthan	71.05	53.43	13.19	28.56	21.32	1.60
27	Sikkim	75.41	62.13	10.16	53.89	46.57	6.15
28	Tamil Nadu	71.35	44.09	17.85	41.42	29.03	6.69
29	Tripura	74.55	60.19	12.94	39.87	35.22	3.28
30	Uttar Pradesh	58.63	37.84	17.34	21.67	15.79	3.65
31	West Bengal	70.75	53.93	15.06	38.93	33.99	3.59

Table 2.6.8. Percentage Distribution of Marginal workers according to education (Rural), India and States, 1981-2001

Sl. No.	State / Union Territories	*1981*					
		Male			*Female*		
		L	*BM*	*AM*	*L*	*BM*	*AM*
	India	66.25	61.50	4.75	11.70	11.56	0.14
01	Andaman & Nicobar	60.94	55.74	5.20	46.49	33.33	13.16
02	Andhra Pradesh	32.71	30.83	1.89	5.54	5.37	0.17
03	Arunachal Pradesh	27.01	23.82	3.20	3.41	3.06	0.35
04	Assam	NA	NA	NA	NA	NA	NA
05	Bihar	34.34	31.93	2.41	3.34	3.02	0.31
06	Chandigarh	48.75	44.31	4.45	6.88	5.64	1.23
07	Dadra and Nagar Haveli	37.78	34.88	2.91	7.61	7.12	0.49
08	Delhi	64.20	51.11	13.09	18.40	12.06	6.34
09	Goa, Daman & Diu	64.50	57.06	7.44	28.14	23.89	4.25
10	Gujarat	50.41	48.76	1.66	15.68	15.24	0.44
11	Haryana	43.67	40.34	3.33	11.83	9.77	2.07
12	Himachal Pradesh	50.97	46.87	4.10	21.24	20.17	1.08
13	Jammu & Kashmir	30.73	28.20	2.53	8.31	7.13	1.18
14	Karnataka	44.63	42.34	2.29	12.77	12.46	0.31
15	Kerala	83.39	78.67	4.73	56.68	50.31	6.37
16	Lakshadweep	84.61	78.54	6.07	60.64	56.44	4.20
17	Madhya Pradesh	35.57	33.00	2.57	5.20	5.03	0.17
18	Maharashtra	55.29	52.52	2.77	31.68	31.41	0.27
19	Manipur	51.36	46.46	4.90	18.59	17.35	1.24
20	Meghalaya	35.09	34.09	1.00	23.47	23.06	0.41
21	Mizoram	77.68	74.65	3.03	65.65	65.13	0.52
22	Nagaland	43.99	41.42	2.56	19.31	18.92	0.38
23	Odisha	47.97	47.24	0.73	5.85	5.37	0.48
24	Pondicherry	60.46	57.40	3.06	14.13	13.01	1.12
25	Punjab	40.19	36.99	3.20	32.78	18.16	14.61
26	Rajasthan	29.79	27.50	2.29	2.72	2.37	0.35
27	Sikkim	41.98	39.53	2.44	11.80	11.32	0.48
28	Tamil Nadu	54.18	52.42	1.76	16.03	15.63	0.39
29	Tripura	52.40	49.44	2.96	14.13	12.30	1.84
30	Uttar Pradesh	35.26	31.49	3.77	6.20	5.56	0.64
31	West Bengal	47.93	44.69	3.25	8.66	7.39	1.27

Sl. No.	State / Union Territories	1991					
		Male			Female		
		L	BM	AM	L	BM	AM
	India	62.66	56.47	6.18	19.49	18.88	0.61
01	Andaman & Nicobar	68.27	60.29	7.99	41.50	40.07	1.44
02	Andhra Pradesh	37.05	33.07	3.98	15.04	14.68	0.37
03	Arunachal Pradesh	39.18	33.20	5.97	15.21	14.68	0.53
04	Assam	49.74	45.61	4.13	30.28	29.42	0.86
05	Bihar	38.95	34.19	4.75	8.85	8.52	0.34
06	Chandigarh	60.91	54.51	6.40	39.29	35.71	3.57
07	Dadra and Nagar Haveli	41.73	36.85	4.88	9.68	9.33	0.35
08	Delhi	73.40	54.28	19.12	35.56	30.72	4.84
09	Goa, Daman & Diu	77.28	57.35	19.93	52.80	35.41	17.38
10	Gujarat	58.79	54.34	4.45	24.40	23.76	0.64
11	Haryana	55.59	50.38	5.21	15.93	15.26	0.67
12	Himachal Pradesh	65.33	59.43	5.91	37.01	36.16	0.84
13	Jammu & Kashmir	NA	NA	NA	NA	NA	NA
14	Karnataka	51.19	46.64	4.55	26.11	25.49	0.62
15	Kerala	91.89	84.33	7.56	79.26	76.56	2.70
16	Lakshadweep	89.03	78.54	10.49	64.71	62.94	1.76
17	Madhya Pradesh	43.86	37.84	6.01	10.14	9.81	0.34
18	Maharashtra	64.75	55.44	9.31	35.87	35.10	0.76
19	Manipur	59.07	50.03	9.03	26.85	23.54	3.31
20	Meghalaya	40.94	36.54	4.40	27.15	26.85	0.31
21	Mizoram	75.13	70.94	4.19	77.91	77.11	0.80
22	Nagaland	51.93	47.45	4.48	46.71	44.18	2.54
23	Odisha	55.70	49.96	5.74	12.57	12.41	0.16
24	Pondicherry	69.12	61.91	7.21	27.16	26.37	0.79
25	Punjab	52.79	48.27	4.52	25.53	24.71	0.81
26	Rajasthan	39.32	34.81	4.51	5.79	5.62	0.18
27	Sikkim	52.90	47.83	5.07	23.95	23.15	0.80
28	Tamil Nadu	59.02	54.73	4.29	29.88	28.95	0.93
29	Tripura	72.16	68.92	3.24	23.93	23.37	0.57
30	Uttar Pradesh	44.75	37.61	7.14	12.04	11.15	0.89
31	West Bengal	53.09	47.88	5.21	32.13	30.94	1.19

Sl. No.	State / Union Territories	2001					
		Male			Female		
		L	BM	AM	L	BM	AM
	India	63.88	44.11	16.52	31.16	24.05	4.53
01	Andaman & Nicobar	82.47	65.94	15.88	60.80	51.71	8.61
02	Andhra Pradesh	51.10	34.12	13.19	25.80	20.57	2.71
03	Arunachal Pradesh	51.99	41.31	8.98	29.54	25.04	3.30
04	Assam	64.77	44.58	18.27	44.97	32.34	11.30
05	Bihar	50.01	28.66	17.43	15.20	10.67	2.92
06	Chandigarh	77.34	48.20	28.48	58.58	36.39	21.45
07	Dadra and Nagar Haveli	44.67	36.56	7.47	15.45	12.35	2.88
08	Delhi	77.41	45.23	31.36	55.64	33.29	21.62
09	Goa, Daman & Diu	79.82	52.82	25.11	55.99	40.86	13.40
10	Gujarat	68.89	49.84	17.88	33.93	27.06	6.28
11	Haryana	70.88	45.69	23.99	36.85	27.79	8.00
12	Himachal Pradesh	85.47	50.74	33.51	61.61	42.35	18.17
13	Jammu & Kashmir	53.05	35.99	12.98	23.21	15.68	4.52
14	Karnataka	62.45	40.87	19.42	34.22	26.41	6.61
15	Kerala	91.46	66.97	23.13	78.11	58.59	18.01
16	Lakshadweep	89.90	74.15	12.81	77.35	64.12	10.59
17	Madhya Pradesh	65.47	50.16	10.87	30.58	23.65	1.62
18	Maharashtra	77.20	51.19	23.76	49.89	39.72	8.32
19	Manipur	75.39	43.57	29.02	48.53	29.57	16.87
20	Meghalaya	54.69	45.11	6.31	47.24	40.78	3.78
21	Mizoram	87.62	75.88	9.70	76.22	67.01	5.13
22	Nagaland	70.28	47.49	20.67	58.56	42.80	13.73
23	Odisha	63.40	46.12	14.78	23.66	19.87	2.58
24	Pondicherry	71.60	48.75	21.33	38.03	31.75	5.15
25	Punjab	61.18	38.64	21.04	44.97	29.89	13.70
26	Rajasthan	70.80	54.29	12.08	28.35	21.21	1.40
27	Sikkim	76.25	63.18	9.79	53.86	46.76	5.93
28	Tamil Nadu	68.33	43.96	15.36	39.02	28.11	5.59
29	Tripura	73.31	60.01	11.82	39.06	34.76	2.94
30	Uttar Pradesh	58.47	38.28	16.69	21.02	15.53	3.30
31	West Bengal	69.72	54.52	13.45	37.62	33.60	2.71

Table 2.6.9. Percentage Distribution of Marginal workers according to education (urban), India and States, 1981-2001

Sl. No.	State / Union Territories	1981					
		Male			Female		
		L	BM	AM	L	BM	AM
	India	69.76	60.61	9.16	28.62	26.56	2.06
01	Andaman & Nicobar	77.33	63.00	14.33	84.69	38.25	46.43
02	Andhra Pradesh	66.71	51.56	15.15	24.15	15.87	8.27
03	Arunachal Pradesh	66.90	51.78	15.12	38.42	24.55	13.86
04	Assam	NA	NA	NA	NA	NA	NA
05	Bihar	66.72	50.68	16.05	29.01	16.00	13.01
06	Chandigarh	74.02	44.99	29.03	74.33	18.20	56.13
07	Dadra and Nagar Haveli	71.35	59.43	11.92	35.43	29.64	5.79
08	Delhi	75.45	49.46	25.99	62.78	18.71	44.07
09	Goa, Daman & Diu	78.14	61.50	16.64	49.49	33.60	15.89
10	Gujarat	77.88	65.88	12.00	45.77	31.75	14.02
11	Haryana	74.06	57.19	16.87	65.46	26.17	39.29
12	Himachal Pradesh	79.79	55.85	23.94	67.43	31.85	35.58
13	Jammu & Kashmir	56.17	40.64	15.53	56.37	28.44	27.93
14	Karnataka	71.43	56.77	14.66	37.49	26.62	10.87
15	Kerala	92.54	62.35	30.19	75.27	54.18	21.09
16	Lakshadweep	85.39	75.41	9.98	65.41	52.47	12.94
17	Madhya Pradesh	72.72	52.68	20.04	27.52	14.81	12.71
18	Maharashtra	79.44	64.14	15.30	49.38	32.79	16.59
19	Manipur	71.26	53.79	17.47	30.95	22.63	8.32
20	Meghalaya	76.15	55.71	20.43	64.21	39.43	24.78
21	Mizoram	92.94	79.09	13.85	88.75	77.36	11.38
22	Nagaland	76.74	64.13	12.62	65.68	52.98	12.69
23	Odisha	72.41	58.30	14.11	23.52	12.94	10.59
24	Pondicherry	79.91	68.07	11.84	47.90	34.40	13.50
25	Punjab	66.24	51.29	14.95	68.89	24.49	44.40
26	Rajasthan	80.28	31.46	48.82	32.56	15.15	17.42
27	Sikkim	68.37	55.15	13.22	59.07	42.34	16.72
28	Tamil Nadu	85.13	71.92	13.21	49.11	40.03	9.08
29	Tripura	88.91	62.05	26.86	71.77	34.55	37.22
30	Uttar Pradesh	60.05	42.83	17.23	45.22	17.20	28.01
31	West Bengal	69.36	54.24	15.12	49.69	28.12	21.57

Sl. No.	*State / Union Territories*	*1991*					
		Male			*Female*		
		L	*BM*	*AM*	*L*	*BM*	*AM*
	India	77.80	64.93	12.88	42.38	37.54	4.83
01	Andaman & Nicobar	82.48	65.07	17.41	62.61	44.35	18.26
02	Andhra Pradesh	69.35	47.91	21.44	30.34	26.86	3.48
03	Arunachal Pradesh	74.71	55.54	19.17	25.83	25.00	0.83
04	Assam	81.50	59.59	21.91	61.75	54.78	6.98
05	Bihar	71.16	47.98	23.17	27.13	23.34	3.79
06	Chandigarh	79.25	44.33	34.91	49.36	30.90	18.45
07	Dadra and Nagar Haveli	85.08	60.41	24.66	33.53	32.33	1.21
08	Delhi	78.13	46.52	31.61	42.73	25.51	17.22
09	Goa, Daman & Diu	82.35	62.27	20.08	52.18	47.80	4.38
10	Gujarat	81.43	63.21	18.22	42.84	39.23	3.61
11	Haryana	77.72	55.26	22.46	33.29	27.44	5.84
12	Himachal Pradesh	85.97	56.01	29.96	66.64	52.46	14.18
13	Jammu & Kashmir	NA	NA	NA	NA	NA	NA
14	Karnataka	77.09	55.65	21.44	42.05	38.04	4.01
15	Kerala	95.33	80.80	14.52	81.78	77.31	4.47
16	Lakshadweep	92.03	80.53	11.50	74.63	72.76	1.87
17	Madhya Pradesh	77.12	49.29	27.82	27.75	23.24	4.51
18	Maharashtra	84.20	63.63	20.58	54.00	46.76	7.24
19	Manipur	78.35	54.72	23.63	28.43	23.52	4.91
20	Meghalaya	82.91	60.67	22.24	65.22	59.97	5.25
21	Mizoram	94.56	82.82	11.74	93.56	91.03	2.53
22	Nagaland	83.11	66.53	16.58	66.22	59.46	6.76
23	Odisha	77.59	57.10	20.48	26.74	24.69	2.04
24	Pondicherry	85.43	65.94	19.49	34.83	32.34	2.49
25	Punjab	72.80	54.50	18.30	44.35	39.79	4.56
26	Rajasthan	74.94	51.12	23.82	19.69	17.03	2.66
27	Sikkim	79.95	60.63	19.32	42.86	39.29	3.57
28	Tamil Nadu	83.84	67.40	16.44	54.58	50.80	3.78
29	Tripura	86.62	60.18	26.44	66.83	56.46	10.37
30	Uttar Pradesh	64.32	41.27	23.05	28.94	22.18	6.75
31	West Bengal	77.96	55.88	22.08	46.44	41.26	5.18

Sl. No.	State / Union Territories	2001					
		Male			Female		
		L	BM	AM	L	BM	AM
	India	72.98	43.74	26.22	47.31	30.59	14.09
01	Andaman & Nicobar	84.60	58.46	25.71	72.50	38.25	33.25
02	Andhra Pradesh	66.21	34.25	28.51	37.72	24.15	10.90
03	Arunachal Pradesh	68.49	41.78	23.96	43.92	25.19	16.24
04	Assam	77.55	46.10	29.98	60.78	35.04	24.02
05	Bihar	63.39	30.34	29.32	27.91	16.30	9.21
06	Chandigarh	76.56	38.25	37.52	63.99	24.06	39.05
07	Dadra and Nagar Haveli	74.62	52.49	21.04	56.78	37.64	18.40
08	Delhi	72.46	43.84	27.43	53.14	26.44	25.35
09	Goa, Daman & Diu	75.30	43.95	29.50	55.99	31.82	22.71
10	Gujarat	78.08	50.21	26.64	53.72	36.77	16.00
11	Haryana	68.19	42.73	24.24	43.84	25.54	17.05
12	Himachal Pradesh	79.99	44.28	34.51	70.92	35.89	33.77
13	Jammu & Kashmir	55.51	27.43	24.10	35.01	15.55	15.65
14	Karnataka	73.11	39.65	31.96	45.28	28.78	15.25
15	Kerala	94.34	65.37	27.91	83.74	57.26	25.18
16	Lakshadweep	91.96	76.75	10.93	85.31	62.11	8.76
17	Madhya Pradesh	73.35	49.57	22.21	35.97	26.42	7.75
18	Maharashtra	82.20	48.76	31.63	56.60	36.74	18.46
19	Manipur	84.15	36.61	45.29	55.12	25.70	27.85
20	Meghalaya	76.01	55.54	18.73	70.07	55.66	13.23
21	Mizoram	97.46	71.58	25.00	96.13	78.72	15.99
22	Nagaland	72.06	43.03	26.89	70.21	42.90	25.22
23	Odisha	73.53	44.74	27.24	32.43	23.02	8.11
24	Pondicherry	85.21	51.77	31.61	57.37	38.02	18.12
25	Punjab	65.22	37.16	26.52	55.03	26.82	26.37
26	Rajasthan	72.69	47.77	20.40	33.30	23.68	6.30
27	Sikkim	63.83	47.53	15.30	56.11	35.07	19.64
28	Tamil Nadu	79.75	44.43	24.78	53.84	33.76	12.37
29	Tripura	87.24	62.04	24.36	66.05	50.01	14.29
30	Uttar Pradesh	59.69	34.88	21.73	35.40	21.20	10.85
31	West Bengal	76.72	50.50	24.43	56.28	39.12	15.35

3

NSS 55th Round (1999-2000) and Census 2001: A Comparison

This chapter presents a comparison of indicators like work participation rate, the incidence of child labour, and educational level of workers for the 55th round of NSS held during 1999-2000 and the Census 2001. Although these are two different data sets, one based on sample while other is a complete enumeration, a comparison is worthwhile to see the conformity or divergence in the results of these two data sets. The usual status definition of workforce employed in the NSS is comparable with the Census, which provides categories like principal and subsidiary status similar to the main and marginal workers of Census.

3.1.1 Work Participation Rates

Table 3.1.1 shows work participation rates according to NSS data and Census 2001 among the total workers. The total workers combine the principal and subsidiary workers of NSS and main and marginal workers of Census. It may be seen from Table 3.1.1 that work participation rates of both sources are very close to each other. The largest difference of two per cent is observed in respect with urban females. The NSS, provides nearly 14 per cent work participation rate of urban females compared to about 12 per cent derived from Census 2001. It has been generally alleged that Census is under enumerating the female workforce in the country, but the Census figures for rural women is very much close to that of

Table 3.1.1. Work participation rate (Total) in states and union territories of India, comparison of NSS 55th round and census 2001

State / UT	*NSS*					
	Rural			*Urban*		
	Persons	*Male*	*Female*	*Persons*	*Male*	*Female*
India	41.7	53.1	29.9	33.7	51.8	13.9
Andhra Pradesh	54.2	60.5	47.8	34.8	51.1	17.8
Arunachal Pradesh	36.9	42.2	31.0	26.7	39.9	10.0
Assam	34.9	52.9	15.1	33.2	52.2	11.2
Bihar	33.8	49.2	17.3	26.6	43.2	7.5
Goa	35.9	53.9	18.1	30.9	49.8	10.6
Gujarat	49.9	58.4	41.3	34.5	53.6	13.5
Mariana	34.6	47.5	20.2	31.4	50.6	9.8
Himachal Pradesh	50.3	53.6	47.1	32.2	49.9	13
Jammu & Kashmir	44.2	54.8	32.7	28.1	47.8	6.2
Karnataka	48.7	59.5	38.0	36.6	54.5	17.8
Kerala	38.7	55.3	23.8	37.3	55.8	20.3
Madhya Pradesh	46.2	53.6	38.2	31.9	48.8	13.4
Maharashtra	48.4	53.1	43.4	34.6	53.2	13.7
Manipur	38.0	49.5	25.3	33	44.5	21.1
Meghalaya	48.6	55.7	41.8	29.6	39.3	19.7
Mizoram	49.9	55.5	44.0	36.3	47.1	25.9
Nagaland	48.2	51.8	44.1	30.5	39.3	19.9
Odisha	42.3	55.1	29.9	31.7	47.5	14.5
Punjab	41.0	53.0	28.0	35.3	54.9	12.5
Rajasthan	44.6	50.0	38.8	32.3	48.6	13.8
Sikkim	38.0	50.2	24.1	37.5	51.9	20.0
Tamil Nadu	51.3	59.4	43.0	39.3	56.3	21.5
Tripura	30.3	50.4	7.3	29.5	49.4	7.5
Uttar Pradesh	34.5	48.1	20.1	30.4	49.0	9.4
West Bengal	34.9	53.4	16.0	35.0	56.7	11.7
A&N Islands	37.1	54.7	18.0	42.2	63.2	20.6
Chandigarh	63.5	78.4	12.8	35.1	54.7	13.6
D&N Haveli	47.0	58.2	35.4	40.4	65.6	11.2
Daman &Diu	50.3	65.5	30.0	37.6	54.9	18.6
Delhi	30.8	52.0	2.9	33.2	52.8	10.5
Lakshadweep	28.5	49.7	11.5	30.8	43.2	17.9
Pondichery	42.5	56.0	28.7	35.2	55.5	16.9

State/UT	*Census*					
	Rural			*Urban*		
	Persons	*Male*	*Female*	*Persons*	*Male*	*Female*
India	41.97	52.36	30.98	32.23	50.85	11.55
Andhra Pradesh	50.92	58.48	43.24	32.22	51.10	12.62
Arunachal Pradesh	46.47	51.13	41.33	34.16	48.99	16.69
Assam	36.45	49.77	22.28	31.98	51.03	10.29
Bihar	34.85	48.43	20.19	25.62	41.93	6.86
Goa	40.70	54.85	26.37	37.05	54.86	17.96
Gujarat	47.55	55.59	39.04	33.07	54.12	9.11
Mariana	43.13	50.88	34.18	31.52	49.52	10.27
Himachal Pradesh	50.63	54.74	46.47	36.89	54.38	14.96
Jammu & Kashmir	37.93	49.14	25.84	32.71	51.80	9.50
Karnataka	49.20	58.32	39.86	35.67	54.11	16.06
Kerala	32.56	50.22	15.88	31.65	50.78	13.55
Madhya Pradesh	47.11	53.08	40.68	30.64	47.64	11.70
Maharashtra	50.43	54.18	46.52	34.00	52.60	12.72
Manipur	46.72	50.07	43.20	38.71	45.17	32.28
Meghalaya	44.58	50.09	38.92	28.74	38.19	19.15
Mizoram	57.22	59.52	54.73	48.09	55.32	40.50
Nagaland	45.08	47.08	42.92	31.91	45.70	14.87
Odisha	40.33	53.38	27.10	30.66	49.37	9.76
Punjab	39.73	54.45	23.15	33.40	53.42	9.74
Rajasthan	45.94	50.82	40.70	29.56	47.64	9.24
Sikkim	49.75	57.75	40.67	40.49	56.27	21.42
Tamil Nadu	50.39	59.38	41.33	37.59	56.37	18.42
Tripura	37.11	50.61	22.86	32.32	51.78	12.09
Uttar Pradesh	34.10	47.84	18.89	26.92	45.08	6.19
West Bengal	37.93	54.30	20.70	33.82	54.07	11.13
A&N Islands	39.20	57.05	18.50	36.33	56.09	12.09
Chandigarh	43.41	63.96	10.32	36.97	55.12	14.06
D&N Haveli	53.85	61.29	45.10	44.74	65.74	14.35
Daman & Diu	52.03	70.89	19.76	35.31	53.83	16.48
Delhi	32.00	49.71	10.12	32.85	52.40	9.08
Lakshadweep	23.77	40.70	6.07	27.28	44.75	8.61
Pondichery	39.20	54.47	23.78	33.08	52.68	13.61

Table 3.1.2. Work participation rate (Main) in states and union territories of India, comparison of NSS 55th round and census 2001

State / UT	*NSS*					
	Rural			*Urban*		
	Persons	*Male*	*Female*	*Persons*	*Male*	*Female*
India	38.0	52.2	23.1	32.4	51.3	11.7
Andhra Pradesh	52.1	59.9	44.3	33.7	50.8	15.9
Arunachal Pradesh	34.2	40.0	27.8	26.7	39.9	10.0
Assam	30.7	50.6	8.7	31.7	50.7	9.7
Bihar	31.6	48.6	13.2	25.8	42.8	6.4
Goa	33.8	53.1	14.8	30.3	49.5	9.8
Gujarat	44.5	57.7	31.1	33.3	53.2	11.4
Mariana	26.4	47.0	3.3	29.6	50.5	5.8
Himachal Pradesh	39.0	50.4	28.1	30.4	49.8	9.6
Jammu & Kashmir	30.0	53.3	4.6	26.8	47.3	4.1
Karnataka	47.4	59.3	35.4	35.9	54.3	16.7
Kerala	33.3	52.6	15.9	33.7	53.4	15.6
Madhya Pradesh	43.4	53.1	33.1	31.1	48.3	12.2
Maharashtra	46.0	52.3	39.3	33.6	52.8	12.2
Manipur	32.8	48.7	15.3	29.1	43.6	14.2
Meghalaya	48.4	55.6	41.4	29.6	39.3	19.6
Mizoram	44.8	52.5	36.7	35.1	46.0	24.6
Nagaland	38.5	50.7	24.5	28.5	39.1	15.8
Odisha	37.0	54.0	20.3	30.0	47.2	11.2
Punjab	29.2	52.6	4.0	32.5	54.1	7.3
Rajasthan	38.7	49.6	27.2	30.1	48.3	9.3
Sikkim	37.5	49.8	23.4	37.3	51.5	20.0
Tamil Nadu	49.6	58.9	40.1	38.2	56.0	19.7
Tripura	30.1	50.2	6.9	29.1	49.0	7.2
Uttar Pradesh	30.0	46.9	12.2	28.8	48.4	6.6
West Bengal	32.3	52.4	11.6	34.0	56.1	10.2
A&N Islands	35.7	54.0	16.0	40.1	62.7	16.9
Chandigarh	62.3	78.3	8.1	33.6	53.7	11.4
D&N Haveli	46.7	58.2	34.7	40.4	65.6	11.2
Daman & Diu	48.4	65.3	25.9	37.1	54.5	18.1
Delhi	30.5	52.0	2.2	32.0	52.6	8.2
Lakshadweep	26.3	49.0	8.1	26.1	41.2	10.3
Pondichery	42.3	55.9	28.3	34.6	55.3	15.9

State / UT	*Census*					
	Rural			*Urban*		
	Persons	*Male*	*Female*	*Persons*	*Male*	*Female*
India	31.03	44.51	16.77	29.30	47.46	9.12
Andhra Pradesh	41.49	51.93	30.87	29.11	47.48	10.03
Arunachal Pradesh	39.28	45.99	31.87	31.53	46.45	13.96
Assam	26.15	41.46	9.86	29.62	48.26	8.40
Bihar	25.75	41.06	9.24	22.39	37.90	4.55
Goa	30.40	45.57	15.05	32.96	50.17	14.51
Gujarat	35.11	50.41	18.93	31.26	52.61	6.97
Mariana	30.20	42.71	15.78	28.20	45.84	7.38
Himachal Pradesh	32.13	42.30	21.88	34.40	51.64	12.78
Jammu & Kashmir	23.78	38.73	7.65	29.45	48.65	6.10
Karnataka	38.66	52.32	24.66	32.92	51.15	13.52
Kerala	25.44	40.96	10.78	27.10	44.54	10.62
Madhya Pradesh	33.30	45.23	20.44	27.12	43.88	8.47
Maharashtra	40.82	47.78	33.57	31.49	49.77	10.58
Manipur	32.69	40.26	24.74	28.50	38.45	18.58
Meghalaya	33.96	41.77	25.93	25.05	34.78	15.16
Mizoram	44.94	51.74	37.61	36.64	46.77	25.99
Nagaland	37.08	40.31	33.62	28.87	42.52	11.99
Odisha	25.82	42.55	8.86	27.56	45.93	7.03
Punjab	32.70	49.35	13.95	31.31	51.14	7.87
Rajasthan	32.26	43.70	19.99	26.29	44.15	6.22
Sikkim	39.57	50.75	26.89	37.21	51.92	19.43
Tamil Nadu	40.98	51.79	30.08	34.49	52.90	15.69
Tripura	28.08	44.49	10.76	30.02	48.92	10.37
Uttar Pradesh	23.81	39.33	6.64	23.47	40.52	4.01
West Bengal	27.91	46.00	8.87	30.90	50.61	8.82
A&N Islands	30.70	49.29	9.13	34.61	53.53	11.39
Chandigarh	41.47	61.77	8.77	35.94	53.89	13.27
D&N Haveli	44.20	56.77	29.41	42.01	64.31	9.72
Daman & Diu	48.16	68.98	12.55	33.29	52.51	13.74
Delhi	29.11	46.37	7.78	31.34	50.34	8.22
Lakshadweep	17.56	30.47	4.07	21.63	36.58	5.66
Pondichery	34.80	50.29	19.16	31.40	50.63	12.28

Table 3.1.3. Work participation rate (Marginal) in major states of India, comparison of NSS 55th round and census 2001

State/UT	*NSS*						*Ccensus*					
	Rural			*Urban*			*Rural*			*Urban*		
	Persons	*Male*	*Female*	*Persons*	*Male*	*Female*	*Persons*	*Male*	*Female*	*Persons*	*Male*	*Female*
India	2.05	0.54	3.58	0.98	0.31	1.69	9.43	6.54	12.37	3.11	3.62	2.59
Andhra Pradesh	4.81	2.40	7.48	1.61	1.56	1.67	10.30	8.31	12.42	2.36	2.77	1.89
Assam	2.39	0.55	4.36	0.83	0.50	1.20	9.09	7.37	10.95	3.23	4.03	2.31
Bihar	6.26	0.66	11.89	1.19	0.41	2.06	12.44	5.19	20.11	1.80	1.51	2.14
Gujarat	9.58	0.57	19.37	3.27	0.05	6.90	12.93	8.18	18.40	3.32	3.68	2.89
Haryana	13.78	4.99	22.02	1.90	0.15	3.79	18.49	12.45	24.59	2.49	2.74	2.18
Himachal Pradesh	14.10	1.66	27.66	1.16	0.49	1.91	14.15	10.41	18.19	3.26	3.15	3.40
Jammu & Kashmir	1.42	0.18	2.66	0.65	0.19	1.14	10.54	5.99	15.21	2.75	2.95	2.54
Karnataka	6.15	3.13	8.88	3.71	2.42	4.90	7.12	9.26	5.10	4.54	6.25	2.93
Kerala	2.95	0.60	5.49	0.91	0.52	1.34	13.81	7.85	20.24	3.52	3.77	3.24

State/UT	*NSS*						*Ccensus*					
	Rural			*Urban*			*Rural*			*Urban*		
	Persons	*Male*	*Female*	*Persons*	*Male*	*Female*	*Persons*	*Male*	*Female*	*Persons*	*Male*	*Female*
Madhya Pradesh	2.64	0.84	4.51	0.76	0.38	1.19	9.61	6.40	12.95	2.51	2.83	2.14
Maharashtra	6.29	1.02	11.36	2.09	0.38	3.95	14.51	10.83	18.24	3.10	3.44	2.73
Odisha	12.15	0.36	24.79	2.81	0.76	5.23	7.03	5.10	9.21	2.09	2.28	1.87
Punjab	6.78	0.52	13.24	2.25	0.32	4.44	13.68	7.12	20.72	3.27	3.49	3.02
Rajasthan	1.83	0.47	3.19	1.04	0.34	1.78	9.41	7.59	11.25	3.10	3.47	2.73
Tamil Nadu	5.04	1.30	8.97	1.74	0.62	2.99	10.29	8.51	12.25	3.45	4.56	2.18
Uttar Pradesh	2.26	1.00	3.57	1.02	0.56	1.51	10.02	8.30	11.83	2.92	3.47	2.31
West Bengal	2.05	0.54	3.58	0.98	0.31	1.69	9.43	6.54	12.37	3.11	3.62	2.59

the NSS. However, at the state level, while male work participation rates are more or less close to Census, this is not true for females. Particularly rural females show a marked level of divergence in the pattern of work participation, with smaller states showing a very high level of dissimilarity in these two data sets. The smaller sample size in small states may be one of the reasons for such a large differences in the participation rates. However, it may be noted that Census 2001 made special efforts like training of enumerators and through media coverage to enumerate female workers. The results are visible in very large increases in female workforce participation rates in the states of Punjab, Haryana and Rajasthan that showed very low levels of participation earlier. This has led Census figures very similar to NSS figures in rural areas and very close to urban areas at the national level. But for several states, this cannot be said to be true particularly for the smaller states.

When principal status workers of NSS are compared with main workers of Census, we find that Census gives us much lower rates of participation. On the other hand, rates of subsidiary status workers of NSS are much lower than the marginal workers of Census. Thus, we see that while total workers derived from NSS and Census are very close, the disaggregation either by states or main and marginal status are not close to each other in most of the cases (see Tables 3.1.2 and 3.1.3). Census figures show in rural areas of Himachal Pradesh (18.49) shows the highest percentage of marginal workers; but according to NSS the Jammu & Kashmir (14.1) occupies the corresponding position. The lowest percentage of workers in marginal work category has been observed in Karnataka (1.42) according to NSS data but Census shows almost 10 per cent of workers fall in marginal work category. The percentage of marginal workers is comparatively low in urban areas by both the data sets.

3.2 Share of Child Labour (5-14) in Total Workforce

We have also calculated proportion of child labour among all workers for both NSS and Census. The results are presented in Tables 3.2 to 3.4. With minor divergence, the results are comparable. Similar to Census results, NSS data also show

Table 3.2. Percentage of child workers (5-14) in total work force in major states of India

State	NSS 55th Round						2001 Census					
	Total		Rural		Urban		Total		Rural		Urban	
	Male	Female	Male	Female	Male	Female	Male	Female	Male	Female	Male	Female
India	1.8	3.2	2.1	3.3	1.1	3.0	1.5	3.0	1.7	3.2	1.0	2.2
Andhra Pradesh	4.0	6.3	4.6	6.6	2.3	4.2	2.9	5.5	3.4	5.7	1.6	3.7
Assam	1.5	2.9	1.6	2.2	1.2	10.7	3.1	5.1	3.4	5.1	1.1	6.2
Bihar	1.8	2.5	1.9	2.3	1.4	5.4	3.5	5.4	3.6	5.5	1.9	4.9
Gujarat	1.7	2.8	2.2	2.8	0.6	3.1	1.7	3.6	2.1	3.8	0.9	2.3
Mariana	1.1	0.6	1.1	0.7	1.2	0.0	2.4	4.5	2.9	4.8	1.0	2.1
Himachal Pradesh	2.4	3.1	2.5	3.2	0.7	0.1	3.1	4.2	3.4	4.3	0.6	1.4
Jammu & Kashmir	0.7	1.0	0.8	0.9	0.6	1.3	3.4	8.0	4.2	8.5	1.1	3.7
Karnataka	2.8	4.8	3.3	5.2	1.4	2.3	2.9	4.6	3.5	5.0	1.7	2.9
Kerala	0.2	0.1	0.2	0.1	0.1	0.1	0.2	0.4	0.2	0.4	0.2	0.4
Madhya Pradesh	2.4	2.7	2.7	2.8	1.0	1.6	3.3	5.5	4.0	5.9	1.1	2.4
Maharashtra	1.5	2.5	2.2	2.7	0.5	1.2	1.5	2.6	2.1	2.8	0.7	1.4
Odisha	1.6	3.5	1.8	3.7	0.6	1.0	1.9	4.3	2.0	4.4	0.9	3.0
Punjab	1.3	1.9	1.4	1.6	1.2	3.4	1.7	2.8	1.9	2.8	1.3	2.7
Rajasthan	3.0	7.9	3.5	8.3	1.3	4.1	3.8	7.8	4.6	8.1	1.2	3.5
Tamil Nadu	1.2	1.8	1.3	1.8	0.9	1.7	1.3	2.0	1.4	2.0	1.0	2.0
Uttar Pradesh	2.1	3.6	2.1	3.5	2.2	4.3	2.9	5.7	3.2	5.7	1.9	5.7
West Bengal	1.7	7.3	2.0	7.3	0.7	7.1	2.2	5.1	2.6	5.2	1.2	4.2

that rural area have higher incidence of child labour and than urban areas. Also, females show higher prevalence of child labour than males in both rural and urban areas. This is true for most of the states and union territories. Both NSS and Census figures show that urban females of Assam reveal the highest percentage of child labour in the range of 6 per cent to nearly 10 per cent estimated based on NSS data. On the other hand in Kerala has the lowest (less than 1 per cent) percentage of child labour in both rural and urban areas and among males and females (see Table 3.2). A high level (up to 8 per cent) of child labour is also observed among rural females in the states of Rajasthan and West Bengal in both the data set.

3.3. Percentage of Non Agricultural workers to Total Workers

Table 3.3 gives the information about the percentage of non-agricultural workers to total workers according to NSS 55th round and Census 2001. It may be seen from the table that in urban areas the percentage of nonagricultural workers to total workers is more than 90 per cent in most of the states, and the two data sources agree on this matter. Both according to NSS and Census the highest percentage of non-agricultural workers has been observed in Kerala. In rural areas also, Kerala tops the states with highest percentage of non-agricultural workforce. The states like Punjab, Tamil nadu, Karnataka and Assam show higher level of non-agricultural workforce in both the NSS and Census results. In the case of urban workers, NSS figures reveal that West Bengal has the highest percentage of non-agricultural workers. This is almost true according to 2001 Census as well. It is surprising to see a very high level of non-agricultural participation in the rural areas of Assam from both the sources. The Census 2001 also shows that participation in non-agricultural activities in the urban areas of Assam turned out to be one of the highest in the country as well. In general in the urban areas, the percentage of non-agricultural workers is higher from the Census than NSS except Bihar, Rajasthan, Tamil Nadu and Uttar Pradesh.

Table 3.3. Percentage of workers (Total) in non agricultural sector according to NSS (38th Round And 55th Round) and census 1981 and 2001.

State	*NSS 38th Round*			*Census 1981*			*NSS 55th Round*			*Census 2001*		
	Person			*Person*			*Person*			*Person*		
	Total	*Rural*	*Urban*	*Total*	*Rural*	*Urban*	*Total*	*Rural*	*Urban*	*Total*	*Rural*	*Urban*
India	NA	NA	NA	29.66	17.13	81.28	41.23	27.05	90.09	42.5	27.23	92.44
Andhra Pradesh	30.7	19.9	84.3	29.3	19.0	83.9	34.5	21.2	90.4	37.8	25.0	94.0
Assam	27.7	20.7	92.6	NA	NA	NA	39.8	32.4	94.1	47.6	40.9	97.9
Bihar	23.5	16.5	85.7	19.9	12.8	82.8	26.9	19.4	88.9	22.8	17.6	84.6
Gujarat	31.3	15.0	82.0	36.3	18.6	90.9	40.3	20.0	90.2	48.4	28.8	96.5
Mariana	35.9	22.9	84.0	35.8	22.0	90.0	47.0	31.6	89.4	48.7	35.2	95.2
Himachal Pradesh	17.2	13.0	87.6	24.3	19.8	90.9	30.4	26.2	89.6	31.5	26.4	97.4
Jammu &Kashmir	31.1	20.3	83.9	28.2	18.4	84.4	37.1	26.3	87.2	51.0	38.9	94.5
Karnataka	30.4	15.6	80.1	33.1	18.8	83.7	43.7	37.2	72.3	44.3	26.5	93.5
Kerala	43.7	37.2	72.3	55.8	49.4	87.9	61.3	51.5	90.4	77.2	71.3	95.1
Madhya Pradesh	20.5	9.7	84.6	22.3	12.0	85.7	26.1	12.8	84.5	28.5	14.5	90.9

State	*NSS 38th Round*			*Census 1981*			*NSS 55th Round*			*Census 2001*		
	Person			*Person*			*Person*			*Person*		
	Total	*Rural*	*Urban*	*Total*	*Rural*	*Urban*	*Total*	*Rural*	*Urban*	*Total*	*Rural*	*Urban*
Maharashtra	33.8	14.2	87.4	35.6	15.6	91.4	43.6	17.3	94.3	45.0	19.7	96.2
Odisha	26.7	20.8	83.8	23.4	17.0	83.2	29.0	21.5	86.7	35.2	27.6	93.6
Punjab	33.2	17.5	86.0	39.5	22.1	88.7	46.6	27.5	91.1	61.1	46.7	94.2
Rajasthan	22.4	13.3	72.7	27.0	16.0	85.9	34.1	22.4	86.9	34.1	22.7	94.7
Tamil Nadu	41.1	25.7	84.6	37.7	20.7	88.0	53.2	31.7	91.0	50.7	29.9	89.1
Uttar Pradesh	28.3	18.0	87.8	22.8	13.2	84.8	36.4	23.9	90.6	34.1	22.4	91.1
West Bengal	43.6	26.4	95.2	44.0	25.9	95.2	53.9	37.0	97.0	55.9	41.4	97.6

Source: The NSS information of 38th round has been taken from Chadha and Sahu (2002). The rest have been calculated from their respective sources.

3.4.1 Distribution of total workers according to educational levels

Table 3.3.1 gives an idea about the percentage distribution of total workers according to educational levels based on NSS and Census figures. Both the sources reveal that broadly one-third of the male workforce and two-third of the female workforce are found illiterate at the national level. It also very encouraging to note that nearly one-fourth of the male workforce have educational level above martic. This figure is only one-tenth of female workforce. Both the data sets broadly agree on this finding. From the NSS and Census figures, it may also be observed that the maximum illiterate workers are found in Bihar but there is nearly five percentage variation observed between the two data sets. On the other hand, as expected, the lowest percentage of illiterate male workers is observed in Kerala and there is virtually little variation between the two sources as well. Among the union territories, except Dadra and Nagar Haveli, the percentage of illiterate workers is comparatively low among male workers. In the case of above matric category, the highest percentages of male workers observed in Delhi and Chandigarh according to NSS figures and Census results also support these results. In the case of female workers, the highest percentage of workers in the educational level matric and above was observed in Chandigarh according to both the data sets. Among the EAG states, Rajasthan shows the higher percentage of workers in the educational level matric category and above both according to NSS and Census figures.

3.4.2 Distribution of rural and urban workers according to educational Level

Table 3.3.2 presents the percentage of workers by level of education in the rural areas. According to NSS nearly 17 per cent of the rural male workforce was found with educational level matric and above compared to 19 per cent as per Census 2001. Similarly, female workforce educated up to matric is in the range of 4 and 5 per cent respectively. Thus we see that both sources match more or less correctly when we compare educational level of work force in the rural areas. At the state level, Bihar shows the highest illiterate workforce and Kerala the least in the rural areas according to both the data sources.

Table 3.4.1. Percentage of Total Workers According to the Education Level in States and Union Territories, Based on NSS 55th round and Census 2001

State / Union Territories	*NSSO*					
	Males			*Females*		
	NL	*BM*	*AM*	*NL*	*BM*	*AM*
India	33.86	42.89	23.25	69.43	23.31	7.26
Andaman & Nicobar	13.67	62.33	24.00	29.71	49.05	21.24
Andhra Pradesh	45.33	34.63	20.04	77.61	17.63	4.76
Arunachal Pradesh	48.40	30.40	21.20	78.30	18.30	3.40
Assam	26.15	55.17	18.68	49.56	39.31	11.13
Bihar	50.00	30.23	19.77	88.69	8.95	2.36
Chandigarh	16.09	29.80	54.11	15.87	14.32	69.82
Dadra	35.75	37.65	26.60	71.30	24.81	3.89
Daman & Diu	12.90	44.50	42.60	43.22	42.90	13.88
Delhi	10.55	35.27	54.17	20.96	28.53	50.51
Goa	13.57	45.12	41.31	39.40	27.28	33.32
Gujarat	24.68	49.07	26.25	61.59	30.04	8.37
Mariana	26.00	39.72	34.28	67.49	22.08	10.42
Himachal Pradesh	20.35	46.17	33.47	43.28	39.78	16.94
Jammu & Kashmir	33.82	40.49	25.69	65.25	25.24	9.51
Karnataka	36.44	38.58	24.97	71.25	20.56	8.19
Kerala	5.25	67.04	27.71	15.41	61.26	23.33
Lakshadweep	6.36	70.62	23.03	17.10	63.88	19.02
Madhya Pradesh	39.95	43.00	17.04	78.95	18.15	2.90
Maharashtra	21.20	47.89	30.91	56.81	33.74	9.45
Manipur	23.16	42.71	34.13	35.42	41.55	23.03
Meghalaya	26.06	63.55	10.39	30.93	61.32	7.75
Mizoram	5.46	70.80	23.73	6.19	76.65	17.16
Nagaland	14.15	55.57	30.27	30.90	50.14	18.96
Odisha	38.94	47.95	13.11	81.71	16.18	2.12
Pondicherry	15.68	45.35	38.97	37.38	42.66	19.96
Punjab	32.81	36.33	30.86	53.78	27.99	18.23
Rajasthan	39.58	41.68	18.74	85.61	11.65	2.74
Sikkim	27.79	55.26	16.95	45.85	35.47	18.68
Tamil Nadu	24.06	50.03	25.91	57.33	32.25	10.42
Tripura	20.75	62.40	16.85	40.41	38.12	21.48
Uttar Pradesh	39.88	37.63	22.49	81.39	13.63	4.97
West Bengal	28.92	52.15	18.93	63.37	29.84	6.79

State / Union Territories	Census					
	Males			Females		
	NL	BM	AM	NL	BM	AM
India	29.50	40.71	26.61	64.30	24.07	8.65
Andaman & Nicobar	16.20	53.94	29.01	31.29	39.09	28.87
Andhra Pradesh	38.00	33.60	25.24	72.19	19.50	5.72
Arunachal Pradesh	40.86	35.28	22.37	74.45	17.90	6.45
Assam	32.67	41.96	23.32	56.72	27.63	14.00
Bihar	45.81	28.06	22.34	84.56	9.68	3.89
Chandigarh	17.39	28.44	53.21	27.28	12.97	58.56
Dadra	32.63	34.40	31.95	81.48	12.13	5.93
Daman & Diu	14.84	46.22	38.54	50.54	33.77	15.32
Delhi	15.08	31.54	52.41	30.23	15.71	52.82
Goa	13.27	39.28	45.21	35.13	29.64	33.58
Gujarat	23.88	45.52	29.71	62.57	26.77	9.88
Mariana	25.56	38.07	35.22	61.87	24.64	12.25
Himachal Pradesh	17.65	43.59	37.33	41.18	38.68	18.65
Jammu & Kashmir	40.10	28.70	28.07	72.44	14.02	10.07
Karnataka	29.89	38.29	30.17	62.12	25.50	11.08
Kerala	5.52	60.79	32.58	17.86	50.51	30.15
Lakshadweep	5.82	60.46	28.73	10.60	47.07	34.47
Madhya Pradesh	28.81	46.30	20.82	68.53	22.04	4.08
Maharashtra	17.30	44.38	36.14	50.67	35.24	12.16
Manipur	21.58	38.04	37.21	49.24	26.89	21.37
Meghalaya	37.41	42.89	16.12	48.75	38.17	9.83
Mizoram	8.88	69.79	19.13	14.05	70.75	12.68
Nagaland	35.18	37.44	24.78	52.71	31.77	13.18
Odisha	29.36	47.21	21.19	74.11	19.35	5.20
Pondicherry	13.00	42.91	42.48	43.02	30.51	24.96
Punjab	29.75	33.21	35.86	49.12	27.56	21.55
Rajasthan	29.41	45.20	20.45	72.53	18.71	2.83
Sikkim	26.30	50.27	20.73	49.35	36.74	12.40
Tamil Nadu	21.33	42.11	26.05	53.50	29.05	10.62
Tripura	22.88	58.86	16.86	57.10	34.01	7.35
Uttar Pradesh	37.36	34.84	24.54	76.50	15.03	5.82
West Bengal	26.86	50.45	20.94	59.68	30.73	8.01

Table 3.4.2. Percentage of Total Workers According to the Education Level in States and Union Territories (Rural), Based on NSS 55th round and Census 2001

State / Union Territories	*NSSO*					
	Males			*Females*		
	NL	*BM*	*AM*	*NL*	*BM*	*AM*
India	39.69	43.66	16.64	73.24	22.54	4.22
Andaman & Nicobar	14.33	65.22	20.45	31.50	56.46	12.03
Andhra Pradesh	53.08	34.48	12.44	79.97	17.14	2.89
Arunachal Pradesh	52.79	30.05	17.16	79.61	18.06	2.33
Assam	28.12	57.02	14.86	31.68	40.99	8.00
Bihar	53.39	30.01	16.60	89.71	8.80	1.48
Chandigarh	33.69	34.00	32.31	26.73	46.37	26.89
Dadra	39.19	38.69	22.13	72.13	24.61	3.26
Daman & Diu	17.16	48.64	34.20	49.95	39.98	10.06
Delhi	8.41	50.83	40.75	18.89	52.22	28.89
Goa	17.51	45.58	36.91	44.29	29.89	25.82
Gujarat	30.30	51.04	18.66	64.66	29.47	5.87
Mariana	29.31	40.28	30.41	70.85	22.20	6.95
Himachal Pradesh	21.29	47.97	30.74	43.80	40.06	16.14
Jammu & Kashmir	37.83	41.08	21.09	66.71	25.64	7.65
Karnataka	43.56	39.56	16.88	76.41	19.64	3.96
Kerala	6.19	68.39	25.42	17.55	62.92	19.53
Lakshadweep	5.98	66.89	27.13	31.84	60.28	7.88
Madhya Pradesh	45.60	43.79	10.61	80.73	17.93	1.34
Maharashtra	28.72	50.49	20.79	61.38	33.91	4.71
Manipur	27.06	46.01	26.93	39.61	43.66	16.73
Meghalaya	28.87	67.30	3.83	33.02	63.06	3.92
Mizoram	7.38	77.06	15.56	8.27	80.41	11.32
Nagaland	17.26	60.13	22.61	33.84	53.89	12.28
Odisha	42.17	48.60	9.23	83.29	15.49	1.22
Pondicherry	22.33	49.19	28.48	47.39	45.16	7.45
Punjab	40.57	34.96	24.47	57.50	28.50	14.00
Rajasthan	46.13	41.88	11.98	87.92	11.01	1.07
Sikkim	29.73	55.74	14.53	47.90	36.40	15.70
Tamil Nadu	31.06	51.94	17.01	63.37	30.73	5.90
Tripura	22.22	63.82	13.96	45.12	40.10	14.77
Uttar Pradesh	43.00	38.11	18.89	83.78	13.13	3.09
West Bengal	32.91	54.23	12.86	67.81	29.21	2.98

State / Union Territories	*Census*					
	Males			*Females*		
	NL	*BM*	*AM*	*NL*	*BM*	*AM*
India	34.71	42.47	19.49	67.86	23.80	5.39
Andaman & Nicobar	18.46	57.98	22.64	35.42	44.60	19.25
Andhra Pradesh	43.49	35.27	17.84	74.55	19.35	3.51
Arunachal Pradesh	47.47	34.76	16.25	77.96	17.34	3.55
Assam	36.09	42.65	19.08	58.68	27.88	11.79
Bihar	48.09	28.14	19.95	85.55	9.48	3.14
Chandigarh	21.30	38.98	38.96	47.98	28.01	23.09
Dadra	40.79	34.96	23.43	85.39	10.73	3.45
Daman & Diu	16.48	48.87	34.30	58.66	32.03	8.90
Delhi	16.00	36.35	46.84	40.82	24.66	33.54
Goa	14.86	45.52	37.62	39.15	34.90	24.16
Gujarat	30.44	47.87	20.72	65.79	26.55	6.93
Mariana	29.07	40.73	28.97	64.60	25.50	8.66
Himachal Pradesh	18.57	45.47	34.49	41.86	39.33	17.32
Jammu & Kashmir	45.88	30.59	20.18	76.27	14.21	6.06
Karnataka	36.44	40.85	20.77	66.59	25.41	6.68
Kerala	6.19	62.90	29.73	19.83	52.85	25.80
Lakshadweep	7.43	62.76	25.27	13.00	49.36	32.84
Madhya Pradesh	33.32	48.67	13.00	70.38	21.92	1.97
Maharashtra	22.27	49.25	25.98	54.21	36.76	7.03
Manipur	24.60	40.13	31.74	52.28	28.17	16.83
Meghalaya	42.60	43.29	10.08	52.47	38.51	5.55
Mizoram	13.71	72.03	11.36	21.86	69.55	5.24
Nagaland	39.25	37.19	20.87	55.03	31.99	10.62
Odisha	31.91	48.97	16.69	75.59	19.32	3.76
Pondicherry	19.60	47.74	31.06	57.46	30.80	10.54
Punjab	34.83	35.20	28.70	52.96	29.47	15.83
Rajasthan	33.50	47.00	14.25	73.86	18.60	1.45
Sikkim	27.75	51.19	18.20	51.09	37.45	9.93
Tamil Nadu	27.93	44.38	18.09	59.33	28.19	6.61
Tripura	25.98	59.80	12.69	61.24	33.14	4.03
Uttar Pradesh	40.07	36.14	20.41	78.91	14.70	3.83
West Bengal	31.22	53.42	13.59	64.21	30.52	3.77

Table 3.4.3. Percentage of Total Workers According to the Education Level in States and Union Territories (Urban), Based on NSS 55th round and Census 2001

State / Union Territories	*NSSO*					
	Males			*Femcles*		
	NL	*BM*	*AM*	*NL*	*BM*	*AM*
India	16.67	40.61	42.72	44.47	28.38	27.14
Andaman & Nicobar	11.95	54.81	33.24	24.96	29.41	45.63
Andhra Pradesh	23.58	35.06	41.36	61.79	20.91	17.30
Arunachal Pradesh	6.46	33.75	59.80	29.20	27.32	43.47
Assam	10.79	40.71	48.50	33.01	20.20	46.79
Bihar	25.00	31.86	43.15	73.06	11.21	15.73
Chandigarh	11.86	28.79	59.36	14.74	10.99	74.27
Dadra	11.38	30.32	58.30	49.84	29.86	20.30
Daman & Diu	5.76	37.53	56.71	30.26	48.50	21.24
Delhi	11.32	29.70	58.99	21.10	26.96	51.95
Goa	9.22	44.61	46.17	30.19	22.37	47.44
Gujarat	12.36	44.75	42.88	39.81	34.09	26.10
Mariana	17.88	38.34	43.78	51.19	21.54	27.28
Himachal Pradesh	10.67	27.63	61.70	22.80	28.84	48.36
Jammu & Kashmir	15.27	37.75	46.98	34.43	16.99	48.58
Karnataka	16.44	35.83	47.74	41.81	25.84	32.34
Kerala	2.62	63.28	34.10	8.29	55.74	35.97
Lakshadweep	6.64	73.34	20.03	9.47	65.72	24.81
Madhya Pradesh	18.70	40.04	41.26	61.33	20.34	18.33
Maharashtra	9.47	43.83	46.70	32.63	32.86	34.51
Manipur	9.67	31.29	59.04	20.57	34.02	45.41
Meghalaya	7.69	39.09	53.22	8.87	42.95	48.18
Mizoram	2.08	59.80	38.12	1.20	67.66	31.15
Nagaland	5.21	42.44	52.35	15.76	30.85	53.39
Odisha	21.11	44.39	34.50	64.10	23.79	12.11
Pondicherry	10.57	42.40	47.03	28.15	40.36	31.49
Punjab	17.66	39.02	43.31	34.20	25.29	40.51
Rajasthan	16.87	40.98	42.15	60.97	18.48	20.55
Sikkim	10.64	51.01	38.35	21.15	24.28	54.57
Tamil Nadu	10.89	46.45	42.66	35.38	37.79	26.83
Tripura	11.68	53.59	34.73	12.99	26.56	60.45
Uttar Pradesh	28.17	35.85	35.99	59.93	18.16	21.91
West Bengal	15.54	45.18	39.28	42.48	32.78	24.73

State / Union Territories	*Census*					
	Males			*Females*		
	NL	*BM*	*AM*	*NL*	*BM*	*AM*
India	15.91	36.11	45.20	39.79	25.92	31.14
Andaman & Nicobar	11.55	45.67	42.05	17.90	21.22	60.03
Andhra Pradesh	21.35	28.53	47.66	51.42	20.80	25.27
Arunachal Pradesh	16.82	37.16	44.61	40.18	23.40	34.72
Assam	11.94	37.73	49.03	27.93	24.04	46.44
Bihar	23.98	27.25	45.14	59.40	14.91	22.86
Chandigarh	16.82	26.90	55.29	25.73	11.84	61.22
Dadra	9.20	32.78	56.42	35.47	28.53	35.07
Daman & Diu	10.11	38.52	50.81	37.82	36.49	25.38
Delhi	15.01	31.21	52.79	29.38	15.00	54.35
Goa	12.60	33.17	52.65	29.06	21.69	47.81
Gujarat	12.95	41.62	44.70	39.61	28.35	30.89
Mariana	16.76	31.41	50.91	40.00	17.75	40.97
Himachal Pradesh	9.94	27.86	61.10	19.65	18.35	60.74
Jammu & Kashmir	24.13	23.47	49.89	41.37	12.52	42.58
Karnataka	16.41	33.03	49.50	40.58	25.93	32.30
Kerala	3.61	54.84	40.62	11.26	42.68	44.72
Lakshadweep	4.02	57.88	32.62	8.43	44.99	35.94
Madhya Pradesh	15.02	39.04	44.73	50.71	23.20	24.29
Maharashtra	10.67	37.89	49.71	33.17	27.75	37.54
Manipur	12.23	31.57	54.11	38.67	22.42	37.19
Meghalaya	13.24	41.04	44.26	20.83	35.67	41.99
Mizoram	3.48	67.28	27.82	3.52	72.35	22.71
Nagaland	15.02	38.66	44.15	20.66	28.79	48.54
Odisha	14.38	36.93	47.54	50.24	19.88	28.50
Pondicherry	9.54	40.39	48.47	30.64	30.26	37.34
Punjab	19.91	29.36	49.71	31.92	19.01	47.14
Rajasthan	15.40	39.03	41.75	53.56	20.36	22.53
Sikkim	14 57	42.80	41.33	22.38	25.62	50.84
Tamil Nadu	12.50	39.07	36.71	37.23	31.44	21.80
Tripura	8.05	54.38	36.82	20.40	41.76	36.78
Uttar Pradesh	26.56	29.68	41.02	50.35	18.65	27.41
West Bengal	15.89	42.98	39.43	37.96	31.71	28.32

Table 3.4.4. Percentage of Main Workers According to the Education Level in States and Union Territories, Based on NSS 55th round and Census 2001

State / Union Territories	*NSSO*					
	Males			*Females*		
	NL	*BM*	*AM*	*NL*	*BM*	*AM*
India	34.21	42.82	22.97	70.35	22.23	7.41
Andaman & Nicobar	13.84	62.51	23.65	28.99	48.41	22.60
Andhra Pradesh	45.48	34.64	19.88	78.54	16.72	4.74
Arunachal Pradesh	47.36	31.43	21.21	77.47	19.12	3.41
Assam	26.95	55.71	17.34	60.30	27.74	11.96
Bihar	50.39	30.04	19.58	89.33	8.08	2.59
Chandigarh	16.30	29.67	54.03	13.89	13.57	72.54
Dadra	35.75	37.65	26.60	71.15	24.92	3.93
Daman & Diu	12.99	44.44	42.56	42.09	45.53	12.38
Delhi	10.57	35.37	54.06	20.12	16.84	63.04
Goa	12.40	45.71	41.89	41.84	22.50	35.66
Gujarat	24.85	49.04	26.10	63.21	28.47	8.31
Mariana	25.86	39.91	34.23	56.06	19.41	24.53
Himachal Pradesh	22.04	45.88	32.08	48.82	37.81	13.37
Jammu & Kashmir	34.72	40.63	24.66	40.68	35.71	23.61
Karnataka	36.47	38.64	24.89	72.02	19.81	8.16
Kerala	5.20	67.69	27.10	16.63	59.67	23.70
Lakshadweep	6.13	70.70	23.17	16.64	53.96	29.40
Madhya Pradesh	40.20	42.93	16.87	79.14	17.99	2.87
Maharashtra	21.32	47.95	30.73	58.25	32.59	9.16
Manipur	23.56	43.36	33.08	37.52	37.75	24.73
Meghalaya	26.07	63.53	10.40	30.93	61.29	7.78
Mizoram	5.56	71.42	23.02	6.29	76.59	17.12
Nagaland	14.37	55.50	30.14	27.68	47.77	24.55
Odisha	39.26	47.94	12.80	83.03	14.07	2.89
Pondicherry	15.72	45.46	38.82	39.12	40.37	20.51
Punjab	33.06	36.19	30.75	37.75	22.74	39.51
Rajasthan	39.72	41.63	18.64	87.36	9.33	3.31
Sikkim	27.98	55.28	16.74	46.24	34.86	18.90
Tamil Nadu	24.22	49.99	25.79	58.49	31.01	10.50
Tripura	20.80	62.42	16.78	39.03	38.62	22.35
Uttar Pradesh	40.64	37.30	22.06	82.45	12.19	5.36
West Bengal	29.31	52.23	18.45	65.36	27.23	7.42

State / Union Territories	*Census*					
	Males			*Females*		
	NL	*BM*	*AM*	*NL*	*BM*	*AM*
India	28.73	40.22	27.87	61.66	23.78	11.29
Andaman & Nicobar	16.07	52.61	30.43	26.30	31.01	41.76
Andhra Pradesh	37.06	33.54	26.30	71.77	18.99	6.64
Arunachal Pradesh	40.35	34.68	23.51	75.86	15.89	7.08
Assam	32.33	41.49	24.10	58.95	22.35	16.70
Bihar	45.24	27.94	23.04	84.63	8.43	4.80
Chandigarh	17.23	28.13	53.67	26.53	11.94	60.31
Dadra	31.34	34.15	33.47	81.42	11.05	6.95
Daman & Diu	14.61	46.06	38.92	47.68	33.38	18.52
Delhi	14.56	31.00	53.48	28.30	14.31	56.15
Goa	12.54	37.74	47.95	31.16	24.90	42.34
Gujarat	23.45	45.20	30.48	60.46	25.97	12.64
Mariana	24.93	36.94	37.00	60.97	21.53	16.08
Himachal Pradesh	18.44	41.74	38.33	44.26	34.82	19.03
Jammu & Kashmir	38.76	27.39	30.92	65.77	11.04	18.99
Karnataka	29.37	38.07	30.95	60.68	24.93	13.04
Kerala	5.01	59.61	34.31	16.57	47.23	34.72
Lakshadweep	4.84	56.29	33.46	6.61	38.89	47.19
Madhya Pradesh	28.12	45.72	22.07	67.99	20.46	5.99
Maharashtra	16.88	43.77	37.18	51.15	33.63	13.25
Manipur	21.28	37.10	38.33	48.52	25.33	23.24
Meghalaya	36.42	42.34	17.58	47.59	36.42	12.42
Mizoram	9.14	69.14	19.38	13.77	69.94	13.93
Nagaland	36.03	35.99	25.31	56.11	28.62	12.84
Odisha	27.86	47.48	22.47	70.45	18.27	9.73
Pondicherry	12.52	42.51	43.36	41.09	29.93	27.43
Punjab	29.06	32.78	37.00	46.46	26.47	25.10
Rajasthan	29.48	44.02	21.50	73.59	16.18	4.03
Sikkim	26.53	48.72	22.12	50.86	32.15	15.32
Tamil Nadu	20.53	41.89	26.96	51.92	29.06	11.85
Tripura	22.57	58.70	17.34	54.29	32.89	11.13
Uttar Pradesh	36.58	34.26	25.93	73.57	13.82	9.30
West Bengal	26.50	49.93	21.82	58.28	27.43	12.47

Table 3.4.5. Percentage of Main Workers According to the Education Level in States and Union Territories (Rural), Based on NSS 55th round and Census 2001

State / Union Territories	*NSSO*					
	Males			*Females*		
	NL	*BM*	*AM*	*NL*	*BM*	*AM*
India	40.18	43.57	16.25	74.82	21.40	3.78
Andaman & Nicobar	14.53	65.61	19.86	31.27	55.21	13.52
Andhra Pradesh	53.31	34.51	12.18	80.88	16.33	2.78
Arunachal Pradesh	51.88	31.18	16.94	78.91	18.88	2.21
Assam	29.03	57.70	13.27	64.25	29.06	6.69
Bihar	53.82	29.80	16.38	90.57	7.93	1.50
Chandigarh	33.40	34.15	32.45	18.69	56.29	25.02
Dadra	39.19	38.69	22.13	71.98	24.73	3.29
Daman & Diu	17.26	48.60	34.14	48.27	44.51	7.22
Delhi	8.42	50.85	40.73	24.77	42.12	33.11
Goa	15.26	46.95	37.79	48.15	24.20	27.65
Gujarat	30.57	50.94	18.50	66.85	28.02	5.12
Mariana	29.19	40.54	30.27	68.87	21.05	10.08
Himachal Pradesh	23.25	47.81	28.94	49.71	38.22	12.07
Jammu & Kashmir	38.97	41.28	19.75	42.56	41.08	16.36
Karnataka	43.57	39.62	16.81	77.24	19.01	3.75
Kerala	6.10	69.16	24.75	19.55	61.22	19.23
Lakshadweep	6.14	66.53	27.33	30.89	59.32	9.79
Madhya Pradesh	45.94	43.64	10.42	80.96	17.82	1.22
Maharashtra	28.98	50.57	20.45	63.08	32.69	4.23
Manipur	27.52	46.79	25.68	41.65	40.54	17.81
Meghalaya	28.89	67.28	3.84	33.04	63.05	3.91
Mizoram	7.56	77.70	14.75	8.77	80.89	10.34
Nagaland	17.58	60.18	22.24	32.80	52.73	14.48
Odisha	42.56	48.58	8.86	84.86	13.55	1.59
Pondicherry	22.39	49.31	28.30	48.01	45.35	6.63
Punjab	40.79	34.82	24.39	46.54	27.81	25.64
Rajasthan	46.31	41.77	11.91	90.32	8.61	1.07
Sikkim	29.93	55.76	14.31	48.38	35.76	15.86
Tamil Nadu	31.31	51.85	16.84	65.04	29.18	5.78
Tripura	22.31	63.79	13.89	43.55	40.82	15.63
Uttar Pradesh	43.96	37.75	18.29	85.50	11.47	3.03
West Bengal	33.42	54.31	12.27	70.55	26.19	3.26

State / Union Territories	*Census*					
	Males			*Females*		
	NL	*BM*	*AM*	*NL*	*BM*	*AM*
India	34.46	42.18	20.02	67.02	23.59	6.12
Andaman & Nicobar	18.61	56.70	23.73	31.57	37.38	30.06
Andhra Pradesh	42.81	35.42	18.42	74.68	18.87	3.83
Arunachal Pradesh	47.41	34.03	17.07	80.15	15.09	3.62
Assam	36.25	42.27	19.24	63.13	22.43	12.39
Bihar	47.75	28.05	20.40	86.41	8.10	3.39
Chandigarh	21.25	38.62	39.37	49.35	26.25	23.44
Dadra	39.61	34.83	24.72	85.83	9.87	3.76
Daman & Diu	16.25	48.74	34.66	55.76	33.18	10.60
Delhi	15.52	35.70	47.96	39.75	22.07	37.11
Goa	13.81	44.03	40.15	36.58	29.86	31.79
Gujarat	30.37	47.66	21.01	65.51	26.01	7.62
Mariana	29.06	39.77	29.93	66.30	22.85	9.42
Himachal Pradesh	19.76	43.91	34.78	45.77	35.94	16.36
Jammu & Kashmir	45.59	29.17	22.07	75.16	11.04	9.39
Karnataka	36.31	40.84	20.93	67.09	24.80	6.72
Kerala	5.66	61.98	31.23	18.86	50.17	29.44
Lakshadweep	6.52	58.88	29.51	8.20	42.02	43.92
Madhya Pradesh	33.11	48.41	13.38	71.33	20.23	2.32
Maharashtra	22.20	48.99	26.28	55.98	35.48	6.47
Manipur	24.60	39.29	32.40	52.99	26.97	16.79
Meghalaya	42.08	42.94	10.80	52.32	37.32	6.47
Mizoram	13.91	71.45	11.61	21.01	70.69	5.28
Nagaland	40.83	35.49	20.91	58.98	28.85	9.72
Odisha	30.72	49.69	17.18	74.09	18.22	6.14
Pondicherry	18.86	47.65	31.88	56.39	30.58	11.82
Punjab	34.42	34.85	29.49	51.66	29.21	17.16
Rajasthan	34.20	45.80	14.60	76.12	15.92	1.51
Sikkim	28.30	49.54	19.36	53.56	32.81	11.93
Tamil Nadu	27.38	44.44	18.49	58.72	28.22	6.99
Tripura	25.89	59.77	12.80	61.56	31.38	5.21
Uttar Pradesh	39.75	35.68	21.21	78.78	13.21	4.78
West Bengal	31.39	53.22	13.62	66.58	26.52	5.15

It may also be observed from Table 3.3.3 that the percentage of illiterate male workers is comparatively low in urban areas in almost all states and union territories. Again among major states, Kerala shows the lowest percentage of illiterate male workers according to both data sources. On the other hand, the highest percentage of illiterate male has been observed in Uttar Pradesh from both the data sources. The NSS data reveals that among the north-eastern states, Mizoram shows the lowest percentage of illiterate male workers in both rural and urban areas, and this is as low as observed in the state of Kerala.

3.4.4 Distribution of main/principal status workers according to education levels

Tables 3.3.4 through 3.4.6 present the educational levels of main workers in the rural and urban areas. The results show the similar trend as revealed by the tables related to all workers described above. However, the educational level of subsidiary/ marginal workers presented in Table 3.4.7 reveals that their educational levels are much lower than the main workers from both NSS and Census sources. But among the subsidiary/marginal workers, the divergence between the two data sources is enormously wide. For example, the states like Punjab, Tamil Nadu and west Bengal show that the percentage of illiterate male workers from NSS is not more than 6 per cent, whereas Census shows this figure as high as more than 25 per cent. The gap between Census and NSS is very wide in most of the states in respect with male workers compared to female workers. It may be remembered here that the work participation rates of main /principal and marginal/subsidiary status also differed markedly between two data sources as discussed in earlier. It is possible that many marginal workers reported in the Census are classified as principal status workers in the NSS. This not only lowers the share of subsidiary workers in the NSS, but affects their educational distribution as well. However, most importantly it must be emphasised that the NSS and Census employs two different approaches of enumerating the marginal/subsidiary workforce, and this may be kept in mind while jumping into the conclusion about the accurateness of the either sources. The definitional differences are as follows:

Table 3.4.6. Percentage of Main Workers According to the Education Level in States and Union Territories (Urban), Based on NSS 55th round and Census 2001

State / Union Territories	*NSSO*					
	Males			*Females*		
	NL	*BM*	*AM*	*NL*	*BM*	*AM*
India	16.74	40.62	42.64	44.05	27.12	28.83
Andaman & Nicobar	12.05	54.48	33.46	22.88	30.22	46.89
Andhra Pradesh	23.59	35.02	41.39	62.45	19.36	18.19
Arunachal Pradesh	6.46	33.75	59.80	29.20	27.32	43.47
Assam	10.95	40.46	48.59	31.83	18.28	49.90
Bihar	25.08	31.77	43.15	72.70	9.99	17.31
Chandigarh	12.11	28.57	59.32	13.55	10.49	75.97
Dadra	11.38	30.32	58.30	49.84	29.86	20.30
Daman & Diu	5.81	37.44	56.75	31.50	47.28	21.22
Delhi	11.35	29.80	58.85	19.82	15.23	64.95
Goa	9.31	44.36	46.34	32.38	19.95	47.66
Gujarat	12.37	44.91	42.72	41.29	31.17	27.54
Mariana	17.79	38.38	43.83	37.41	17.03	45.56
Himachal Pradesh	10.70	27.71	61.59	22.44	25.50	52.07
Jammu & Kashmir	15.43	37.65	46.92	32.23	11.42	56.35
Karnataka	16.50	35.88	47.62	42.41	24.37	33.22
Kerala	2.74	63.66	33.60	8.57	55.39	36.04
Lakshadweep	6.11	73.82	20.08	7.44	50.53	42.03
Madhya Pradesh	18.59	40.28	41.14	61.97	19.61	18.42
Maharashtra	9.47	43.90	46.64	33.18	32.07	34.74
Manipur	9.85	31.45	58.70	24.57	29.02	46.41
Meghalaya	7.69	39.09	53.22	8.89	42.85	48.26
Mizoram	2.14	60.68	37.18	1.27	67.88	30.86
Nagaland	5.23	42.19	52.58	7.97	28.72	63.31
Odisha	21.28	44.40	34.32	65.66	19.07	15.27
Pondicherry	10.60	42.50	46.90	30.44	35.50	34.06
Punjab	17.88	38.88	43.24	27.59	16.88	55.53
Rajasthan	16.96	41.15	41.88	56.19	16.88	26.93
Sikkim	10.74	51.02	38.24	21.15	24.28	54.57
Tamil Nadu	10.92	46.50	42.59	34.46	37.71	27.82
Tripura	11.42	53.93	34.65	13.38	26.20	60.42
Uttar Pradesh	28.40	35.65	35.95	59.47	17.62	22.91
West Bengal	15.64	45.35	39.01	44.01	31.48	24.51

State / Union Territories	*Census*					
	Males			*Females*		
	NL	*BM*	*AM*	*NL*	*BM*	*AM*
India	15.11	35.55	46.57	36.42	24.71	35.59
Andaman & Nicobar	11.37	45.05	42.84	17.26	20.08	61.82
Andhra Pradesh	20.38	28.08	49.15	48.68	19.96	28.89
Arunachal Pradesh	16.09	36.92	45.65	37.05	23.05	38.36
Assam	11.38	37.29	50.04	25.59	21.76	51.09
Bihar	22.62	26.92	46.84	53.08	14.21	29.66
Chandigarh	16.65	26.62	55.73	25.02	10.99	62.76
Dadra	8.81	32.30	57.27	31.87	24.30	42.80
Daman & Diu	9.89	38.32	51.24	38.02	33.63	27.99
Delhi	14.49	30.68	53.85	27.53	13.78	57.43
Goa	11.41	32.14	54.90	25.35	19.59	53.65
Gujarat	12.68	41.36	45.24	37.59	25.80	35.40
Mariana	15.53	30.48	53.07	33.89	14.81	50.01
Himachal Pradesh	9.40	26.97	62.53	18.03	15.33	65.38
Jammu & Kashmir	22.77	23.21	51.61	29.81	11.04	55.75
Karnataka	15.79	32.64	50.55	37.92	25.39	35.51
Kerala	3.33	53.37	42.40	9.90	38.70	50.05
Lakshadweep	3.11	53.62	37.51	5.14	35.99	50.20
Madhya Pradesh	14.01	38.12	46.70	45.70	21.99	30.53
Maharashtra	10.26	37.28	50.73	31.12	25.95	41.36
Manipur	11.61	30.70	55.64	34.31	20.11	43.74
Meghalaya	12.30	39.77	46.49	18.67	30.92	48.83
Mizoram	3.65	66.49	28.34	3.32	68.85	26.41
Nagaland	13.95	38.30	45.58	18.61	25.62	53.77
Odisha	13.46	36.34	49.08	43.74	18.71	36.14
Pondicherry	9.33	39.92	49.15	29.36	29.44	39.39
Punjab	19.22	28.99	50.80	28.94	17.23	51.87
Rajasthan	14.44	38.33	43.47	47.43	18.82	30.09
Sikkim	12.92	42.43	43.32	20.39	24.75	53.73
Tamil Nadu	11.99	38.72	37.50	35.71	31.05	23.41
Tripura	7.77	53.93	37.54	18.15	40.39	40.51
Uttar Pradesh	24.98	29.08	43.24	43.23	17.38	35.68
West Bengal	15.36	42.44	40.51	36.48	29.81	31.64

Table 3.4.7. Percentage of subsidiary workers (Total) according to educational classification in major states according to NSS 55th round and Census 2001

State	*NSS 55th Round*						*Census 2001*					
	Male			*Female*			*Male*			*Female*		
	NL	*BM*	*AM*	*NL*	*BM*	*AM*	*NL*	*BM*	*AM*	*NL*	*BM*	*AM*
Andhra Pradesh	26.80	33.25	39.95	66.53	28.48	4.99	46.25	34.14	15.88	73.32	20.83	3.32
Assam	8.68	43.25	48.06	35.41	54.55	10.04	34.62	44.65	18.84	54.7	32.39	11.57
Bihar	16.15	47.13	36.72	86.71	11.65	1.65	49.15	28.76	18.18	84.5	10.80	3.07
Gujarat	8.00	51.83	40.18	57.16	34.32	8.52	29.66	49.90	19.27	64.88	27.64	6.86
Haryana	41.34	18.18	40.48	70.14	22.70	7.16	29.54	45.23	24.03	62.73	27.65	8.55
Karnataka	27.00	21.37	51.63	60.79	30.72	8.49	35.33	40.62	22.04	64.9	26.60	7.30
Kerala	6.10	55.41	38.49	12.97	64.43	22.60	7.99	66.67	24.04	20.95	58.36	19.21
Madhya Pradesh	17.97	49.35	32.67	77.79	19.13	3.08	33.35	50.07	12.56	69.13	23.80	1.96
Maharashtra	11.93	42.96	45.11	44.12	43.88	12.00	21.54	50.58	25.75	49.43	39.42	9.34
Odisha	20.21	48.82	30.97	79.33	19.94	0.73	36.03	46.04	15.48	76.12	19.95	2.72
Punjab	5.09	52.39	42.52	57.66	29.26	13.08	38.02	38.34	22.13	54.05	29.59	14.93
Rajasthan	24.97	46.64	28.39	82.15	16.23	1.61	24.59	62.13	10.16	46.11	46.57	6.15
Tamil Nadu	1.92	55.49	42.59	43.46	47.19	9.35	25.45	60.19	12.94	60.13	35.22	3.28
Uttar Pradesh	8.81	50.90	40.29	79.92	15.65	4.43	41.37	37.84	17.34	78.33	15.79	3.65
West Bengal	5.82	47.38	46.80	56.42	38.99	4.59	29.25	53.93	15.06	61.07	33.99	3.59

According to Census, marginal workers are those who are engaged in any economic activity less than six months in the year preceding the date of Census. But NSS defines subsidiary workers on the following two criteria :

1. A person could be engaged for a relatively longer period during the last 365 days in one economic/non-economic activity and for a relatively shorter period in another economic activity.
2. A person could be pursuing one economic activity/non-economic activity almost throughout the year in the principal usual activity status, and simultaneously pursue another economic activity for a relatively shorter period in a subsidiary capacity (NSS report No. 458).

4

District Level Trends and Patterns

In the second chapter it has been observed that there are significant differences between states and union territories with respect to the indicators of work participation and the structure of the workforce related to age composition, sex, residence and educational levels. In this chapter, we are providing the crude work participation rates and share of non-agricultural sector by sex, rural and urban areas. The results have been plotted on district level maps, and the variations and very much obvious. We have also calculated co-efficient of variations to show whether inter-district variability over the Census year 1981 to 2001 is increasing or declining.

4.1. Work Participation Rates at the District Level

Among the major states, the crude work participation was found to be as high as 57 per cent in Erode (Periyar) district of Tamil Nadu and as low as 24 per cent in Mallapuram district of Kerala in 2001. Similar low participation is also observed in the districts like Siwan (27 per cent) and Saran (27 per cent) of Bihar. Outside the major states, the most of the districts of Himachal Pradesh shows a very high participation rates ranging from 63 per cent n Kangra to 86 per cent in Kinnaur. The figures of the districts of Himachal Pradesh stand outliers when we study the geographical variation in work participation rates in the country.

Malappuram not only showed the lowest rate in the country but it has declined from 25 per cent in 1981 to 24 per cent in

2001. The female work participation in Mallapuram was also one of lowest (7 per cent) in country. Such low participation of females is also seen in several districts of Uttar Pradesh namely in Shahjahanpur, Pilibhit, Mainpuri and Etah etc. In other two states of south India, namely Andhra Pradesh and Karnataka, the participation rates was as high as 52 per cent in Vizianagaram in Andhra Pradesh and 51 per cent in Timkur in Karnataka. On lower side, the district of Hyderabad (29 per cent) and Bidar (37 per cent) both part of the erstwhile princely states of Nizam showed one of the lowest rates in the respective states. However, in most of the districts of south India, more than half of the male population has been found working. It is observed from Table 4.1.1 that in Erode 66 per cent of males have been working in 1981, which declined to 65 per cent in 1991, but slightly increased to 66 per cent in 2001.

The districts of hilly states like Uttarakhand, Himachal Pradesh, and Ladakh region show much higher participation rates, and it is also true for north-eastern states. In these districts, female work participation rates are also found higher. Compared to them, districts north of Vindhayan range falling in the upper and middle Gangetic plain the participation rates are much lower and female work participation is abysmally low. On the other hand, districts falling in mid-Indian belt belong to the states of Maharasthra, Madhya Pradesh, Chhattisgarh, Jharkhand and Orissa, the participation rates are moderately high compared to the average picture of the country. For example, in Maharashtra, the highest work participation is observed in the district of Bhandara (48 per cent). Similarly, Gujarat the highest participation rate is found in the tribal district of The Dangs (50 per cent) in 2001. The district of Koraput in Orissa shows a high work participation rate (49 per cent). On the other hand, urban districts like Mumbai, Chennai and Hyderabad depict much lower work participation ranging from 29 per cent in Hyderabad to 34 per cent in Chennai and 37 per cent in Mumbai in 2001. However, there is an improvement in the rates particularly from 1991 to 2001. When compared with other urban territories like Delhi and Chandigarh, the level is more or less uniform across them. In Chandigah work participation was found 37 per cent compared to 32 per cent in Delhi in 2001. There is virtually

Table 4.1.1. Crude Work Participation Rate (Total), Districts Level, India, 1981-2001

Sl. No.	State/Union Territory	1981			1991			2001		
		Total	Male	Female	Total	Male	Female	Total	Male	Female
Andaman & Nicobar Islands										
01	Andaman	36.02	56.89	8.18	34.51	53.09	11.71	37.13	55.99	14.79
02	Nicobar	41.38	55.72	23.70	39.73	54.82	21.76	46.65	60.92	29.99
Andhra Pradesh										
03	Adilabad	46.53	57.41	35.43	44.37	52.98	35.58	45.15	52.80	37.41
04	Nizamabad	50.92	57.53	44.39	49.65	54.20	45.17	49.44	54.36	44.59
05	Karimnagar	50.55	58.98	42.06	50.32	56.23	44.33	49.02	54.75	43.27
06	Medak	49.49	58.40	40.42	47.77	55.00	40.32	48.45	55.34	41.38
07	Hyderabad	27.86	47.48	6.55	27.36	46.03	7.36	29.24	47.28	9.90
08	Rangareddi	45.94	56.12	35.28	40.75	52.35	28.43	40.21	53.35	26.29
09	Mahbubnagar	51.81	58.74	44.77	50.20	55.33	44.94	51.89	56.24	47.41
10	Nalgonda	49.44	59.15	39.43	48.31	54.81	41.56	49.10	54.94	43.05
11	Warangal	47.76	57.00	38.17	47.78	54.32	40.97	48.25	54.35	41.98
12	Khammam	45.04	56.92	32.63	45.87	55.53	35.82	48.25	56.70	39.59
13	Srikakulam	49.06	59.06	39.29	48.64	56.45	40.92	47.36	56.44	38.41

Sl. No.	State/Union Territory	1981			1991			2001		
		Total	Male	Female	Total	Male	Female	Total	Male	Female
Andaman & Nicobar Islands										
14	Vizianagaram	48.49	59.90	37.13	50.33	58.98	41.69	52.20	59.84	44.63
15	Visakhapatnam	43.49	57.45	29.25	43.11	56.25	29.63	41.82	55.41	28.03
16	East Godavari	40.61	58.98	22.10	38.48	56.75	20.17	39.58	58.41	20.62
17	West Godavari	43.27	59.03	27.36	43.35	58.02	28.58	44.13	59.95	28.16
18	Krishna	43.14	57.93	27.92	43.29	57.04	29.11	43.97	58.16	29.47
19	Guntur	47.37	58.53	35.89	47.86	57.31	38.13	49.05	59.09	38.85
20	Prakasam	48.73	57.84	39.41	48.64	55.67	41.39	50.26	57.65	42.64
21	Nellore	46.44	59.08	33.50	45.62	57.10	33.90	45.41	58.31	32.29
22	Cuddapah	44.85	57.71	31.45	43.95	55.68	31.67	44.80	58.31	32.71
23	Kurnool	46.70	56.08	36.96	46.51	54.69	37.93	49.45	58.31	42.36
24	Anantapur	45.69	56.70	34.04	46.20	55.83	36.02	48.83	58.31	39.42
25	Chittoor	45.75	59.26	31.76	45.93	57.69	33.76	46.80	58.31	35.37
Arunachal Pradesh										
26	West Kameng (West Kamenga + Tawang)	52.11	61.04	41.69	66.50	57.81	36.01	49.41	59.94	35.60
27	East Kameng	57.97	63.80	51.80	50.77	53.98	47.43	45.38	48.62	42.10

Sl. No.	State / Union Territory	1981			1991			2001		
		Total	Male	Female	Total	Male	Female	Total	Male	Female
28	Lower Subansiri (Lower Subansiri + Papun Pare)	55.15	59.03	50.77	45.50	52.52	37.66	40.65	46.97	33.90
29	Upper Subansiri	54.36	56.01	52.65	47.38	51.37	42.78	40.50	44.50	36.34
30	West Siang	48.80	53.28	43.89	43.14	50.20	35.05	41.46	47.26	35.10
31	East Siang (East Siang + Upper Siang)	49.95	56.55	42.17	44.35	52.42	34.99	41.95	48.68	34.53
32	Dibang Valley	59.94	68.33	47.25	45.77	56.11	32.65	44.53	52.80	34.63
33	Lohit	48.42	59.29	34.49	44.12	55.31	30.09	42.05	51.34	31.20
34	Tirap (Tirap + Changlang)	52.58	57.38	47.04	48.49	54.43	41.60	48.34	52.57	43.67
Assam										
35	Goalpara (Goalpara + Kokrajhar + Dhubri + Bongariagaon)	N.A.	N.A.	N.A.	64.72	73.40	55.78	53.86	64.63	42.67
36	Kamrup (Kamrup + Nailbari + Barpeta)	N.A.	N.A.	N.A.	84.15	87.49	80.75	73.66	81.04	70.51

Sl. No.	State / Union Territory	1981			1991			2001		
		Total	Male	Female	Total	Male	Female	Total	Male	Female
Assam										
37	Darrang (Darrang + Sonipur)	N.A.	N.A.	N.A.	87.14	89.20	85.04	45.61	81.79	73.46
38	Nagaon (Nagaon + Marigaon)	N.A.	N.A.	N.A.	94.93	96.10	93.75	47.68	92.69	88.30
39	Sibsagar (Sibsagar + Goalghat + Jorhat)	N.A.	N.A.	N.A.	80.76	83.19	78.26	45.81	76.48	66.93
40	Lakhimpur (Lakhimpur + Dhemaji)	N.A.	N.A.	N.A.	92.44	92.64	92.24	48.48	87.41	85.18
41	Dibrugarh (Dibrugarh + Tinsukia)	N.A.	N.A.	N.A.	88.88	90.25	87.47	46.91	83.39	77.68
42	Karbi Anglong /Mikir Hills	N.A.	N.A.	N.A.	42.78	51.08	33.63	40.63	48.98	31.62
43	North Cachar Hills	N.A.	N.A.	N.A.	42.05	52.35	30.03	37.32	48.61	24.56
44	Cachar (Cachar + Karimganj + Hailakandi)	N.A.	N.A.	N.A.	85.41	89.06	81.70	43.42	81.47	70.33
Bihar										
45	Patna	28.56	46.29	8.63	27.48	44.06	8.36	30.21	44.94	13.33
46	Nalanda	31.27	47.32	13.95	32.80	46.46	17.59	38.10	48.26	26.98

Sl. No.	State / Union Territory	1981			1991			2001		
		Total	Male	Female	Total	Male	Female	Total	Male	Female
47	Nawada	32.80	49.03	16.59	31.73	47.36	15.04	37.26	48.14	25.77
48	Gaya (Gaya + Jehanabad)	32.63	48.42	16.22	32.07	46.66	16.23	37.26	47.60	26.21
49	Aurangabad	30.15	47.23	12.27	29.48	45.52	11.97	33.33	45.64	20.15
50	Rohtas (Rohtas + Kaimur)	5.54	47.33	0.94	29.47	45.97	10.96	31.74	46.01	16.01
51	Bhojpur (Bhojpur + Buxar)	26.93	44.84	7.96	26.61	43.48	7.78	29.13	44.28	12.31
52	Gopalganj	26.73	47.64	5.94	26.58	45.61	6.90	29.81	44.58	15.05
53	Siwan	24.40	43.57	6.48	23.90	41.70	6.40	26.91	41.48	12.78
54	Saran	24.40	42.94	6.20	24.23	41.93	5.86	26.50	42.08	10.37
55	Vaishali	26.22	46.55	5.77	25.55	45.02	4.39	28.79	45.25	10.91
56	Pashchim Champaran	34.58	52.85	14.53	34.95	51.91	15.61	37.92	50.85	23.57
57	Purba Champaran	31.29	53.07	7.75	30.86	50.34	8.79	32.66	48.78	14.69
58	Sitamarhi (Sitamarhi + Sheohar)	29.65	54.14	3.41	29.88	51.50	5.37	31.77	50.32	10.97
59	Muzaffarpur	29.78	50.98	7.76	28.94	48.46	7.35	30.42	46.72	12.71
60	Begusarai	29.34	48.81	8.61	28.23	46.45	7.92	31.76	46.19	15.93

Sl. No.	State / Union Territory	1981			1991			2001		
		Total	Male	Female	Total	Male	Female	Total	Male	Female
61	Samastipur	28.95	50.15	7.14	28.10	46.99	7.70	31.58	46.84	15.13
62	Darbhanga	28.91	49.68	7.68	29.49	47.55	9.66	31.21	46.12	14.88
63	Madhubani	5.46	51.00	0.83	32.49	48.95	14.83	34.34	47.75	20.10
64	Saharsa (Saharsa + Madhepura + Supaul)	38.22	53.44	21.87	37.55	50.37	23.17	41.99	50.31	32.89
65	Purnia (Purnia + Araia + Kishanganj)	35.61	55.88	13.70	35.19	53.98	14.56	37.20	51.74	21.36
66	Katihar	34.36	53.97	13.24	33.71	51.51	14.14	37.55	50.86	23.06
67	Munger (Munger + Khagarai + Jamuli)	32.06	49.07	13.65	32.93	47.30	16.57	36.56	47.30	24.52
68	Bhagalpur (Bhagalpur + Banka)	31.96	49.29	12.94	32.77	47.52	15.93	37.00	48.42	24.16
69	Santhal Pargana (Dumka + Godda + Sahibganj + Deogarh + Pakaur)	40.70	55.30	25.45	40.64	52.25	28.22	41.60	51.55	31.03
70	Dhanbad	30.01	48.28	7.57	27.63	44.34	7.39	27.70	43.64	9.47

Sl. No.	*State / Union Territory*	*1981*			*1991*			*2001*		
		Total	*Male*	*Female*	*Total*	*Male*	*Female*	*Total*	*Male*	*Female*
Bihar										
71	Giridih (Giridih + Bokaro)	34.22	50.66	17.55	33.80	47.28	19.45	31.34	44.68	17.13
72	Hazaribagh (Hazaribagh + Chatra + Kodarma)	33.99	50.10	17.21	33.29	46.60	19.00	36.24	41.30	24.70
73	Palamu (Palamu + Garhwa)	35.48	51.46	18.78	35.31	48.10	21.57	38.18	47.19	28.55
74	Ranchi (Ranchi + Gumla + Lohardaga)	41.75	52.94	30.14	41.75	49.97	33.06	42.02	49.14	34.57
75	Sinhabhumi (Pashchimi Singhbhum + Purbi Sinhabhumi)	39.24	52.18	25.50	39.55	50.20	28.18	39.61	49.93	28.78
Chandigarh										
76	Chandigarh	34.84	54.22	25.45	34.94	54.33	10.39	37.80	56.11	14.22
Dadra & Nagar Haveli										
77	Dadra and Nagar Haveli	48.92	56.32	41.33	53.25	57.50	48.79	51.76	62.33	38.74
Delhi										
78	Delhi	32.19	52.67	6.84	31.64	51.72	7.36	32.14	51.21	8.89

Sl.No.	*State/Union Territory*	*1981*			*1991*			*2001*		
		Total	*Male*	*Female*	*Total*	*Male*	*Female*	*Total*	*Male*	*Female*
Goa, Damn & Diu										
79	Goa (North Goa + South Goa)	35.35	48.48	21.88	35.28	49.56	20.52	38.80	54.60	22.36
80	Diu	36.19	46.42	26.14	41.24	54.75	26.44	31.35	44.90	19.23
81	Daman	28.48	41.22	17.29	31.94	46.35	18.41	51.70	71.47	18.26
Gujarat										
82	Jamnagar	34.80	52.40	16.24	36.60	53.03	19.29	38.56	54.68	21.43
83	Rajkot	34.36	51.64	16.11	36.88	53.28	19.55	39.27	55.94	21.36
84	Surendranagar	37.78	52.62	21.88	40.49	52.96	26.96	42.74	54.02	30.53
85	Bhavnagar	35.72	52.18	18.55	38.34	53.15	22.72	38.25	53.42	22.05
86	Amreli	37.31	51.84	22.44	39.86	53.86	25.60	43.10	55.02	31.02
87	Junagadh (Junagarh + Porbandar)	34.20	50.48	17.16	38.51	52.90	23.52	40.74	54.82	25.97
88	Kachchh	35.93	52.62	19.22	36.28	51.68	20.31	38.25	53.63	21.93
89	Banas Kantha	35.28	53.24	17.52	39.25	51.90	25.69	43.61	51.20	35.46

Sl.No.	State / Union Territory	1981			1991			2001		
		Total	Male	Female	Total	Male	Female	Total	Male	Female
Goa, Damn & Diu										
90	Sabar Kantha	39.32	51.82	26.51	43.90	51.71	35.82	45.16	52.28	37.63
91	Mahesana (Mahesana + Patan)	36.31	50.06	22.14	42.63	52.46	32.29	45.08	53.53	35.98
92	Gandhinagar	31.25	49.84	11.14	32.96	49.68	14.72	41.54	53.07	28.89
93	Ahmadabad	31.92	50.89	10.63	33.16	51.26	13.03	34.55	53.09	13.75
94	Kheda (Kheda + Anand)	35.38	52.73	16.43	41.49	53.96	27.92	43.62	55.08	31.12
95	Panch Mahals (Panch Mahals + Dohad)	44.97	54.94	34.57	47.06	51.79	42.09	48.92	52.63	45.05
96	Vadodara	37.39	54.79	18.38	40.54	55.35	24.32	41.71	55.86	26.31
97	Bharuch (Bharuch + Narmada)	42.12	55.68	27.73	43.22	56.24	29.24	44.02	56.53	30.54
98	Surat	42.55	57.95	25.88	43.17	58.60	26.03	43.69	60.68	23.34
99	Valsad (Valsad + Navsari)	43.08	54.55	31.40	45.63	56.61	34.16	45.28	56.99	32.77
100	The Dangs	50.62	56.96	44.08	50.55	53.51	47.53	49.80	52.36	47.21

Sl.No.	State/Union Territory	1981			1991			2001		
		Total	*Male*	*Female*	*Total*	*Male*	*Female*	*Total*	*Male*	*Female*
Goa, Damn & Diu										
Haryana										
101	Ambala (Ambala + Panchkula)	29.61	52.29	3.56	28.94	50.80	4.24	33.93	52.10	12.65
102	Kurukshetra (Kurukshetra + Yamunanagar + Kaithal)	31.63	52.14	7.87	29.28	50.26	5.18	36.15	50.68	19.26
103	Karnal (Karnal + Panipat)	30.50	51.19	6.27	29.72	49.67	6.51	37.39	50.55	21.90
104	Sonipat	32.21	47.61	14.42	30.65	47.89	10.15	40.89	49.65	30.44
105	Jind	35.20	50.45	17.35	32.42	48.88	12.77	43.87	51.56	34.85

Sl.No.	State / Union Territory	1981			1991			2001		
		Total	Male	Female	Total	Male	Female	Total	Male	Female
Haryana										
106	Rohtak (Rohtak + Rewari + Jhajar)	31.33	46.12	14.57	30.49	45.78	12.90	42.29	50.15	33.17
107	Gurgaon	31.67	49.34	11.58	32.06	46.52	15.46	37.92	46.84	27.72
108	Faridabad	31.22	50.85	7.05	30.34	48.07	8.91	35.80	48.32	20.90
109	Mahendragarh	29.44	45.01	12.71	31.01	44.76	15.90	43.31	48.00	38.20
110	Bhiwani	33.42	47.31	17.95	32.47	45.36	17.81	42.76	49.24	35.38
111	Hisar (Hisar + Fatehabad)	32.71	51.76	10.72	32.91	50.34	12.67	43.89	52.74	33.63
112	Sirsa	31.86	53.93	6.70	34.45	52.76	13.75	42.59	53.05	30.73
Himachal Pradesh										
113	Chamba	48.72	59.09	37.63	48.58	53.98	42.90	77.89	83.95	71.58
114	Kangra	34.34	48.02	20.89	34.37	46.08	22.94	62.93	74.94	51.92
115	Lahul & Spiti	66.83	70.50	62.06	64.93	68.90	60.07	84.88	88.62	79.86
116	Kullu	52.29	58.19	45.87	47.93	54.05	41.28	84.98	89.57	79.95
117	Mandi	46.24	51.70	40.77	45.72	49.11	42.38	73.63	78.24	69.23
118	Hamirpur	37.12	42.14	32.75	41.87	44.15	39.81	70.86	75.93	66.64

Sl.No.	State / Union Territory	1981			1991			2001		
		Total	Male	Female	Total	Male	Female	Total	Male	Female
119	Una	28.02	46.10	10.45	33.45	48.66	18.50	65.49	79.20	52.47
120	Bilaspur	41.65	49.27	34.05	44.60	48.39	40.83	70.21	76.32	64.25
121	Solan	42.13	53.68	29.70	45.05	54.14	35.06	75.50	86.49	62.20
122	Sirmaur	46.34	60.07	30.63	46.59	55.64	36.50	75.69	85.87	64.16
123	Shimla	51.60	59.04	43.11	48.62	55.18	41.29	72.33	80.50	63.05
124	Kinnaur	57.26	62.75	51.05	52.42	60.08	43.48	85.58	90.90	79.^2
Jammu & Kashmir										
125	Kupwara	48.86	56.93	39.46	N.A.	N.A.	N.A.	32.67	45.34	18.69
126	Baramula	45.44	56.66	32.56	N.A.	N.A.	N.A.	31.76	46.83	15.06
127	Srinagar	34.90	52.62	14.60	N.A.	N.A.	N.A.	31.99	50.14	10.68
128	Badgam	48.73	58.65	37.46	N.A.	N.A.	N.A.	35.91	48,53	22.34
129	Pulwama	50.70	56.53	44.19	N.A.	N.A.	N.A.	32.58	46.95	17.36
130	Anantanag	42.44	56.18	27.27	N.A.	N.A.	N.A.	33.69	45.95	20.39
131	Leh (Ladakh)	50.39	59.46	40.15	N.A.	N.A.	N.A.	49.58	58.32	38.97

Sl.No.	State / Union Territory	1981			1991			2001		
		Total	Male	Female	Total	Male	Female	Total	Male	Female
132	Kargil	54.94	59.53	49.57	N.A.	N.A.	N.A.	46.64	50.08	42.53
133	Doda	43.36	55.52	29.90	N.A.	N.A.	N.A.	46.00	52.72	38.56
134	Udhampur	54.58	62.04	46.35	N.A.	N.A.	N.A.	49.28	57.83	39.35
135	Punch	46.54	56.04	35.86	N.A.	N.A.	N.A.	53.97	57.68	49.93
136	Rajauri	44.98	55.18	33.73	N.A.	N.A.	N.A.	45.15	52.15	37.19
137	Jammu	39.43	52.64	25.02	N.A.	N.A.	N.A.	33.25	50.56	13.32
138	Kathua	43.40	55.34	30.37	N.A.	N.A.	N.A.	37.34	50.64	22.58
Karnataka										
139	Bangalore(Bangalore + Bangalore rural)	33.82	52.05	13.91	36.51	53.99	17.39	41.09	58.33	22.32
140	Belgaum	41.32	58.10	25.87	42.35	54.41	29.71	44.56	55.90	32.74
141	Bellary	42.71	54.85	30.24	45.13	53.76	36.19	45.42	54.61	35.94
142	Bidar	40.39	53.28	27.06	39.87	48.82	30.46	37.11	47.50	26.17
143	Bijapur(Bijapur+Bagalkot)	41.80	54.44	28.53	41.64	50.89	32.04	41.57	51.99	30.76
144	Chikmagalur	44.60	57.12	31.45	44.97	57.54	32.11	45.29	59.43	30.92

Sl. No.	State / Union Territory	1981			1991			2001		
		Total	*Male*	*Female*	*Total*	*Male*	*Female*	*Total*	*Male*	*Female*
Karnataka										
145	Chitradurga (Chitradurga + Davangere)	42.95	55.29	29.88	43.04	53.93	31.50	45.50	56.86	33.59
146	Dakshin Kannada (Dakshin Kannada + Udupi)	41.84	49.57	34.54	43.16	51.70	35.13	47.66	57.12	38.74
147	Dharwad (Dharwad + Gadag + Haveri)	41.72	55.10	27.63	42.14	53.41	30.18	45.05	58.86	32.65
148	Gulbarga	45.25	55.38	34.96	43.07	51.22	34.60	43.12	51.06	34.90
149	Hassan	40.52	55.61	25.23	44.25	56.13	32.37	50.23	60.79	39.70
150	Kodagu	47.27	59.58	34.08	47.12	58.71	35.27	48.56	60.91	36.16
151	Kolar	39.49	54.29	24.26	43.42	55.05	31.37	48.70	58.10	39.02
152	Mandya	36.82	55.86	16.97	44.50	57.48	31.03	47.65	61.21	33.90
153	Mysore (Mysore + Chamaraja nagar)	37.77	56.46	18.08	40.20	59.96	22.61	43.22	59.04	26.83
154	Raichur (Raichur + Koppal)	43.89	56.88	30.75	44.43	53.62	35.04	44.92	53.21	36.48
155	Shimoga	38.04	54.18	20.99	40.89	55.19	26.00	43.51	58.68	28.00
156	Tumkur	41.36	55.68	26.47	47.69	56.91	38.06	50.95	60.24	41.35

Sl. No.	State / Union Territory	1981			1991			2001		
		Total	Male	Female	Total	Male	Female	Total	Male	Female
157	Uttara Kannada	38.43	53.74	22.45	38.78	53.35	23.69	42.94	57.63	27.81
Kerala										
158	Kasaragod(Kasaragod + Kannur)	29.93	43.92	16.39	30.31	45.11	16.11	32.80	49.65	17.13
159	Wayanad	38.58	51.08	24.30	38.76	53.24	23.76	39.53	55.82	23.17
160	Kozhikode	27:10	43.15	11.38	26.57	44.59	9.02	27.89	48.66	8.24
161	Malappuram	25.17	40.37	10.73	24.29	40.70	8.71	24.12	42.76	6.63
162	Palakkad	35.36	47.09	24.26	35.48	48.58	23.13	36.11	51.99	21.20
163	Thrissur	29.63	41.81	18.55	31.96	47.18	17.94	32.12	50.58	15.21
164	Ernakulam	31.68	46.94	16.37	33.44	51.50	15.38	35.97	55.11	17.18
165	Idukki	37.77	51.51	23.49	39.71	55.19	23.84	43.16	58.11	28.10
166	Kottayam	29.82	46.89	12.75	31.22	50.37	12.13	32.87	52.24	13.97
167	Alappuzha	31.93	43.92	20.52	34.09	46.83	21.96	34.30	49.41	20.29
168	Kollam(Kollam + Pathanamithitta)	30.27	44.77	16.13	31.32	47.81	15.53	31.28	48.10	15.66
169	Thiruvananthapuram	30.21	46.39	14.49	32.60	50.23	15.58	32.40	51.38	14.50

Sl.		1981			1991			2001		
No.	State / Union Territory	Total	Male	Female	Total	Male	Female	Total	Male	Female
Lakshadweep										
170	Lakshadweep	24.39	39.24	9.16	26.43	44.17	7.60	25.32	42.41	7.28
Madhya Pradesh & Chattisgarh										
171	Morena (Morena + Sheopur)	31.31	50.31	8.52	31.51	47.31	12.37	38.09	48.39	25.84
172	Bhind	27.60	48.16	2.75	27.37	46.29	4.16	36.78	48.31	22.87
173	Gwalior	31.17	49.21	9.80	30.92	47.48	11.02	32.51	47.65	14.66
174	Datia	32.69	50.67	11.62	36.81	50.67	20.44	50.30	56.37	43.23
175	Shivpuri	38.80	54.42	20.54	42.47	52.74	30.37	45.24	52.05	37.30
176	Guna	36.31	53.99	16.27	37.04	51.52	20.51	40.98	51.44	29.15
177	Tikamgarh	42.12	54.47	28.13	42.78	51.28	33.02	47.06	52.20	41.27
178	Chhatarpur	40.18	55.27	22.71	41.02	51.65	28.60	40.18	49.28	29.70
179	Panna	40.92	55.07	25.42	41.60	53.20	28.67	43.62	51.26	35.14
180	Sagar	39.66	52.14	25.66	39.07	50.38	26.23	41.53	51.38	30.40
181	Damoh	40.10	53.40	25.72	40.94	52.50	28.17	44.88	53.06	35.80
182	Satna	41.77	52.96	29.81	40.35	49.88	29.96	39.85	48.41	30.60

Sl. No	State/Union Territory	1981 Total	1981 Male	1981 Female	1991 Total	1991 Male	1991 Female	2001 Total	2001 Male	2001 Female
	Madhya Pradesh & Chattisgarh									
183	Rewa	39.63	49.86	29.08	37.75	46.36	28.51	43.73	49.39	37.72
184	Shahdol (Shahdol + Umaria)	43.85	56.72	30.27	43.49	53.78	32.55	43.01	5.37	33.84
185	Sidhi	44.57	55.81	32.76	43.02	51.55	33.77	41.37	48.02	34.24
186	Mandsaur (Mandsaur + Neemuch)	45.12	54.95	34.67	46.56	54.41	38.26	48.10	55.55	40.29
187	Ratlam	43.04	55.47	29.92	45.99	54.88	36.62	45.08	53.57	36.21
188	Ujjain	39.05	53.35	23.62	39.80	52.39	26.24	44.14	53.77	33.88
189	Shajapur	43.56	54.90	31.37	44.66	53.79	34.72	48.80	55.08	42.01
190	Dewas	43.02	53.96	31.25	41.04	50.98	30.29	44.37	51.76	36.42
191	Jhabua	53.38	57.99	48.71	54.04	56.22	51.80	52.51	54.30	50.69
192	Dhar	46.22	54.00	38.17	46.73	52.87	40.27	46.62	52.48	40.49
193	Indore	33.75	50.26	15.37	34.34	50.83	16.14	36.24	51.84	19.14
194	West Nimar (West Nimar + Barwani)	43.90	53.14	34.22	45.88	52.39	39.02	47.04	52.59	41.25

Sl. No	State/Union Territory	1981			1991			2001		
		Total	Male	Female	Total	Male	Female	Total	Male	Female
	Madhya Pradesh & Chhattisgarh									
195	East Nimar	43.39	54.82	31.22	43.69	53.05	33.71	43.94	52.83	34.43
196	Rajgarh	43.76	57.10	29.43	46.97	54.95	38.32	49.88	54.57	44.84
197	Vidisha	35.29	54.05	14.00	37.50	52.09	20.80	37.19	51.15	21.23
198	Bhopal	31.90	49.31	11.97	31.83	48.13	13.50	32.08	47.43	14.94
199	Sehore	40.09	53.14	25.72	42.02	50.67	32.38	41.84	48.85	34.14
200	Raisen	37.35	53.53	19.53	37.38	50.91	21.99	36.59	49.55	21.88
201	Betul	48.40	56.42	40.17	46.66	53.24	39.84	44.15	51.01	37.05
202	Hoshangabad (Hoshangabad + Harda)	36.99	52.37	20.05	37.47	50.85	22.58	38.52	50.35	25.41
203	Jabalpur (Jabalpur + Katni)	37.20	51.05	22.03	36.99	49.77	23.03	38.67	50.71	25.56
204	Narsimhapur	38.97	53.82	23.01	39.57	52.45	25.45	42.13	53.95	29.13
205	Mandla (Mandla + Dindori)	53.88	59.19	48.58	51.20	55.37	46.98	53.92	56.88	50.95
206	Chhindwara	43.34	54.26	32.02	43.45	52.28	34.19	42.15	50.85	33.02
207	Seoni	49.49	56.44	42.42	49.19	54.34	43.91	48.78	53.98	43.48

Sl. No	State / Union Territory	1981 Total	1981 Male	1981 Female	1991 Total	1991 Male	1991 Female	2001 Total	2001 Male	2001 Female
208	Balaghat	52.00	57.03	46.99	49.78	54.12	45.46	50.31	54.35	46.35
209	Surguja (Surguja+Koriya)	47.68	61.87	32.93	47.44	56.73	37.74	49.32	55.51	42.92
210	Bilaspur (Bilaspur + Jangir -Champa + Korba)	45.93	54.56	37.25	44.68	51.71	37.50	43.08	50.13	35.88
211	Raigarh (Raigarh + Jashpur)	48.79	60.70	36.95	49.16	57.79	40.54	49.76	56.43	43.06
212	Rajnandgaon (Rajnandgaon + Kanwardha)	53.29	56.52	50.12	52.44	54.87	50.05	50.38	53.38	47.43
213	Durg	46.05	52.78	39.18	43.92	50.73	36.88	41.38	49.22	33.38
214	Raipur (Raipur + Mahasamud + Dhamtari)	49.19	55.56	42.87	47.14	53.37	40.88	42.46	50.42	34.38
215	Bastar (Bastar + Kanker + Dhamtari)	51.74	61.53	41.97	53.65	58.64	48.67	53.02	57.20	48.89
Maharashtra										
216	Mumbai (Greater Mumbai + Suburban)	35.21	55.45	8.97	35.25	55.08	11.02	37.27	56.87	13.06
217	Thane	40.27	55.33	23.23	39.85	54.90	22.73	39.11	55.81	19.62
218	Raigarh	41.75	50.60	33.30	43.87	51.57	36.25	41.40	52.70	29.81
219	Ratnagiri (Ratnagiri + Sindhudurg)	40.55	45.74	36.35	45.87	48.96	43.26	45.54	52.39	39.41
220	Nashik	43.93	52.62	34.65	43.59	50.96	35.75	43.77	52.79	34.03
221	Dhule (Dhule+Nandurbar)	43.63	53.39	33.51	45.58	51.51	39.39	44.64	51.80	37.17

Sl. No.	State / Union Territory	1981			1991			2001		
		Total	Male	Female	Total	Male	Female	Total	Male	Female
Maharashtra										
222	Jalgaon	42.28	52.13	31.91	42.89	50.30	35.02	42.47	51.27	33.03
223	Pune	38.52	50.96	25.24	40.32	51.31	28.55	40.85	53.49	27.10
224	Ahmadnagar	45.68	53.33	37.70	45.95	51.12	40.50	45.96	52.59	38.90
225	Solapur	41.58	53.41	29.02	43.07	51.27	34.29	45.28	53.08	36.93
226	Satara	41.44	48.61	34.68	44.52	49.54	39.63	46.41	53.67	39.11
227	Sangli	38.90	52.95	24.36	44.12	53.17	34.67	47.17	56.09	37.85
228	Kolhapur	36.89	52.62	20.64	46.13	54.61	37.31	46.92	56.60	36.72
229	Aurangabad (Aurangabad + Jalna)	46.06	54.32	37.34	44.60	50.60	38.20	41.99	49.69	33.74
230	Parbhani (Parbhani + Hingoli)	49.77	58.62	40.63	45.67	51.60	39.45	43.93	50.09	37.49
231	Bid	46.56	55.58	37.21	47.00	50.71	43.08	44.31	49.08	39.21
232	Nanded	49.36	57.15	41.26	44.73	50.09	39.07	41.79	48.73	34.42
233	Osmanabad (Osamanabad + Latur)	44.92	55.01	34.39	44.49	50.15	38.48	41.89	49.64	33.58
234	Buldana	50.59	56.98	43.92	47.64	52.13	42.92	45.51	52.00	38.65

Sl. No.	*State / Union Territory*	*1981*			*1991*			*2001*		
		Total	*Male*	*Female*	*Total*	*Male*	*Female*	*Total*	*Male*	*Female*
Maharashtra										
235	Akola (Akola + Wahsim)	44.80	54.33	34.75	43.77	51.41	35.63	41.64	51.45	31.18
236	Amravati	43.00	54.39	30.83	44.39	54.06	34.07	42.02	53.81	29.46
237	Yavatmal	48.93	55.80	41.76	47.71	53.05	42.08	45.52	53.32	37.23
238	Wardha	45.22	54.61	35.31	44.56	52.93	35.65	44.50	54.56	33.75
239	Nagpur	38.17	50.27	25.07	37.50	49.84	24.12	37.82	51.85	22.77
240	Bhandara (Bhandara + Gondiya)	50.50	54.60	46.39	50.13	52.78	47.45	47.78	53.06	42.46
241	Chandrapur (Chandrapur + Gadchiroli)	50.03	56.61	43.22	48.50	53.73	43.04	46.95	54.05	39.53
Manipur										
242	Manipur North (Senapati)	54.05	53.99	54.11	51.88	51.62	52.15	45.93	50.21	41.43
243	Manipur West (Tamenglong)	51.13	49.58	52.71	46.02	45.60	46.47	45.62	46.60	44.55
244	Manipur South (Churachandpur)	44.32	49.85	38.36	44.07	48.51	39.32	43.60	48.41	38.51
245	Bishnupur (Bishnupur + Thoubal + Imphal East + Imphal West)	39.32	43.92	34.69	38.94	42.80	34.98	42.64	47.82	37.45

Sl.		1981			1991			2001		
No.	*State / Union Territory*	*Total*	*Male*	*Female*	*Total*	*Male*	*Female*	*Total*	*Male*	*Female*
246	Ukhrul	50.65	49.90	51.47	46.05	47.26	44.68	47.25	48.83	45.53
247	Tengnoopal (Chandel)	54.67	58.07	48.47	52.56	55.27	49.59	46.10	48.88	43.26
Meghalaya										
248	Jaintia Hills	49.36	55.90	42.67	46.44	52.65	40.05	42.42	47.95	36.86
249	East Khasi Hills (East Khasi Hills + Ribhoi)	41.62	52.44	30.17	39.20	49.70	28.11	40.53	49.28	31.52
250	West Khasi Hills	51.24	54.05	48.28	43.82	47.46	40.00	43.61	46.36	40.76
251	East Garo Hills	45.59	52.36	38.40	44.09	48.66	39.32	44.69	47.97	41.30
252	West Garo Hills (East Garo Hills+South Grao hills)	48.21	55.85	40.29	44.66	51.15	37.90	41.37	48.31	34.16
Mizoram										
253	Aizawl (Aizawl + Kolasib + Champhal + Serchhip + Mamit)	N.A.	N.A.	N.A.	48.59	53.65	43.12	54.21	59.00	49.12
254	Lunglei	N.A.	N.A.	N.A.	50.19	55.61	44.24	52.32	57.29	46.92
255	Chhimtulpul/Saiha (Saihal + Lawngtial)	N.A.	N.A.	N.A.	49.02	52.99	44.66	45.35	49.50	40.85

Sl. No.	State / Union Territory	1981			1991			2001		
		Total	Male	Female	Total	Male	Female	Total	Male	Female
Nagaland										
256	Kohima (Kohima + Dimapur)	45.95	55.08	34.41	39.26	47.28	29.89	38.50	46.79	29.09
257	Phek	52.82	51.35	54.51	24.69	39.77	10.75	48.18	48.43	47.91
258	Mon	58.66	62.41	54.35	51.38	54.23	48.10	50.20	52.88	47.15
259	Tuensang	51.89	53.44	50.14	45.24	47.08	43.17	44.58	46.06	42.93
260	Mokokchung	41.47	45.85	36.64	38.64	43.10	33.75	47.08	50.46	43.40
261	Zunheboto	46.23	47.92	44.49	42.54	44.04	40.99	36.88	39.35	34.28
262	Wokha	42.88	43.38	42.34	39.74	41.52	37.81	34.89	37.63	31.94
Odisha										
263	Sambalpur(Sambalpur + Bargarh + Jharsuguda + Debagarh)	43.66	59.27	27.60	43.41	56.99	29.36	43.41	54.61	31.84
264	Sundargarh	38.99	54.89	21.93	39.44	53.15	24.80	40.36	51.33	28.88
265	Kendujhar	38.98	55.26	22.42	38.82	52.90	24.35	39.77	51.22	28.05
266	Mayurbhanj	47.77	57.63	37.79	45.82	54.45	37.00	46.23	52.44	39.89
267	Baleswar (Baleswar + Bhadrak)	29.02	51.33	6.19	28.38	49.96	6.07	30.68	50.47	10.09
268	Cuttack (Cuttack + Jajpur + Kendrapara + Jagatsinghpur)	29.20	51.71	6.06	27.51	48.93	5.25	30.97	50.45	10.80

Sl. No.	State / Union Territory	1981			1991			2001		
		Total	Male	Female	Total	Male	Female	Total	Male	Female
269	Dhenkanal (Dhenkanal + Angul)	36.59	55.50	16.85	35.62	53.10	17.18	36.71	51.60	21.04
270	Phulbani (Kandhamal + Boudh)	47.99	61.18	34.78	47.31	57.53	37.04	46.69	53.59	39.78
271	Balangir (Balangir+ Sonpur)	41.10	59.97	22.08	41.67	58.20	24.80	42.40	54.89	29.64
272	Kalahandi (Kalahandi + Nuapara)	41.87	61.55	22.39	45.24	60.78	29.71	46.37	56.64	36.12
273	Koraput (Koraput + Nabarangapur + Mlakangiri+Rayagarh)	48.23	62.17	34.20	48.99	59.80	38.11	48.70	55.95	41.46
274	Ganjam (Ganjam+Gajapati)	42.04	53.84	30.59	41.41	53.18	29.74	42.98	52.38	33.61
275	Puri (Puri+Nayagarh+Khordha)	30.98	53.81	7.21	30.24	52.04	7.01	30.95	51.56	8.85
Pondicherry										
276	Yanam	33.98	50.92	16.57	33.71	51.75	15.11	31.56	52.32	10.28
277	Pondicherry	30.45	46.98	13.34	33.92	50.94	16.27	36.16	53.65	18.50
278	Mahe	20.50	36.30	6.69	22.10	39.34	7.18	25.27	44.81	8.24
279	Karaikal	32.28	49.52	15.41	32.01	51.15	13.02	33.70	52.65	15.16
Punjab										
280	Gurdaspur	27.57	49.68	3.20	28.09	51.32	2.34	33.30	51.29	13.08
281	Amritsar	30.96	53.97	4.53	30.67	55.04	2.75	35.92	52.76	16.69

Sl. No.	State / Union Territory	1981			1991			2001		
		Total	Male	Female	Total	Male	Female	Total	Male	Female
282	Firozpur (Firozpur+Moga)	33.42	56.08	7.77	32.13	54.65	6.94	38.15	53.49	20.82
283	Ludhiana	31.72	54.65	5.03	31.26	55.52	2.53	37.91	55.55	16.49
284	Jalandhar (Jalandhar + Nawanshahr)	29.29	51.21	4.75	29.96	52.96	4.38	36.88	54.11	17.59
285	Kapurthala	54.77	52.39	4.34	31.22	54.04	5.75	34.82	52.82	14.56
286	Hoshiarpur	29.33	49.83	6.92	28.86	51.02	4.74	34.67	50.63	17.61
287	Rupnagar	30.50	51.89	5.65	30.07	52.24	4.59	39.18	52.59	23.80
288	Patiala (Patiala + Fatehgarh Sahib)	31.13	53.97	4.68	30.15	53.42	3.71	37.27	53.89	18.06
289	Sangrur	34.92	57.60	8.55	32.23	56.24	4.64	40.70	54.73	24.59
290	Bathinda (Bhathinda+Mansa)	35.40	56.65	10.81	33.32	56.27	7.24	41.78	54.86	26.80
291	Faridkot (Farikot+Muktsar)	33.66	55.56	8.82	32.61	55.85	6.26	39.09	54.36	21.89

Sl. No.	State / Union Territory	1981			.1991			2001		
		Total	Male	Female	Total	Male	Female	Total	Male	Female
Rajasthan										
292	Ganganagar	33.07	53.24	10.01	37.24	52.45	19.91	40.76	52.69	27.24
293	Bikaner	33.09	50.90	13.10	35.84	49.09	20.87	39.51	50.17	27.52
294	Churu	34.96	49.42	19.80	38.57	47.21	29.35	44.38	50.01	38.44
295	Jhunjhunun	34.35	45.20	23.00	33.42	42.75	23.41	39.76	46.53	32.61
296	Alwar	36.19	48.09	22.85	40.37	47.76	31.97	48.74	53.05	43.88
297	Bharatpur	32.59	48.44	13.52	33.15	46.43	16.97	41.57	48.56	33.30
298	Sawai Madhopur	34.14	49.19	16.77	38.41	47.15	28.17	40.93	46.21	34.87
299	Jaipur	32.84	48.16	15.69	34.20	46.85	20.01	36.64	47.04	25.05
300	Sikar	30.84	45.01	16.12	31.65	42.92	19.74	38.81	45.81	31.45
301	Ajmer	38.78	52.10	24.34	39.62	50.41	27.88	39.27	49.79	27.97
302	Tonk	41.11	52.93	28.37	41.54	50.23	32.12	43.96	49.28	38.27
303	Jaisalmer	36.31	56.22	11.76	36.85	50.08	20.45	41.65	51.73	29.37
304	Jodhpur	33.84	50.20	15.85	36.49	47.95	23.63	38.28	48.43	27.09
305	Nagaur	37.81	50.67	24.38	39.74	48.21	30.74	40.70	48.07	32.93
306	Pali	94.88	99.38	90.13	38.14	48.27	27.55	39.82	48.53	30.94

Sl.		1981			1991			2001		
No.	State / Union Territory	Total	Male	Female	Total	Male	Female	Total	Male	Female
307	Barmer	41.38	54.77	26.58	44.39	51.52	36.39	46.81	51.30	41.78
308	Jalor	33.72	51.58	14.76	41.25	50.37	31.56	50.19	54.14	46.09
309	Sirohi	35.13	50.61	19.06	38.39	50.34	25.80	40.41	50.12	30.11
310	Bhilwara	44.86	57.74	31.18	46.73	56.12	36.78	46.67	54.42	38.61
311	Udaipur	39.60	52.98	25.92	43.28	53.12	33.09	41.51	51.47	31.33
312	Chittaurgarth	48.00	57.49	38.02	49.03	55.97	41.73	51.58	56.75	46.23
313	Dungarpur	44.43	50.99	38.15	44.66	51.32	37.97	47.97	51.35	44.67
314	Banswara	42.18	50.99	33.22	46.39	51.88	40.73	47.24	50.49	43.92
315	Bundi	37.80	54.16	19.36	40.17	51.73	27.17	51.58	56.75	46.23
316	Kota	33.98	50.61	15.25	36.21	49.35	21.39	37.75	48.49	25.83
317	Jhalawar	39.66	53.92	24.26	43.69	54.13	32.32	47.00	53.90	39.55
Sikkim										
318	North	52.49	62.16	40.25	44.13	53.86	32.38	57.38	64.59	47.79
319	West	51.89	55.73	47.64	44.86	51.74	37.34	43.23	52.15	33.61
320	South	50.33	58.03	41.31	42.78	51.82	32.66	52.99	58.91	46.60
321	East	44.30	56.60	28.86	38.51	50.23	24.86	47.56	57.97	35.20

Sl. No.	State / Union Territory	1981			1991			2001		
		Total	Male	Female	Total	Male	Female	Total	Male	Female
Tamil Nadu										
322	Chennai	28.31	48.42	6.80	30.54	51.18	8.44	34.27	54.12	13.52
323	Chengalpattu / Kancheepuram (Kancheepuram + Thituvellur)	37.81	54.21	20.68	38.06	53.70	21.77	38.74	55.10	21.93
324	Vellore/North Arcot (Vellore + Tiruvanamalai)	42.03	56.53	27.22	42.52	54.78	30.02	44.00	55.87	32.09
325	South Arcot / Cuddalore (Cuddalore + Villuppuram)	41.78	56.40	26.75	43.68	55.16	31.81	46.10	56.54	35.50
326	Dharmapuri	44.50	59.17	29.20	47.60	57.22	37.39	49.48	57.90	40.50
327	Salem(Salem + Namakkal)	47.93	61.77	33.34	49.25	61.01	36.69	50.94	61.64	39.57
328	Erode(Pariyar)	51.78	66.38	36.51	52.30	65.37	38.66	55.56	66.49	44.32
329	Coimbatore	45.08	61.11	28.19	45.13	62.48	26.91	46.29	63.22	28.72
330	The Nilgiris	38.85	50.38	26.81	40.67	51.41	29.75	45.06	54.86	35.39
331	Madurai (Madurai + Dindlgul Anna + Theni)	43.86	56.60	30.78	45.72	57.09	33.99	46.15	65.21	34.01
332	Tiruchirappalli (Tiruchirapalli + Perambalur + Karur)	43.96	58.30	29.41	46.39	57.79	34.81	47.47	58.54	36.45

Sl. No.	State / Union Territory	1981			1991			2001		
		Total	Male	Female	Total	Male	Female	Total	Male	Female
Tamil Nadu										
333	Thanjavur(Thanjavur + Nagapattinam + Thiruvarur)	39.06	56.29	21.63	40.58	56.18	24.87	40.51	56.29	25.01
334	Pudukkottai	41.12	55.85	26.49	44.25	55.56	33.00	46.47	57.62	35.49
335	Ramanathapuram (Ramanathapuram + Sivaganga)	44.21	55.89	32.80	47.54	32.97	23.04	46.79	57.15	36.70
336	Tirunelveli (Tiruneveli + Toothukudi)	42.83	54.46	31.70	45.13	54.14	36.46	45.62	55.68	35.99
337	Kanniyakumari	29.04	48.44	9.34	30.50	49.80	11.03	32.70	52.95	12.72
Tripura										
338	West Tripura	31.13	49.05	12.35	30.29	48.02	11.52	34.86	50.55	18.37
339	North Tripura (North Tripura + Dhalai	32.71	52.08	11.97	32.52	49.36	14.59	35.77	49.45	21.30
340	South Tripura	33.88	52.30	14.37	31.30	45.09	16.80	39.57	52.14	26.27

Sl. No.	State / Union Territory	1981 Total	1981 Male	1981 Female	1991 Total	1991 Male	1991 Female	2001 Total	2001 Male	2001 Female
Uttar Pradesh & Uttarakhand										
341	Uttarkashi	55.30	58.80	51.32	50.66	51.99	49.21	46.07	48.28	43.71
342	Chamoli (Chamoli Rudraprayag)	50.07	48.03	52.03	46.90	46.12	47.67	44.62	43.95	45.27
343	Tehri Garhwal	50.84	48.46	53.03	45.31	44.37	46.19	43.77	45.06	42.54
344	Dehradun	39.37	53.31	15.08	34.54	51.23	14.75	31.23	47.78	12.57
345	Garhwal	43.46	44.19	42.79	39.44	42.04	36.99	38.71	40.79	36.84
346	Pithoragarh (Pithoragarh + Chamawat)	46.16	47.52	44.82	48.52	47.59	49.46	42.07	43.43	40.74
347	Almora (Almora+Bageshwar)	39.70	43.03	36.62	47.08	44.36	49.59	46.71	44.70	48.47
348	Nainital (Nainital + Udam Singh Nagar)	33.79	52.38	11.67	38.58	52.51	22.56	33.58	48.04	17.58
349	Saharanpur (Saharanpur + Hardwar)	29.60	52.31	2.30	29.59	51.41	3.90	28.61	47.16	7.16
350	Muzaffarnagar	28.82	51.11	2.37	33.37	51.44	12.33	33.11	49.00	14.86
351	Bijnor	28.39	50.47	2.80	28.36	49.96	3.57	28.24	46.45	7.92

Sl. No.	State / Union Territory	1981			1991			2001		
		Total	Male	Female	Total	Male	Female	Total	Male	Female
352	Meerut (Meerut+Bhatpat)	28.29	49.42	3.07	30.51	49.69	8.00	30.67	46.85	11.95
353	Ghaziabad	27.67	48.42	2.66	30.23	48.24	8.58	28.51	45.63	8.62
354	Bulandshahar (Bulandshahar+ Gautam Buddha Nagar)	26.15	47.05	1.96	28.97	47.41	7.42	37.36	49.60	23.26
355	Moradabad (Moradabad + Jyotiba Phule Nagar)	28.77	51.55	1.72	29.18	50.20	4.52	31.26	47.85	12.37
356	Rampur	29.69	53.58	1.37	30.99	52.74	5.66	28.30	47.11	6.90
357	Budaun	31.65	56.08	1.45	31.60	54.15	3.74	30.04	48.94	7.59
358	Bareilly	29.02	52.17	1.13	29.16	51.77	2.23	30.26	48.62	9.18
359	Pilibhit	30.02	54.49	1.10	30.25	52.23	4.48	28.04	47.76	5.56
360	Shahjahanpur	31.22	55.69	1.10	31.23	55.16	1.89	28.63	48.81	4.66
361	Aligarh	26.74	47.84	1.64	29.95	48.26	8.22	30.62	45.53	13.31
362	Mathura (Mathura+Hathras)	28.03	48.70	2.58	29.15	48.01	6.04	34.10	47.08	18.77
363	Agra (Agra +Firozabad)	27.67	49.21	1.66	27.86	48.50	3.05	27.20	44.24	7.11
364	Etah	28.36	50.88	1.14	30.83	51.00	6.38	28.76	46.47	7.90

Sl. No.	State/Union Territory	1981			1991			2001		
		Total	Male	Female	Total	Male	Female	Total	Male	Female
Uttar Pradesh & Uttarakhand										
365	Mainpuri	27.21	49.11	0.76	27.69	49.21	1.87	27.51	45.68	6.30
366	Farrukhabad (Farrukhabad + Kannauj)	29.00	51.42	1.83	29.72	51.09	4.13	31.10	48.37	10.94
367	Etawah (Etawah + Auraiya)	26.43	47.24	1.39	27.43	48.78	1.75	30.05	46.99	10.28
368	Kanpur (Kanpur Dehat + Kanpur Nagar)	28.46	49.08	3.63	27.82	47.87	3.74	30.73	47.52	11.06
369	Fatehpur	33.20	51.23	13.08	37.00	50.99	21.12	37.67	48.55	25.48
370	Allahabad (Allahabad + Kaushambi)	30.25	48.25	10.02	33.79	46.82	18.89	34.97	44.19	24.52
371	Jalaun	30.78	49.57	8.31	33.62	49.34	14.65	35.95	49.22	20.32
372	Jhansi	30.13	47.94	9.64	34.95	48.78	18.91	37.02	49.13	23.12
373	Lalitpur	39.66	55.77	20.89	41.84	53.04	28.86	43.20	50.44	34.99
374	Hamirpur (Hamirpur+Mahoba)	34.50	51.24	14.94	40.03	51.54	26.36	40.43	49.77	29.54
375	Banda (Banda + Chitrakoot)	37.34	52.22	20.13	43.19	52.24	32.45	40.95	48.51	32.20
376	Kheri	31.36	56.85	1.23	31.93	55.47	3.96	31.45	51.10	8.88
377	Sitapur	31.12	56.07	1.64	32.16	55.16	4.54	31.09	50.61	8.51
378	Hardoi	30.44	54.58	1.27	32.05	54.11	5.10	32.30	51.12	10.01
379	Unnao	31.04	52.56	6.85	33.54	52.74	11.55	34.30	50.04	16.79

Sl. No.	State / Union Territory	1981			1991			2001		
		Total	Male	Female	Total	Male	Female	Total	Male	Female
380	Lucknow	29.85	51.00	4.87	29.59	48.56	7.68	29.78	46.95	10.44
381	Rae Bareli	34.62	53.04	15.05	35.33	51.00	18.50	35.63	47.93	22.71
382	Bahraich (Bahraich +Shravasti)	32.80	57.98	3.33	38.77	56.90	17.22	37.41	53.01	19.37
383	Gonda (Gonda +Balrampur)	32.71	56.28	6.23	36.75	54.51	16.42	37.17	51.21	21.59
384	Barabanki	33.53	56.70	6.55	35.52	55.43	12.31	36.80	51.72	19.96
385	Faizabad (Faizabad + Ambedkar Nagar)	29.46	50.13	7.34	31.68	49.36	12.53	36.49	47.63	29.62
386	Sultanpur	30.20	49.77	10.04	31.74	48.87	13.39	32.12	44.65	19.33
387	Pratapgarh	27.99	46.58	9.52	31.86	45.73	17.81	33.53	42.89	24.21
388	Basti (Basti +Sant Kabir Nagar + Siddharthnagar)	33.70	53.35	12.52	34.37	50.66	16.55	36.08	46.63	24.99
389	Gorakhpur (Gorakpur + Maharajganj)	30.38	48.91	10.68	32.10	47.19	15.67	33.43	44.55	21.72
390	Deoria (Deoria+Kushinagar)	34.83	50.24	19.22	31.18	46.31	15.53	31.47	43.10	19.62
391	Azamgarh	32.31	46.93	17.98	29.90	44.46	15.44	30.45	40.90	20.22
392	Jaunpur	27.21	45.51	9.07	27.94	42.98	12.81	31.07	40.40	21.88
393	Ghazipur	26.62	44.02	8.96	30.16	44.30	15.38	31.39	41.73	20.80
394	Ballia(Ballia + Mau)	27.43	45.01	9.65	29.20	43.98	13.77	30.20	41.69	18.31

Sl. No.	State/Union Territory	1981			1991			2001		
		Total	*Male*	*Female*	*Total*	*Male*	*Female*	*Total*	*Male*	*Female*
395	Varanasi (Varansi + Sant Ravidas Nagar + Chandauli)	28.85	48.00	7.68	31.61	46.44	15.06	30.94	43.81	16.81
396	Mirzapur (Mirzapur + Sonbhadra)	36.15	53.98	16.08	37.88	50.91	22.99	35.00	46.28	22.43
West Bengal										
397	Koch Bihar	29.80	53.63	4.32	32.14	53.57	9.21	38.99	54.91	22.22
398	Jalpaiguri	33.60	52.00	13.38	33.79	50.62	15.64	38.31	52.27	23.50
399	Darjiling	36.24	49.55	21.24	34.22	47.13	20.09	35.39	48.51	21.38
400	Dakshin Dinajpur (Dakshin Dinjapur+West Dinjapur	32.05	54.16	8.46	34.50	54.46	13.04	39.25	53.31	24.34
401	Maldah	30.31	50.08	9.47	34.69	51.51	16.77	40.75	52.55	28.29
402	Murshidabad	28.75	50.09	6.50	31.51	51.49	10.33	34.18	51.14	16.37
403	Nadia	27.19	48.87	3.83	29.34	52.00	5.13	35.09	54.96	14.07
404	24 Parganas (North 24 Parganas+South 24 Parganas)	27.21	48.57	3.57	28.56	49.48	5.75	33.02	53.01	11.55
405	Kolkata	35.19	55.74	6.33	33.01	53.86	6.91	37.56	58.06	12.84

Sl. No.	State/Union Territory	1981			1991			2001		
		Total	Male	Female	Total	Male	Female	Total	Male	Female
West Bengal										
406	Haora	26.91	48.42	2.26	29.10	51.47	3.73	33.67	55.85	9.19
407	Hugli	29.75	50.23	7.22	31.14	52.31	8.05	36.88	56.50	16.16
408	Medinipur	29.72	48.41	10.07	35.19	51.90	17.50	39.03	54.50	22.82
409	Bankura	32.92	49.96	15.24	35.91	51.79	19.21	44.70	56.75	32.04
410	Puruliya	38.27	51.00	24.98	43.15	51.24	34.61	44.45	52.31	36.21
411	Birbhum	30.52	51.47	8.75	33.15	52.45	12.75	37.42	54.30	19.65
412	Barddhaman	30.61	50.01	8.99	30.66	50.10	9.01	35.55	53.53	16.03

no increase in participation rate in Delhi, whereas there is an increase of about 2 percentage points from 1991 to 2001.

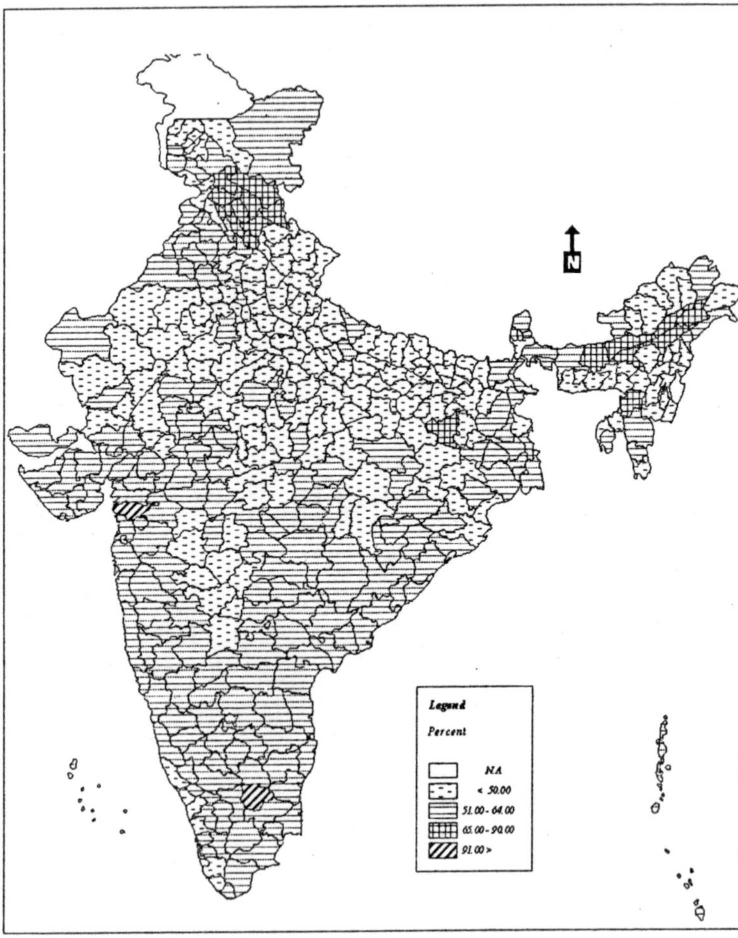

Map 4.1.1. Crude Work Participation Rate (Total, Male), District, India, 2001

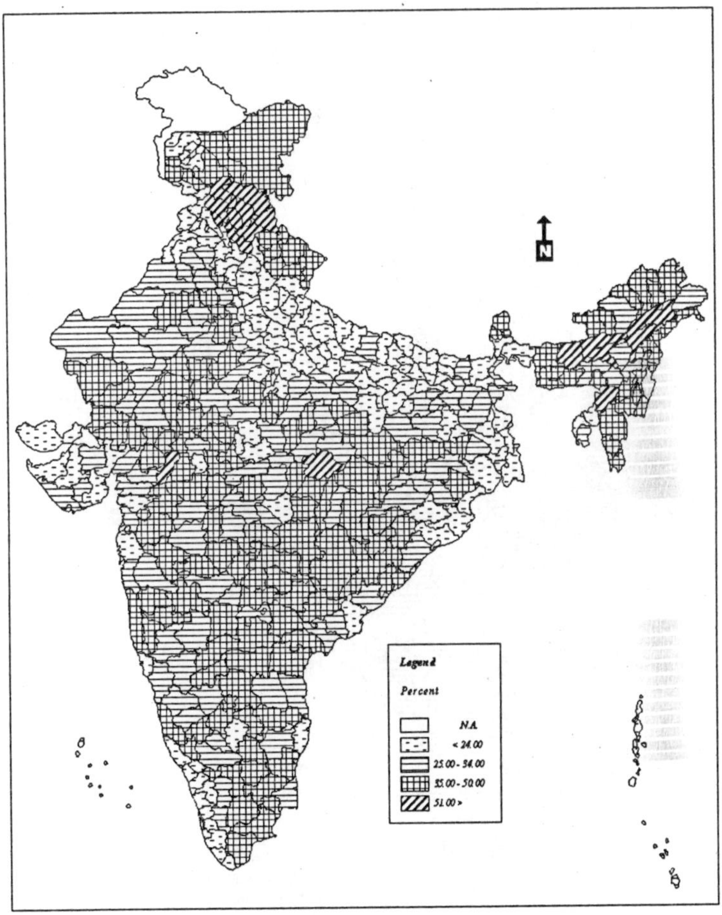

Map 4.1.2. Crude Work Participation Rate (Total Female), District, India, 2001

Map 4.1.1 and 4.1.2 show the work participation rates of male and female workers respectively. Maps reveal that the work participation rates of both males and females are lower in northern and parts of central India. It may also be observed that rates vary from 35 per cent to 50 per cent in most of the districts in 2001. Compared to northern and central India, work participation rates are higher in the Himalayan region, north-eastern and south India. This pattern is also true when we study the variations in work participation rates by even rural and urban areas. (See Maps 4.1.3 to 4.1.6).

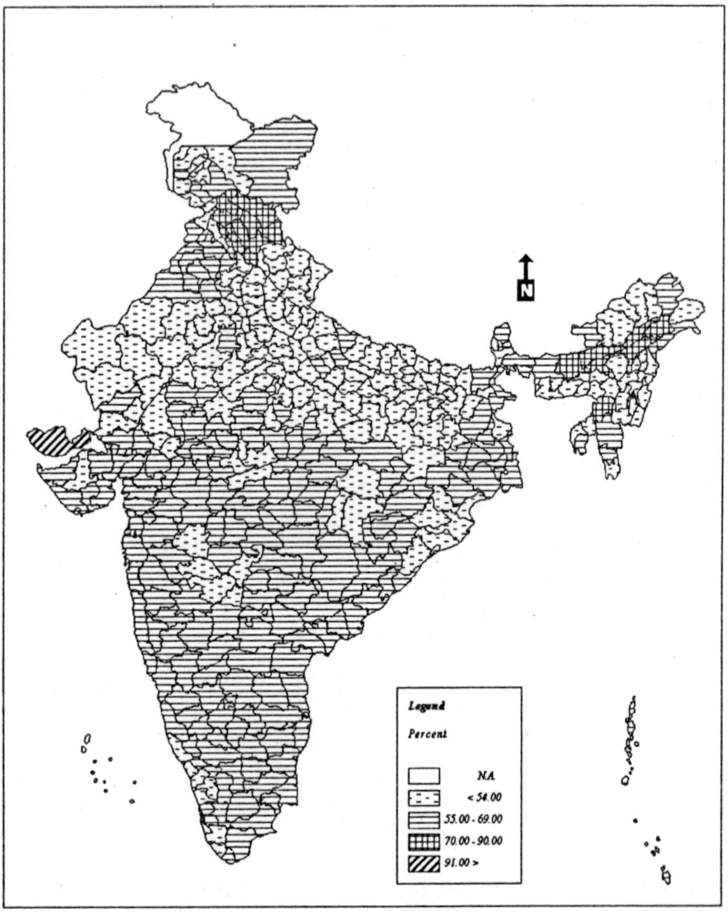

Map 4.1.3. Crude Work Participation Rate (Total), Rural (Male), District, India, 2001

Map 4.1.3 depicts male work participation rate in rural areas at the district level in 2001.It may be seen that the work participation rate of males is about 55 per cent to 69 per cent in most of the districts. Rural areas of most of the districts in Uttar Pradesh, Haryana, Bihar Rajasthan and Kerala show less than 50 per cent work participation rates among males, which was lower than the national average of 52 per cent in 2001. It may also be observed from Map 4.1.4 that the female work participation rates are highest in most of districts of Himachal Pradesh and Assam. Generally the rates vary from about 41 to 59 per cent in most the districts in 2001. In the case of female work participation also most of the districts of Uttar Pradesh, Punjab, Sikkim, Bihar and Kerala show one of the lowest rates.

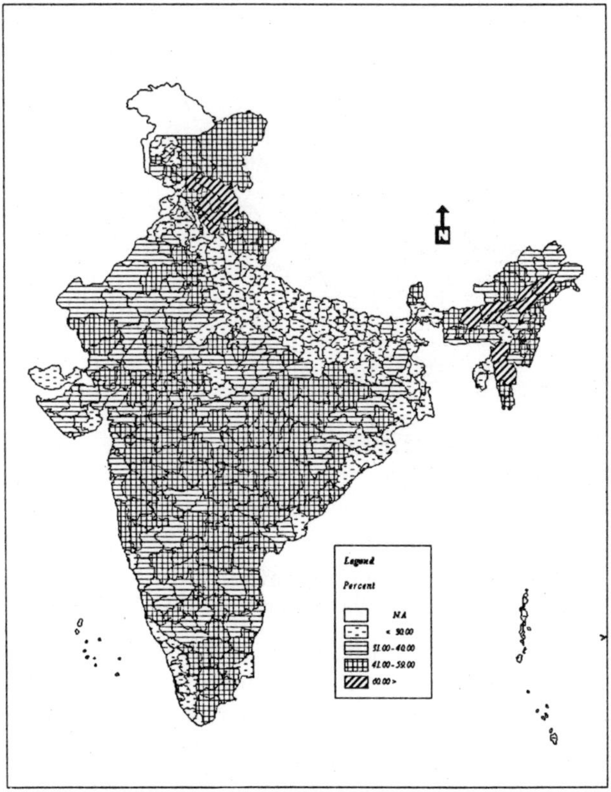

Map 4.1.4. Crude Work Participation Rate to Total Workers, Rural (Female), District, India, 2001

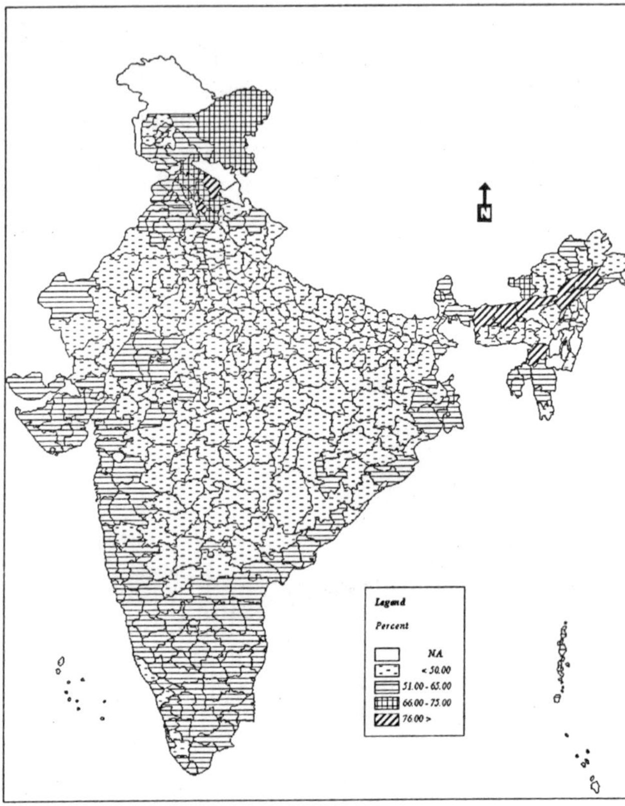

Map 4.1.5. Crude Work Participation Rate to Total Workers, Urban (Male), District, India, 2001

Map 4.1.5 depicts crude work participation rate of male workers in urban areas at the district level in 2001. It may be observed from the map that work participation rate of males is highest in Kullu (Jammu and Kashmir) and most of districts of Assam. We also found that the work participation rate is about in the range of 66 per cent to 75 per cent in majority of the district of the country. On the other hand, in northern India, most of the districts have less than 50 per cent of male work participation rate in urban areas. Map 4.1.6 depicts the female work participation rate in urban areas at the district level in 2001.From the map it may be observed that the female work participation rate is highest in most of the districts of north-east India. But, in most of districts in India the crude work participation rate is below 14 per cent in 2001.

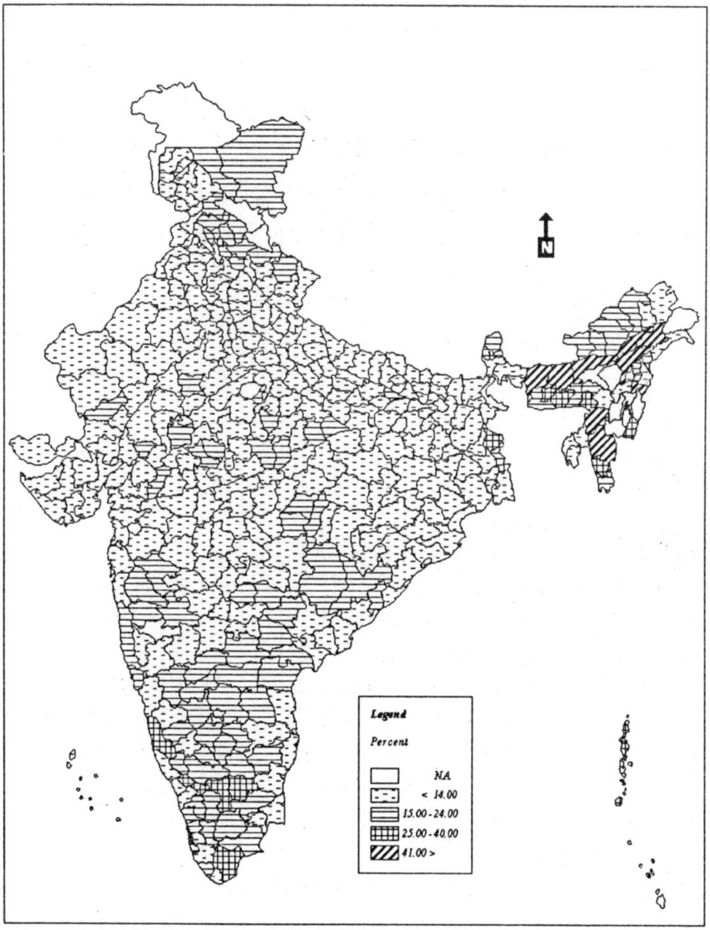

Map 4.1.6. Crude Work Participation Rate to Total Workers, Urban (Female), District, India, 2001

4.2 Co-efficients of variations at the District Level

When we are analysing the work participation rates at the district level it is important to know the nature of disparity among the districts over time. For this we have calculated the co-efficients of variations for the period 1981 to 2001 and

Table 4.1.2. Crude Work Participation Rate (Rural) Districts Level, India 1981-2001

Sl. No.	*State / Union Territory*	*1981*			*1991*			*2001*		
		Total	*Male*	*Female*	*Total*	*Male*	*Female*	*Total*	*Male*	*Female*
Andaman & Nicobar Islands										
01	Andaman	35.80	56.58	8.62	34.39	52.60	12.61	37.61	56.02	16.25
02	Nicobar	41.38	55.72	23.70	39.73	54.82	21.76	46.65	60.92	29.99
Andhra Pradesh										
03	Adilabad	50.42	59.46	41.30	49.31	55.30	43.26	50.91	55.27	46.53
04	Nizamabad	54.66	59.75	49.72	53.82	56.42	51.30	52.93	55.89	50.05
05	Karimnagar	53.68	60.88	46.49	54.94	58.57	51.29	52.94	56.45	49.44
06	Medak	51.94	60.04	43.75	50.85	56.53	45.01	51.24	56.32	46.06
07	Hyderabad	0.00	0.00	0.00	0.00	0.00	0.00	0.00	0.00	0.00
08	Rangareddi	50.47	58.10	42.60	49.53	55.22	43.58	49.06	55.78	42.08
09	Mahbubnagar	57.71	60.20	55.19	46.72	50.28	43.06	54.17	57.28	50.98
10	Nalgonda	51.84	60.79	42.69	50.75	56.04	45.26	51.79	56.05	47.39
11	Warangal	51.57	59.62	43.28	52.20	56.76	47.48	52.10	55.89	48.22
12	Khammam	48.54	58.95	37.70	50.24	57.63	42.54	52.47	58.36	46.42

Sl. No.	State / Union Territory	1981			1991			2001		
		Total	Male	Female	Total	Male	Female	Total	Male	Female
13	Srikakulam	51.08	60.24	42.16	50.76	57.44	44.17	48.98	57.04	41.04
14	Vizianagaram	51.75	61.77	41.81	54.21	60.79	47.62	56.11	61.29	50.97
15	Visakhapatnam	50.54	62.14	38.89	52.06	60.70	43.37	49.39	58.61	40.18
16	East Godavari	43.11	60.79	25.32	40.88	58.26	23.45	41.94	59.87	23.82
17	West Godavari	45.98	60.77	31.08	45.95	59.44	32.35	46.60	61.20	31.77
18	Krishna	48.55	60.67	36.12	49.49	59.64	38.99	49.21	60.32	37.83
19	Guntur	52.44	60.98	43.68	53.43	59.46	47.19	54.35	60.79	47.78
20	Prakasam	51.15	59.00	43.15	51.43	56.69	46.00	52.74	58.34	46.96
21	Nellore	49.68	60.74	38.42	49.55	58.68	40.22	48.92	59.47	38.19
22	Cuddapah	47.54	59.03	35.59	47.75	57.34	37.68	48.09	57.80	38.10
23	Kurnool	51.29	58.43	43.91	51.58	57.13	45.76	53.77	57.89	49.50
24	Anantapur	49.74	58.78	40.21	50.72	57.62	43.41	53.56	59.44	47.39
25	Chittoor	48.68	61.13	35.86	49.58	59.54	39.31	50.75	59.78	41.59
Arunachal Pradesh										
26	West Kameng (West Kamenga + Tawang)	52.85	61.15	43.28	48.65	58.07	37.39	49.06	58.28	37.63
27	East Kameng	57.97	63.80	51.80	50.77	53.98	47.43	49.49	50.15	48.84

Sl. No.	State/Union Territory	1981			1991			2001		
		Total	Male	Female	Total	Male	Female	Total	Male	Female
28	Lower Subansiri (Lower Subansiri + Papun Pare)	56.37	57.59	55.05	48.90	52.36	45.18	43.07	46.02	40.02
29	Upper Subansiri	54.36	56.01	52.65	47.38	51.37	42.78	44.22	44.99	43.45
30	West Siang	49.35	52.39	46.22	44.19	49.59	38.30	42.48	45.57	39.23
31	East Siang (East Siang + Upper Siang)	52.28	57.31	46.57	45.98	52.50	38.59	44.47	49.36	39.09
32	Dibang Valley	59.90	68.33	47.17	47.86	57.22	36.31	46.90	53.67	38.95
33	Lohit	49.52	59.45	37.02	45.98	·54.92	35.27	44.49	52.03	35.77
34	Tirap (Tirap + Changlang)	52.58	57.38	47.04	48.82	54.09	42.76	50.06	52.31	45.41
Assam										
35	Goalpara (Goalpara + Kokrajhar + Dhubri + Bongariagaon)	N.A.	N.A.	N.A.	55.51	66.50	44.13	55.68	65.75	45.25
36	Kamrup (Kamrup + Nailbari + Barpeta)	N.A.	N.A.	N.A.	75.15	80.42	69.76	76.73	81.66	71.69
37	Darrang (Darrang + Sonipur)	N.A.	N.A.	N.A.	80.09	83.19	76.89	79.26	82.79	75.67
38	Nagaon (Nagaon + Marigaon)	N.A.	N.A.	N.A.	91.02	93.09	88.94	90.91	92.99	88.83

Sl. No.	*State / Union Territory*	*1981*			*1991*			*2001*		
		Total	*Male*	*Female*	*Total*	*Male*	*Female*	*Total*	*Male*	*Female*
Assam										
39	Sibsagar (Sibsagar + Goalghat + Jorhat)	N.A.	N.A.	N.A.	72.92	76.07	69.67	74.26	78.03	70.39
40	Lakhimpur (Lakhimpur + Dhemaji)	N.A.	N.A.	N.A.	86.91	87.28	86.53	87.22	88.09	86.35
41	Dibrugarh (Dibrugarh + Tinsukia)	N.A.	N.A.	N.A.	83.89	85.51	82.23	83.82	85.52	82.07
42	Karbi Anglong /Mikir Hills	N.A.	N.A.	N.A.	44.14	51.29	36.36	41.85	49.38	33.78
43	North Cachar Hills	N.A.	N.A.	N.A.	45.15	53.68	35.46	39.41	48.49	29.53
44	Cachar (Cachar + Karimganj + Hailakandi)	N.A.	N.A.	N.A.	77.09	82.90	71.16	77.20	82.36	71.93
Bihar										
45	Patna	30.01	47.97	10.65	29.59	46.22	10.78	33.72	47.46	18.34
46	Nalanda	32.33	48.16	15.33	34.34	47.69	19.54	39.90	49.40	29.54
47	Nawada	33.36	49.49	17.36	32.39	47.93	15.84	38.28	48.78	27.24
48	Gaya (Gaya + Jehanabad)	33.60	49.22	17.54	33.09	47.54	17.53	38.75	48.53	28.39

Sl. No.	State/Union Territory	1981			1991			2001		
		Total	Male	Female	Total	Male	Female	Total	Male	Female
49	Aurangabad	48.79	47.48	50.16	29.96	46.00	12.49	34.19	46.20	21.36
50	Rohtas (Rohtas + Kaimur)	29.85	47.87	10.18	30.21	46.61	11.83	32.66	46.72	17.21
51	Bhojpur (Bhojpur + Buxar)	27.26	45.20	8.43	27.14	44.04	8.38	29.90	44.94	13.34
52	Gopalganj	26.76	47.69	6.06	26.72	45.79	7.09	30.06	44.74	15.47
53	Siwan	24.41	43.59	6.62	24.29	42.02	6.10	27.09	41.58	13.14
54	Saran	24.48	43.06	6.49	23.95	41.76	6.57	26.75	42.24	10.85
55	Vaishali	26.24	46.59	5.92	25.65	45.22	4.46	29.07	45.50	11.26
56	Pashchim Champaran	35.20	53.47	15.24	35.75	52.63	16.55	39.01	51.52	25.15
57	Purba Champaran	31.50	53.45	7.93	31.20	50.85	9.00	33.12	49.20	15.26
58	Sitamarhi (Sitamarhi + Sheohar)	29.77	54.46	3.43	30.15	51.94	5.51	32.05	50.59	11.28
59	Muzaffarpur	5.55	51.88	0.81	29.46	49.28	7.69	30.92	47.21	13.33
60	Begusarai	29.81	49.30	9.22	28.70	47.02	8.40	32.11	46.47	16.41
61	Samastipur	29.09	50.44	7.25	28.26	47.24	7.84	31.81	47.02	15.45
62	Darbhanga	29.49	50.67	8.08	30.17	48.42	10.23	31.91	46.72	15.75
63	Madhubani	29.96	51.21	8.41	32.74	49.20	15.09	34.63	47.95	20.52
64	Saharsa (Sahasa + Madhepura + Supaul)	38.78	53.90	22.66	38.23	50.96	24.04	42.94	50.86	34.32

Sl. No.	State / Union Territory	1981			1991			2001		
		Total	Male	Female	Total	Male	Female	Total	Male	Female
65	Purnia (Purnia + Araia + Kishanganj)	36.11	56.45	14.35	35.93	54.77	15.36	38.09	52.40	22.61
66	Katihar	35.10	54.84	14.15	34.68	52.57	15.15	38.83	51.77	24.82
67	Munger (Munger + Khagarai + Jamuli)	33.27	50.29	15.02	34.19	48.30	18.18	38.31	48.42	27.05
68	Bhagalpur (Bhagalpur + Banka)	32.91	50.25	14.06	33.94	48.40	17.48	38.49	49.28	26.39
69	Santhal Pargana (Dumka + Godda + Sahibganj + Deogarh + Pakaur)	41.81	56.21	26.89	41.86	53.06	29.96	42.96	52.38	33.02
70	Dhanbad	31.59	49.11	11.14	28.92	45.33	10.28	30.73	45.48	14.51
71	Giridih (Giridih+ Bokaro)	35.20	51.17	19.28	35.25	48.14	21.83	33.88	46.12	21.21
72	Hazaribagh (Hazaribagh + Chatra + Kodarma)	34.90	50.60	19.20	34.81	47.34	21.79	5.87	46.52	28.63
73	Palamu (Palamu + Garhwa)	36.03	51.93	19.54	35.92	48.51	22.45	38.92	47.53	29.74
74	Ranchi (Ranchi + Gumla + Lohardaga)	45.66	55.63	35.67	46.37	52.62	39.92	47.07	51.68	42.38
75	Sinhabhumi (Pashchimi Singhbhum + Purbi Sinhabhumi)	45.45	56.60	34.20	46.40	53.85	38.76	46.52	53.06	39.85

Sl. No.	*State / Union Territory*	*1981*			*1991*			*2001*		
		Total	*Male*	*Female*	*Total*	*Male*	*Female*	*Total*	*Male*	*Female*
Chandigarh										
76	Chandigarh	36.16	58.58	3.57	41.54	64.43	5.34	43.64	63.88	11.08
Dadra & Nagar Haveli										
77	Dadra and Nagar Haveli	49.42	56.39	42.31	54.29	57.42	51.05	53.84	61.26	45.13
Delhi										
78	Delhi	30.15	47.49	8.75	29.12	48.23	5.46	31.27	48.11	10.42
Goa, Damn & Diu										
79	Goa (North Goa + South Goa)	36.07	47.37	24.89	36.40	48.80	23.92	40.53	54.51	26.39
80	Diu	41.19	48.13	34.34	45.50	56.45	33.02	33.57	44.01	23.79
81	Daman	28.04	40.28	17.07	35.75	48.37	23.27	57.38	76.34	18.32
Gujarat										
82	Jamnagar	38.40	53.88	22.25	41.32	54.18	27.94	44.53	56.32	32.23
83	Rajkot	38.98	53.23	23.99	43.27	54.92	31.10	46.74	57.67	35.21
84	Surendranagar	40.82	53.96	26.81	44.90	54.41	34.58	46.77	55.02	37.89
85	Bhavnagar	39.60	53.90	24.83	43.21	54.85	31.04	42.09	53.49	30.24
86	Amreli	39.44	52.72	25.93	42.27	54.67	29.74	46.18	55.86	36.51
87	Junagadh (Junagarh + Porbandar)	37.23	51.96	21.83	43.12	54.67	31.14	45.49	56.33	34.20

Sl.		*1981*			*1991*			*2001*		
No.	*State / Union Territory*	*Total*	*Male*	*Female*	*Total*	*Male*	*Female*	*Total*	*Male*	*Female*
88	Kachchh	37.96	53.21	23.08	38.77	51.79	25.57	40.68	53.58	27.14
89	Banas Kantha	36.69	53.78	18.64	40.60	52.42	27.93	45.41	51.59	38.79
90	Sabar Kantha	40.60	52.30	28.68	45.69	52.17	39.01	46.82	52.62	40.73
91	Mahesana (Mahesana + Patan)	38.35	50.79	25.61	46.34	53.36	39.01	48.59	54.31	42.48
92	Gandhinagar	32.05	50.90	12.09	36.63	52.07	20.11	47.24	55.21	38.63
93	Ahmadabad	39.13	53.58	23.66	44.21	54.97	32.53	44.46	55.32	32.64
94	Kheda(Kheda+Anand)	37.21	53.85	19.02	45.21	55.43	34.06	46.99	56.36	36.78
95	Panch Mahals (Panch Mahals + Dohad)	47.20	55.93	38.12	49.22	52.27	46.01	51.29	53.17	49.34
96	Vadodara	41.96	57.35	25.38	48.31	58.75	36.99	49.53	58.69	39.67
97	Bharuch (Bharuch + Narmada)	44.63	56.87	31.73	46.71	57.62	35.06	47.37	57.68	36.32
98	Surat	48.71	58.82	38.41	52.43	60.21	44.29	51.49	59.60	42.93
99	Valsad (Valsad + Navsari)	45.77	54.80	36.80	49.62	57.53	41.50	48.59	57.16	39.68
100	The Dangs	50.62	56.96	44.08	52.97	54.41	51.52	49.80	52.36	47.21
Haryana										
101	Ambala (Ambala + Panchkula)	29.85	53.05	3.04	29.34	52.17	2.96	34.52	52.09	13.96

Sl. No.	*State / Union Territory*	*1981*			*1991*			*2001*		
		Total	*Male*	*Female*	*Total*	*Male*	*Female*	*Total*	*Male*	*Female*
102	Kurukshetra (Kurukshetra + Yamunanagar + Kaithal)	32.26	52.64	8.66	29.82	50.91	5.56	38.65	51.55	23.70
103	Karnal (Karnal + Panipat)	30.59	51.00	6.56	29.88	49.45	6.92	39.05	49.91	26.33
104	Sonipat	33.15	47.57	16.55	31.65	48.29	11.62	44.59	50.98	36.95
105	Jind	36.42	50.81	19.55	33.57	49.45	14.53	47.28	52.74	40.87
106	Rohtak (Rohtak + Rewari + Jhajar)	32.39	46.11	16.87	31.25	45.53	14.81	46.20	51.06	40.59
107	Gurgaon	32.71	49.88	13.24	33.08	46.35	17.78	39.58	46.10	32.13
108	Faridabad	30.14	48.28	8.78	30.68	45.78	12.74	41.83	46.92	35.90
109	Mahendragarh	29.74	44.64	13.85	31.67	44.62	17.46	45.19	48.11	42.03
110	Bhiwani	34.42	46.92	20.65	33.71	45.26	20.58	45.65	49.92	40.83
111	Hissar (Hissar+Fatehabad)	33.53	52.01	12.33	34.00	50.69	14.62	47.38	53.72	40.06
112	Sirsa	32.43	54.43	7.63	36.02	53.36	16.47	46.34	53.87	37.83
Himachal Pradesh										
113	Chamba	49.90	59.69	39.47	49.90	54.41	45.17	80.61	85.30	75.77

Sl. No.	*State / Union Territory*	*1981*			*1991*			*2001*		
		Total	*Male*	*Female*	*Total*	*Male*	*Female*	*Total*	*Male*	*Female*
Himachal Pradesh										
114	Kangra	34.50	47.96	21.33	34.70	46.12	23.61	63.97	75.40	53.60
115	Lahul & Spiti	66.83	70.50	62.06	64.93	68.90	60.07	84.88	88.62	79.86
116	Kullu	53.34	58.24	48.10	48.69	53.84	43.15	88.04	91.05	84.79
117	Mandi	47.25	51.67	42.90	46.62	49.05	44.24	75.93	79.30	72.76
118	Hamirpur	37.28	41.64	33.56	42.59	44.05	41.29	72.88	76.78	69.70
119	Una	28.01	45.90	10.78	33.80	48.49	19.45	67.24	79.77	55.49
120	Bilaspur	42.01	49.17	34.93	45.08	48.19	42.01	71.52	76.76	66.47
121	Solan	42.75	53.18	31.75	46.40	54.14	38.01	79.16	87.29	70.19
122	Sirmaur	47.91	61.15	32.79	48.46	56.46	39.56	80.06	88.43	70.60
123	Shimla	53.56	58.49	47.73	50.35	54.19	46.27	79.10	83.31	74.62
124	Kinnaur	57.26	62.75	51.05	52.42	60.08	43.48	85.58	90.90	79.02

Sl. No.	*State / Union Territory*	*1981*			*1991*			*2001*		
		Total	*Male*	*Female*	*Total*	*Male*	*Female*	*Total*	*Male*	*Female*
Jammu & Kashmir										
125	Kupwara	48.87	56.93	39.47	N.A.	N.A.	N.A.	32.53	44.95	18.97
126	Baramula	47.46	57.64	35.76	N.A.	N.A.	N.A.	32.18	46.93	16.00
127	Srinagar	52.32	59.87	43.77	N.A.	N.A.	N.A.	31.42	47.02	14.34
128	Badgam	51.44	60.21	41.49	N.A.	N.A.	N.A.	36.24	48.51	23.20
129	Pulwama	51.90	56.89	46.33	N.A.	N.A.	N.A.	32.33	46.23	17.74
130	Anantanag	43.60	56.38	29.20	N.A.	N.A.	N.A.	34.10	45.44	21.98
131	Leh (Ladakh)	50.41	58.74	44.79	N.A.	N.A.	N.A.	49.47	55.45	42.86
132	Kargil	55.09	59.60	49.85	N.A.	N.A.	N.A.	46.83	49.16	44.16
133	Doda	44.08	55.88	31.08	N.A.	N.A.	N.A.	46.82	52.72	40.39
134	Udhampur	57.11	63.26	50.34	N.A.	N.A.	N.A.	51.05	57.27	44.12
135	Punch	47.83	56.77	37.77	N.A.	N.A.	N.A.	55.39	58.28	52.29
136	Rajauri	45.53	55.31	34.79	N.A.	N.A.	N.A.	45.74	51.88	38.84
137	Jammu	43.66	54.46	32.05	N.A.	N.A.	N.A.	33.56	49.66	15.70
138	Kathua	45.16	56.07	33.30	N.A.	N.A.	N.A.	38.39	50.84	24.75

Sl. No.	State / Union Territory	1981			1991			2001		
		Total	Male	Female	Total	Male	Female	Total	Male	Female
Karnataka										
139	Bangalore (Bangalore + Bangalore rural)	40.04	56.68	22.49	43.68	56.67	29.77	48.02	60.24	35.08
140	Belgaum	44.33	58.14	30.01	45.68	55.80	35.12	48.06	56.96	38.82
141	Bellary	47.51	57.65	37.21	49.97	55.65	44.13	50.82	55.85	45.67
142	Bidar	43.43	55.67	30.90	43.30	50.73	35.62	40.22	49.03	31.01
143	Bijapur (Bijapur + Bagalkot)	44.94	56.75	33.05	45.58	52.56	38.37	44.86	52.98	36.45
144	Chikmagalur	47.08	58.22	35.50	47.41	58.60	36.06	47.58	60.23	34.80
145	Chitradurga (Chitradurga + Davangere)	47.01	57.77	35.77	47.72	56.15	38.90	49.34	58.40	39.88
146	Dakshin Kannada (Dakshin Kannada + Udupi)	43.27	49.97	37.03	44.55	51.79	37.69	50.18	57.79	43.15
147	Dharwad (Dharwad + Gadag + Haveri)	46.79	58.43	34.66	47.79	56.11	39.00	51.45	59.66	42.80

Sl. No.	State / Union Territory	1981 Total	1981 Male	1981 Female	1991 Total	1991 Male	1991 Female	2001 Total	2001 Male	2001 Female
148	Gulbarga	50.11	57.77	41.57	47.94	53.81	41.91	48.33	53.69	42.84
149	Hassan	42.50	57.04	27.95	47.10	57.58	36.74	53.83	62.45	45.32
150	Kodagu	49.20	60.33	37.40	49.17	59.45	38.74	50.23	61.52	38.97
151	Kolar	43.44	57.44	29.12	47.91	57.57	37.94	53.60	60.14	46.67
152	Mandya	38.19	57.27	18.45	46.73	58.75	34.33	49.94	62.50	37.25
153	Mysore (Mysore + Chamarajanagar)	40.95	59.63	21.20	44.00	59.94	27.35	47.34	61.56	32.60
Karnataka										
154	Raichur (Raichur + Koppal)	46.54	58.70	34.34	47.91	55.24	40.48	48.43	54.31	42.48
155	Shimoga	41.16	56.37	25.23	44.62	57.19	31.63	46.34	60.63	35.83
156	Tumkur	43.07	57.04	28.65	50.50	58.50	42.27	54.29	61.62	46.76
157	Uttara Kannada	41.22	55.55	26.38	41.88	55.26	28.06	46.75	59.59	33.54
158	Kasaragod (Kasaragod+Kannur)	31.22	44.94	18.57	32.11	46.15	18.41	34.54	50.43	19.49
159	Wayanad	38.04	51.08	24.30	38.75	53.21	23.79	39.48	55.76	23.13

Sl.		1981			1991			2001		
No.	State / Union Territory	Total	Male	Female	Total	Male	Female	Total	Male	Female
Kerala										
160	Kozhikode	27.93	43.39	12.85	26.96	44.11	10.28	27.38	47.36	8.50
161	Malappuram	25.32	40.39	11.03	24.43	40.75	8.95	24.10	42.69	6.67
162	Palakkad	35.95	47.23	25.30	36.16	48.65	24.42	36.46	51.97	21.92
163	Thrissur	29.94	41.53	19.49	32.40	47.09	18.94	32.21	50.46	15.56
164	Ernakulam	33.43	47.69	19.17	34.97	46.08	30.03	37.53	55.95	19.37
165	Idukki	38.10	51.64	24.03	40.07	55.35	24.39	43.67	58.39	28.83
166	Kottayam	29.95	47.16	12.72	31.51	50.77	12.31	33.25	52.69	14.24
167	Alappuzha	32.72	44.37	21.66	34.19	46.97	22.07	33.75	48.50	20.18
168	Kollam (Kollam + Pathanamithitta)	30.69	45.29	16.47	31.72	48.20	15.97	31.44	48.07	16.07
169	Thiruvananthapuram	31.01	47.39	15.17	33.63	51.54	16.40	32.36	51.75	14.23
Lakshadweep										
170	Lakshadweep	25.25	39.01	11.29	25.28	42.86	6.96	23.77	40.63	6.20

Sl. No.	State / Union Territory	1981			1991			2001		
		Total	Male	Female	Total	Male	Female	Total	Male	Female
Madhya Pradesh & Chattisgarh										
171	Morena (Morena + Sheopur)	32.22	51.23	9.45	33.13	48.42	14.62	40.86	49.61	30.43
172	Bhind	28.09	48.96	2.90	28.09	47.27	4.50	40.04	50.11	27.85
173	Gwalior	36.32	53.50	15.30	36.40	50.93	18.64	38.29	50.02	24.22
174	Datia	33.85	51.99	12.47	39.57	52.32	24.40	55.03	58.56	50.88
175	Shivpuri	40.41	55.64	22.61	45.05	53.96	34.54	48.68	53.50	43.04
176	Guna	37.56	55.26	17.49	39.16	52.93	23.42	44.08	52.94	34.05
177	Tikamgarh	43.66	55.68	30.03	45.18	52.49	36.76	49.45	53.26	45.14
178	Chhatarpur	42.00	56.79	24.92	43.59	53.08	32.50	42.93	50.38	34.35
179	Panna	41.99	55.99	26.74	43.24	54.24	31.03	45.62	52.20	38.34
180	Sagar	42.58	54.54	29.28	41.77	52.01	30.19	44.53	52.94	34.96
181	Damoh	41.71	54.95	27.48	43.01	54.15	30.75	47.35	54.46	39.47
182	Satna	43.52	53.63	32.91	42.38	50.50	33.63	41.89	48.81	34.50
183	Rewa	40.96	50.56	31.28	39.14	46.91	30.92	46.16	50.48	41.63

Sl. No.	State / Union Territory	1981			1991			2001		
		Total	Male	Female	Total	Male	Female	Total	Male	Female
184	Shahdol (Shahdol + Umaria)	46.66	58.42	34.52	47.45	55.88	38.67	47.64	54.05	41.04
185	Sidhi	44.87	56.02	33.20	43.84	51.63	35.50	43.42	48.55	38.01
186	Mandsaur (Mandsaur + Neemuch)	48.81	56.76	40.41	50.82	55.92	45.47	52.09	56.76	47.22
187	Ratlam	48.95	58.49	38.97	53.34	57.84	48.63	51.33	55.57	46.94
188	Ujjain	45.56	57.38	32.99	46.90	55.67	37.52	52.36	56.94	47.51
189	Shajapur	45.85	56.31	34.64	47.60	55.03	39.52	52.19	56.12	47.96
190	Dewas	45.89	55.33	35.81	44.62	51.91	36.80	49.42	53.29	45.28
191	Jhabua	55.36	59.02	51.68	56.08	57.09	55.05	54.40	54.95	53.84
192	Dhar	48.43	55.00	41.68	48.81	53.34	44.09	49.16	52.63	45.59
193	Indore	43.05	54.14	31.12	43.90	53.56	33.39	45.64	53.35	37.42
194	West Nimar (West Nimar + Barwani)	46.25	54.19	37.99	48.53	53.19	43.65	49.65	53.16	46.01

Sl. No.	*State / Union Territory*	*1981*			*1991*			*2001*		
		Total	*Male*	*Female*	*Total*	*Male*	*Female*	*Total*	*Male*	*Female*
Madhya Pradesh & Chhattisgarh										
195	East Nimar	48.39	57.23	39.02	49.32	55.33	42.93	49.14	54.67	43.24
196	Rajgarh	45.96	58.64	32.40	50.37	56.54	43.70	53.65	55.98	51.17
197	Vidisha	36.81	55.72	15.40	39.97	53.75	24.17	39.48	52.51	24.54
198	Bhopal	41.20	54.80	25.85	42.73	52.29	31.77	42.19	49.41	34.03
199	Sehore	41.89	54.24	28.36	44.87	51.63	37.36	44.86	49.69	39.56
200	Raisen	38.21	54.35	20.53	38.75	51.68	24.11	38.11	50.20	24.43
201	Betul	51.72	57.88	45.52	51.15	55.24	46.99	48.01	52.57	43.34
202	Hoshangabad (Hoshangabad + Harda)	40.26	54.61	24.67	41.30	52.92	28.44	42.48	52.02	31.95
203	Jabalpur (Jabalpur + Katni)	43.70	54.27	32.73	44.26	53.19	34.74	44.99	52.96	36.50
204	Narsimhapur	40.61	55.07	25.14	41.39	53.43	28.23	44.30	55.04	32.48
205	Mandla (Mandla + Dindori)	55.72	60.24	51.24	52.97	56.21	49.71	55.91	57.72	54.11
206	Chhindwara	47.37	56.88	37.70	48.01	54.72	41.06	46.22	52.42	39.75
207	Seoni	51.30	57.40	45.14	51.42	55.34	47.41	51.01	54.92	47.04

Sl. No.	State / Union Territory	1981			1991			2001		
		Total	Male	Female	Total	Male	Female	Total	Male	Female
208	Balaghat	53.79	57.98	49.66	51.84	55.05	48.67	52.88	55.39	50.44
209	Surguja (Surguja + Koriya)	49.51	63.24	35.39	50.32	58.44	41.94	52.45	57.09	47.70
210	Bilaspur (Bilaspur + Jangir - Champa + Korba)	48.34	55.56	41.16	47.59	52.66	42.47	46.83	51.03	42.60
211	Raigarh (Raigarh + Jashpur)	50.49	61.92	39.23	51.09	58.88	43.37	51.95	57.44	46.48
212	Rajnandgaon (Rajnandgaon + Kanwardha)	56.36	57.99	54.78	55.95	56.24	55.66	53.11	54.14	52.10
213	Durg	53.00	54.90	51.14	51.43	52.62	50.25	48.59	51.15	46.06
214	Raipur (Raipur + Mahasamud + Dhamtari)	52.73	57.10	48.47	50.89	54.60	47.21	47.58	51.51	43.71
215	Bastar (Bastar + Kanker + Dhamtari)	52.98	62.29	43.75	55.35	59.44	51.29	54.82	57.90	51.79
Maharashtra										
216	Mumbai (Greater Mumbai + Suburban)	0.00	0.00	0.00	0.00	0.00	0.00	0.00	0.00	0.00
217	Thane	45.48	56.20	33.99	49.62	55.18	43.81	48.04	55.67	39.93
218	Raigarh	43.10	50.34	36.34	46.25	51.44	41.23	43.71	52.41	35.07

Sl. No.	State/Union Territory	1981			1991			2001		
		Total	*Male*	*Female*	*Total*	*Male*	*Female*	*Total*	*Male*	*Female*
219	Ratnagiri (Ratnagiri + Sindhudurg)	41.61	45.74	38.34	47.30	49.07	45.82	46.89	52.35	42.08
220	Nashik	49.89	54.61	44.98	51.16	53.05	49.19	51.07	54.31	47.64
221	Dhule (Dhule + Nandurbar)	47.43	55.66	39.01	50.33	53.53	47.03	48.93	53.23	44.48
222	Jalgaon	46.95	54.31	39.25	48.15	51.93	44.17	47.54	52.66	42.08
223	Pune	45.28	52.66	37.82	49.03	53.20	44.70	50.00	55.49	44.20
224	Ahmadnagar	47.74	53.94	41.34	48.49	51.60	45.23	48.98	53.17	44.55
225	Solapur	89.33	56.28	34.92	48.06	53.52	42.20	50.61	55.37	45.47
226	Satara	43.19	49.06	37.78	46.67	50.06	43.43	48.74	54.50	43.02
227	Sangli	41.26	54.19	28.06	47.43	54.10	40.52	51.45	57.66	44.98
228	Kolhapur	39.33	53.59	24.96	50.88	55.57	46.10	52.73	58.27	46.97
229	Aurangabad (Aurangabad + Jalna)	51.08	57.10	44.83	50.32	52.55	47.97	47.83	51.42	44.03
230	Parbhani (Parbhani + Hingoli)	53.95	60.83	46.89	50.79	53.78	47.69	49.42	52.26	46.47
231	Bid	49.66	57.38	41.74	51.13	52.28	49.93	48.03	50.32	45.60
232	Nanded	54.09	60.06	47.94	49.30	52.09	46.37	46.20	50.38	41.79
233	Osamanabad (Osamanabad + Latur)	47.86	56.87	38.53	48.25	51.79	44.53	45.57	51.19	39.57
234	Buldana	54.79	58.99	50.44	51.90	53.50	50.23	49.65	53.33	45.77

Sl.		1981			1991			2001		
No.	State / Union Territory	Total	Male	Female	Total	Male	Female	Total	Male	Female
	Maharashtra									
235	Akola (Akola +Wahsim)	50.09	56.95	42.92	49.64	53.43	45.63	46.87	52.99	40.35
236	Amravati	48.32	57.41	38.65	51.06	57.25	44.48	47.80	56.15	38.91
237	Yavatmal	52.48	57.77	47.02	51.44	54.55	48.20	48.89	54.36	43.09
238	Wardha	50.96	58.01	43.57	50.26	55.54	44.66	49.35	56.63	41.58
239	Nagpur	50.76	56.90	44.22	50.50	55.19	45.47	50.02	56.77	42.81
240	Bhandara (Bhandara + Gondiya)	53.32	56.10	50.55	52.93	54.00	51.86	50.32	54.12	46.52
241	Chandrapur (Chandrapur + Gadchiroli)	53.17	58.15	48.06	53.69	55.84	51.48	52.05	55.97	48.01
	Manipur									
242	Manipur North (Senapati)	54.08	53.93	54.24	51.88	51.62	52.15	45.93	50.21	41.43
243	Manipur West (Tamenglong)	52.27	50.19	54.39	46.02	45.60	46.47	45.62	46.60	44.55
244	Manipur South Churachandpur)	47.18	50.67	43.49	47.52	50.98	43.77	43.60	48.41	38.51

Sl. No.	State / Union Territory	1981			1991			2001		
		Total	Male	Female	Total	Male	Female	Total	Male	Female
245	Bishnupur (Bishnupur + Thoubal + Imphal East + Imphal West)	41.51	45.34	37.65	41.84	44.43	39.18	45.27	49.69	40.80
246	Ukhrul	51.33	50.29	52.46	46.05	47.26	44.68	47.25	48.83	45.53
247	Tengnoopal (Chandel)	63.28	67.50	55.85	54.48	55.81	53.04	47.71	49.55	45.84
Meghalaya										
248	Jaintia Hills	50.61	56.76	44.31	47.66	53.64	41.50	43.56	49.01	38.06
249	East Khasi Hills (East Khasi Hills + Ribhoi)	46.41	54.88	37.66	42.43	50.63	33.97	44.42	51.13	37.44
250	West Khasi Hills	51.48	54.05	48.79	44.67	47.93	41.23	44.96	47.33	42.50
251	East Garo Hills	45.94	52.50	39.02	44.97	49.19	40.60	46.19	48.74	43.55
252	West Garo Hills (East Garo Hills + South Grao Hills)	50.44	57.25	43.44	46.68	52.46	40.70	42.86	49.16	36.35
Mizoram										
253	Aizawl (Aizawl + Kolasib + Champhal + Serchhip + Mamit)	N.A.	N.A.	N.A.	51.27	55.02	47.14	61.26	63.29	59.07

Sl. No.	State / Union Territory	1981			1991			2001		
		Total	Male	Female	Total	Male	Female	Total	Male	Female
254	Lunglei	N.A.	N.A.	N.A.	51.25	55.62	46.54	57.62	60.17	54.85
255	Chhimtulpul / Saiha (Saihal + Lawngtial)	N.A.	N.A.	N.A.	50.95	54.11	47.49	47.98	51.33	44.34
Nagaland										
256	Kohima (Kohima + Dimapur)	49.22	55.15	42.13	41.83	46.03	37.20	41.66	46.92	35.83
257	Phek	52.82	51.35	54.51	76.33	42.74	113.56	48.08	47.61	48.57
258	Mon	60.33	62.89	57.51	52.91	54.90	50.66	51.35	53.63	48.78
259	Tuensang	53.47	53.92	52.97	46.31	46.94	45.62	45.98	46.63	45.26
260	Mokokchung	44.18	46.54	41.63	40.14	42.85	37.23	48.91	50.95	46.72
261	Zunheboto	47.85	47.58	48.12	44.39	44.36	44.42	38.13	39.56	36.66
262	Wokha	45.28	43.81	46.79	42.21	41.69	42.77	38.64	39.97	37.24
Odisha										
263	Sambalpur (Sambalpur + Bargarh + Jharsuguda + Debagarh)	45.74	60.87	30.47	46.13	58.78	33.27	46.36	56.13	36.41
264	Sundargarh	42.71	57.45	27.79	44.88	56.38	33.23	46.60	53.92	39.22
265	Kendujhar	39.74	55.88	23.58	40.07	53.62	26.37	41.27	51.70	30.71
266	Mayurbhanj	48.73	58.24	39.20	46.87	54.95	38.67	47.39	52.75	41.97
267	Baleshwar (Baleshwar + Bhadrak)	29.02	51.59	6.14	28.45	50.25	6.08	30.91	50.82	10.30

Sl. No.	*State / Union Territory*	*1981*			*1991*			*2001*		
		Total	*Male*	*Female*	*Total*	*Male*	*Female*	*Total*	*Male*	*Female*
Odisha										
268	Cuttack (Cuttack + Jajpur + Kendrapara +Jagatsinghpur)	28.94	51.71	6.08	27.22	48.87	5.22	30.91	50.34	11.14
269	Dhenkanal (Dhenkanal +Angul)	36.79	55.65	17.45	36.28	53.59	18.30	37.47	51.83	22.55
270	Phulbani (Kandhamal + Boudh)	48.92	61.89	36.03	48.40	58.25	38.57	47.77	54.07	41.49
271	Balangir (Balangir + Sonpur)	42.19	61.07	23.29	42.89	59.30	26.28	43.89	55.73	31.86
272	Kalahandi (Kalahandi + Nuapara)	42.51	62.27	23.06	46.25	61.56	31.02	47.45	57.14	37.84
273	Koraput (Koraput + Nabarangapur + Mlakangiri + Rayagarh)	49.98	63.40	36.58	51.22	61.08	41.37	50.81	56.76	44.92
275	Puri (Puri + Nayagarh + Khordha)	31.11	54.65	7.26	30.21	52.82	6.97	30.67	51.92	8.65
Pondicherry										
276	Yanam	0.00	0.00	0.00	0.00	0.00	0.00	0.00	0.00	0.00

Sl. No.	*State / Union Territory*	*1981*			*1991*			*2001*		
		Total	*Male*	*Female*	*Total*	*Male*	*Female*	*Total*	*Male*	*Female*
277	Pondicherry	35.24	50.48	19.17	40.41	53.95	26.22	40.97	54.75	26.87
278	Mahe	19.86	34.96	6.64	0.00	0.00	0.00	0.00	0.00	0.00
279	Karaikal	34.64	51.11	18.35	33.26	51.91	14.78	35.06	53.41	17.11
Punjab										
280	Gurdaspur	27.73	50.04	3.17	28.30	52.11	1.98	34.05	51.53	14.57
281	Amritsar	31.57	54.74	5.10	30.91	56.05	2.05	38.26	53.34	21.22
282	Firozpur (Firozpur + Moga)	34.71	57.63	8.82	33.10	55.93	7.65	39.79	53.86	24.02
283	Ludhiana	31.77	54.59	5.82	30.24	55.32	1.69	40.17	53.68	24.81
284	Jalandhar (Jalandhar + Nawanshahr)	29.36	51.10	5.34	30.11	53.69	4.13	38.96	54.38	22.07
285	Kapurthala	29.39	52.40	4.37	31.35	54.45	5.97	35.25	52.55	16.24
286	Hoshiarpur	29.44	49.84	7.33	28.83	51.24	4.60	35.37	50.55	19.32
287	Rupnagar	30.41	52.15	5.30	29.99	52.91	3.63	42.56	53.96	29.45
288	Patiala (Patiala + Fatehgarh Sahib)	31.66	55.23	4.38	30.52	54.77	2.78	39.14	54.79	21.07
289	Sangrur	36.32	59.14	9.61	33.14	57.57	4.95	43.69	55.69	29.92
290	Bathinda (Bhathinda + Mansa)	36.71	57.71	12.48	34.41	57.66	8.02	44.98	56.15	32.22

Sl. No.	State / Union Territory	1981			1991			2001		
		Total	Male	Female	Total	Male	Female	Total	Male	Female
291	Faridkot (Farikot Muktsar)	35.01	56.80	10.19	33.63	57.27	6.77	41.95	55.52	26.72
Rajasthan										
292	Ganganagar	34.16	54.13	11.68	39.62	53.32	24.11	43.96	53.52	33.21
293	Bikaner	37.75	54.77	18.97	41.67	51.27	30.94	45.41	51.52	38.61
294	Churu	39.11	51.68	25.96	43.95	48.48	39.14	50.86	52.00	49.66
295	Jhunjhunun	37.06	46.28	27.56	35.87	43.42	27.86	43.67	48.09	39.05
296	Alwar	37.33	48.46	24.97	42.20	47.74	35.95	51.61	53.80	49.17
297	Bharatpur	33.87	49.24	15.32	34.64	46.87	19.61	44.54	49.42	38.74
298	Sawai Madhopur	35.44	50.04	18.61	40.38	47.77	31.72	43.64	46.81	39.98
299	Jaipur	35.82	48.88	21.48	38.08	46.53	28.73	41.17	46.04	35.81
300	Sikar	32.73	46.09	18.89	33.60	43.21	23.50	42.15	46.33	37.79
301	Ajmer	46.55	56.30	36.27	46.94	52.86	40.60	45.72	51.22	39.94
302	Tonk	43.50	54.20	32.03	44.27	51.29	36.68	47.38	50.23	44.32
303	Jaisalmer	32.50	55.81	4.14	38.15	50.34	23.18	43.49	51.99	33.22
304	Jodhpur	37.68	52.75	21.44	40.93	48.24	32.94	42.96	48.59	36.84
305	Nagaur	39.76	51.59	27.49	42.16	48.80	35.16	43.52	48.80	37.99
306	Pali	93.93	99.28	88.35	40.37	48.37	32.14	42.21	48.53	35.90
307	Barmer	42.66	55.50	28.58	46.21	52.11	39.63	48.22	51.54	44.52
308	Jalor	34.30	52.12	15.49	42.21	50.82	33.13	51.73	54.76	48.60
309	Sirohi	36.62	51.48	21.49	40.76	50.94	30.22	42.50	50.28	34.41

Sl. No.	*State/Union Territory*	*1981*			*1991*			*2001*		
		Total	*Male*	*Female*	*Total*	*Male*	*Female*	*Total*	*Male*	*Female*
Rajasthan										
310	Bhilwara	47.38	59.26	34.85	50.18	57.46	42.57	50.08	55.21	44.83
311	Udaipur	41.52	53.97	29.00	45.88	54.00	37.61	43.62	51.74	35.46
312	Chittaurgarth	50.65	58.92	42.06	52.45	57.25	47.45	55.19	58.01	52.30
313	Dungarpur	45.77	51.69	40.15	45.94	51.73	40.17	49.22	51.70	46.81
314	Banswara	43.06	51.21	34.84	47.97	52.40	43.42	48.61	50.77	46.41
315	Bundi	39.96	55.84	22.05	42.73	53.07	31.08	55.19	58.01	52.30
316	Kota	36.56	51.98	19.52	40.44	50.73	28.94	43.18	49.82	35.87
317	Jhalawar	41.31	55.08	26.49	46.56	55.58	36.77	49.95	54.95	44.56
Sikkim										
318	North	53.43	62.20	42.45	43.95	53.51	32.52	57.75	64.72	48.54
319	West	52.23	55.70	48.44	45.06	51.71	37.82	43.25	52.04	33.81
320	South	51.00	57.66	43.33	42.95	51.70	33.21	53.44	59.00	47.47
321	East	45.37	54.99	33.95	38.31	49.31	25.85	49.60	58.75	38.78
Tamil Nadu										
322	Chennai	0.00	0.00	0.00	0.00	0.00	0.00	0.00	0.00	0.00

Sl. No.	State / Union Territory	1981			1991			2001		
		Total	Male	Female	Total	Male	Female	Total	Male	Female
323	Chengalpattu /Kancheepuram (Kancheepuram + Thituvellur)	42.63	57.12	27.75	43.90	56.12	31.38	43.86	56.46	31.13
324	Vellore/North Arcot (Vellore + Tiruvanamalai)	45.42	58.32	32.26	46.30	56.31	36.06	48.22	57.39	38.99
325	South Arcot/ Cuddalore (Cuddalore + Villuppuram	44.30	57.98	30.25	46.26	56.23	35.98	49.88	57.74	41.88
326	Dharmapuri	45.85	59.91	31.20	49.07	57.54	40.08	51.65	58.40	44.43
327	Salem (Salem + Namakkal)	51.97	63.10	40.24	53.26	61.74	44.15	56.61	62.84	49.91
328	Erode(Pariyar)	55.24	68.11	41.84	56.59	67.06	45.68	61.33	68.38	54.04
329	Coimbatore	53.76	66.18	40.94	53.19	66.31	39.61	54.07	66.17	41.67
330	The Nilgiris	41.48	50.49	32.33	44.28	52.21	36.31	50.68	56.69	44.82
331	Madurai (Madurai + Dindlgul Anna + Theni)	50.66	60.10	41.08	52.51	59.55	45.27	53.83	60.10	47.43
332	Tiruchirappalli (Tiruchirapalli + Perambalur + Karur)	8.83	60.95	3.60	51.52	59.89	43.05	54.62	60.86	48.41
333	Thanjavur (Thanjavur+ Nagapattinam + Thiruvarur)	41.91	58.27	25.37	43.61	57.76	29.36	43.38	57.53	29.44

Sl. No.	*State / Union Territory*	*1981*			*1991*			*2001*		
		Total	*Male*	*Female*	*Total*	*Male*	*Female*	*Total*	*Male*	*Female*
334	Pudukkottai	43.22	57.19	29.41	46.78	56.64	37.00	49.29	58.64	40.10
335	Ramanathapuram (Ramanathapuram + Sivaganga)	47.73	57.50	38.32	52.23	57.43	47.13	50.66	57.67	43.88
336	Tirunelveli (Tiruneveli + Toothukudi)	47.20	56.57	38.36	50.29	55.96	44.89	50.01	56.69	43.71
337	Kanniyakumari	28.93	48.53	8.99	30.70	50.16	11.03	33.53	53.53	13.75
Tripura										
338	West Tripura	31.72	49.71	12.83	30.77	48.13	12.27	35.72	50.15	20.46
339	North Tripura (North Tripura + Dhalai)	33.15	52.56	12.36	32.74	49.37	15.01	36.16	49.29	22.28
340	South Tripura	34.39	52.78	14.95	31.53	45.05	17.32	40.07	52.13	27.34
Uttar Pradesh & Uttarakhand										
341	Uttarkashi	56.50	59.03	53.73	51.79	52.06	51.50	47.10	48.47	45.68
342	Chamoli (Chamoli + Rudraprayag)	50.62	47.08	53.88	47.49	45.08	49.78	45.28	42.98	47.37
343	Tehri Garhwal	51.35	47.95	54.38	45.58	43.25	47.71	44.43	43.40	45.35

Sl. No.	State / Union Territory	1981			1991			2001		
		Total	*Male*	*Female*	*Total*	*Male*	*Female*	*Total*	*Male*	*Female*
Uttar Pradesh & Uttarakhand										
344	Dehradun	37.05	55.01	15.65	38.93	52.71	22.93	33.23	47.44	17.67
345	Garhwal	44.60	43.16	45.86	40.20	40.31	40.10	40.27	40.07	40.45
346	Pithoragarh (Pithoragarh + Chamawat)	46.86	47.34	46.39	49.80	47.72	51.88	44.01	43.08	44.88
347	Almora(Almora + Bageshwar)	39.91	41.98	38.06	47.63	43.47	51.35	47.82	44.28	50.85
348	Nainital (Nainital + Udam Singh Nagar)	35.76	53.62	14.71	43.19	54.12	30.82	36.65	49.06	23.12
349	Saharanpur (Saharanpur + Hardwar)	30.12	53.38	2.25	30.44	52.69	4.15	29.16	47.47	8.03
350	Muzaffarnagar	29.39	51.94	2.44	35.12	52.47	14.76	35.14	50.06	17.92
351	Bijnor	28.81	51.21	2.61	29.06	50.89	3.82	29.26	47.04	9.35
352	Meerut (Meerut + Bhatpat)	48.17	49.58	31.24	32.24	50.74	10.19	33.37	47.93	16.41
353	Ghaziabad	27.33	48.09	2.46	30.98	48.13	10.38	30.63	46.07	12.64
354	Bulandshahar (Bulandshahar + Gautam Buddha Nagar)	26.28	47.31	1.81	29.64	47.74	8.33	39.94	50.24	28.10

Sl. No.	State / Union Territory	1981			1991			2001		
		Total	Male	Female	Total	Male	Female	Total	Male	Female
355	Moradabad (Moradabad + Jyotiba Phule Nagar)	29.41	52.68	1.48	29.86	51.12	4.61	32.82	48.40	14.98
356	Rampur	30.33	54.63	1.04	31.86	53.68	6.07	28.49	47.19	7.02
357	Budaun	32.50	57.45	1.25	32.52	55.32	3.88	30.95	49.71	8.38
358	Bareilly	29.93	53.84	0.70	30.33	53.58	2.04	31.70	49.62	10.91
359	Pilibhit	30.64	55.70	0.92	30.91	53.18	4.69	28.44	48.40	5.64
360	Shahjahanpur	32.26	57.36	0.92	32.42	56.95	1.75	29.38	50.04	4.67
361	Aligarh	27.11	48.48	1.51	31.15	49.19	9.53	32.69	46.52	16.53
362	Mathura (Mathura + Hathras)	28.44	49.22	2.60	29.91	48.62	6.61	36.26	47.66	22.73
363	Agra (Agra + Firozabad)	28.26	50.01	1.46	28.26	49.01	2.88	28.01	45.03	7.79
364	Etah	28.80	51.67	0.86	31.63	51.97	6.67	29.42	47.13	8.37
365	Mainpuri	27.45	49.59	0.62	28.13	49.89	1.82	28.18	46.48	6.67
366	Farrukhabad (Farrukhabad + Kannauj)	29.13	51.73	1.57	29.93	51.84	3.45	31.62	49.02	11.16
367	Etawah (Etawah + Auraiya)	26.59	47.63	1.09	27.80	49.41	1.57	31.15	47.85	11.51
368	Kanpur (Kanpur Dehat + Kanpur Nagar)	29.33	50.39	4.61	29.57	50.44	4.76	33.84	48.81	16.31

Sl. No.	State / Union Territory	1981			1991			2001		
		Total	Male	Female	Total	Male	Female	Total	Male	Female
369	Fatehpur	33.85	51.76	13.92	38.09	51.56	22.83	38.98	49.15	27.58
370	Allahabad (Allahabad + Kaushambi)	31.29	49.32	11.46	35.87	48.02	22.20	37.24	45.18	28.41
371	Jalaun	31.81	50.43	9.53	35.69	50.48	17.71	38.75	50.63	24.66
372	Jhansi	32.41	50.55	11.22	40.08	51.68	26.47	42.39	51.58	31.82
373	Lalitpur	41.52	57.21	23.17	44.16	54.33	32.32	45.55	51.22	39.10
374	Hamirpur (Hamirpur + Mahoba)	35.82	52.36	16.51	42.10	52.62	29.56	43.02	50.80	33.91
375	Banda (Banda + Chitrakoot)	38.52	52.94	21.92	45.16	53.13	35.72	43.17	49.32	36.05
376	Kheri	31.75	57.61	1.18	32.49	56.29	4.13	32.02	51.70	9.43
377	Sitapur	31.52	56.93	1.45	32.85	56.23	4.65	31.78	51.44	8.89
378	Hardoi	30.82	55.32	1.09	32.73	54.96	5.36	32.92	51.72	10.52
379	Unnao	31.59	53.18	7.36	34.50	53.58	12.62	35.60	50.87	18.60
380	Lucknow	32.04	54.41	6.08	34.36	53.43	12.10	33.57	49.10	16.07
381	Rae Bareli	35.34	53.80	15.87	36.17	51.55	19.74	36.64	48.44	24.29
382	Bahraich (Bahraich + Shravasti)	33.30	58.76	3.44	39.71	57.68	18.28	38.37	53.72	20.58
383	Gonda (Gonda + Balrampur)	33.15	56.94	6.51	37.61	55.28	17.39	38.07	51.86	22.82
384	Barabanki	34.05	57.43	6.82	36.20	56.14	12.86	37.71	52.45	21.08

Sl. No.	State / Union Territory	1981			1991			2001		
		Total	Male	Female	Total	Male	Female	Total	Male	Female
Uttar Pradesh & Uttarakhand										
385	Faizabad (Faizabad + Ambedkar Nagar)	29.51	50.42	7.47	32.25	49.74	13.50	37.55	47.89	26.86
386	Sultanpur	30.32	49.90	10.24	31.96	49.07	13.71	32.45	44.81	19.89
387	Pratapgarh	28.07	46.58	9.82	32.19	45.85	18.45	33.95	42.94	25.05
388	Basti (Basti + Sant Kabir Nagar + Siddharthnagar)	34.00	53.70	12.85	34.76	51.02	17.03	36.70	46.92	25.98
389	Gorakhpur (Gorakpur + Maharajganj)	31.07	49.66	11.53	33.33	48.09	17.44	35.06	45.28	24.42
390	Deoria (Deoria+ Kushinagar)	35.33	50.57	20.04	31.70	46.63	16.35	32.07	43.33	20.66
391	Azamgarh	32.44	47.16	18.19	30.19	44.61	15.98	30.82	40.95	20.97
392	Jaunpur	27.35	45.63	9.39	28.24	43.11	13.39	31.53	40.34	22.93
393	Ghazipur	26.88	44.24	9.38	30.70	44.64	16.23	31.92	41.87	21.80
394	Ballia (Ballia + Mau)	27.68	45.28	10.00	29.66	44.32	14.43	30.33	41.72	18.63
395	Varanasi (Varansi + Sant Ravidas Nagar + Chandauli)	29.72	48.66	9.28	33.36	46.90	18.47	31.93	43.48	19.44

Sl.		1981			1991			2001		
No.	State / Union Territory	Total	Male	Female	Total	Male	Female	Total	Male	Female
396	Mirzapur (Mirzapur + Sonbhadra)	37.15	54.58	17.87	39.42	51.59	25.64	36.59	46.73	25.42
West Bengal										
397	Koch Bihar	30.04	54.29	4.12	32.46	54.11	9.26	39.64	55.14	23.28
398	Jalpaiguri	34.52	52.59	14.74	34.63	50.79	17.24	39.59	52.24	26.20
399	Darjiling	38.65	49.83	26.37	36.17	46.77	24.82	37.04	47.92	25.65
400	Dakshin Dinajpur (Dakshin Dinjapur + West Dinjapur)	33.16	55.40	9.54	35.71	55.98	14.02	40.31	63.17	29.58
401	Maldah	30.55	50.40	9.66	35.26	51.88	17.56	41.46	52.69	29.60
402	Murshidabad	28.87	50.64	6.14	31.41	51.94	9.61	33.47	51.27	14.74
403	Nadia	27.63	50.79	3.09	29.48	52.93	4.24	34.75	55.06	13.17

Sl. No.	State / Union Territory	1981			1991			2001		
		Total	Male	Female	Total	Male	Female	Total	Male	Female
404	24 Parganas (North 24 Parganas + South 24 Parganas)	25.90	49.56	2.93	28.78	50.09	6.06	33.02	52.61	12.22
405	Kolkata	0.00	0.00	0.00	0.00	0.00	0.00	0.00	0.00	0.00
406	Haora	24.59	46.17	1.89	28.14	50.95	3.90	33.39	55.52	10.29
407	Hugli	30.32	50.95	8.44	32.13	53.69	9.32	38.59	57.75	18.91
408	Medinipur	30.08	48.77	10.53	35.91	52.40	18.53	39.94	54.96	24.26
409	Bankura	33.42	50.31	15.94	36.57	52.15	20.22	45.58	57.05	33.53
410	Puruliya	39.50	51.63	26.89	44.84	51.88	37.44	46.22	52.94	39.20
411	Birbhum	30.88	51.99	9.02	33.70	52.99	13.35	37.88	54.54	20.35
412	Barddhaman	30.12	50.32	8.47	32.67	52.68	11.22	38.79	56.51	19.98

Table 4.1.3. Crude Work Participation Rate (Urban) District Level, India, 1981-2001

Sl. No.	State / Union Territory	1981			1991			2001		
		Total	Male	Female	Total	Male	Female	Total	Male	Female
Andaman & Nicobar Islands										
01	Andaman	36.48	57.56	7.20	34.78	54.13	9.60	46.65	60.92	29.99
02	Nicobar	0.00	0.00	0.00	0.00	0.00	0.00	0.00	0.00	0.00
Andhra Pradesh										
03	Adilabad	30.33	49.12	10.23	27.94	45.43	9.56	29.19	46.05	11.72
04	Nizamabad	35.16	48.55	20.99	33.21	45.67	20.44	33.63	47.64	19.25
05	Karimnagar	33.86	49.15	17.71	32.48	47.35	16.97	32.77	47.84	17.14
06	Medak	31.50	46.73	15.13	29.62	46.09	12.20	31.79	49.58	12.98
07	Hyderabad	27.86	47.48	6.55	27.36	46.03	7.36	29.24	47.28	9.90
08	Rangareddi	31.45	49.97	11.18	30.94	49.19	11.21	32.73	51.34	12.70
09	Mahbubnagar	33.71	47.20	19.06	31.31	44.77	17.08	32.54	47.49	16.88
10	Nalgonda	30.77	46.85	12.97	30.23	45.80	13.49	31.59	47.80	14.43
11	Warangal	29.44	44.63	13.17	29.36	44.26	13.77	32.04	47.90	15.69
12	Khammam	27.92	47.10	7.62	28.62	47.20	9.44	31.18	49.97	11.95

Sl. No.	State / Union Territory	1981			1991			2001		
		Total	Male	Female	Total	Male	Female	Total	Male	Female
13	Srikakulam	32.51	49.49	15.49	33.80	49.54	18.07	34.21	51.59	17.02
14	Vizianagaram	31.26	50.12	12.20	31.71	50.24	13.29	34.80	53.39	16.49
15	Visakhapatnam	28.00	47.39	7.57	29.58	49.69	8.38	30.45	50.69	9.40
16	East Godavari	31.86	52.65	10.80	30.80	51.94	9.65	31.91	53.63	10.29
17	West Godavari	32.94	52.45	13.14	33.37	52.54	14.21	34.08	54.78	13.72
18	Krishna	31.94	52.29	10.83	32.19	52.35	11.46	32.89	53.58	11.79
19	Guntur	34.01	52.11	15.37	34.18	52.00	15.93	35.96	54.88	16.89
20	Prakasam	35.00	51.34	17.89	34.47	50.49	18.05	36.50	53.81	18.86
21	Nellore	34.07	52.86	14.49	33.04	52.05	13.63	33.28	54.33	11.94
22	Cuddapah	33.66	52.24	14.10	31.94	50.39	12.73	33.53	52.35	14.31
23	Kurnool	32.56	48.89	15.30	31.96	47.71	15.38	35.10	50.96	18.70
24	Anantapur	30.30	48.86	10.39	31.49	49.99	12.06	34.84	53.04	16.00
25	Chittoor	31.31	50.21	11.25	31.15	50.26	11.08	32.49	51.73	12.66
Arunachal Pradesh										
26	West Kameng (West Kamenga + Tawang)	40.65	59.43	14.73	37.77	54.36	15.46	51.70	69.05	18.26

Sl. No.	State / Union Territory	1981			1991			2001		
		Total	Male	Female	Total	Male	Female	Total	Male	Female
27	East Kameng	0.00	0.00	0.00	0.00	0.00	0.00	33.84	44.56	21.87
28	Lower Subansiri (Lower Subansiri + Papun Pare)	46.64	67.41	12.90	35.58	52.96	13.80	35.91	48.76	21.36
29	Upper Subansiri	0.00	0.00	0.00	0.00	0.00	0.00	31.15	43.33	17.23
30	West Siang	44.29	58.99	17.26	37.06	53.27	12.25	37.48	53.29	16.83
31	East Siang (East Siang + Upper Siang)	34.26	52.01	7.86	34.90	51.96	12.10	30.63	45.65	13.72
32	Dibang Valley	0.00	0.00	0.00	34.95	50.76	11.74	33.33	48.87	13.01
33	Lohit	37.20	57.74	5.91	37.22	56.65	8.28	31.41	48.39	10.59
34	Tirap (Tirap + Changlang)	0.00	0.00	0.00	40.43	61.78	8.81	36.04	54.33	12.98
Assam										
35	Goalpara (Goalpara + Kokrajhar + Dhubri + Bongariagaon)	N.A.	N.A.	N.A.	87.37	90.50	84.19	87.33	90.70	83.90

Sl. No.	State / Union Territory	1981			1991			2001		
		Total	Male	Female	Total	Male	Female	Total	Male	Female
36	Kamrup (Kamrup + Nailbari + Barpeta)	N.A.	N.A.	N.A.	97.85	98.37	97.33	97.96	98.49	97.42
37	Darrang (Darrang + Sonipur)	N.A.	N.A.	N.A.	97.37	98.00	96.74	96.53	97.47	95.58
Assam										
38	Nagaon (Nagaon + Marigaon)	N.A.	N.A.	N.A.	99.42	99.56	99.28	99.45	99.59	99.31
39	Sibsagar (Sibsagar + Goalghat + Jorhat)	N.A.	N.A.	N.A.	93.83	95.15	92.48	92.98	94.80	91.13
40	Lakhimpur (Lakhimpur + Dhemaji)	N.A.	N.A.	N.A.	99.66	99.68	99.63	98.54	98.85	98.23
41	Dibrugarh (Dibrugarh + Tinsukia)	N.A.	N.A.	N.A.	95.30	96.39	94.20	94.21	95.74	92.65
42	Karbi Anglong/Mikir Hills	N.A.	N.A.	N.A.	31.41	49.41	9.02	31.10	45.94	14.20
43	North Cachar Hills	N.A.	N.A.	N.A.	31.59	48.12	10.52	32.81	48.86	13.04
44	Cachar (Cachar+ Karimganj + Hailakandi)	N.A.	N.A.	N.A.	97.31	97.96	96.65	97.28	97.97	96.58

Sl. No.	State / Union Territory	1981			1991			2001		
		Total	Male	Female	Total	Male	Female	Total	Male	Female
Bihar										
45	Patna	26.11	43.60	4.99	24.05	40.62	4.30	25.28	41.49	6.08
46	Nalanda	24.52	42.05	5.05	23.96	39.49	6.28	27.83	41.85	12.18
47	Nawada	24.68	42.81	4.91	22.93	39.81	4.04	24.99	40.69	7.51
48	Gaya (Gaya + Jehanabad)	0.58	0.43	0.76	23.97	39.88	5.59	26.09	40.91	9.23
49	Aurangabad	25.89	44.07	5.44	23.72	39.84	5.51	24.08	39.68	6.74
50	Rohtas (Rohtas + Kaimur)	24.20	42.54	2.29	22.97	40.33	3.10	23.35	39.70	4.75
51	Bhojpur (Bhojpur + Buxar)	24.18	41.93	3.79	22.46	39.21	3.03	23.53	39.68	4.55
52	Gopalganj	26.24	46.68	3.62	24.26	42.78	3.76	25.91	42.26	8.29
53	Siwan	24.26	43.18	2.97	23.64	41.10	3.41	23.88	39.87	6.10
54	Saran	23.62	42.01	2.62	23.04	40.70	3.19	24.01	40.58	5.38
55	Vaishali	25.93	46.10	3.42	24.03	42.32	3.33	25.06	41.98	6.04
56	Pashchim Champaran	26.67	45.30	5.17	27.81	45.56	7.18	28.28	44.95	9.46
57	Purba Champaran	26.92	45.67	3.67	25.24	42.02	5.23	25.88	42.76	6.14
58	Sitamarhi (Sitamarhi + Sheohar)	27.14	47.62	3.02	25.33	44.21	2.97	27.09	45.68	5.55

Sl. No.	State / Union Territory	1981			1991			2001		
		Total	Male	Female	Total	Male	Female	Total	Male	Female
59	Muzaffarpur	24.81	41.64	3.85	23.96	40.77	3.92	25.55	42.11	6.40
60	Begusarai	25.34	44.78	3.28	23.82	41.36	3.45	24.29	40.50	5.67
61	Samastipur	25.82	43.95	4.60	24.95	42.33	4.95	25.50	42.23	6.46
62	Darbhanga	22.87	40.02	3.19	22.28	38.57	3.52	23.31	39.47	4.89
63	Madhubani	25.66	44.84	3.43	26.09	42.39	7.72	26.29	42.53	8.09
64	Saharsa (Sahasa + Madhepura + Supaul)	29.02	46.31	7.75	28.24	42.72	10.51	26.84	41.87	9.25
65	Purnia (Purnia + Araia + Kishanganj)	29.85	49.69	5.67	26.77	45.29	5.07	26.98	44.52	6.55
66	Katihar	27.22	46.21	3.74	24.40	41.66	3.94	24.78	41.99	4.98
67	Munger (Munger + Khagarai + Jamuli)	24.64	41.84	5.00	25.21	41.26	6.54	24.85	39.97	7.34
68	Bhagalpur (Bhagalpur + Banka)	24.78	42.29	4.15	24.31	41.24	4.56	26.73	38.95	8.48

Sl. No.	State / Union Territory	1981			1991			2001		
		Total	Male	Female	Total	Male	Female	Total	Male	Female
69	Santhal Pargana (Dumka +Godda + Sahibganj + Deogarh + Pakaur)	25.73	43.72	4.48	25.14	42.36	4.86	25.87	42.27	6.92
70	Dhanbad	29.07	47.53	4.20	26.42	43.46	4.45	24.95	42.02	4.71
71	Giridih (Giridih + Bokaro)	27.06	44.48	6.04	25.85	42.88	5.37	3.21	5.48	4.20
72	Hazaribagh (Hazaribagh + Chatra + Kodarma)	28.84	47.64	4.35	26.41	43.53	5.06	25.67	42.39	5.82
73	Palamu (Palamu + Garhwa)	2.71	2.24	3.27	24.65	41.14	5.11	25.12	41.28	6.73
74	Ranchi (Ranchi + Gumla + Lohardaga)	26.99	43.58	7.25	25.65	41.19	7.68	26.36	41.67	9.05

Sl. No.	State / Union Territory	1981			1991			2001		
		Total	Male	Female	Total	Male	Female	Total	Male	Female
Bihar										
75	Sinhabhumi (Pashchimi Singhbhum + Purbi Sinhabhumi)	26.08	43.49	5.46	25.84	43.31	5.54	27.04	44.46	7.70
Chandigarh										
76	Chandigarh	34.83	54.50	9.46	34.18	53.05	10.89	37.13	55.12	14.54
Dadra & Nagar Haveli										
77	Dadra and Nagar Haveli	41.94	55.30	26.84	41.98	58.21	22.10	44.75	65.63	14.54
Delhi										
78	Delhi	32.46	53.08	6.74	31.92	52.11	7.57	32.23	51.52	8.74
Goa, Daman & Diu										
79	Goa (North Goa +South Goa)	33.81	50.73	15.13	33.68	50.62	15.45	37.04	54.68	18.17
80	Diu	29.63	44.16	15.44	35.67	52.42	18.23	29.02	45.89	14.65
81	Daman	29.70	43.94	17.87	28.47	44.40	14.18	39.27	57.94	18.18
Gujarat										
82	Jamnagar	28.77	49.96	6.06	29.63	51.37	6.30	30.94	52.64	7.32
83	Rajkot	27.79	49.40	4.84	29.70	51.45	6.40	32.17	54.33	7.95
84	Surendranagar	30.22	49.32	9.53	30.21	49.59	9.16	31.61	51.29	9.93
85	Bhavnagar	27.95	48.80	5.77	29.34	50.05	7.19	31.94	53.31	8.13
86	Amreli	29.00	48.43	8.62	31.09	50.97	10.25	32.46	52.21	11.46

Sl. No.	State / Union Territory	1981			1991			2001		
		Total	Male	Female	Total	Male	Female	Total	Male	Female
87	Junagadh (Junagarh + Porbandar)	27.29	47.10	6.45	28.96	49.25	7.60	30.91	51.72	8.75
88	Kachchh	30.19	51.03	7.70	30.67	51.45	7.97	32.59	53.77	9.51
89	Banas Kantha	27.26	47.53	5.52	27.42	47.36	5.72	29.10	48.10	8.05
90	Sabar Kantha	27.68	47.58	6.16	28.70	47.91	8.16	31.43	49.58	11.69
91	Mahesana (Mahesana+ Patan)	28.21	47.20	8.03	29.50	49.34	8.05	32.26	50.73	11.83
92	Gandhinagar	28.32	46.17	7.50	27.65	46.29	6.72	30.95	49.18	10.42
93	Ahmadabad	29.09	49.86	5.32	29.42	50.03	6.31	32.09	52.55	9.00
94	Kheda (Kheda + Anand)	28.13	48.28	6.14	28.90	48.93	7.28	32.67	50.94	12.78
95	Panch Mahals(Panch Mahals + Dohad)	27.10	47.12	5.80	28.89	47.77	8.61	30.10	48.41	10.43
96	Vadodara	29.67	50.55	6.30	30.23	50.88	7.32	32.22	52.46	9.91
97	Bharuch (Bharuch + Narmada)	31.12	50.57	9.95	53.87	51.16	56.82	31.77	52.39	9.07
98	Surat	34.30	56.87	7.80	34.11	57.10	7.02	38.49	61.34	8.68
99	Valsad (Valsad + Navsari)	33.50	53.70	10.96	33.30	53.87	10.70	36.42	56.57	13.22
100	The Dangs	0.00	0.00	0.00	31.05	46.57	13.84	0.00	0.00	0.00
Haryana										
101	Ambala (Ambala + Panchkula)	29.11	50.74	4.61	28.21	48.25	6.47	32.99	52.12	10.52
102	Kurukshetra (Kurkshetra + Yamunanagar + Kaithal)	28.47	49.59	3.89	27.58	48.24	3.99	29.76	48.45	7.85

Sl. No.	State / Union Territory	1981			1991			2001		
		Total	Male	Female	Total	Male	Female	Total	Male	Female
103	Karnal (Karnal + Panipat)	30.25	51.74	5.49	29.28	50.25	5.43	33.97	51.86	12.64
104	Sonipat	27.90	47.77	4.54	27.42	46.54	5.52	29.84	45.67	11.15
105	Jind	27.62	48.15	3.70	26.87	46.13	4.44	30.46	46.89	11.29
106	Rohtak (Rohtak+ Rewari + Jhajar)	27.05	46.14	5.21	27.39	46.82	5.22	30.90	47.51	11.31
107	Gurgaon	32.78	54.41	4.40	28.05	47.18	6.47	32.14	49.38	12.12
108	Faridabad	27.47	47.20	4.87	29.97	50.46	4.79	31.01	49.41	8.67
Haryana										
109	Mahendragarh	27.47	47.42	4.88	26.33	45.75	4.77	31.21	47.26	13.02
110	Bhiwani	28.16	49.28	3.28	26.52	45.82	4.46	30.39	46.38	11.78
111	Hissar (Hissar + Fatehabad)	29.26	50.72	3.87	28.82	49.04	5.42	32.25	49.49	12.03
112	Sirsa	29.62	52.04	2.97	28.61	50.55	3.58	32.06	50.74	10.73
Himachal Pradesh										
113	Chamba	32.60	51.09	12.08	32.55	48.92	14.39	47.57	69.68	21.92
114	Kangra	31.27	49.05	11.87	28.13	45.29	9.76	45.35	67.95	20.70
115	Lahul & Spiti	0.00	0.00	0.00	0.00	0.00	0.00	0.00	0.00	0.00
116	Kullu	38.63	57.61	12.01	37.75	56.58	13.74	53.16	75.60	23.47
117	Mandi	33.46	52.02	10.31	34.12	49.76	16.12	44.98	65.99	21.83

Sl. No.	State/Union Territory	1981			1991			2001		
		Total	Male	Female	Total	Male	Female	Total	Male	Female
118	Hamirpur	34.03	50.21	14.26	30.87	45.49	14.07	46.16	67.09	22.59
119	Una	28.11	48.32	6.27	29.77	50.41	7.78	47.78	73.83	19.67
120	Bilaspur	34.41	51.00	13.79	36.72	51.48	19.08	52.00	70.73	30.34
121	Solan	37.03	57.50	10.79	35.54	54.18	12.82	60.66	83.83	19.24
122	Sirmaur	29.96	48.95	7.65	29.80	48.34	8.59	42.14	66.42	14.20
123	Shimla	42.31	61.63	13.36	41.90	58.60	18.89	51.42	72.84	21.56
124	Kinnaur	0.00	0.00	0.00	0.00	0.00	0.00	0.00	0.00	0.00
Jammu & Kashmir										
125	Kupwara	48.69	56.72	39.14	N.A.	N.A.	N.A.	36.19	53.78	10.61
126	Baramula	32.43	50.31	11.87	N.A.	N.A.	N.A.	29.68	46.38	10.24
127	Srinagar	30.68	50.87	7.48	N.A.	N.A.	N.A.	32.15	50.95	9.64
128	Badgam	32.27	49.19	12.84	N.A.	N.A.	N.A.	33.29	48.74	15.21
129	Pulwama	38.54	52.88	22.65	N.A.	N.A.	N.A.	34.66	52.92	13.99
130	Anantanag	32.77	52.04	11.18	N.A.	N.A.	N.A.	31.26	48.88	10.34
131	Leh (Ladakh)	50.23	63.93	31.52	N.A.	N.A.	N.A.	49.92	65.84	23.89
132	Kargil	52.28	58.42	44.18	N.A.	N.A.	N.A.	44.67	57.91	20.98
133	Doda	31.90	50.04	10.38	N.A.	N.A.	N.A.	34.91	52.71	10.41
134	Udhampur	30.61	50.65	8.01	N.A.	N.A.	N.A.	39.79	60.48	9.53
135	Punch	27.40	45.21	7.50	N.A.	N.A.	N.A.	33.34	49.87	11.16

Sl. No.	State / Union Territory	1981			1991			2001		
		Total	Male	Female	Total	Male	Female	Total	Male	Female
136	Rajauri	35.08	52.80	13.53	N.A.	N.A.	N.A.	37.31	55.43	12.68
137	Jammu	29.38	48.43	7.90	N.A.	N.A.	N.A.	32.87	51.67	10.16
138	Kathua	29.70	49.75	7.27	N.A.	N.A.	N.A.	31.05	49.46	8.99
Karnataka										
139	Bangalore (Bangalore + Bangalore rural)	30.40	49.58	9.06	33.24	52.78	11.64	38.56	57.64	17.57
140	Belgaum	30.99	49.22	11.35	31.50	49.92	11.91	33.47	52.55	13.37
141	Bellary	32.99	49.26	15.89	33.76	49.37	17.31	35.34	52.32	17.60
142	Bidar	26.38	42.55	8.79	25.74	41.27	8.48	26.69	42.46	9.60
143	Bijapur (Bijapur + Bagalkot)	31.07	47.33	13.97	28.83	45.50	11.28	31.86	49.08	13.93
144	Chikmagalur	32.94	52.10	11.77	32.94	52.42	12.18	35.85	56.18	14.67
145	Chitradurga (Chitradurga + Davangere)	29.74	47.45	10.13	30.38	48.08	11.02	33.80	52.18	14.28
146	Dakshin Kannada (Dakshin Kannada + Udupi)	37.43	48.37	26.64	39.65	51.48	27.85	42.08	55.68	28.64

Sl. No.	State / Union Territory	1981			1991			2001		
		Total	*Male*	*Female*	*Total*	*Male*	*Female*	*Total*	*Male*	*Female*
Karnataka										
147	Dharwad(Dharwad + Gadag + Haveri)	32.41	49.06	14.50	31.61	48.42	13.70	34.60	52.27	16.07
148	Gulbarga	28.86	47.32	11.91	27.33	43.04	10.35	29.20	44.16	13.21
149	Hassan	29.01	47.66	8.65	30.72	49.49	10.79	33.46	53.27	12.91
150	Kodagu	36.76	55.64	15.41	36.31	54.90	16.50	38.06	57.16	18.06
151	Kolar	25.85	43.53	7.30	26.65	46.62	9.57	33.74	51.89	14.97
152	Mandya	29.32	48.37	8.71	32.97	51.00	13.69	35.66	54.55	16.12
153	Mysore(Mysore+Chamarajanagar)	29.33	47.67	9.76	31.21	49.96	11.33	34.19	53.51	14.22
154	Raichur(Raichur+Koppal)	32.80	49.41	15.34	31.18	47.55	13.94	32.18	49.28	14.39
155	Shimoga	29.03	47.98	8.52	30.56	49.73	10.10	34.45	55.03	13.16
156	Tumkur	30.68	47.38	12.36	33.51	49.23	15.91	37.19	54.68	18.75
157	Uttara Kannada	30.19	48.48	10.72	29.01	47.36	9.87	33.45	52.76	13.53
Kerala										
158	Kasaragod (Kasaragod + Kannur)	25.71	42.76	9.26	27.60	27.60	12.70	30.20	48.46	13.67
159	Wayanad	0.00	0.00	0.00	38.95	38.95	22.97	40.79	57.14	24.34
160	Kozhikode	24.88	42.51	7.39	25.95	25.95	6.98	28.71	50.76	7.82
161	Malappuram	23.27	40.04	6.92	22.94	22.94	6.28	24.35	43.45	6.35
162	Palakkad	30.14	45.84	14.95	31.82	31.82	16.17	33.88	52.14	16.59

Sl. No.	State / Union Territory	1981			1991			2001		
		Total	Male	Female	Total	Male	Female	Total	Male	Female
163	Thrissur	28.45	42.85	14.99	30.71	30.71	15.10	31.89	50.87	14.29
164	Ernakulam	28.99	45.80	12.07	31.61	12.73	34.24	34.24	54.18	14.77
165	Idukki	30.78	48.75	12.37	32.35	32.35	12.66	33.65	52.82	14.71
166	Kottayam	28.57	44.28	13.07	29.90	29.90	11.27	30.76	49.73	12.50
167	Alappuzha	27.73	41.54	14.43	33.85	33.85	21.70	35.60	51.54	20.57
168	Kollam(Kollam + Pathanamithitta)	27.50	41.35	13.90	29.32	29.32	13.31	30.38	48.28	13.33
169	Thiruvananthapuram	27.83	43.44	12.49	30.60	30.60	13.97	32.49	50.66	15.05
Lakshadweep										
170	Lakshadweep	23.39	39.50	6.65	27.31	45.17	8.10	27.24	44.62	8.65
Madhya Pradesh & Chhattisgarh										
171	Morena(Morena + Sheopur)	25.59	44.52	2.71	25.21	43.00	3.66	27.08	43.53	7.68
172	Bhind	25.26	44.33	1.99	24.56	42.47	2.90	26.27	42.46	7.06
173	Gwalior	26.95	45.60	5.44	27.07	45.03	5.76	28.70	46.06	8.44
174	Datia	27.90	45.16	8.20	27.26	44.89	7.07	33.45	48.47	16.19
175	Shivpuri	27.91	46.19	6.37	28.07	45.89	7.16	27.95	44.67	8.82
176	Guna	28.77	46.30	8.90	28.33	45.70	8.49	29.49	45.89	11.21

Sl. No.	*State / Union Territory*	*1981*			*1991*			*2001*		
		Total	*Male*	*Female*	*Total*	*Male*	*Female*	*Total*	*Male*	*Female*
177	Tikamgarh	31.02	45.70	14.46	30.95	45.25	14.82	35.93	47.22	23.38
178	Chhatarpur	30.29	47.07	10.65	30.24	45.66	12.35	30.39	45.36	13.26
179	Panna	28.27	44.56	9.28	30.67	46.39	12.57	29.75	44.83	12.76
180	Sagar	32.09	46.01	16.11	32.53	46.47	16.59	34.28	47.56	19.43
181	Damoh	30.57	44.42	15.07	31.58	45.14	16.43	34.24	47.06	19.98
182	Satna	32.71	49.67	12.83	32.10	47.44	14.57	32.00	46.90	15.10
183	Rewa	30.81	45.63	13.01	30.01	43.41	14.38	31.23	43.99	16.69
184	Shahdol (Shahdol + Umaria)	30.86	49.30	9.37	28.68	46.28	8.41	27.52	44.36	8.81
185	Sidhi	30.17	46.51	8.02	31.14	50.51	5.86	29.04	45.02	10.25
186	Mandsaur (Mandsaur + Neemuch)	30.62	47.95	11.71	32.37	49.44	13.98	34.10	51.34	15.64
Madhya Pradesh & Chhattisgarh										
187	Ratlam	29.70	48.74	9.20	30.29	48.63	10.61	30.69	49.00	11.27
188	Ujjain	28.21	46.76	7.65	28.94	47.42	8.80	31.15	48.81	12.07
189	Shajapur	30.48	46.90	12.31	31.03	48.05	12.31	33.88	50.56	15.75
190	Dewas	30.56	48.13	10.99	30.81	48.36	11.28	30.98	47.73	12.74
191	Jhabua	31.63	47.24	14.16	32.53	47.35	16.41	32.63	47.74	16.34
192	Dhar	30.90	47.27	13.01	32.94	49.84	14.00	33.85	51.78	13.35

Sl. No.	State / Union Territory	1981			1991			2001		
		Total	Male	Female	Total	Male	Female	Total	Male	Female
193	Indore	28.94	48.30	7.01	30.14	49.65	8.46	32.25	51.22	11.22
194	West Nimar (West Nimar + Barwani)	30.41	47.30	11.79	30.91	47.99	12.27	32.33	49.43	13.97
195	East Nimar	29.73	48.30	9.73	28.86	47.07	9.31	29.75	47.82	10.43
196	Rajgarh	29.12	47.00	9.44	30.14	47.17	11.33	31.86	47.93	14.30
197	Vidisha	27.86	45.94	7.05	27.68	45.48	7.47	28.78	46.14	9.21
198	Bhopal	29.00	47.62	7.59	29.10	47.07	8.98	29.62	46.95	10.33
199	Sehore	28.37	46.09	8.03	29.01	46.29	9.45	28.04	45.00	9.19
200	Raisen	29.56	46.27	10.25	30.04	46.82	10.41	29.85	46.68	10.42
201	Betul	30.09	48.89	8.12	27.01	44.88	7.22	27.23	44.35	8.54
202	Hoshangabad (Hoshangabad + Harda)	27.26	45.87	5.83	27.30	45.39	6.86	28.29	46.06	8.48
203	Jabalpur (Jabalpur + Katni)	29.26	47.34	8.13	28.30	45.78	8.61	30.99	48.04	11.98
204	Narsimhapur	28.52	45.95	9.12	29.16	46.91	9.36	30.76	48.20	11.47
205	Mandla (Mandla + Dindori)	29.67	46.00	12.05	29.85	45.53	12.99	31.15	47.51	13.87
206	Chhindwara	28.33	44.90	9.90	28.30	44.40	10.53	29.60	46.06	11.81
207	Seoni	2.80	45.51	8.38	27.90	45.02	9.30	29.46	46.03	11.71
208	Balaghat	33.16	47.57	17.46	30.17	45.62	13.69	33.02	47.62	17.96
209	Surguja (Surguja + Koriya)	28.46	48.33	5.43	26.50	44.91	5.21	26.78	44.55	6.94

Sl. No.	*State / Union Territory*	*1981*			*1991*			*2001*		
		Total	*Male*	*Female*	*Total*	*Male*	*Female*	*Total*	*Male*	*Female*
210	Bilaspur (Bilaspur + Jangir-Champa + Korba)	30.98	48.60	11.73	30.48	47.23	12.31	25.85	47.22	12.69
211	Raigarh (Raigarh + Jashpur)	30.28	48.16	10.40	30.73	47.81	12.14	30.29	47.75	11.67
212	Rajnandgaon (Rajnandgaon + Kanwardha)	31.50	46.56	15.57	33.72	47.73	19.22	34.71	49.15	19.80
213	Durg	31.15	48.57	11.42	30.16	47.48	10.72	29.69	46.23	11.88
214	Raipur (Raipur + Mahasamud + Dhamtari)	32.11	48.50	14.62	31.90	48.50	14.24	31.15	48.11	12.90
215	Bastar (Bastar + Kanker + Dhamtari)	32.55	50.30	13.05	31.44	48.55	13.20	32.29	49.43	14.21
Maharashtra										
216	Mumbai (Greater Mumbai+ Suburban)	35.21	55.45	8.97	35.25	55.08	11.02	37.27	56.87	13.06
217	Thane	33.73	54.29	8.82	34.50	54.76	10.40	35.73	55.86	11.41
218	Raigarh	33.56	52.03	13.12	33.03	52.11	11.94	34.15	53.55	12.25
219	Ratnagiri (Ratnagiri + Sindhudurg)	28.48	45.78	11.15	30.49	47.87	12.86	34.30	52.64	15.07
220	Nashik	30.68	48.37	10.77	29.85	47.25	10.84	32.25	50.46	12.02
221	Dhule (Dhule + Nandurbar)	27.97	44.34	10.09	27.31	43.95	9.15	28.97	46.69	9.80

Sl. No.	State / Union Territory	1981			1991			2001		
		Total	Male	Female	Total	Male	Female	Total	Male	Female
Maharashtra										
223	Pune	31.00	49.18	10.41	31.87	49.52	12.34	34.25	52.08	14.42
224	Ahmadnagar	31.87	49.42	12.15	32.44	48.63	14.74	33.80	50.28	15.65
225	Solapur	30.30	46.58	14.74	30.69	45.66	14.85	33.86	48.11	18.96
226	Satara	29.71	45.82	12.13	29.94	46.23	12.36	32.30	48.86	14.45
227	Sangli	30.29	48.58	10.39	32.88	50.06	14.44	34.00	51.29	15.65
228	Kolhapur	29.52	49.82	6.84	32.84	52.01	11.87	33.24	52.76	12.00
229	Aurangabad (Aurangabad + Jalna)	28.35	44.86	9.82	28.94	45.40	10.54	28.94	45.89	10.35
230	Parbhani (Parbhani+ Hingoli)	31.66	49.23	12.86	28.05	44.26	10.48	27.80	43.78	10.75
231	Bid	29.61	46.04	11.69	28.12	43.68	10.94	27.23	43.45	9.67
232	Nanded	28.87	44.85	11.47	28.29	43.02	12.15	27.80	43.58	10.74
233	Osamanabad (Osamanabad +Latur)	28.78	45.06	10.92	27.53	42.94	10.42	27.42	43.59	9.83
234	Buldana	32.08	48.30	14.56	31.17	46.91	14.31	30.14	47.09	11.97
235	Akola (Akola + Wahsim)	28.92	46.54	9.87	29.14	46.44	10.48	29.66	47.93	10.15
236	Amravati	30.15	47.17	11.73	30.62	47.52	12.32	31.06	49.38	11.45
237	Yavatmal	28.94	45.02	11.35	29.69	45.98	12.08	30.76	48.80	11.50
238	Wardha	27.96	44.51	10.18	28.79	45.76	10.56	30.90	48.76	11.71

Sl. No.	State / Union Territory	1981			1991			2001		
		Total	Male	Female	Total	Male	Female	Total	Male	Female
239	Nagpur	28.57	45.28	10.25	29.46	46.56	10.78	31.03	49.12	11.59
240	Bhandara (Bhandara+Gondiya)	31.80	44.90	18.17	31.54	44.85	17.56	31.68	46.50	16.30
241	Chandrapur (Chandrapur+ Gadchiroli)	28.50	46.43	8.75	30.20	46.55	12.05	30.85	48.15	12.10
Manipur										
245	Manipur North (Senapati)	53.53	54.86	51.97	0.00	0.00	0.00	0.00	0.00	0.00
246	Manipur West (Tamenglong)	35.58	41.77	28.41	0.00	0.00	0.00	0.00	0.00	0.00
247	Manipur South (Churachandpur)	31.84	46.43	14.90	29.47	37.71	21.08	0.00	0.00	0.00
248	Bishnupur (Bishnupur + Thoubal + Imphal East + Imphal West)	35.23	41.28	29.10	34.39	40.26	28.39	38.66	44.96	32.43
249	Ukhrul	41.65	44.81	38.05	0.00	0.00	0.00	0.00	0.00	0.00
250	Tengnoopal (Chandel)	39.62	61.12	15.27	40.36	51.93	27.06	34.94	44.32	25.21
Meghalaya										
248	Jaintia Hills	35.49	46.30	24.60	34.62	43.04	25.98	29.95	36.00	24.16

Sl. No.	*State / Union Territory*	*1981*			*1991*			*2001*		
		Total	*Male*	*Female*	*Total*	*Male*	*Female*	*Total*	*Male*	*Female*
249	East Khasi Hills (East Khasi Hills + Ribhoi)	32.85	48.11	16.04	33.14	48.03	16.70	33.00	45.66	20.21
250	West Khasi Hills	55.39	79.22	25.42	31.70	40.68	22.15	33.39	38.96	27.73
251	East Garo Hills	34.76	48.37	17.12	31.17	41.32	19.57	35.77	43.44	27.73
252	West Garo Hills (East Garo Hills + South Grao hills)	29.55	44.62	12.56	28.04	40.72	14.00	29.14	41.50	16.03
Mizoram										
253	Aizawl (Aizawl + Kolasib + Champhal + Serchhip + Mamit)	N.A.	N.A.	N.A.	46.32	52.47	39.80	49.29	55.97	42.28
254	Lunglei	N.A.	N.A.	N.A.	48.60	55.59	40.69	45.06	53.34	36.10
255	Chhimtulpul/Saiha(Saihal + Lawngtial)	N.A.	N.A.	N.A.	36.85	45.97	26.73	30.12	38.78	20.87
Nagaland										
256	Kohima (Kohima+Dimapur)	37.07	54.91	10.66	33.35	49.90	11.14	31.43	46.52	13.49

Sl. No.	*State / Union Territory*	*1981*			*1991*			*2001*		
		Total	*Male*	*Female*	*Total*	*Male*	*Female*	*Total*	*Male*	*Female*
Nagaland										
257	Phek	0.00	0.00	0.00	37.26	10.70	40.25	49.26	56.21	40.08
258	Mon	41.17	58.29	11.52	31.65	46.53	10.24	33.24	42.23	22.21
259	Tuensang	33.74	48.70	11.01	34.45	48.38	14.60	26.46	39.18	10.23
260	Mokokchung	28.56	42.76	10.82	30.59	44.38	13.29	35.31	47.48	20.42
261	Zunheboto	34.97	49.93	14.08	28.91	41.82	13.62	29.80	38.25	19.61
262	Wokha	28.41	41.13	9.79	28.02	40.76	11.96	22.58	30.38	13.35
Odisha										
263	Sambalpur(Sambalpur + Bargarh + Jharsuguda + Debagarh)	32.31	51.07	10.95	30.28	48.77	9.43	30.27	48.07	10.85
264	Sundargarh	30.56	49.58	7.19	28.58	47.18	6.48	28.44	46.65	7.97
265	Kendujhar	33.03	50.72	12.64	30.07	48.17	9.21	30.31	48.35	10.47
266	Mayurbhanj	31.91	48.32	12.61	29.89	47.26	9.97	30.70	48.50	10.83
267	Baleshwar (Baleswar + Bhadrak)	29.03	48.69	6.76	27.73	47.28	5.99	28.73	47.61	8.31
268	Cuttack (Cuttack + Jajpur + Kendrapara + Jagatsinghpur)	31.46	51.63	5.91	29.62	49.33	5.56	31.31	51.09	8.61
269	Dhenkanal (Dhenkanal + Angul)	34.18	53.85	8.86	29.59	48.99	6.03	30.78	49.91	8.66

Sl. No.	State / Union Territory	1981			1991			2001		
		Total	Male	Female	Total	Male	Female	Total	Male	Female
270	Phulbani (Kandhamal + Boudh)	31.22	49.18	10.62	29.96	46.71	11.25	30.05	46.44	12.44
271	Balangir (Balangir + Sonpur)	30.23	49.38	9.64	30.14	48.24	10.36	29.49	47.75	9.90
272	Kalahandi (Kalahandi + Nuapara)	31.73	50.74	11.43	30.78	50.01	10.02	31.92	50.21	12.45
273	Koraput (Koraput + Nabarangapur + Mlakangiri + Rayagarh)	34.50	52.83	14.82	31.28	49.93	11.51	32.45	49.90	14.09
274	Ganjam (Ganjam + Gajapati)	30.03	46.64	12.61	28.66	46.00	10.33	30.25	47.60	11.86
275	Puri (Puri + Nayagarh + Khordha)	30.24	49.38	6.86	30.37	49.15	7.20	31.80	50.50	9.53
Pondicherry										
276	Yanam	33.98	50.92	16.57	33.71	51.75	15.11	31.56	52.32	10.28
277	Pondicherry	26.75	44.24	8.90	30.57	49.37	11.18	33.97	53.14	14.74
278	Mahe	21.77	38.92	6.78	22.10	39.34	7.18	25.27	44.81	8.24
279	Karaikal	28.12	46.68	10.28	30.31	50.13	10.62	31.94	51.67	12.62

Sl. No.	State / Union Territory	1981			1991			2001		
		Total	Male	Female	Total	Male	Female	Total	Male	Female
Punjab										
280	Gurdaspur	26.99	48.39	3.31	27.32	48.53	3.64	31.09	50.62	8.63
281	Amritsar	29.73	52.42	3.36	30.20	53.07	4.09	32.35	51.90	9.67
282	Firozpur (Firozpur + Moga)	29.29	51.32	4.22	29.01	50.61	4.67	32.89	52.33	10.45
283	Ludhiana	31.65	54.73	3.92	32.26	55.70	3.39	36.11	56.95	9.49
284	Jalandhar (Jalandhar + Nawanshahr)	29.02	51.42	3.32	29.67	51.65	4.84	33.72	53.71	10.58
285	Kapurthala	30.28	52.37	4.28	30.84	52.90	5.10	33.94	53.34	10.96
286	Hoshiarpur	28.64	49.78	4.37	29.00	49.85	5.56	31.83	50.92	10.40
287	Rupnagar	30.80	50.96	6.91	30.32	50.26	7.40	32.17	49.73	12.07
288	Patiala (Patiala + Fatehgarh Sahib)	29.89	50.99	5.39	29.29	50.23	5.88	33.54	52.10	12.05
289	Sangrur	30.16	52.32	5.03	29.42	52.06	3.71	33.46	52.39	11.70
290	Bathinda (Bhathinda + Mansa)	30.94	53.06	5.07	29.59	51.52	4.53	32.85	51.28	11.65
291	Faridkot (Farikot + Muktsar)	29.36	51.57	4.52	29.62	51.65	4.78	32.28	51.62	10.26
Rajasthan										
292	Ganganagar	28.88	49.93	3.26	28.33	49.23	3.87	29.99	49.95	6.73

Sl. No.	State/Union Territory	1981			1991			2001		
		Total	Male	Female	Total	Male	Female	Total	Male	Female
Rajasthan										
293	Bikaner	25.94	45.08	3.91	27.00	45.83	5.37	28.79	47.75	7.16
294	Churu	24.92	43.98	4.81	25.33	44.12	5.03	27.62	44.91	9.13
295	Jhunjhunun	23.97	41.21	5.03	23.96	40.23	5.64	24.75	40.71	7.05
296	Alwar	26.98	45.23	5.10	29.09	47.89	6.47	31.87	48.79	11.61
297	Bharatpur	26.38	44.56	4.91	26.71	44.50	5.83	28.90	44.86	10.39
298	Sawai Madhopur	25.72	43.68	4.88	27.06	43.57	8.00	27.25	43.13	9.28
299	Jaipur	27.66	46.93	5.39	28.25	47.33	6.42	30.27	48.42	9.65
300	Sikar	23.38	40.77	5.12	24.34	41.82	5.41	25.99	43.84	6.68
301	Ajmer	28.40	46.66	7.84	28.96	46.91	8.90	29.64	47.72	9.58
302	Tonk	30.49	47.38	11.83	30.28	45.89	13.19	31.02	45.63	15.52
303	Jaisalmer	60.63	58.77	63.12	29.81	48.70	5.09	31.24	50.32	6.94
304	Jodhpur	26.64	45.55	5.03	28.41	47.44	6.09	29.14	48.12	7.57
305	Nagaur	26.40	45.40	5.60	27.03	45.21	6.87	27.14	44.63	8.07
306	Pali	99.11	99.80	98.33	30.11	47.94	10.36	31.08	48.57	11.96
307	Barmer	28.08	47.46	4.74	28.09	46.42	6.44	29.17	48.37	6.69
308	Jalor	27.08	45.62	5.99	28.95	44.90	10.86	31.47	46.89	14.11
309	Sirohi	28.31	46.82	7.31	28.59	47.95	6.78	30.67	49.39	9.11
310	Bhilwara	29.86	48.92	8.80	32.50	50.79	12.12	33.55	51.48	13.56

Sl. No.	*State / Union Territory*	*1981*			*1991*			*2001*		
		Total	*Male*	*Female*	*Total*	*Male*	*Female*	*Total*	*Male*	*Female*
311	Udaipur	28.80	47.68	7.47	30.68	49.06	10.05	31.25	50.21	10.38
312	Chittaurgarth	30.48	48.42	10.31	30.55	49.25	9.73	32.70	50.31	13.60
313	Dungarpur	25.05	41.59	6.68	28.35	46.29	8.36	32.19	47.19	15.87
314	Banswara	28.86	47.85	7.26	27.52	45.86	7.54	29.44	46.91	10.70
315	Bundi	27.25	45.93	6.29	27.99	45.31	8.67	32.70	50.31	13.60
316	Kota	28.49	47.77	5.88	28.82	46.95	8.05	29.26	46.43	9.97
317	Jhalawar	27.18	45.30	7.07	28.35	46.48	8.31	29.29	47.66	8.95
Sikkim										
318	North	47.31	60.94	21.27	50.81	65.16	26.10	45.51	60.83	20.75
319	West	36.89	57.20	7.25	33.83	53.25	8.28	41.50	59.01	18.95
320	South	41.55	62.45	10.82	36.75	55.83	9.22	38.39	56.32	17.05
321	East	41.93	59.89	16.39	39.40	54.20	19.90	40.11	55.18	22.12
Tamil Nadu										
322	Chennai	0.00	0.00	0.00	30.54	51.18	8.44	34.27	54.12	13.52

Sl. No.	*State / Union Territory*	*1981*			*1991*			*2001*		
		Total	*Male*	*Female*	*Total*	*Male*	*Female*	*Total*	*Male*	*Female*
323	Chengalpattu/Kancheepuram (Kancheepuram + Thituvellur)	30.26	49.74	9.34	30.89	50.77	9.74	34.36	53.95	13.93
324	Vellore/North Arcot (Vellore + Tiruvanamalai)	30.68	50.56	10.34	30.37	49.84	10.70	34.23	52.33	16.19
325	South Arcot/ Cuddalore (Cuddalore + Villuppuram	28.29	47.96	7.87	29.86	49.52	9.33	33.10	52.37	13.61
326	Dharmapuri	31.42	52.03	9.65	33.60	54.22	11.85	38.06	55.23	20.04
327	Salem (Salem + Namakkal)	37.99	58.47	16.39	39.49	59.21	18.74	43.39	60.02	26.04
328	Erode (Pariyar)	39.52	60.27	17.46	39.23	60.23	17.17	48.86	64.30	33.07
329	Coimbatore	36.55	56.23	15.43	37.87	59.08	15.30	42.29	61.72	21.98
330	The Nilgiris	36.10	50.27	20.85	37.03	50.62	23.06	41.25	53.64	28.95

Sl. No.	State / Union Territory	1981			1991			2001		
		Total	Male	Female	Total	Male	Female	Total	Male	Female
Tamil Nadu										
331	Madurai (Madurai+ Dindlgul Anna+Theni)	31.88	50.53	12.41	34.09	52.89	14.49	37.97	55.89	19.71
332	Tiruchirappalli (Tiruchirapalli + Perambalur + Karur)	31.03	50.93	10.27	32.24	52.05	11.86	36.64	55.01	18.31
333	Thanjavur (Thanjavur + Nagapattinam + Thiruvarur)	29.54	49.70	9.15	30.38	50.86	9.77	32.77	52.92	13.07
334	Pudukkottai	27.42	47.31	7.10	29.14	49.16	8.94	32.72	52.68	12.90
335	Ramanathapuram (Ramanathapuram + Sivaganga)	35.25	51.90	18.42	36.46	53.35	19.34	39.41	56.17	22.80
336	Tirunelveli (Tiruneveli + Toothukudi)	34.58	50.55	18.87	35.62	50.85	20.67	40.45	54.50	26.78
337	Kanniyakumari	29.57	48.01	11.04	29.52	48.03	11.03	32.26	52.65	12.18
Tripura										
338	West Tripura	27.89	45.47	9.69	28.81	47.66	9.23	32.50	51.66	12.71

Sl.		*1981*			*1991*			*2001*		
No.	*State / Union Territory*	*Total*	*Male*	*Female*	*Total*	*Male*	*Female*	*Total*	*Male*	*Female*
339	North Tripura (North Tripura +Dhalai	26.74	45.60	6.78	30.26	49.25	10.17	31.86	51.14	11.46
340	South Tripura	27.30	46.32	6.88	27.61	45.74	8.36	32.99	52.27	11.92
Uttar Pradesh & Uttarakhand										
341	Uttarkashi	39.14	56.27	9.16	36.07	51.17	13.97	33.77	46.28	16.53
342	Chamoli (Chamoli + Rudraprayag)	43.75	56.53	23.22	40.91	54.57	19.02	37.98	51.96	18.00
343	Tehri Garhwal	39.07	57.07	6.64	40.69	58.28	9.45	37.83	56.79	7.63
344	Dehradun	31.22	51.58	5.23	30.20	49.80	6.47	29.46	48.08	7.90
345	Garhwal	32.98	51.62	5.66	33.83	52.34	7.56	28.19	44.89	7.86
346	Pithoragarh (Pithoragarh + Chamawat)	34.24	50.08	12.13	32.51	46.12	15.14	29.75	45.42	10.94
347	Almora (Almora + Bageshwar)	36.56	55.22	7.82	39.16	54.98	17.65	32.12	49.23	10.15
348	Nainital (Nainital + Udam Singh Nagar)	28.58	49.18	3.51	29.06	49.24	5.10	27.52	46.06	6.37
349	Saharanpur (Saharanpur + Hardwar)	28.20	49.44	2.44	27.33	47.97	3.27	27.17	46.35	4.85

Sl. No.	*State / Union Territory*	*1981*			*1991*			*2001*		
		Total	*Male*	*Female*	*Total*	*Male*	*Female*	*Total*	*Male*	*Female*
350	Muzaffarnagar	26.76	48.06	2.11	27.99	48.25	5.06	27.18	45.88	6.05
351	Bijnor	27.11	48.17	3.37	26.28	47.15	2.82	25.09	44.58	3.52
352	Meerut (Meerut + Bhatpat)	27.83	49.06	2.96	27.58	47.86	4.37	26.69	45.25	5.43
353	Ghaziabad	28.33	49.05	3.03	29.36	48.38	6.48	26.80	45.26	5.36
354	Bulandshahar (Bulandshahar + Gautam Buddha Nagar)	25.63	45.93	2.56	26.44	46.16	4.03	30.52	47.92	10.30
355	Moradabad (Moradabad + Jyotiba Phule Nagar)	27.00	48.44	2.37	27.41	47.73	4.29	27.42	46.48	6.00
356	Rampur	27.93	50.61	2.23	28.56	50.01	4.53	27.74	46.85	6.55
357	Budaun	27.24	48.68	2.42	27.30	48.46	3.16	25.92	45.32	4.14
358	Bareilly	26.78	47.98	2.15	26.78	47.94	2.60	27.33	46.56	5.72
359	Pilibhit	26.82	48.18	2.04	27.31	47.97	3.56	26.22	44.82	5.21
360	Shahjahanpur	26.91	48.50	1.85	26.67	48.01	2.42	25.75	44.01	4.61
361	Aligarh	25.49	45.68	2.07	26.36	45.42	4.38	25.53	43.08	5.50
362	Mathura (Mathura+Hathras)	26.52	46.72	2.49	26.69	45.97	4.27	27.61	45.32	6.96
363	Agra (Agra+Firozabad)	26.72	47.87	1.98	27.13	47.55	3.34	25.92	42.98	6.04

Sl. No.	State / Union Territory	1981			1991			2001		
		Total	Male	Female	Total	Male	Female	Total	Male	Female
Uttar Pradesh & Uttarakhand										
364	Etah	25.99	46.44	2.59	26.87	46.01	4.95	25.61	43.24	5.71
365	Mainpuri	25.26	45.22	1.86	24.81	44.65	2.20	23.58	40.86	4.18
366	Farrukhabad (Farrukhabad + Kannauj)	28.38	49.78	3.18	28.77	47.75	7.02	28.95	45.62	10.05
367	Etawah (Etawah + Auraiya)	25.51	44.95	3.06	25.48	45.30	2.71	25.33	43.24	5.12
368	Kanpur (Kanpur Dehat + Kanpur Nagar)	27.45	47.60	2.46	25.88	45.06	2.60	27.69	46.26	5.97
369	Fatehpur	26.60	45.99	4.43	27.06	45.90	5.50	26.26	43.30	7.28
370	Allahabad (Allahabad + Kaushambi)	26.16	44.27	4.12	25.88	42.42	5.74	26.31	40.56	9.00
371	Jalaun	26.53	46.10	3.25	26.31	45.24	4.01	26.81	44.55	6.35
372	Jhansi	26.40	43.58	7.11	27.12	44.30	7.60	29.24	45.56	10.49
373	Lalitpur	27.53	46.27	6.28	27.61	44.99	8.05	29.35	45.81	11.05

Sl. No.	State / Union Territory	1981			1991			2001		
		Total	Male	Female	Total	Male	Female	Total	Male	Female
373	Lalitpur	27.53	46.27	6.28	27.61	44.99	8.05	29.35	45.81	11.05
374	Hamirpur (Hamirpur + Mahoba)	27.85	45.64	7.08	30.19	46.35	11.24	29.24	45.26	10.79
375	Banda (Banda + Chitrakoot)	28.58	46.93	6.39	29.83	46.25	10.08	27.25	43.55	8.28
376	Kheri	27.65	49.68	1.74	27.24	48.53	2.57	26.67	46.18	4.37
377	Sitapur	27.66	48.51	3.26	27.07	47.17	3.70	26.07	44.39	5.84
378	Hardoi	27.41	48.49	2.75	26.95	47.52	3.28	27.74	46.60	6.35
379	Unnao	26.98	47.95	3.01	27.44	47.38	4.78	27.12	45.43	6.72
380	Lucknow	27.88	47.99	3.76	26.75	45.63	5.07	27.61	45.72	7.23
381	Rae Bareli	27.77	47.90	4.20	26.90	45.58	5.59	26.08	43.18	7.37
382	Bahraich (Bahraich + Shravasti)	26.22	47.53	1.98	27.77	47.56	5.12	25.82	44.31	4.98
383	Gonda (Gonda + Balrampur)	27.11	48.10	2.64	26.01	44.88	4.24	25.85	43.26	5.84
384	Barabanki	28.26	49.33	3.81	28.91	48.35	7.03	27.84	44.61	9.19
385	Faizabad (Faizabad + Ambedkar Nagar)	29.06	47.89	6.25	27.37	46.57	4.84	28.11	45.65	8.15

Sl. No.	State / Union Territory	1981			1991			2001		
		Total	Male	Female	Total	Male	Female	Total	Male	Female
386	Sultanpur	26.76	46.26	3.85	27.06	44.74	6.22	25.43	41.62	7.29
387	Pratapgarh	26.60	46.68	3.33	26.21	43.81	6.20	25.97	42.13	8.44
388	Basti (Basti + Sant Kabir Nagar + Siddharthnagar)	27.81	46.61	5.70	27.33	44.34	7.64	25.06	41.63	6.66
389	Gorakhpur (Gorakpur + Maharajganj)	24.64	42.92	3.00	24.46	41.82	4.27	23.63	40.36	4.92
390	Deoria (Deoria + Kushinagar)	27.69	45.89	6.92	24.69	42.42	4.63	23.67	40.20	5.58
391	Azamgarh	30.98	44.80	15.76	26.13	42.68	7.99	25.93	40.31	10.51
392	Jaunpur	25.29	43.96	4.32	23.85	41.27	4.48	25.31	41.15	7.95
393	Ghazipur	24.03	41.83	4.49	26.40	42.07	9.36	24.97	40.18	8.28
394	Ballia (Ballia + Mau)	24.63	41.99	5.36	23.47	39.92	5.07	29.34	41.47	16.22
395	Varanasi (Varanasi +Sant Ravidas Nagar + Chandauli)	26.49	46.27	3.09	26.93	45.24	5.66	28.14	44.72	9.19
396	Mirzapur (Mirzapur + Sonbhadra)	29.50	50.24	3.36	28.19	46.77	5.54	26.41	43.96	5.78

Sl. No.	State / Union Territory	1981			1991			2001		
		Total	Male	Female	Total	Male	Female	Total	Male	Female
West Bengal										
397	Koch Bihar	26.62	44.73	7.07	28.41	47.24	8.61	32.53	52.67	11.65
398	Jalpaiguri	27.98	48.41	4.91	29.50	49.77	7.40	32.44	52.43	11.00
399	Darjiling	29.91	48.86	7.06	29.78	47.92	8.89	31.94	49.72	12.16
400	Dakshin Dinajpur (Dakshin Dinjapur + West Dinjapur	25.47	43.81	5.12	26.69	44.83	6.51	46.43	49.66	12.23
401	Maldah	25.49	43.93	5.59	27.26	46.62	6.31	31.73	50.81	11.59
402	Murshidabad	27.65	44.77	9.98	32.36	47.61	16.45	39.12	50.23	27.67
403	Nadia	26.90	46.35	6.51	28.88	48.78	8.12	36.33	54.57	17.37
404	24 Parganas (North 24 Parganas + South 24 Parganas)	27.41	47.09	4.17	28.15	48.36	5.14	33.03	53.67	10.41
405	Kolkata	35.19	55.74	6.33	33.01	53.86	6.91	37.56	58.06	12.84
406	Haora	29.65	50.81	2.77	30.08	51.97	3.54	33.95	56.16	8.05
407	Hugli	28.39	48.61	4.11	28.96	49.41	5.11	33.48	54.13	10.46
408	Medinipur	25.85	44.63	5.02	28.69	47.49	7.90	31.01	50.58	10.08
409	Bankura	26.82	45.81	6.67	28.54	47.84	7.95	33.72	53.04	13.42
410	Puruliya	25.87	44.74	5.01	26.98	45.23	6.67	28.66	46.76	9.00
411	Birbhum	26.59	45.83	5.68	27.56	47.05	6.52	32.52	51.83	12.20
412	Barddhaman	31.81	49.31	10.33	26.94	45.58	4.70	30.02	48.59	9.09

Table 3.3.1. Percentage of Workers in Non-Agricultural Sector, Districts Level, India, 2001 (All Areas)

State / Union Territory	*Total*			*Main*			*Marginal*		
	Total	*Male*	*Female*	*Total*	*Male*	*Female*	*Total*	*Male*	*Female*
Andaman & Nicobar Islands									
Andamans	77.80	80.64	64.87	82.19	82.44	80.73	47.95	60.93	31.00
Nicobars	98.45	98.15	99.15	98.00	98.07	97.58	97.90	97.30	98.32
Andhra Pradesh									
Adilabad	38.57	44.43	30.10	41.77	46.00	34.40	27.22	36.88	21.20
Anantapur	32.31	40.50	19.76	35.40	42.50	21.58	18.45	25.71	14.74
Chittoor	33.66	41.03	21.26	36.04	42.74	22.35	23.37	29.83	19.18
Cuddapah	36.52	44.38	22.44	40.84	46.82	26.38	20.10	27.17	15.95
East Godavari	37.76	41.17	27.90	40.86	42.95	32.51	23.22	27.12	20.06
Guntur	32.90	42.25	18.36	35.59	43.84	20.32	19.21	28.38	14.02
Hyderabad	99.73	99.74	99.69	98.49	98.92	96.07	96.47	97.43	94.44
Karimnagar	40.79	46.03	34.09	44.07	48.51	37.54	25.56	32.54	21.80
Khammam	27.93	37.39	13.92	29.81	38.18	15.10	18.21	29.93	11.05

State / Union Territory	Total			Main			Marginal		
	Total	Male	Female	Total	Male	Female	Total	Male	Female
Krishna	40.85	49.76	22.75	44.65	51.79	26.36	19.34	29.06	13.61
Kurnool	31.56	40.81	18.73	34.06	42.33	20.81	18.23	27.32	13.17
Mahbubnagar	26.63	35.11	16.20	28.76	36.32	17.58	18.39	27.83	13.43
Medak	32.35	38.60	23.74	33.94	39.70	24.55	24.87	33.02	19.61
Nalgonda	32.15	42.62	18.34	35.38	44.35	20.14	18.85	29.40	14.48
Nellore	37.44	45.18	23.14	41.45	47.36	27.16	21.19	29.77	15.81
Nizamabad	42.84	42.08	43.76	45.28	43.98	47.01	31.39	30.90	31.72
Prakasam	31.52	39.39	20.48	33.43	40.48	21.62	21.33	28.94	17.53
Rangareddi	59.75	70.58	35.66	61.69	70.96	38.50	43.68	61.38	29.21
Srikakulam	31.56	39.63	19.81	36.63	42.77	23.63	17.87	23.85	14.48
Visakhapatnam	46.48	56.15	26.85	48.75	56.89	28.48	37.30	51.42	25.11
Vizianagaram	31.54	41.32	18.48	35.04	43.01	20.73	19.56	29.52	14.85
Warangal	31.63	41.80	17.96	35.02	43.81	20.41	18.28	29.39	12.70
West Godavari	30.60	35.10	20.83	32.55	36.38	21.98	21.17	24.57	19.01
Arunachal Pradesh									
Changlang	24.66	33.17	12.98	27.84	35.35	14.85	11.77	16.37	9.45

State / Union Territory	Total			Main			Marginal		
	Total	Male	Female	Total	Male	Female	Total	Male	Female
Dibang Valley	38.83	49.72	19.07	42.72	52.05	22.43	20.09	32.45	11.64
East Kameng	26.30	38.93	11.52	26.32	39.38	9.46	32.71	36.91	30.86
East Siang	41.99	50.79	28.22	43.68	52.31	27.94	34.79	41.25	30.89
Lohit	35.83	45.39	17.43	39.64	46.60	21.78	16.94	33.63	9.21
Lower Subansiri	24.40	37.15	10.53	28.66	41.31	13.21	12.83	16.07	10.73
Papum Pare	72.28	80.37	55.37	77.12	83.39	61.87	45.00	50.48	40.81
Tawang	54.89	70.14	27.19	58.11	72.13	29.09	29.72	41.46	19.82
Tirap	23.93	36.53	7.98	25.31	37.82	8.40	13.23	21.34	7.15
Upper Siang	32.53	45.82	12.20	35.80	49.77	13.34	11.17	10.23	12.08
Upper Subansiri	29.27	42.80	12.12	31.12	44.07	13.68	23.22	35.06	16.63
West Kameng	60.59	72.03	30.59	66.71	74.97	38.61	28.39	37.20	21.49
West Siang	34.75	46.42	17.47	37.76	49.86	17.30	30.95	35.59	27.76
Assam									
Barpeta	43.13	41.08	50.54	45.04	43.02	60.87	38.06	31.62	42.20
Bongaigaon	43.45	46.10	34.48	47.70	47.83	46.93	27.07	33.40	22.68
Cachar	65.57	62.74	76.56	67.26	64.82	80.91	50.02	48.48	51.85

State / Union Territory	*Total*			*Main*			*Marginal*		
	Total	*Male*	*Female*	*Total*	*Male*	*Female*	*Total*	*Male*	*Female*
Assam									
Darrang	38.61	38.12	39.86	41.44	38.69	56.82	32.21	35.64	30.36
Dhemaji	19.06	24.42	11.55	25.85	29.33	16.46	9.99	11.35	9.28
Dhubri	39.09	38.11	45.38	40.69	39.13	57.40	29.57	29.22	30.02
Dibrugarh	63.04	67.62	54.51	74.01	74.58	72.45	35.38	40.32	31.71
Goalpara	44.97	45.38	43.78	47.34	46.70	50.93	36.48	36.41	36.51
Golaghat	42.52	46.31	35.72	51.53	50.79	53.92	28.13	32.62	25.45
Hailakandi	50.93	47.52	61.77	53.56	49.82	73.74	41.81	36.89	46.31
Jorhat	54.45	60.45	42.56	66.25	67.79	61.19	28.21	32.24	25.36
Kamrup	65.57	66.08	63.69	70.79	69.89	76.31	45.02	45.58	44.55
Karbi Anglong	26.79	29.83	21.65	30.57	32.84	23.89	20.56	20.37	20.65
Karimganj	60.73	57.46	74.74	61.89	59.30	81.74	52.94	45.93	61.86
Kokrajhar	34.36	35.94	31.15	37.28	38.28	33.63	28.03	29.90	26.80
Lakhimpur	24.90	31.88	15.76	36.04	40.24	25.72	9.97	10.19	9.85

State / Union Territory	*Total*			*Main*			*Marginal*		
	Total	*Male*	*Female*	*Total*	*Male*	*Female*	*Total*	*Male*	*Female*
Marigaon	27.15	27.49	26.04	30.29	29.40	36.98	19.58	19.14	19.85
Nagaon	41.56	40.58	45.74	45.86	43.80	62.15	27.18	24.91	29.64
Nalbari	48.45	49.22	46.25	51.27	50.84	53.55	37.25	37.83	36.83
North Cachar Hills	45.47	52.54	29.37	51.43	55.52	36.69	27.23	36.28	22.15
Sibsagar	56.74	62.03	46.84	73.69	72.59	77.14	25.53	27.62	23.93
Sonitpur	53.08	54.28	50.45	58.89	56.80	67.38	38.00	42.90	34.90
Tinsukia	62.60	67.44	53.57	70.43	71.98	66.39	39.19	44.99	34.64
Bihar									
Araria	11.89	14.11	6.96	12.97	14.56	6.83	8.40	10.52	7.34
Aurangabad	21.09	24.08	13.67	23.45	25.25	14.97	14.71	18.99	11.59
Banka	14.55	16.56	10.60	17.23	18.32	12.50	9.70	10.64	9.08
Begusarai	33.53	35.44	27.34	35.56	36.62	30.12	24.89	28.66	20.95
Bhagalpur	31.97	36.25	21.10	37.99	39.67	29.09	19.03	22.63	16.04
Bhojpur	25.72	27.50	18.81	28.63	29.50	22.13	17.35	20.14	14.17

State / Union Territory	*Total*			*Main*			*Marginal*		
	Total	*Male*	*Female*	*Total*	*Male*	*Female*	*Total*	*Male*	*Female*
Buxar	23.89	25.32	17.79	26.16	26.50	23.31	16.75	20.50	12.29
Darbhanga	26.06	28.80	17.14	29.16	30.14	22.80	16.53	21.08	11.91
Gaya	21.64	26.27	12.28	23.03	26.92	11.59	17.86	25.35	13.32
Gopalganj	18.54	21.96	8.40	21.61	23.45	11.07	11.59	17.66	6.18
Jamui	37.17	29.14	49.75	33.79	29.69	45.05	43.73	28.65	52.67
Jehanabad	19.77	22.69	14.21	20.30	23.06	11.54	17.80	22.85	15.04
Kaimur (Bhabua)	17.12	18.56	13.45	19.06	20.01	14.73	13.08	13.57	12.66
Katihar	16.47	19.42	9.37	18.77	20.06	12.00	10.41	16.07	7.67
Khagaria	19.61	23.02	11.41	23.04	24.59	15.63	11.75	16.59	8.51
Kishanganj	15.77	15.43	17.66	15.89	15.79	16.89	16.49	15.25	17.62
Lakhisarai	23.91	27.80	15.07	26.00	28.65	16.62	17.80	24.50	13.31
Madhepura	10.39	14.16	4.66	11.96	14.49	5.09	6.38	12.65	4.19
Madhubani	16.63	19.52	9.25	19.29	20.54	12.20	10.33	14.89	7.52
Munger	42.21	46.25	27.14	48.22	49.94	37.01	27.87	33.30	19.97
Muzaffarpur	28.92	31.49	18.38	31.48	32.71	23.29	19.01	24.41	12.59
Nalanda	22.18	26.39	13.88	23.94	27.17	14.31	16.83	23.39	13.11
Nawada	19.33	23.40	11.31	20.63	23.72	10.49	16.00	23.30	12.08
Pashchim Champaran	16.40	19.86	8.16	18.96	21.11	9.38	9.35	14.45	5.88

State / Union Territory	*Total*			*Main*			*Marginal*		
	Total	*Male*	*Female*	*Total*	*Male*	*Female*	*Total*	*Male*	*Female*
Bihar									
Patna	44.83	49.84	25.11	49.66	52.48	32.67	24.90	33.05	16.22
Purba Champaran	17.85	19.78	10.53	19.35	20.49	11.85	12.76	16.90	9.07
Purnia	13.71	16.89	6.07	14.97	17.28	6.34	8.95	14.86	5.93
Rohtas	26.45	28.55	18.53	29.30	29.94	24.17	19.55	23.96	14.89
Saharsa	15.87	20.53	7.01	18.90	21.31	8.94	9.27	16.99	5.87
Samastipur	24.42	26.70	17.26	27.42	28.02	23.63	18.37	22.70	15.24
Saran	26.67	29.10	16.28	29.87	31.18	20.35	17.47	21.38	11.72
Sheikhpura	20.14	24.20	11.52	21.91	24.93	12.20	14.46	20.72	10.76
Sheohar	12.58	12.22	14.61	12.87	12.54	16.93	13.90	14.36	13.41
Sitamarhi	20.77	21.31	17.97	20.99	21.03	20.57	18.66	22.35	15.78
Siwan	24.68	27.97	14.19	28.52	30.37	17.43	17.11	21.45	12.20
Supaul	11.16	15.13	4.50	12.73	15.06	5.15	6.21	12.41	4.05
Vaishali	27.26	28.81	20.11	29.07	29.96	22.02	20.80	23.99	16.95
Chandigarh									
Chandigarh	99.42	99.37	99.69	99.32	99.31	99.33	95.98	96.61	94.83
Chhatisgarh									
Bastar	19.62	24.11	14.30	23.19	24.92	18.47	14.70	21.52	12.23

State/Union Territory	*Total*			*Main*			*Marginal*		
	Total	*Male*	*Female*	*Total*	*Male*	*Female*	*Total*	*Male*	*Female*
Bilaspur	26.67	36.87	12.11	32.80	40.68	16.69	10.16	17.03	6.40
Dantewada	11.65	16.28	6.28	13.35	17.29	6.81	7.04	10.20	5.82
Dhamtari	20.40	28.48	10.97	24.11	30.89	13.55	8.48	12.72	6.52
Durg	35.39	49.14	14.63	39.19	51.44	16.74	16.73	28.56	9.75
Janjgir-Champa	16.85	24.26	7.14	21.18	26.90	9.88	6.19	10.86	3.96
Jashpur	11.86	16.06	6.99	15.95	17.77	11.73	4.37	7.50	3.46
Kanker	15.39	18.99	11.40	16.82	20.27	11.18	11.65	11.66	11.65
Kawardha	12.80	19.20	5.79	14.80	20.51	6.82	5.47	9.73	3.71
Korba	35.62	46.06	18.57	43.06	50.19	23.00	18.26	25.54	14.48
Koriya	28.06	38.88	11.74	38.13	43.15	21.12	9.00	17.32	5.77
Mahasamund	15.77	22.20	7.16	19.71	23.77	10.67	5.31	11.02	3.39
Raigarh	20.16	26.71	10.75	24.87	28.66	15.31	8.42	13.83	6.42
Raipur	37.06	49.60	17.77	44.08	53.53	23.66	14.76	24.74	9.29
Rajnandgaon	20.07	30.21	8.77	21.95	31.68	9.74	9.18	15.70	5.78
Surguja	13.81	19.11	6.90	18.74	20.51	13.11	4.14	7.02	3.19
Dadra & Nagar Haveli									
Dadra & Nagar Haveli	52.45	69.05	19.43	59.21	71.75	23.58	16.64	27.42	12.84

State/Union Territory	Total			Main			Marginal		
	Total	Male	Female	Total	Male	Female	Total	Male	Female
Daman & Diu									
Daman	94.71	96.51	82.53	96.09	96.62	91.83	62.61	86.47	42.29
Diu	85.01	94.99	63.96	91.29	95.58	75.48	54.52	76.12	50.29
Delhi									
Central	99.88	99.92	99.58	99.82	99.85	99.57	99.50	99.62	99.16
East	99.68	99.75	99.16	99.63	99.70	99.14	99.35	99.63	98.56
New Delhi	99.95	99.95	99.95	99.74	99.78	99.54	99.31	99.59	98.35
North	99.00	99.20	97.32	99.11	99.29	97.53	96.10	96.93	93.95
North East	99.72	99.73	99.57	99.66	99.67	99.46	99.11	99.40	98.38
North West	97.71	98.05	95.27	98.06	98.26	96.54	91.50	93.56	86.57
South	99.60	99.62	99.51	99.54	99.57	99.35	99.13	99.33	98.45
South West	97.12	97.76	92.99	97.83	98.10	95.99	83.54	89.32	70.13
West	99.58	99.67	99.03	99.53	99.61	99.05	98.26	99.01	96.14
Goa									
North Goa	82.35	88.29	67.95	90.87	92.72	84.77	51.70	63.34	40.97
South Goa	84.87	89.45	72.09	89.40	91.72	81.61	59.28	70.63	46.80
Gujarat									
Ahmadabad	81.77	86.04	62.83	85.99	87.26	77.61	46.14	59.47	39.51
Amreli	36.29	47.25	16.49	42.48	48.32	21.94	14.82	33.00	11.51

State / Union Territory	Total			Main			Marginal		
	Total	Male	Female	Total	Male	Female	Total	Male	Female
Anand	43.39	41.36	47.78	46.03	43.08	57.27	34.61	26.55	37.70
Banas Kantha	33.52	31.68	36.38	35.27	32.28	44.02	28.18	25.05	28.83
Bharuch	44.87	52.23	26.90	49.62	53.95	32.56	23.37	30.76	20.38
Bhavnagar	55.03	66.32	25.48	61.87	67.50	34.57	23.54	46.35	17.65
Dohad	17.27	22.46	11.58	21.46	23.88	15.62	10.73	16.12	9.08
Gandhinagar	59.82	56.96	65.63	63.09	58.56	75.69	42.12	37.77	44.02
Jamnagar	50.33	59.89	23.83	54.21	59.58	29.93	23.47	46.66	16.47
Junagadh	36.00	45.76	14.89	42.35	46.82	22.01	13.92	32.64	9.66
Kachchh				61.18	64.41	45.86	42.36	46.77	40.97
Kheda	41.13	36.30	49.73	43.62	37.73	61.78	33.51	24.64	36.61
Mahesana	52.03	48.22	58.23	54.97	49.61	68.29	40.91	34.90	42.73
Narmada	20.76	25.87	13.84	24.65	26.93	18.58	12.16	15.09	11.16
Navsari	43.36	53.49	24.27	48.40	54.76	31.00	17.02	33.03	12.07
Panch Mahals	22.18	27.64	14.90	28.59	29.54	25.21	11.71	17.23	10.23
Patan	36.03	38.78	31.71	40.84	40.32	42.42	22.57	24.02	22.21
Porbandar	49.05	57.82	26.74	55.29	59.18	35.89	24.40	41.60	19.38
Rajkot	56.20	66.80	24.88	60.77	67.11	32.44	25.61	48.30	18.82
Sabar Kantha	37.01	32.93	42.99	40.25	34.48	57.48	29.97	24.21	31.65
Surat	66.12	75.96	35.26	70.27	77.34	40.65	26.93	37.52	23.19

State / Union Territory	Total			Main			Marginal		
	Total	Male	Female	Total	Male	Female	Total	Male	Female
Surendranagar	37.84	46.52	21.14	42.52	47.61	24.88	20.89	33.58	17.58
The Dangs	13.96	19.54	7.68	16.38	19.99	10.17	7.77	17.57	4.69
Vadodara	46.79	55.16	27.29	54.40	57.57	40.65	18.60	29.28	14.82
Valsad	47.86	59.78	25.78	56.55	63.36	35.45	18.48	27.10	15.12
Haryana									
Ambala	70.10	69.07	76.16	72.95	70.97	89.12	57.60	60.16	53.13
Bhiwani	35.92	41.76	26.68	41.52	44.50	33.47	23.59	29.40	20.56
Faridabad	64.70	74.34	39.32	73.71	77.25	56.63	38.51	55.37	26.94
Fatehabad	32.51	37.84	22.94	35.65	39.25	24.01	25.05	31.16	22.09
Gurgaon	59.63	65.77	47.77	66.19	68.03	59.88	41.46	52.85	35.73
Hisar	41.13	48.54	27.47	45.15	50.09	31.07	28.05	37.41	23.57
Jhajjar	42.41	51.18	27.49	49.28	54.91	34.20	27.00	36.12	21.21
Jind	33.32	40.42	20.93	37.72	42.13	24.09	23.22	31.62	19.01
Kaithal	36.97	40.71	28.29	40.60	41.32	36.70	28.27	38.91	23.22
Karnal	49.60	52.47	40.73	54.45	54.59	53.71	32.93	39.62	27.78
Kurukshetra	53.58	51.34	59.82	55.78	52.24	72.00	43.99	43.32	44.36
Mahendragarh	34.04	44.19	20.16	44.68	49.20	29.71	19.62	27.54	16.03
Panchkula	77.23	80.36	65.59	82.30	82.04	83.70	49.00	62.34	37.49

State / Union Territory	*Total*			*Main*			*Marginal*		
	Total	*Male*	*Female*	*Total*	*Male*	*Female*	*Total*	*Male*	*Female*
Haryana									
Panipat	62.19	67.43	49.62	67.95	69.97	58.35	44.66	48.54	42.74
Rewari	42.00	52.79	25.78	55.00	59.09	40.60	21.97	29.33	18.55
Rohtak	48.76	57.61	30.09	54.01	59.66	36.79	32.15	45.42	22.87
Sirsa	38.49	39.56	36.37	42.38	41.05	46.72	26.86	32.14	24.32
Sonipat	46.85	54.25	32.40	54.20	57.90	42.55	27.31	35.86	21.85
Yamunanagar	66.97	63.76	83.48	66.63	63.77	87.76	65.06	59.43	73.22
Himachal Pradesh									
Bilaspur	29.51	48.71	7.27	39.00	55.31	11.60	11.40	25.94	3.29
Chamba	26.21	39.64	9.79	42.78	50.10	22.24	6.13	10.74	4.02
Hamirpur	28.42	51.46	6.58	42.11	64.62	11.05	9.47	21.21	2.94
Kangra	36.36	52.95	14.42	53.63	64.43	25.92	13.30	22.52	7.89
Kinnaur	31.13	45.09	12.21	37.57	51.64	14.50	7.86	10.90	5.81

State/Union Territory	Total			Main			Marginal		
	Total	*Male*	*Female*	*Total*	*Male*	*Female*	*Total*	*Male*	*Female*
Kullu	21.22	31.51	8.58	25.64	35.82	10.33	7.09	9.52	5.55
Lahul & Spiti	45.32	61.09	21.97	47.07	62.65	22.30	29.11	36.22	23.74
Mandi	25.91	42.69	7.83	38.60	51.19	14.57	7.79	17.29	3.34
Shimla	32.84	46.54	13.01	38.39	50.36	16.79	8.60	15.65	4.84
Sirmaur	25.82	37.28	8.44	30.44	40.20	10.65	9.92	18.56	4.97
Solan	42.94	59.51	15.00	60.16	67.33	32.10	10.83	21.74	5.97
Una	37.18	52.77	14.78	53.84	60.56	30.77	13.38	25.78	7.51
Jammu and Kashmir									
Anantanag	47.24	46.07	50.18	51.09	50.37	56.58	42.29	35.07	46.45
Badgam	54.64	52.30	60.42	56.20	54.44	66.53	50.59	44.11	54.51
Baramula	53.93	51.32	63.31	58.86	56.85	71.09	44.81	36.04	55.45
Doda	31.13	37.35	21.73	41.90	43.74	36.13	15.62	18.83	13.85
Jammu	68.54	73.38	46.78	77.10	77.18	76.41	33.32	46.67	22.35

State/Union Territory	Total			Main			Marginal		
	Total	*Male*	*Female*	*Total*	*Male*	*Female*	*Total*	*Male*	*Female*
Kargil	49.21	63.21	32.23	63.97	75.28	40.71	27.34	36.11	21.75
Kathua	42.90	48.38	29.26	47.95	51.54	35.44	29.22	38.14	21.11
Kupwara	36.69	38.33	32.42	50.26	50.44	48.72	26.00	24.81	27.19
Leh (Ladakh)	58.14	71.09	33.97	73.57	82.20	49.55	26.19	31.15	21.89
Pulwama	43.32	41.63	48.49	46.14	44.83	55.91	40.24	34.43	44.01
Punch	29.90	29.53	30.37	43.97	39.05	68.23	20.13	15.43	22.66
Rajauri	29.52	34.75	21.37	44.60	42.76	60.31	14.72	14.70	14.73
Srinagar	87.19	87.34	86.32	91.02	91.22	89.17	68.87	58.72	79.82
Udhampur	35.08	40.57	25.84	43.85	45.32	37.78	19.97	21.60	19.34
Jharkhand									
Bokaro	55.33	61.80	28.43	69.28	70.94	52.44	28.62	36.81	16.30
Chatra	18.29	21.46	12.78	20.49	22.57	13.91	15.18	19.49	12.07
Deoghar	35.07	38.39	27.50	44.04	45.28	37.17	20.45	22.69	18.95
Dhanbad	76.23	82.59	41.75	87.23	88.22	76.20	44.11	57.84	21.81
Dumka	18.19	23.26	10.02	24.33	26.86	15.92	8.89	12.50	6.66
Garhwa	15.95	21.05	7.23	22.30	24.53	12.41	7.80	12.71	4.88
Giridih	25.73	32.80	10.62	36.20	38.98	19.05	14.23	20.93	8.10
Godda	19.06	22.51	12.46	26.14	27.10	21.46	10.22	11.71	9.10
Gumla	13.04	16.83	8.55	15.49	18.14	10.33	8.94	12.82	7.34
Hazaribagh	38.26	50.66	12.92	49.08	54.59	23.25	16.08	31.81	7.54

State / Union Territory	*Total*			*Main*			*Marginal*		
	Total	*Male*	*Female*	*Total*	*Male*	*Female*	*Total*	*Male*	*Female*
Jharkhand									
Kodarma	37.14	49.59	14.32	48.42	53.44	25.18	18.52	35.08	9.60
Lohardaga	19.14	26.07	9.96	23.52	28.48	12.57	11.14	17.56	7.79
Pakaur	33.13	30.86	36.60	37.69	33.51	49.15	22.63	19.15	24.39
Palamu	20.24	24.99	11.57	26.39	28.77	16.45	12.60	16.71	9.40
Pashchimi Singhbhum	27.30	35.87	15.06	36.86	41.82	22.71	14.35	20.11	10.88
Purbi Singhbhum	53.93	63.95	27.63	69.67	73.16	51.56	23.71	33.73	13.79
Ranchi	36.71	46.91	18.86	44.49	50.90	26.05	19.78	30.59	12.93
Sahibganj	36.46	34.14	40.40	38.86	35.66	48.36	30.94	26.98	32.88
Karnataka									
Bagalkot	34.76	43.16	20.83	40.19	45.26	27.15	16.40	26.41	12.61
Bangalore	94.26	95.17	91.09	95.10	95.47	93.71	80.75	86.93	72.43
Bangalore Rural	37.95	42.62	29.45	40.72	43.33	34.07	27.32	39.98	21.60
Belgaum	30.95	39.53	15.58	34.67	40.27	19.80	14.89	31.04	9.53

Bellary	33.15	42.42	18.51	35.80	43.50	21.03	17.81	31.96	11.83
Bidar	37.44	46.15	20.83	40.76	47.05	22.63	27.56	41.40	18.97
Bijapur	29.29	36.84	15.03	34.37	38.70	21.42	14.85	26.04	9.50
Chamarajanagar	28.82	30.94	24.42	32.05	32.80	29.84	20.70	25.12	17.25
Chikmagalur	50.03	50.53	49.03	53.25	51.42	58.16	35.67	46.48	30.22
Chitradurga	27.90	34.45	17.46	31.31	35.82	21.09	15.61	25.22	11.62
Dakshina Kannada	90.33	88.37	93.01	90.75	88.79	93.69	86.30	83.54	88.03
Davanagere	34.32	39.79	23.39	38.24	41.43	29.22	20.01	29.33	14.92
Dharwad	46.67	57.04	25.07	50.75	58.25	30.18	24.07	44.10	14.77
Gadag	30.15	39.89	15.10	33.47	41.12	18.02	12.67	24.52	8.70
Gulbarga	32.71	41.77	18.90	37.70	43.36	24.16	18.95	32.86	13.06
Hassan	30.16	35.80	21.56	33.61	36.51	27.16	16.06	30.27	11.82
Haveri	25.55	31.39	14.77	28.85	32.65	18.39	13.70	21.52	10.22
Kodagu	88.24	87.79	89.01	88.82	88.13	90.07	74.20	75.25	73.38
Kolar	35.75	42.88	24.72	38.83	44.24	27.83	22.61	32.42	18.33

State / Union Territory	Total			Main			Marginal		
	Total	Male	Female	Total	Male	Female	Total	Male	Female
Koppal	27.07	34.24	16.95	31.10	36.67	19.28	14.98	25.82	10.79
Mandya	26.27	29.38	20.51	28.76	30.18	24.95	16.96	25.31	13.48
Mysore	41.18	46.62	28.03	45.59	48.48	36.00	21.55	33.19	14.34
Raichur	26.64	34.45	14.52	32.16	36.98	20.26	11.97	19.55	8.59
Shimoga	37.87	44.62	23.26	42.13	45.89	30.19	20.00	34.86	12.96
Tumkur	30.26	35.98	21.60	33.50	37.03	25.73	18.30	27.46	15.10
Udupi	62.20	68.66	52.86	66.16	70.05	59.52	38.18	53.08	30.21
Uttara Kannada	60.76	66.59	48.25	64.44	67.39	54.53	47.58	60.60	40.32
Kerala									
Alappuzha	82.33	82.45	82.08	87.54	87.52	87.60	66.84	64.65	69.76
Ernakulam	86.80	88.14	82.55	89.07	89.46	87.54	76.36	80.47	70.10
Idukki	51.79	49.93	55.69	53.56	51.14	59.49	43.62	42.01	45.33
Kannur	80.23	83.44	70.56	84.27	85.98	77.93	65.07	70.99	56.82
Kasaragod	85.20	84.60	86.55	86.96	86.27	88.91	77.64	75.51	80.02
Kollam	78.53	74.13	90.49	82.41	78.45	93.71	63.64	56.85	78.66
Kottayam	78.97	77.95	82.73	81.14	79.80	86.83	67.49	66.76	68.90
Kozhikode	88.42	88.74	86.56	91.07	90.99	91.56	78.15	79.11	75.15

State/Union Territory	*Total*			*Main*			*Marginal*		
	Total	*Male*	*Female*	*Total*	*Male*	*Female*	*Total*	*Male*	*Female*
Kerala									
Malappuram	75.69	76.91	68.19	79.11	79.63	75.16	62.43	65.15	53.81
Palakkad	57.24	66.27	36.27	61.34	69.09	40.14	40.10	50.55	27.68
Pathanamthitta	66.54	62.87	78.61	70.71	66.87	85.49	52.04	47.67	60.57
Thiruvananthapuram	79.42	78.20	83.57	87.42	85.96	92.73	68.97	66.84	74.35
Thrissur	83.15	85.52	75.79	85.75	87.13	80.84	69.73	75.18	61.43
Wayanad	52.55	52.43	52.85	56.66	55.46	60.54	43.00	43.88	41.85
Lakshadweep									
Lakshadweep	100.0	100.0	100.0	100.0	100.0	100.0	100.0	100.0	100.0
Madhya Pradesh									
Balaghat	21.51	29.56	12.24	27.52	33.13	17.18	9.96	14.69	7.74
Barwani	15.43	22.12	7.08	18.40	23.55	8.87	7.59	13.64	5.24
Betul	20.46	28.85	8.46	26.36	31.85	12.91	8.10	15.52	4.47
Bhind	27.64	25.67	32.69	28.00	25.96	38.69	27.25	26.74	27.51
Bhopal	77.01	82.29	57.87	81.96	83.93	72.41	50.62	69.20	31.38

State/Union Territory	Total			Main			Marginal		
	Total	Male	Female	Total	Male	Female	Total	Male	Female
Chhatarpur	24.66	29.51	15.37	27.48	29.63	19.44	16.82	30.61	11.76
Chhindwara	25.57	34.53	11.04	31.27	36.63	16.34	11.64	23.03	6.32
Damoh	42.36	38.33	49.03	42.84	38.93	54.72	40.87	34.60	43.46
Datia	21.81	27.04	13.85	24.92	28.22	16.00	14.34	20.27	11.99
Dewas	22.95	32.65	8.13	28.33	34.69	12.33	8.84	19.86	4.35
Dhar	18.25	26.60	6.87	22.28	28.33	9.28	7.42	15.03	4.42
Dindori	9.61	13.36	5.54	10.71	14.34	6.01	6.27	9.25	4.62
East Nimar	24.62	33.70	9.65	27.23	34.65	11.42	11.50	22.70	6.19
Guna	21.86	26.61	12.33	26.26	28.03	19.06	11.37	19.46	7.93
Gwalior	59.66	65.03	38.64	65.30	66.51	57.44	32.44	51.98	17.81
Harda	19.63	27.70	6.89	24.69	29.14	11.14	7.54	17.63	3.97
Hoshangabad	36.62	42.11	21.65	41.91	43.78	32.51	19.73	30.84	12.46
Indore	68.33	76.84	42.51	73.32	78.59	52.51	40.66	60.13	25.10
Jabalpur	59.82	66.14	44.11	65.99	69.47	53.62	36.82	45.06	29.84
Jhabua	12.77	17.00	8.17	14.32	17.38	9.01	9.81	15.59	7.41

State/Union Territory	*Total*			*Main*			*Marginal*		
	Total	*Male*	*Female*	*Total*	*Male*	*Female*	*Total*	*Male*	*Female*
Madhya Pradesh									
Shajapur	18.79	27.44	6.56	24.43	29.14	10.78	6.34	15.54	3.58
Sheopur	18.85	23.39	10.89	22.89	23.90	17.72	11.37	21.66	8.12
Shivpuri	17.10	23.09	7.33	19.29	23.36	9.03	11.05	23.27	6.22
Sidhi	17.79	25.01	6.90	22.10	26.69	9.73	7.23	14.26	4.59
Tikamgarh	18.47	23.26	11.61	21.38	23.40	15.21	12.60	24.73	9.46
Ujjain	32.22	42.84	14.19	37.06	44.42	18.66	16.56	31.67	9.24
Umaria	23.13	29.96	12.11	28.39	32.88	15.38	13.83	20.22	9.96
Vidisha	25.31	28.47	16.47	29.36	29.95	26.23	13.62	21.08	9.08
Maharashtra									
West Nimar	18.50	26.83	6.86	20.24	27.41	7.57	8.89	18.92	4.71
Ahmadnagar	29.95	39.80	16.53	31.24	40.54	15.58	24.15	36.63	17.62
Akola	31.89	41.93	12.28	33.75	42.38	13.50	23.19	37.65	12.81

State / Union Territory	Total			Main			Marginal		
	Total	Male	Female	Total	Male	Female	Total	Male	Female
Amravati	29.20	37.74	13.60	32.38	39.42	14.83	16.02	25.05	9.86
Aurangabad	36.75	49.03	16.69	39.85	50.80	17.70	24.64	40.26	15.07
Bhandara	28.85	39.20	16.09	36.76	44.65	22.17	14.05	19.58	10.60
Bid	22.22	32.22	9.50	23.27	32.83	8.48	16.73	28.54	10.61
Buldana	19.03	28.58	6.16	20.07	29.16	5.66	13.83	23.39	8.24
Chandrapur	34.37	47.25	15.54	41.77	51.72	19.58	16.44	27.25	9.59
Dhule	28.88	39.92	12.19	33.82	42.37	14.04	14.48	23.70	9.98
Gadchiroli	18.00	25.08	9.97	21.63	28.10	10.34	9.68	14.41	6.98
Gondiya	31.45	37.97	23.78	38.53	42.93	30.63	18.61	20.30	17.66
Hingoli	16.57	25.04	6.09	17.52	25.45	6.17	13.51	23.59	8.07
Jalgaon	28.51	39.82	10.75	31.79	41.50	11.49	16.16	27.79	9.34
Jalna	21.88	31.25	9.67	22.98	31.38	8.87	18.27	34.11	11.49
Kolhapur	42.00	52.02	26.68	44.13	53.27	25.08	30.45	40.98	25.69
Latur	26.58	35.96	11.84	29.31	36.81	12.56	13.43	29.08	7.93

State / Union Territory	Total			Main			Marginal		
	Total	Male	Female	Total	Male	Female	Total	Male	Female
Mumbai	99.96	99.97	99.91	99.84	99.87	99.64	99.38	99.45	99.22
Mumbai (Suburban)	99.92	99.93	99.89	99.84	99.86	99.67	99.56	99.65	99.32
Nagpur	61.02	71.73	36.02	65.65	73.62	41.05	39.74	55.60	25.12
Nanded	25.72	34.96	12.65	28.56	36.53	12.67	16.24	25.64	11.52
Nandurbar	18.04	26.01	7.82	21.90	28.54	9.81	8.04	12.37	5.99
Nashik	37.22	49.53	17.62	39.63	50.96	17.43	23.48	35.58	16.28
Osmanabad	20.89	27.85	11.08	22.07	28.61	10.17	17.16	26.83	12.55
Parbhani	23.51	34.40	8.35	26.45	35.94	9.15	16.77	36.27	9.61
Pune	59.34	70.50	36.46	62.68	72.15	39.26	41.43	59.43	27.99
Raigarh	51.00	64.37	28.18	59.48	69.67	32.12	28.71	39.79	20.69
Ratnagiri	34.28	50.58	16.63	39.49	54.48	16.46	18.80	31.43	12.43
Sangli	30.40	38.90	17.87	34.41	41.14	18.86	17.32	23.42	14.89
Satara	30.26	41.33	15.72	32.97	42.45	15.48	18.48	31.96	12.65
Sindhudurg	34.12	44.19	21.78	44.23	51.56	27.88	19.68	26.73	15.15
Solapur	36.80	45.51	23.94	39.22	46.60	25.38	24.83	37.60	18.31
Thane	77.72	85.86	51.89	83.12	88.39	60.46	43.30	56.80	31.43
Wardha	30.99	40.89	14.96	34.96	42.85	16.60	18.14	30.42	10.13
Washim	15.69	23.93	4.62	17.40	24.63	5.26	8.42	15.72	4.80
Yavatmal	22.47	31.47	9.68	24.58	32.63	9.90	12.43	22.11	6.85

State / Union Territory	*Total*			*Main*			*Marginal*		
	Total	*Male*	*Female*	*Total*	*Male*	*Female*	*Total*	*Male*	*Female*
Manipur									
Bishnupur	52.73	48.80	57.91	61.23	59.58	65.21	47.98	36.51	53.43
Chandel	31.31	33.71	28.55	29.22	34.91	20.58	36.96	29.82	40.81
Churachandpur	34.00	36.42	30.77	33.61	38.83	24.05	38.66	30.90	43.25
Imphal East	65.61	65.40	65.90	72.49	70.73	76.72	50.67	43.04	54.50
Imphal West	69.74	69.60	69.93	77.20	76.61	78.38	54.51	46.53	58.51
Senapati	16.49	19.26	13.31	23.98	27.57	17.04	25.59	21.87	27.47
Tamenglong	20.36	28.18	11.62	20.62	29.77	9.52	22.61	22.17	22.95
Thoubal	38.52	36.97	40.32	44.38	45.56	42.17	36.75	26.36	41.35
Ukhrul	26.74	35.96	15.93	28.28	38.92	14.35	26.82	27.60	26.20
Meghalaya									
East Garo Hills	16.91	19.00	14.42	20.50	24.07	14.23	18.72	18.34	18.91
East Khasi Hills	68.25	71.03	63.66	65.62	69.01	58.91	46.70	49.98	44.16
Jaintia Hills	23.87	25.41	21.87	27.53	27.19	28.08	14.32	18.70	11.42

State / Union Territory	Total			Main			Marginal		
	Total	Male	Female	Total	Male	Female	Total	Male	Female
Ri Bhoi	25.31	30.25	18.25	25.95	30.82	17.58	20.96	22.14	20.32
South Garo Hills	25.67	32.69	16.75	27.76	34.91	14.34	23.33	28.75	20.19
West Garo Hills	27.62	33.39	18.65	31.40	35.94	22.21	21.44	24.75	19.49
West Khasi Hills	14.79	18.68	10.52	17.45	21.48	12.09	13.32	13.29	13.35
Mizoram									
Aizawl	62.44	67.35	55.73	66.08	70.59	58.24	60.97	64.09	58.93
Champhai	19.41	23.54	14.85	23.44	29.05	15.50	14.79	13.66	15.50
Kolasib	32.23	38.05	24.40	34.65	40.20	24.05	30.00	30.32	29.88
Lawngtlai	22.20	28.25	13.97	25.39	31.42	13.55	15.19	16.16	14.78
Lunglei	31.75	39.51	21.47	33.24	40.63	21.73	27.12	32.50	24.22
Mamit	39.27	42.79	34.87	19.20	23.01	12.58	11.55	13.76	10.78
Saiha	27.26	37.46	14.67	31.05	39.76	16.69	14.82	23.34	10.80
Serchhip	21.31	26.91	14.91	24.91	29.85	18.52	15.89	14.78	16.65

State / Union Territory	*Total*			*Main*			*Marginal*		
	Total	*Male*	*Female*	*Total*	*Male*	*Female*	*Total*	*Male*	*Female*
Nagaland									
Dimapur	67.07	73.34	47.64	70.50	74.90	52.40	44.83	56.28	35.41
Kohima	41.02	51.44	27.39	43.84	55.52	27.03	27.74	28.75	26.99
Mokokchung	33.57	41.17	24.01	36.53	45.78	23.20	25.46	26.89	24.24
Mon	11.48	15.92	5.85	14.72	19.85	7.37	11.58	13.95	9.81
Phek	25.36	36.28	13.44	27.21	40.24	11.91	20.99	20.52	21.39
Tuensang	14.34	20.44	7.16	16.01	22.93	7.30	19.73	22.15	17.55
Wokha	33.94	46.50	18.16	35.68	48.81	17.69	35.51	37.64	33.96
Zunheboto	52.65	52.17	53.19	35.56	48.03	18.64	18.78	19.14	18.53
Odisha									
Anugul	41.96	48.76	27.67	50.94	53.48	39.36	23.70	30.17	19.47
Balangir	28.75	33.03	20.24	37.11	36.51	40.52	15.06	19.58	12.65
Baleshwar	32.99	33.24	31.79	36.33	35.65	43.23	22.67	21.25	24.56
Bargarh	24.51	28.37	17.30	31.07	30.92	31.82	12.72	16.21	11.15
Baudh	21.89	24.40	17.87	27.69	26.71	31.76	12.60	15.12	11.51
Bhadrak	32.09	31.17	37.96	34.44	33.17	51.66	24.98	22.82	28.42
Cuttack	56.87	58.11	51.75	61.52	60.78	67.67	40.62	41.76	39.48
Debagarh	21.61	27.23	13.66	30.64	32.08	25.37	10.33	13.53	8.69
Dhenkanal	40.15	42.94	30.26	44.84	44.99	43.61	26.40	31.23	22.05

State/Union Territory	Total			Main			Marginal		
	Total	Male	Female	Total	Male	Female	Total	Male	Female
Gajapati	21.91	28.51	14.62	26.83	31.44	18.39	13.18	17.33	11.46
Ganjam	36.85	45.75	21.94	47.21	50.64	34.14	19.04	27.37	14.62
Jagatsinghapur	45.55	45.41	46.18	48.87	47.87	57.96	34.80	33.79	36.18
Jajapur	44.08	43.62	47.39	47.01	45.89	63.43	33.22	32.49	34.73
Jharsuguda	53.28	57.77	42.45	61.60	61.99	59.72	34.00	37.67	31.40
Kalahandi	20.00	24.56	12.73	26.89	27.19	25.50	9.10	13.17	7.49
Kandhamal	30.54	33.07	27.43	34.64	35.83	31.04	25.02	23.51	25.61
Kendrapara	32.54	32.41	33.19	35.30	34.07	54.06	23.83	23.54	24.12
Kendujhar	30.67	35.28	22.03	38.85	39.19	37.25	16.37	19.77	14.51
Khordha	69.72	69.89	68.57	75.15	74.18	83.92	42.47	41.21	45.11
Koraput	27.05	33.14	18.54	35.32	37.38	29.32	14.40	18.48	12.50
Malkangiri	16.31	16.99	15.39	17.55	18.12	15.89	15.42	15.34	15.45
Mayurbhanj	33.58	32.44	35.11	35.94	35.14	38.22	30.25	24.10	33.19
Nabarangapur	17.04	20.51	12.35	23.81	23.44	25.43	9.42	11.86	8.33

State/Union Territory	*Total*			*Main*			*Marginal*		
	Total	*Male*	*Female*	*Total*	*Male*	*Female*	*Total*	*Male*	*Female*
Nayagarh	37.74	35.57	49.32	40.66	38.82	63.24	29.44	23.22	39.96
Nuapada	22.27	26.34	16.19	28.17	28.11	28.48	9.65	12.72	8.12
Puri	39.95	39.04	46.40	41.86	40.50	59.03	30.51	29.03	32.93
Rayagada	24.62	30.54	16.95	31.25	34.57	22.70	14.11	18.32	12.26
Sambalpur	46.34	45.81	47.17	53.82	50.66	62.81	31.70	26.40	34.52
Sonapur	22.58	24.93	18.56	28.50	28.25	29.62	13.04	15.56	11.86
Sundargarh	40.62	50.87	21.54	53.79	56.67	41.53	16.16	26.28	10.63
Karaikal	66.82	71.10	52.00	70.74	73.33	60.24	32.40	40.68	23.80
Mahe	97.47	97.68	96.44	97.76	97.96	96.69	93.79	94.97	91.35
Pondicherry	76.80	81.28	63.46	78.76	82.45	67.00	51.42	60.41	41.23
Yanam	74.95	77.11	63.44	77.12	78.29	70.16	48.12	61.36	30.12
Amritsar	61.18	60.40	64.12	63.33	62.08	70.33	52.10	51.16	52.80
Bathinda	48.73	44.22	59.44	49.54	45.43	65.32	45.33	38.28	47.93
Faridkot	44.84	39.81	59.59	54.20	48.04	78.66	50.60	44.63	54.67

State/Union Territory	*Total*			*Main*			*Marginal*		
	Total	*Male*	*Female*	*Total*	*Male*	*Female*	*Total*	*Male*	*Female*
Fatehgarh Sahib	65.71	58.76	90.37	65.00	59.47	89.36	74.06	60.65	85.32
Firozpur	43.25	43.16	43.55	45.48	44.36	51.80	34.96	37.31	33.76
Gurdaspur	65.14	62.97	75.12	67.10	65.27	80.53	58.43	50.66	67.29
Hoshiarpur	59.30	59.90	57.44	63.35	62.34	68.03	42.27	43.90	40.82
Jalandhar	75.08	74.64	77.28	76.55	75.80	81.22	63.28	62.92	63.70
Kapurthala	63.82	61.68	72.94	65.00	63.09	75.16	58.05	56.93	59.25
Ludhiana	80.19	77.83	90.42	80.16	78.15	90.31	76.04	67.65	84.48
Mansa	40.85	34.59	56.35	41.00	35.28	65.97	41.79	36.12	43.75
Moga	47.59	39.05	69.24	47.41	40.03	72.51	51.59	41.76	57.84
Muktsar	41.07	37.18	51.91	42.46	38.32	59.43	34.93	32.98	35.75
Nawanshahr	67.40	58.72	83.40	67.52	58.89	85.14	67.16	64.46	69.05
Patiala	61.05	59.07	68.09	62.55	59.92	75.94	53.15	55.04	51.91
Rupnagar	70.46	67.36	78.41	71.29	68.22	80.23	62.72	58.96	65.76
Sangrur	52.91	44.89	74.04	52.80	45.71	77.21	57.58	49.43	61.37

presented in Table 4.2. The co efficient of variation is a ratio of standard deviation to its mean expressed in percentage terms. The higher co-efficient shows an increasing disparity and the vice-versa. In 1981, Rajasthan shows the maximum variation in work participation rate between districts (about 30 percent), but it has declined 11 per cent in 1991 and further down to 10 per cent in 2001. Except Pondicherry and Andaman and Nicobar Islands, the union territories show an increase in the disparity of work participation rates between districts during 1981 to 2001. In 1981, among the southern states, Tamil Nadu (14.11) showed the maximum variations, but is replaced by Kerala (14.18) in 2001. Among the north-eastern region, most of the states experience a decreasing trend in the variation during the reference period. In the case of male workers, the disparity is comparatively low in all the states and union territories. In the case of female workers, all states showed a very high disparity during the reference period, but showed a very sharp decline during the reference period. The declining disparity in most of the states in the levels of female work participation rates shows that female work participation has increased in those districts during 1981 to 2001, and also indicates the improvement of enumeration of female workforce in the country.

5

Summary and Conclusions

5.1 Introduction

An important objective of development planning in India has been to provide increasing employment opportunities not only to the unemployed but also to the new additions to the labour force. The age structure of the population, labour force and employment are closely interrelated. Any change in the size, composition and distribution of population will affect the structure of the work force in any nation. Cultural norms about seeking and participation in work are also very important for the country like India. Women are not supposed to work, and even if they work, it is not valued as work. Thus, what constitutes a work has certain market, but uncertain non-market determinants. However, in a country like India, an understanding of the past trend and the present level and patterns are likely to provide the state of the economy and changes in it.

Indian economy has been predominantly agricultural. In the recent past, a major shift in the economic policy has taken place in 1991 with the liberalisation and globalisation of Indian economy. This was expected to bring a major qualitative shift in the occupational structure of the workforce. After 1991, the Indian economy has witnessed a series of reforms, encompassing all major sectors of the economy; it has marked a steady break from the past policy regimes of control, regulation and license raj. This has boosted up economic growth during the 1990s as the economy grew on an average 6 per cent rate during this period. What are the reflections of this high economic growth rate on the trend, structure and pattern of participation of work force in the Indian economy? The 2001 Census provides an opportunity to assess these aspects at the country, state and the district levels.

5.2. Major Trends and Patterns

The work participation rate among males remained almost static, whereas among females it has seen a significant increase during 1981-2001. This is true for almost all states. As a result, the disparity in work participation rates between males and females has been declining over the last two decades. This is true for both rural and urban areas. The northern states of Punjab, Haryana, Delhi, Chandigarh and Uttar Pradesh show very low percentage of work participation among females. Punjab recorded the lowest participation rates over the decades from 1981 to 2001. On the other hand, the hilly states of Himachal Pradesh, Uttarakhand and northern-eastern states show very high work participation rates. In south India, Kerala does not record a high work participation rates in spite of very high literacy. On the other hand, comparatively a very high work participation rate is seen in Andhra Pradesh. The geography of work participation goes well with high altitude, tribal inhabited and high rainfall areas devoted to rice cultivation showing higher participation rates.

It is important to know the changes in work participation rates by main and marginal work status separately. Main workers are those who have worked more than 183 days preceding the Census operation, and those who have worked for less than 183 days are termed as marginal workers. The extent of marginal workforce shows the incidence of part time or short duration jobs in an economy. It has been observed that at the national level, a declining trend is observed in the work participation rates of male main workers; it was around 52 per cent in 1981 which declined by 1 percentage point in 1991 (51 per cent) and further by 6 percentage points in 2001 (45 per cent). The female main workers also experienced a setback during 1991-2001, but only in rural areas. There has been a spectacular increase of marginal workforce among both males and females in both rural and urban areas. But even after a very high growth of marginal work force among males, their participation rate has not shown any increase during the 1990s due to steep decline in the main work category.

On the other hand, in some states like Haryana and Punjab, female workforce in main category has increased 2 and 6 times respectively.

Unlike main workers, marginal workforce among both males and females has shown a very high increase during 1991-2001 in both rural and urban areas. The increase may be partly attributed to the efforts made by Census to enumerate women workforce in the country, which went unreported in earlier censuses, and partly due to the availability of short duration jobs under various government programmes in the rural areas. However, the decline in participation rates of male main workers and concomitant jump in the marginal workforce in urban areas also reflects the changing job market during the 1990s. Now the short duration jobs, more significantly in urban areas, is gaining prominence consistent with policy of globalisation and liberalisation of Indian economy.

India is in the process of completing the demographic transition. As a result, the age structure of the population is changing. While the population below age 14 is declining, the share of elderly is increasing in the country. According to 2001 Census, nearly 7.5 per cent of India's population (77 million) falls in the age 60 and above. So, it would be worthwhile to look into the age composition of workforce as well. It is found that the proportion of both male and female elderly workers (age group 60 and above) has increased faster, particularly in the last decade 1991-2001. It is worrying to note that the poor states like Bihar and Uttar Pradesh show very high work participation of the elderly in 2001. Uttar Pradesh further shows a very high proportion of rural male elderly workers (12 per cent) in 2001. On the other hand, it is encouraging to note that the proportion of workers in age below 14 has declined during 1981-2001. All the states and union territories demonstrate this trend. But females show higher incidence of child labour than males. The Census 2001 further shows that southern states have the lowest incidence of child labour with Kerala showing the least. On the other hand, north-eastern states like Meghalaya, Mizoram and Nagaland show high level of participation of children in the labour force. Meghalaya has the highest proportion of male child workers (more than 6 per cent of male child workers in 2001). In the case of female child workers, the incidence of child labour goes up to 8 per cent of the workforce in the states of Jammu and Kashmir and Sikkim. The northern states like Madhya Pradesh, Rajashthan, and Bihar also have higher incidence of child labour. It is interesting to note that there is a preponderance of marginal workers among both child and elderly workers. As mentioned above, females show higher level of child labour than males, but this is true for main workers only. Among marginal workers, the proportion of male child labour outstrips females in most of states and union territories.

As mentioned above, the growth rates of marginal workers during 1991-2001 has been very glaring. Some researchers felt that it might be a result of the increase in the workforce participation of those who are not in the labour force such as child and elderly population (Kumar and Sharma 2002). The age composition of marginal work force and changes during 1981 to 2001 refutes this conjecture.

It is also important to know in which sectors the changes have been higher comparatively. For that, we have analysed the growth rates of workers by industrial classification. It is revealed from the analysis that service sector (other workers) shows the maximum increase at the national level during 1991-2001. Even in rural areas, the service sector shows a very high growth rate (about 20 per cent). In the case of female workers, the growth rates are high in household industry for both rural and urban areas.

In order to ascertain the shift in occupational structure, we have calculated changes in the share of workers in the non-agricultural sector during 1981-2001. It has been found that the percentage of workers engaged in non-agricultural sector has increased considerably over the decades at the national and state levels. In 1981, nearly one third of the male workforce was engaged in non-agricultural activities; however, in 2001, around half of the male workers were retuned as non-agricultural workers. North eastern states like Assam, Meghalaya and Mizoram have lower share of non-agricultural workers than the national level. On the other hand, states like Punjab and Kerala have gained about 20 per cent increase in non-agricultural workforce during 1981 to 2001. In Kerala, where half of the total workforce was engaged in non-agricultural activities in 1981, by 2001, this figure went up to three-fourth. Similarly in Punjab, where the share of the nonagricultural workforce was two-fifth in 1981, by 2001, it went up to three-fifth. In other developed states like Gujarat, Haryana, Maharashtra, Karnataka and West Bengal, the increase was in the range of 10 per cent from 1981 to 2001.

The percentage of main workers in non-agricultural sector has increased considerably over the decades at the national level and all states and union territories. As per 1981 Census, around one third of total main workers are engaged in the non-agricultural activities, however, the percentage of main workers involved in non-agricultural activities increased remarkably to more than 40 per cent in 2001 at all India level. This trend in the increase of main workers in non-agricultural activities is observed for all the states and union territories. In rural areas, the percentage of main workers in the non-agricultural category was very low in 1981 (17 per cent), which increased to 27 per cent in 2001.

In the case of marginal workers also, there is an increasing trend observed in the percentage of non-agricultural workers during 1981-2001. In 1981, around 9 per cent of marginal workers were engaged in non-agricultural sector in the rural areas at the all India level, however it increased to around 20 per cent in 2001. Even if the percentages of both male and female marginal workers have increased over the periods in the rural areas, the gender gap remained unchanged. The percentage of marginal non-agricultural workers in urban areas was around 27 per cent in 1981, which increased to around 47 per cent in 1991 and further to 80 per cent in 2001 at the national level.

The educational level of workforce has been increasing from 1981 to 2001 at the national as well as state levels. The percentage of literate male workers has increased from 49.6 per cent in 1981 to 70.5 per cent in 2001. It is interesting to observe that among those literate male workers the educational level of matric and above has increased from about 5 per cent in 1981 to nearly 26 per cent in 2001. In the case of female workers, the literacy rate increased from 14 per cent in 1981 to nearly 36 per cent in 2001. On the other hand, those literates who were in the educational level of matric and above were 2 per cent in 1981, which increased to nearly 9 per cent in 2001 among female workers. Thus, the pace of change in educational levels of male and female workforce has been more or less same during 1981 to 2001. Moreover, this is true for most of the states and union territories. The states of Kerala and Mizoram have very high (more than 80 per cent) percentage of literate workforce among both males and females. Main workers are more literate than marginal workers in 2001, which marks a reversal of the pattern, observed during 1981 to 1991. In the rural areas, the proportion of male literate marginal workers was two times greater than the proportion of female literate marginal workers. The share of both male and female marginal workers with educational level of matric and above has increased more than two times from 1991 to 2001.

We have tried to compare the results of 2001 Census with that of the NSS 55th round (1999-2000) with respect to indicators like work participation rates, proportion of child labour, share of workforce in non-agricultural sector and the educational levels of workers. The results show a very close correspondence in most of the indicators at the national level except the comparison of subsidiary workers of NSS with that of the marginal workers of the Census. At the state level, several states, particularly smaller states, show a marked divergence between the two data sets, probably due to smaller sample size for smaller states in the NSS.

At the district level, there has been a high inter-district variation observed for both males and females. However, the inter-district variations in female work participation rates have declined in most of the states due to sharp rise in female work participation rates in 2001.

5.3 Salient Findings

- Male work participation rates (main +marginal) remained almost static around 52 per cent during 1981 to 2001, whereas female work participation showed an increasing trend from 20 per cent in 1981 to 26 per cent in 2001.

The increase in female workforce is the result of spectacular increase in marginal workforce in both rural and urban areas, and due to a rise in the main workforce in urban areas. On the other hand, main workforce among males has declined very steeply in rural areas, and has not changed in urban areas. Thus, in spite of spectacular increase in marginal workers among males both in rural and urban areas, the overall work participation rates among males remained static during 1981-2001.

- A very high growth rate of marginal workforce among females during 1981-2001 shows an improvement of Census enumeration of women workers. On the other hand, the increase in marginal workforce among males indicates about the changing employment of short duration because of greater casualisation of male workforce in both rural and urban areas. This is also accompanied by rapid decline in regular jobs among males in the rural areas during 1990s.
- Disparities between male and female work participation rates are declining in both rural and urban areas in recent times. This has been possible due to the rising trend in the work participation rates among females.
- The share of workers in non-agricultural sector has increased remarkably from nearly one third of the workforce in eighties to two-fifth in 1990s. This shows that sectoral transformation of the workforce towards non-agricultural activities has been rapid during the phase of liberalisation and privatisation of Indian economy during the 1990s.
- The child workers among both males and females (age group 5-14) have declined consistently from 1981 to 2001. The child labour constitutes 2.4 per cent of the male workforce and 4.6 per cent of female workforce according to 2001 Census. On the other hand, there is considerable increase in the workforce of the elderly among both males and females in 2001. When we look at the age composition of main and marginal workers separately, it is found that child workers are predominantly employed as marginal workers, whereas elderls are engaged equally as main and marginal workers.

- Increasing decline in the share of illiterate workers among both males and females has been a noteworthy feature of the consecutive censuses. The share of the matriculate and above among male workforce has increased from 6 per cent in 1981 to 10 per cent in 1991 and further to 27 per cent in 2001. Similarly, the percentage of female workers with educational level of matriculate and above has increased from 2 per cent in 1981 to 3 per cent in 1991 and further to 9 per cent in 2001. This shows that the educational level of the workforce has increased very speedily during the 1990s among both males and females.
- The work participation rates derived from 2001 Census is consistent with NSS work participation rates (1999-2000) for both males and females, but when we compare the marginal work force of 2001 Census with that of the subsidiary workforce of NSS, the divergence between the two sources of data has been significant. It may be noted that the 2001 Census took a special effort to enumerate women workforce in the country, and the spectacular growth of marginal workforce among both males and females shows the success of the Census in enumerating marginal female workforce particularly in 2001 Census compared to earlier ones.

References

Bhole, L.M. and P. Dash. 2002. "Employment-Unemployment in India", *Indian Journal of Labor Economics*. 45(2): pp. 273-86.

Chanda G.K and Sahu P.P 2002. "Post Reform Setbacks in Rural Employment Issues That Need Further Scrutiny", *Economic and Political Weekly,* 37(21): pp. 1998-2026.

Dev, S.Mahendra. 2004. "Female Work Participation and Child Labour Occupational from NFHS". *Economic and Political Weekly,* 39(7): pp. 736-744

Dubey Amaresh, Pale Veronica and Thomas Eugene D. 2004. "Work force Participation on Women in Rural India–The Role of Education", *The Indian Journal of Labour Economics* 47(4), pp. 749-760.

Ghosh Ajit K. 2004. "The Employment Challenge in India" *Economic and Political Weekly* 39(48): pp. 5106-5116.

Kapila, Uma .2003. "Economic Reforms: A Medium Term Perspective (Recommendations of Prime Ministers Economic Advisory Council April 2001)" In Kapila Uma (Ed.) *Indian Economy since Independence*, Academic Foundation (15th Edition), New Delhi.

Kumar, Sanjay and Sharma, N.K. 2002. " Workers in Census 2001: Some Pertinent Issues" *Economic and Political Weekly*, May 2002, pp. 1712-1713.

Kundu, A. 1997. "Trends and Structure of Employment in the 1990s: Implications for Urban Growth", *Economic and Political Weekly*, June 14, 1997, pp. 1399-1405.

Lauterbach, Albert (1977). "Employment, Unemployment and Underemployment: A Conceptual Re-examination" *American Journal of Economics and Sociology*, Vol. 36, No. 3, pp. 283-298.

Papola, T.S. 2004. "Globalisation, Employment and Social Protection: Emerging Perspectives for the Indian Workers" *The Indian Journal of Labour Economics*, Vol. 47, No. 3. 2004, pp. 541-550.

Rayappa, P.H. and Erpenshade. T.J. 1975. "Determinants of Labour supply in a Developing Economy: An Integration or Demographic and Non-Demographic Factors". *Demography India* 4(1): pp. 16-48.

Sen, Abhijit, 1996. "Economic Reforms, Employment and Poverty: Terms and Options" *Economic and Political Weekly*, Special Number, September, pp. 2459-2477.

Singh, Ajit Kumar, 2004. "Changing Workforce Structure in India 1981-2001: An Interstate Study". Paper presented in the 45th Annual Conference of the Indian Society of Labour Economics held during December 15-17, 2003 at Jadavpur University, Calcutta.

Sikiri, D.K. (2005). "Challenges of 2001 Census in India and Future Issues" (http://www.ancdsaap.org/cencon2005/papers/India/India. D.K. Sikiri.pdf) accessed on 13th March, 2007.

Sinha, J.N. (1982). "1981 Census Economic Data: A Note", *Economic and Political Weekly*, Februray 6, 1982, pp. 195-203.

Sundaram, K. (2001) "Employment-Unemployment Situation in the Nineties", *Economic and Political Weekly*, Auguast 11, pp. 931-940.

Sundaram, K., Tendulkar, Suresh D. 2004. "The Poor in the Indian Labour Force – Scenario in the 1990s", *Economic and Political Weekly*, 39 (48): pp. 5125-5132.

Subramanian, M.S. 1990. "Work Force Participation of Child Labour in the Rural Economy of India", *The Indian Journal of Labour Economics* 33(4): pp. 263-271.

Visaria Pravin, 2003. "Demographic Aspects of Development: the Indian Experience", in Kapila Uma (Ed.) *Indian Economy since Independence*, Academic Foundation, New Delhi.

Index